The Medieval French Alexander

D1547392

SUNY series in Medieval Studies
Paul E. Szarmach, Editor

The Medieval French Alexander

EDITED BY

Donald Maddox
and
Sara Sturm–Maddox

State University of New York Press

Published by
State University of New York Press, Albany

© 2002 State University of New York

For information, address State University of New York Press,
90 State Street, Suite 700, Albany, NY 12207

Production by Diane Ganeles
Marketing by Anne M. Valentine

Library of Congress Cataloging-in-Publication Data

The Medieval French Alexander / Donald Maddox and Sara Sturm-Maddox, eds.
    p.   cm. — (SUNY series in medieval studies)
    Includes index.
    ISBN 0-7914-5443-6 (alk. paper). — ISBN 0-7914-5444-4 (pbk. : alk. paper)
    1. French literature—To 1500—History and criticism. 2. Alexander, the
Great, 356–323 B.C.—Romances—History and criticism. I. Maddox, Donald.
II. Sturm-Maddox, Sara. III. Series.

PQ1423.M38 2002
840.9'351—dc21   2001049518

10 9 8 7 6 5 4 3 2 1

Contents

Illustrations

Abbreviations

Editions and Translations

AdeP — Albéric de Pisançon. See *MFRA III*, pp. 37–60.

Alexandreis — *Galteri de Castellione "Alexandreis,"* ed. M. L. Colker (Padova: Antenore, 1978).

AetP — *Li Romanz d'Athis et Prophilias (L'Estoire d'Athenes)*, ed. Alfons Hilka [Gesellschaft für romanische Literatur, 29 and 40] (Halle: Niemeyer, 1912; 1916).

Fais — *"Les Fais et Concquestes du Noble Roy Alexandre,"* Edition du manuscrit 836 de la Bibliothèque Municipale de Besançon, ed. R. Nicolet-Licinsky (Ann Arbor: University Microfilms, 1980).

FG — *"Le Roman du Fuerre de Gadres" d'Eustache* (see *MFRA IV*).

MFRA I — *The Medieval French "Roman d'Alexandre,"* vol. I: *Text of the Arsenal and Venice Versions*, ed. Milan S. La Du [Elliott Monographs 36] (Princeton: Princeton University Press, 1937; New York: Kraus Reprints, 1965).

MFRA II — *The Medieval French "Roman d'Alexandre,"* vol. II: *Version of Alexandre de Paris*, ed. Edward C. Armstrong, Douglas L. Buffum, Bateman Edwards, L. F. H. Lowe [Elliott Monographs 37] (Princeton: Princeton University Press, 1938; New York: Kraus Reprints, 1965).

MFRA III — *The Medieval French "Roman d'Alexandre,"* vol. III: *Version of Alexandre de Paris: Variants and Notes to Branch I*, ed. Alfred Foulet [Elliott Monographs 38] (Princeton: Princeton University Press, 1949; New York: Kraus Reprints, 1965).

MFRA IV — *The Medieval French "Roman d'Alexandre,"* vol. IV: *"Le Roman du Fuerre de Gadres" d'Eustache*, ed. Edward C. Armstrong and Alfred Foulet [Eliott Monographs 39] (Princeton: Princeton University Press, 1942; New York: Kraus Reprints, 1965).

MFRA V   *The Medieval French "Roman d'Alexandre,"* vol. V: *Version of
              Alexandre de Paris. Variants and Notes to Branch II, with an
              Introduction,* ed. Frederick B. Agard [Elliott Monographs 40]
              (Princeton: Princeton University Press, 1942; New York: Kraus
              Reprints, 1965).

MFRA VI   *The Medieval French "Roman d'Alexandre,"* vol. VI: *Version of
              Alexandre de Paris: Variants and Notes to Branch III,* ed. Alfred
              Foulet [Elliott Monographs 42] (Princeton: Princeton Univer-
              sity Press, 1976).

MFRA VII   *The Medieval French "Roman d'Alexandre,"* vol. VII: *Version of Alexandre
              de Paris: Variants and Notes to Branch IV,* ed. Bateman Edwards and
              Alfred Foulet [Elliott Monographs 41] (Princeton: Princeton
              University Press, 1955; New York: Kraus Reprints, 1965).

Parfait   Carey, R. J., ed., *Jean de la Mote. Le Parfait du Paon* (Chapel Hill:
              University of North Carolina Press, 1972).

Prise   *La Prise de Defur and Le Voyage d'Alexandre au Paradis terrestre,*
              ed. Lawton P. G. Peckham and Milan S. La Du [Elliott Mono-
              graphs 35] (Princeton: Princeton University Press, 1935; New
              York: Kraus Reprints, 1965).

Prosa   *Der Altfranzösische Prosa-Alexanderroman,* ed. Alfons Hilka (Halle:
              Niemeyer, 1920; rpt. Geneva: Slatkine, 1974).

RA   *Le Roman d'Alexandre,* ed. (from the text of *MFRA II*) and trans.
              Laurence Harf-Lancner [Livre de Poche, "Lettres Gothiques"
              4542] (Paris: Librairie Générale Française, 1994).

Restor   *Jean le Court dit Brisebare, "Le Restor du Paon,"* ed. R. J. Carey
              (Geneva: Droz, 1966).

RTC   *The Anglo-Norman Alexander: "Le Roman de Toute Chevalerie" by
              Thomas of Kent,* ed. Brian Foster and Ian Short. 2 vols. (Lon-
              don: Anglo-Norman Text Society, 1976–1977).

Voeux   *Les "Voeux du Paon" by Jacques de Longuyon: An Edition of the
              Manuscripts of the P Redaction,* ed. Camillus Casey (Ann Arbor:
              University Microfilms, 1965).

Studies

AGMA   *Alexander the Great in the Middle Ages: Ten Studies on the Last
              Days of Alexander in Literary and Historical Writing,* ed. W. J.

Aerts, Jos. M. M. Hermans, and Elizabeth Visser (Niemeyer: Alfa, 1978).

Alessandro *Alessandro nel Medioevo Occidentale*, ed. Mariantonia Liborio, Piero Boitani, Corrado Bologna, and Adele Cipolla; intro. Peter Dronke (Verona: Mondadori, 1997).

Alexandre *Alexandre le Grand dans les littératures Occidentales et Proche-Orientales: Actes du Colloque de Paris, 27–29 novembre 1997*, ed. Laurence Harf-Lancner, Claire Kappler, and François Suard [*Littérales* Hors Série—1999] (Paris: Centre des Sciences de la Littérature, Université de Paris X, Nanterre, 1999).

Cary Cary, George, *The Medieval Alexander* (Cambridge: Cambridge University Press, 1967).

Frontières Gaullier-Bougassas, Catherine, *Les Romans d'Alexandre. Frontières de l'épique et du romanesque* (Paris: Champion, 1998).

Ross Ross, David J. A., *Alexander Historiatus: A Guide to Medieval Illuminated Alexander Literature* (London: Warburg Institute, 1963).

Légende Gosman, Martin, *La Légende d'Alexandre le Grand dans la littérature française du 12e siècle. Une réécriture permanente* (Amsterdam: Rodopi, 1997).

Studies Ross, D. J. A., *Studies in the Alexander Romance* (London: Pindar, 1985).

Introduction:
Alexander the Great in the French Middle Ages

Donald Maddox and Sara Sturm-Maddox

The figure of Alexander "the Great" is extraordinary on any terms. The global dimensions of that "greatness" are aptly summed up by Laurence Harf-Lancner, a contributor to this volume:

> On June 13 in the year 323 B.C., Alexander died in Babylon at the age of thirty-three. He had conquered a great part of the known world and had, by advancing through India as far as the Ganges basin, pushed back the eastern limits of the universe. His accomplishments were also to give rise to a myth about his own person that after his death would proliferate and endure to our own time.[1]

The awesome magnitude of Alexander the Great thus obtains in two spheres that are in most contexts inextricably interrelated: in ancient history, but also in the expansive mythic strands that proliferate outward from the historical record. The powerful legendary matrix resulting from this blend of history and myth is by no means an ideological monolith, however, for over the *longue durée* it retains a remarkable elasticity, capable of accommodating an astonishing variety of contrastive, and sometimes contradictory, worldviews. As David Williams has observed, Alexander is the only hero whose appeal seems truly multicultural and transhistorical.[2] Indeed, across a vast expanse of space and time, throughout Europe and the Near East and from Alexander's own century through the Middle Ages and beyond, his adventures continued to yield rich veins that generations of writers exploited in a strikingly diverse array of literary and didactic texts. For a schematic overview of the medieval French Alexander texts and their principal antecedents, see the Chronology at the end of this introduction.

Throughout the Middle Ages, Alexander's adventures found prominence in a wide variety of historical and literary settings. The medieval European

1

tradition originates in the third century A.D. with a Greek romance known as the "Pseudo-Callisthenes," which brought together history and legend in a combination that was to have enormous influence. Translated into Latin in the fourth century and abridged in the ninth,[3] it affords the essential elements of the vernacular image of Alexander that emerges shortly after 1100 and thereafter looms large in both Latin and vernacular texts. In influential works like the Latin *Alexandreis* of Gautier de Châtillon (ca. 1170, extant in some 200 manuscripts), depictions of Alexander helped to shape medieval attitudes toward history. He figures among the legendary Nine Worthies in the late medieval canon of heroes—a theme of long duration that was itself introduced in an Alexander romance;[4] Chaucer's Monk proclaims that "The storie of Alisaundre is so commune/ That every wight that hath discrecioun/ Hath herd somewhat or al of his fortune."[5] By the end of the Middle Ages his importance had by no means diminished; of particular interest in this regard is the popularity of Alexander texts in fifteenth-century Burgundy, where he "plays a key role in the rich political reflections of the theoreticians of power" connected with Philippe le Bon and Charles le Téméraire.[6]

Already in the mid-tenth century, the legend of Alexander was recognized by clerical authors as an apt vehicle for addressing a wide range of contemporary concerns. A telling example of this is examined in this volume by Michel Zink, who explores the ways in which the author of the Prologue to the Latin translation of the Pseudo-Callisthenes sets forth the combats and victories of the great pagan heroes as models for emulation by Christians, but models nonetheless to be transcended through the exercise of Christian virtues.[7] Here a figurative implementation of the legend of Alexander transforms chivalric combat into spiritual *agon*, casting clerics as "officers" and the lay public as "simple soldiers" in a striking metaphor whose repercussions will be evident in numerous texts, including Saint Bernard's *Praise of the New Militia*. The potential of the Macedonian's heroic legend for development in positive or negative didactic commentary was to have a long posterity in secular texts as well, and Zink discusses one early vernacular example of its prominent reappearance, in the prologue to the late-twelfth-century *Conte du Graal* of Chrétien de Troyes in which the poet's patron, Philip of Flanders, is favorably compared to Alexander in terms of the practice of largesse.

Almost half a century ago, the substantial corpus of medieval texts devoted to Alexander was surveyed by George Cary; in 1963, D. J. A. Ross assessed the illustrated Alexander manuscripts.[8] Subsequently, a few sporadic contributions addressed specific features of the legend in medieval contexts.[9] In recent years, a quickening of scholarly interest has produced much new work on the figure of Alexander as represented both in the ancient world and thereafter.[10] The present volume partakes of this renewal. As the first systematic collective study of the medieval French Alexander tradition and its background, it provides an essential complement to comparative study of the larger textual archive in the comprehensive medieval Alexandrian tradition that includes, for example, the Castilian adaptations of the legend[11] and its avatars in medieval Britain, Persia, and elsewhere.[12] And a substantial inquiry devoted exclusively to the medieval French corpus of works dealing with Alexander the Great is fully justified: within the richly variegated plurality of Latin and vernacular texts that comprise the Alexandrian tradition from late antiquity through the later Middle Ages, the corpus of French texts that engage the Macedonian's legend is unique in terms of both its amplitude and its diachronic scope. It involves a substantial number of works that together span nearly the entire period of medieval French literary production, from the early-twelfth century through the late fifteenth—hence a thread whose multiple strands are intricately woven into the fabric of medieval literary history.

This volume is the product of an international initiative, and its contributors include many of the major participants in the recent renewal of scholarly attention to the medieval Alexander. Most of the essays are revised contributions to an international colloquium held at the University of Massachusetts, Amherst. That gathering provided a provocative forum for collaborative rethinking of how the classical legacy was repeatedly renewed and transformed in a corpus of narratives spanning four centuries. The contributions subject the various types of medieval writing exemplified, in this substantial and important group of works, to sensitive textual analyses informed by a variety of methodological perspectives: anthropology, art history, codicology, the history of mentalities, postcolonial theory, and sociology are among the disciplines represented. The topics addressed include the generic interplay between romance and epic conventions; the ideological implications of successive rewritings of ancient history; the composition of a "mirror for the prince" in the accounts of the hero's education and accomplishments; the thirteenth-century *mise en prose* of the heroic story; the fourteenth-century cyclification of the legend's components; the use of a legendary hero as warrant for the historicity of a character in later Arthurian romance, notably the monumental *Roman de Perceforest*; and medieval beliefs and phantasms concerning the fabulous and exotic Orient. We also see how legend was tendentiously recast in particular episodes, such as Alexander's visit to Jerusalem and his battles against Persians assimilated to Saracens, so as to appropriate the classical hero's engagements as a prefiguration of the conflicts of the Crusade era.

Within the full context of the medieval French Alexander, the twelfth century stands out as the powerfully formative period. From the beginning to the end of the century, a number of texts in verse develop the basic elements of the legend and add new ones. The earliest of these, dating from near the beginning of the century, is a Franco-Provençal work by Albéric de Pisançon of which only the opening survives, a fragment of 105 octosyllables in fifteen monorhymed *laisses* depicting the hero's *enfances*.[13] Albéric's poem was subsequently adapted in a decasyllabic Poitevin *Roman d'Alexandre*, also portraying only the *enfances* (ca. 1160),[14] followed, during the 1170s, by three dodecasyllabic works unknown in their original states: *Le Roman du Fuerre de Gadres*, an account, attributed to Eustache, of a raid on Gaza (*MFRA IV* and *MFRA V*); an *Alixandre en Orient* by Lambert le Tort of Châteaudun; and an anonymous *Mort Alixandre*. The Poitevin *enfances* and the latter two works were amalgamated into a composite *Roman d'Alixandre*.[15] Late in the century, Alexandre de Paris drew substantially upon these earlier works in order to elaborate a massive dodecasyllabic poem of some 16,000 verses in monorhymed laisses treating the comprehensive biography of the hero in four "branches."[16] The enormous success of this so-called "Vulgate" version is evident in the number of interpolations and continuations by poets, moralists and historians that appear throughout the Middle Ages. It is reflected too in the designation of the French twelve-syllable verse in which it is cast as "alexandrine"—a designation dating from the fifteenth century.[17]

This twelfth-century corpus as synthesized in the monumental achievement of Alexandre de Paris comprises the dense and intricate "core" that has received the lion's share of the textual scholarship devoted to the medieval French Alexander during the twentieth century. Much of this emerged from a single project with multiple editors, *MFRA I-VII* published in the Elliott Monograph Series between 1927 and 1976, an achievement that provides an invaluable frame of reference for study of the entire tradition.[18] Despite the seminal vitality of that editorial project, however, scholarship on the French Alexander material during the twentieth century is relatively modest compared to that devoted to other areas of medieval French narrative.

Why, in view of the impressive size of the medieval French Alexander corpus, did it not command considerably more attention until near the end of the century? One reason may be that the twelfth-century *Alexandre* is a *roman* that embodies many formal and thematic features of Old French epic, such as monorhyming *laisses* and lengthy segments devoted to collective combat.[19] The coexistence of epic and romance elements throughout the poem precludes any uncomplicated identification with a single genre.[20] In recent decades, an intensified scholarly interest in questions relating to medieval genres has disclosed the myriad ways in which the fluidity of *matières* in medieval vernacular writing persistently defies modern textbook notions of generic purity, prompting a new interest in Alexander de Paris's composite poem.

Mindful of this generic lability, Emmanuèle Baumgartner turns her attention to the vast epic canvas of the Gadres episode, which Alexandre de Paris extensively reworks into the second branch of his narrative. Her interest is kindled precisely by the fact that, even though this lengthy episode redolent of Old French epic enjoyed considerable popularity in the Middle Ages, it has generally been overshadowed by modern readings centered on the poem's affinities with romance. Baumgartner shows that, while in terms of its generic properties the episode in many ways compares favorably with the *chansons de geste*, it conveys a didactic and ideological perspective that is fundamentally at odds with an epic worldview. Here we discover many subtle, though powerful, intimations of a cautionary perspective on the unbridled fervor of conquest for its own sake. According to Alexander's rewriting, the exercise of individual and collective prowess to win personal glory and to benefit from the conquerer's legendary largesse untimately proves vain in the absence of transcendental ideals. To provide an effective vehicle for this lesson, in Baumgartner's view, the extensive recourse to the technical and thematic elements of epic would most likely have maximized the appeal of this episode to a chivalric public.

Thus we see that the values represented by this colossal—and in some respects monstrous—story from the ancient world were to find an accommodation through medieval epic discourse that was procrustean at best. This generic incommensurability partakes of a larger tendency apparent in the medieval reception of the Alexandrian legend, whose inherent ambiguities were sometimes met with ambivalence on the part of medieval authors.[21] At first glance, Alexander's most fundamental traits would seem to be relatively stable, whether he be considered an "epic" or a "romance" hero: a largesse deemed exemplary in texts ranging from epic and troubadour lyric to romance;[22] an indomitable drive to conquer; and an equally insatiable desire for knowledge. From the earliest accounts of his life and adventures, however, the story of this "greatest of rulers" is rich in ambiguities, some of them profoundly disquieting. First there is the question of his birth: was Alexander the son of the mighty conqueror Philip of Macedonia, and thus his legitimate heir, or was he the son of the Egyptian Pharaoh and magician-astrologer Nectanabus, who seduced Alexander's mother in the guise of Ammon—a divinity with whom Alexander himself often proclaimed his filiation?[23] Or again, were his temperament and his inclinations shaped by that eminent philosopher Aristotle, who served as his tutor and later as his advisor, or were they formed by Nectanabus's pretensions to all-embracing knowledge? Was his largesse a primordial trait of his character, as Aristotle affirms—"Largesse estoit ta mere et tu ieres ses fis:/ En doner iert ta gloire, ta joie et tes delis" (br. IV, 51, 1032–33: Largesse was your mother, and you were her son. In giving was your glory, joy, and delight)—or was it the calculated gesture later held up as an example for the Prince by a cynical Machiavelli?[24]

It is of course true that we also find ambiguities in some representations of the two other rulers, Charlemagne and Arthur, whose legends were tributary to major medieval French narrative traditions. In some poems Charles is the object of mild humor, or subject to lapses of temper or judgment, or even, according to one legendary current, guilty of incest; Arthur's fortunes in the hands of medieval authors are also variable, and include moments of weakness, lethargy, and, again, the shadow of incest. But these ambiguities are far less culturally remote than those of a colossal hero who could be portrayed, on the one hand, as representative of the best of the pagan past and a *figura Christi*,[25] and on the other, as at the hands of a twelfth-century clerical writer expanding upon Old Testament implications, as a figure of the Antichrist.[26] Unlike the more "exotic" Macedonian, Charlemagne and Arthur were both readily perceived in proximity to medieval religious and social institutions: in terms of values, Charlemagne is most often depicted as the Christian Emperor who through both piety and conquest represents God and France; Arthur is characteristically portrayed as a monarch whose *regnum*, however problematic politically and socially, was impelled by, and in many ways exemplified, ideals of chivalry, courtliness and social order. Thus the fact that twentieth-century scholarship devoted to medieval French narrative traditions accorded considerably more attention to the Carolingian and Arthurian material than to the Alexandrian legacy may to some degree be attributable to the latter's greater originary remoteness from medieval institutions and values, rendering its reception more difficult to apprehend and interpret.[27] It is worthy of note that that remoteness would finally be mitigated, in the fourteenth-century *Roman de Perceforest*, by making Alexander Arthur's ancestor, a development that Michelle Szkilnik explores in this volume.

Branch III of the Vulgate *Alexandre* offers a particularly interesting example of the difficulties involved in interpreting medieval perceptions of Alexander's story. In an extensive rewriting of the *Alixandre en Orient* of Lambert le Tort, Alexandre de Paris variously illustrates the question of Alexander's relentless curiosity about the universe in terms of his oriental adventures. Here, descriptions of the farthest known reaches of civilization are, as Emmanuèle Baumgartner points out, "designed to awaken, as well as to satisfy, the medieval public's curiosity and in this regard are among the very first instances of literary exoticism in the vernacular."[28] The conqueror and his forces encounter widespread evidence of supernatural influences. Among them are three fountains: one that restores youth, one that revives the dead, and one that confers immortality. This romance, which in the expansive adaptation from Lambert le Tort introduces the theme of the "Fountain of Youth" into vernacular literature, makes of this triad of fountains a special case, a triple adventure considerably amplified with regard to earlier versions, to become "the very symbol of Alexander's quest, and of that obsession with transcending the human condition the Greeks called *hybris* and the French of the twelfth century *outrage*, hence a symbol of Alexander's excess."[29] Or we may consider the introduction, in his Eastward itinerary, of the "bornes Artu" which he has sought to reach, a name suggestively introducing the prestige of Arthur while evoking the pillars of Hercules set in place by that hero to mark the limits beyond which man should not pass.[30] Dante was to render memorably in the *Commedia* the fateful consequences of willfully passing that limit.[31] His Ulysses, whose affinities with Alexander have been observed,[32] embodies that type of hunger for knowledge—that "turpis curiositas"—condemned by Saint Bernard as "the first degree of pride."[33]

Yet despite the Macedonian's ironclad will, the marvelous Orient refuses to yield, and finally closes back upon its own enigmas; soon thereafter, Alexander will learn of his impending death from another marvel, the Trees of the Sun and the Moon.[34] If Chaucer's Monk finds Alexander's insatiable ambition a sign of his greatness, demanding "Who shal me yeven teeris to compleyne/ The death of gentillesse and of franchise,/ That all the world weelded in his demeyne,/ And yet hym thoughte it myghte nat suffise?" (1663–66), two Latin Alexander texts draw different conclusions. The twelfth-century *Iter Alexandri ad Paradisum*, which will appear with some variation in two Old French versions, is a prime example.[35] Reaching a reputed Paradise of Delights at the source of the Ganges, Alexander learns from an aged Jew that his boundless ambition can never be satisfied, whereupon he renounces all forms of greed and ambition.[36] We find a more somber moment in the Latin *Alexandreis* of Gautier de Châtillon, which otherwise tends to exalt the Macedonian hero: after a triumphant Alexander at last declares himself eager to conquer other worlds, since all the earth is subject to his power, Nature herself conspires with Leviathan to exact vengeance.[37]

It is hardly surprising, then, that even Alexander's splendid education, which had already earned special praise from the earliest of the French authors, Albéric de Pisançon, frequently comes under unfavorable scrutiny. As might be expected, the reservations have less to do with its substance than with the values reflected in its applications by Alexander. Douglas Kelly examines this question in the Vulgate *Alexandre* and the *Roman de Toute Chevalerie*, specifically in terms of the interplay of ideals of *chevalerie* and *clergie* as they inform the motivation and implementation of the Macedonian's conquests. He begins with a lesser-known romance also attributed to Alexandre de Paris, *Athis et Prophilias*, in which the "humanistic" view of *clergie* proves less than ideal for the formation of the knight or nobleman. In both the Vulgate *Alexandre* and Thomas's *Roman*, although *clergie* is indeed vital to the hero's brilliant education as well as to his active life, the intellectual component ultimately facilitates and glorifies the vast agenda of militant conquest. In terms of what motivates Alexander and what he accomplishes, Kelly concludes that in these two late-twelfth-century works it is *chevalerie*, not *clergie*, that prevails as an ideal.

Catherine Gaullier-Bougassas also considers the question of Alexander's education, with emphasis on the role of Aristotle, in a selection of texts from the twelfth to the fifteenth century.[38] Whereas in numerous didactic texts the complementarity of monarch and philosopher is more consistently praised, these literary works show a greater diversity of attitudes and tend to take more nuanced—and often far less optimistic—positions. At times, Aristotle does serve to project a favorable view of the influence of clerics on rulers, as is initially the case in the Vulgate *Alexandre* in which his functions as Alexander's tutor, and later as his advisor, are crucial. Yet in due course he acquires dubious associations with the magician Nectanabus, while in the final branch his image undergoes "symbolic destruction" when his idolatrous panegyric of the late ruler reveals how extensively his wisdom has been corrupted by the latter's excesses. An ambivalent image of the philosopher also features in the later *Voyage d'Alexandre au Paradis terrestre*, while in the *Lai d'Aristote* Henri d'Andeli subjects him to pitiless ridicule.

In general, then, valorizations of the conqueror's education range between two extremes, the one demonstrating how it enhances the learned king's profile and furthers his achievements, the other condemning his rampant ambition and lack of restraint. Here again, we see the persistence of ambiguity and ambivalence in these medieval literary reconfigurations of ancient traditions. Despite the continued emphasis in French texts on Alexander's acquired learning, these texts also accord considerable attention to his innate gifts—to his *nature* as well as to his *noreture*—as manifested in the inexhaustible curiosity that motivates his explorations but also in the cleverness he displays in his dealings with others. François Suard focuses on this aspect of his character. We see how Alexandre de Paris individualizes and nuances the traditional image of the omnipotent conqueror in his adaptation of two scenes, inspired by classical sources, in which the hero presents himself to an adversary in disguise. The medieval author's rewriting of each of these otherwise quite different scenes introduces the humorous vein of the *gab* found in the early epico-romanesque tradition. His aim in depicting the disguised Alexander as both learned and clever, associating his mastery of ruse and of language with his mastery of prowess, is, Suard suggests, not only literary but didactic, and deliberately enigmatic, so as to heighten the exemplary nature of the scenes by suggesting them to the reader as instructive.

In the social and political spheres too, the portrait is ambiguous. Is Alexander the embodiment of prideful ambition and an agent of destruction, as the Old Testament depicts him[39]—a role that seems to find an echo in Gautier de Châtillon's designation as "that bloody sword of the Fates"?[40] Or is he a civilizing hero whose extraordinary military and intellectual accomplishments are due to Providence? For Dante, his was the closest approximation before the Roman Empire to a universal monarchy (*De Monarchia* II, 8. 8). But was he conquering hero, or conquering oppressor?[41] Fashioned by the courtly French tradition as the embodiment of *courtoisie* and held up by some authors as a model for princes because of his celebrated largesse and learning, Alexander was identified by others as a cautionary figure because of his insatiable hunger for both knowledge and power.

Medieval implementations of his legend also transformed it into a powerful medium for direct expression or symbolic representation of contemporary social and political aspirations and—more commonly—anxieties. Alexandre de Paris, in his prologue, presents Alexander—his "riche estoire"—to those who would "prendre bon essample" with regard not only to prowess but to what to love and to hate, and how to keep one's friends and do harm to one's enemies (br. I, vv. 1–8). In the twelfth-century vernacular romances, subtle semantic changes detectible within a modest, though culturally charged, lexicon inherited from early epic discourse provide valuable indices of social change, as Rupert T. Pickens demonstrates in his examination of how terms relating to *vasselage* and *cortoisie* are variably semanticized as we move from the decasyllabic texts to the Vulgate *Alexandre*. His inquiry discloses a major transition from the epic celebration, typical of the early *chansons de geste*, of *vasselage*— a feudal value centered in male strength and loyalty to the overlord—to a more "courtly" concept in which *vasselage* is subsumed into elegant speech and refined manners, in a form of *courtoisie* strongly identified with women. On the ideological plane, Pickens proposes, we may also discern an attempt to revitalize a conservative ethos.

Evidence of such a tendency is also apparent in William W. Kibler's study of the Vulgate *Alexandre*, which was the first to introduce the legend to the economically volatile Paris region. In Alexandre's poem Kibler identifies striking reflections of the profound institutional changes taking place on the French political horizon. While the text can be categorized as one of the many "mirrors for the prince" written during the medieval period, it also reflects the anxieties of the French aristocracy, which in the latter decades of the twelfth century was progressively being displaced by a rising monied class elevated by the Capetian monarchy to the status of administrators and advisors. In response to this major economic shift, the romance tenders a conservative ideal of kingship valorizing traditional forms of largesse while also repeatedly emphasizing the perils of reliance on low-born men rather than on the higher aristocracy.

Institutionalized largesse is addressed by Stephen D. White, who considers the *Roman d'Alexandre* in the light of current theoretical discussions of models for the study of feudal society. He examines in particular the lengthy deathbed scene in Branch IV of the Vulgate, where Alexander makes generous gifts of land, as promised, to each of his twelve peers. White suggests ways in which, by holding up Alexander's fief-giving as an example of largesse and contrasting it with the bribe-like gifts of avaricious lords, Alexandre de Paris draws on a long-standing and complex feudal discourse. In this text the Eastern potentates encountered by Alexander are generally framed not only as his opposites but as counterexamples to his own exemplary conduct.[42] White shows how the Vulgate *Alexandre*, by radically dichotomizing Alexander's expansive largesse and Darius's avaricious use of bribes to procure selfish ends, oversimplifies and moralizes real political experience. He concludes that the romance reproduces and mystifies, but fails to resolve, a fundamental underlying ambiguity between honorable fief-giving and bribery camouflaged as largesse.

Together, then, the late-twelfth-century corpus reflects acutely felt tensions engendered by accelerated social change, as these found expression within a conceptual sphere encompassing such basic yet mutable notions as *clergie*, *chevalerie*, *vasselage*, *courtoisie*, and *largesse*. And while the early Alexander texts

afford considerable insight into the definition of an ethos, the texts that derive
from that fertile legacy and focus on this same gigantic figure during the three
ensuing centuries offer equally suggestive views of its metamorphosis over
time.

We begin to note new attitudes toward the Alexandrian legend early in
the next century. According to Michelle R. Warren, the political preoccupa-
tions apparent in the twelfth-century verse romance shift in the thirteenth-
century prose version, adaptively translated from the tenth-century Latin prose
Historia de Preliis. In essence, Warren suggests, the prose *Alexandre* moves
significantly away from courtly concerns toward embodiment of a more resolutely expansionist ideology. Her essay on relations of unequal power and the
coercive dynamics that sustain them is usefully informed by contemporary
postcolonial studies. She argues, moreover, that prose is particularly well suited
to the kind of totalizing effects cultivated in this thirteenth-century text's
representation of imperial desire and colonial ambition.

Much recent scholarship has disclosed that the emergence of French
prose around the turn of the thirteenth century owes a great deal to increasing
concern with the writing of history in the vernacular. Catherine Croizy-
Naquet shows how the figure of Alexander comes into prominence in this
regard, as Roman history enters upon the French historiographic horizon with
the *Faits des Romains* at the beginning of the thirteenth century. The compiler
of this text attaches the Roman material to elements of ancient story that were
already well-known, notably the legend of Troy and the great deeds of Alexander.
Although Alexander's presence in the text is limited, evocations of his heroic
career in the account of the life of Caesar enable the compiler to redefine the
contours of both exemplary figures. This essay demonstrates that the thirteenth-
century reconfiguration of Alexander also played an important role in the
development of medieval historiography.

The late medieval "epigones," works that derive from the earlier French
tradition while also modifying it in multiple ways, comprise an important
subset of texts which Martin Gosman addresses.[43] While retaining the basic
legendary *fabula*, these epigonic writers, who for the most part nourish an
optimistic view of the tradition's political implications, variously reinvest it
with illustrations of social order founded on the principle of *utilitas regis*.
Hence a corpus of late-medieval narratives that resonate profoundly with a
period in which monarchy definitively transforms itself from a weak feudal
institution into a highly theorized sociopolitical machine. In literary and
pseudohistoriographical texts from across this period, Gosman discloses the
conservative as well as the innovative functions of works that produce idealized
images of monarchy, operative within a courtly framework emphasizing political cohesiveness sustained by protocol, ritual, and pageant. These works are thus
indicative of how major political transformations in late-medieval France were
conspicuously valorized in its cultural productions.

Among these epigones, three of the works in Gosman's corpus, composed in the fourteenth century, form an ensemble inserted into Branch II of the *Roman d'Alexandre* and generally referred to as the "Cycle du Paon." While in general they are marked by a "spirit of idyllic courtesy which pervades the knightly atmosphere," as John L. Grigsby observed,[44] the last of the three, Jean de la Mote's *Parfait du Paon* (1340), reintroduces elements that underline the ambiguous traits of the hero.[45] Here Renate Blumenfeld-Kosinski looks closely at the nature of the poetic project involved in the *Parfait*, which in its network of references to earlier Alexander texts in many ways represents the endpoint of the tradition. In the episode of the *chambre amoureuse*, she suggests, the description of the elaborate murals provides through *ekphrasis*—word painting—a reading of both the Alexander and the related *Paon* cycles, while also configuring a legendary memory inviting readers to reflect on the tradition in new ways. Though they are part of only one interlude in a larger canvas of bloodshed and destruction, these highly allusive figural reminiscences also allow the temporary emergence of a different figure of Alexander: now himself engaged in poetic creation, he is dramatically transformed into a dynamic artificer commemorating, and consecrating, the sort of culture represented in the chamber itself, thus investing a role that in turn generates new texts.

Two other contributions focus on one monumental fourteenth-century text, the *Roman de Perceforest*, which is progressively becoming available in modern editions. Michelle Szkilnik considers how in the *Perceforest* Alexander is at last integrated into the Arthurian tradition: here he becomes not only Arthur's ancestor, but the founder of the rites of Arthurian society. Not only does he institute an illustrious lineage and establish a brilliant civilization; he initiates the recording of events that constitute the very material of romance. It is in this linkage and through its demonstration of Alexander's adoption of Arthurian values, Szkilnik argues, that the Macedonian hero's name and enterprise are saved for the Western legacy.

Implementing methodologies of sociology and feminist theory, Jane H. M. Taylor examines an episode in the *Perceforest* that is new in the tradition and represents Alexander as lover: the account of his clandestine, idyllic love affair in England with Sibille. In earlier Alexander texts, Taylor points out, women were perceived either as marginal or as dangerous distractions to male autonomy in an ideal social order based on masculine chivalric identity. The *Perceforest* makes the tensions between public and private spheres, between eros and empire-building, even more explicit. It also brings more fully into prominence a dichotomous universe, one in which the bond of "brotherliness" is ultimately incompatible with erotic love. Yet here again the male, homosocial ethos prevails, with the systematic exclusion of the lady from the public arena. Taylor situates this eventuality within the context of a much larger assortment of medieval French narratives that show similar tendencies.

The *Perceforest* is one example of how, during the later Middle Ages, the Alexandrian material continued to offer writers, as it had to Lambert le Tort, Alexandre de Paris, and the anonymous architect of the prose *Alexandre*, a powerful vehicle for depicting engagements with geographical and cultural alterities. "Alterity," writes Corrado Bologna, "is the measure of Alexander. Bent upon knowing and on conquering, on taking the measure of reality, Alexander is one of the most extraordinary mediators of alterity for the ancient and medieval West" (*Alessandro*, p. 167). Eventually, the legend's luxuriant "exotic" landscape began to intersect, often contrastively, with later medieval eyewitness descriptions of travel to remote lands. Developing a comparative perspective on one of the most important of these accounts, the *Devisement du monde* of Marco Polo, Laurence Harf-Lancner discovers two quite distinct approaches to the marvels of the Orient and to that which is, more generally, "other." The Alexander romances magnify the emblematic, often exemplary or cautionary figure of the discoverer avid for knowledge, who enters marvelous worlds that ultimately escape his capacity to master them fully. In contrast, the originality of the *Devisement* lies in its tendency to classify, and thus to demystify, the Oriental *merveilleux*, though without in any way diminishing the sense of wonder and awesome strangeness that prevails throughout. The intricate and arresting manuscript illustrations of the two works also show contrasts. While Marco Polo's text tends to reduce the marvelous to the exotic—the never-before-seen, the unheard-of—his imagers, recurring to earlier practices reflected in many *Alexandre* manuscripts, sometimes contradict his text so as to remain faithful to the traditional iconography of *mirabilia*, marvelous objects and events. Hence, in this essay, we find many detailed examples of the frequently subtle interplay between texts and their manuscript illuminations.

Like Harf-Lancner, Keith Busby is attentive to the evidence afforded by manuscripts, and in addressing the complex textual history of the *Roman d'Alexandre* he makes the codex containing each known version of a work the central object of study. The threads of his wide-ranging inquiry converge in a typology of the French *Alexandre* manuscripts, and he offers many suggestive comments on codicological features that might cast light on the reception of the legend within the historical context that produced a given manuscript. For manuscripts in which the *Roman d'Alexandre* figures among other works, Busby argues that close scrutiny of the manuscript's material properties and the way it contextualizes a given work may be required in order to apprehend the latter's intrinsic significance and larger implications.

In sum, these essays invite us to rethink medieval literary history and the norms of medieval culture from the multiple vantage points offered by the medieval French Alexander. As an ensemble, these works enable us to revisit, by working through one of its richest veins, the entire opening period of French literary history, from its inception near the beginning of the twelfth century to its glorious late-medieval expansion and diversification and its anticipation of early modern syntheses and transformations. The medieval French engagement with the legend of Alexander the Great, as it moves us in successive phases across the medieval centuries, emerges as a barometer of social and political change; as a measure of the complex coherence of mentalities and even a few pockets of local knowledge; and, on occasion, as a skeleton key for gaining access to contradictions within the social formation. The object of both adulation and censure even in his own time, Alexander emerges from these depictions as a figure about whom crystallize configurations, variously valorized, of an ideal whose ramifications are both political and personal. For it is Alexander—more than Charlemagne, more than Arthur, despite the celebrity of both of these rulers—who serves as a mirror, or perhaps better, as a prism, in which both the ancient world and the medieval are refracted in multiple and monumental ways.

Notes

1. *RA*, p. 5; translation by the editors.

2. David Williams, "Alexandre le Grand dans la littérature anglaise médiévale. De l'ambivalence à la polyvalence," in *Alexandre*, p. 356.

3. Pseudo-Callisthenes, *The Romance of Alexander the Great*, trans. A. M. Wolohojian (New York: Columbia University Press, 1969); *Julii Valerii Epitomè*, ed. J. Zacher (Halle, 1867).

4. See Laurence Harf-Lancner on Jacques de Longuyon's *Voeux du paon* (1312) in "Alexandre et l'Occident médiéval," in *Alexandre*, p. 19. The Nine Worthies are Hector, Alexander, and Caesar; Joshua, David, and Judas Maccabeus; Arthur, Charlemagne, and Godefroy de Bouillon.

5. Geoffrey Chaucer, "The Monk's Tale" (vv. 743–45), *The Canterbury Tales*, in *The Riverside Chaucer*, ed. Larry D. Benson (Boston: Houghton-Mifflin, 1987).

6. Christine Raynaud, "Alexandre dans les bibliothèques bourguignonnes," in *Alexandre*, p. 187.

7. On the prologue see also A. Frugoni, "La biblioteca di Giovanni III duca di Napoli (Dal *Prologus* dell'arciprete Leone al *Romanzo di Alessandro*)," in C. Settis Frugoni, *La fortuna di Alessandro Magno dall'antichità al Medioevo* (Firenze: La Nuova Italia, 1978), pp. 133–41.

8. Cary, *The Medieval Alexander*; Ross, *Alexander Historiatus*. See also idem., "Alexander historiatus: A Supplement," *Journal of the Warburg and Courtauld Institutes* 30 (1967), 383–88.

9. These concern specific matters such as his extraterrestrial voyages; the eulogies spoken in his memory; his horse Bucephalus; or his tent. On the latter, see Aimé Petit, "Le pavillon d'Alexandre dans le *Roman d'Alexandre* (ms. B. Venise, Museo Civico VI, 665)," *Bien dire et bien aprandre* 6 (1988), 77–96.

10. The scope of this tradition is illustrated in *Alexandre*; see the introductory essays by Claire Kappler and Laurence Harf-Lancner.

11. See Christine Abril, "Les Enfances d'Alexandre: Essai de comparaison entre le *Roman d'Alexandre* et le *Libro de Alexandre*," *PRIS-MA* 13 (1997), 1–12; Amaia Arizaleta, "La figure d'Alexandre comme modèle d'écriture dans la littérature médiévale castillane," in *Alexandre*, pp. 173–86, and her *La Translation d'Alexandre. Recherches sur la genèse et signification du "Libro de Alexandre"* (Paris: Klincksieck, 1999).

12. For recent syntheses on the comprehensive Alexandrian tradition, with special emphases on the medieval heritage, see *Alessandro*; *Alexandre*; and the article "Alessandro Magno" in *Miti e personaggi del Medioevo: Dizionario di storia, letteratura, arte, musica*, ed. Willem P. Gerritsen and Anthony G. van Melle; Italian ed. Gabriella Agrati and Maria Letizia Magini (Milan: Mondadori, 1999), pp. 4–16. On the British Alexander, see Gerrit H. V. Bunt, *Alexander the Great in the Literature of Medieval Britain* (Groningen: Egbert Forsten, 1994).

13. See *MFRA III*, pp. 37–60, for the text, along with a French translation of Lamprecht's Middle High German adaptation, the *Alexanderlied* (ca. 1155).

14. Only the beginning of this poem survives, in two manuscripts: Arsenal 3472 and Venice, Museo Civico, VI, 665. For a reconstruction of the decasyllabic archetype see *MFRA III*, pp. 61–100. In ms. BNF fr. 789, components of the decasyllabic poem and Alexandre de Paris's Branch I are combined with new material. See *MFRA III*, pp. 101–54, and *RA*, pp. 20–21.

15. Evidence of this "archetype" is found in three manuscripts. See *MFRA I* for the texts of mss. Arsenal 3472 and Venice, Museo Civico, VI, 665 (which also recounts the "Fuerre de Gadres" episode). For the first 72 laisses of ms. BN fr. 789, see *MFRA III*, pp. 101–54. For a fac-simile of the Venice ms.: *Le Roman d'Alexandre: Riproduzione del ms. Venezia Biblioteca Museo Correr 1493*, ed. Roberto Benedetti (Udine: Roberto Vattori, 1998), with an introduction by Emmanuèle Baumgartner.

16. The four components of Alexandre de Paris's poem were identified as "branches" by Paul Meyer, "Etude sur les manuscrits du *Roman d'Alexandre*," *Romania* 11 (1882), 213–332. Each branch is clearly representative of antecedent works: Br. I, the *enfances*, reflects the decasyllabic *Alexandre*; Br. II draws on the "Fuerre de Gadres" episode by Eustache; Br. III, on the expedition to the Orient, extensively reworks Lambert le Tort; and Br. IV, on the death of Alexander, is a rewriting of the anonymous *Mort Alixandre*. *MFRA II* gives the text of BN fr. 24365 for Branch I, and of BN fr. 25517 for Branches II–IV. *RA* follows the text of BN fr. 25517 exclusively, giving substantial excerpts from branches I, II, and III and all of Branch IV. See *RA*, pp. 59–61.

17. See Catherine Gaullier-Bougassas, "Jean Wauquelin et Vasque de Lucène: le 'roman familial' d'Alexandre et l'écriture de l'histoire au XVe siècle," in *Cahiers de Recherches médiévales (XIIIe–XVe siècle)*, 5 (1998), 125–38.

18. In addition to *MFRA I–VII*, other works in the French Alexander tradition appear in the Elliott Monograph Series (Princeton: Princeton University Press): Gui de Cambrai, *Le Vengement Alixandre*, ed. Bateman Edwards (23, 1928); Jean le Nevelon,

Venjance Alexandre, ed. Edward Billings Ham (37, 1931); *La Prise de Defur* and *Le Voyage d'Alexandre au Paradis Terrestre*, ed. Lawton P. G. Peckham and Milan S. La Du (35, 1935). All except *MFRA VI* (1976) were subsequently reprinted (New York: Kraus Reprints, 1965).

19. See Harf-Lancner's discussion of "Chanson de geste ou roman?" in *RA*, pp. 27–43.

20. For a sensitive discussion of the question of genre, see François Suard, "Alexandre est-il un personnage de roman?" *Bien dire et bien aprandre*, 7 (1989), 77–87, esp. p. 79.

21. On the legend's ambiguities see also, in *Alessandro*, Peter Dronke's "Introduzione" (pp. xv–lxxv).

22. See Corrado Bologna, "La generosità cavalleresca di Alessandro Magno," *L'Immagine riflessa* 12 (1989), 367–404.

23. See Catherine Gaullier-Bougassas, "Nectanabus et la singularité d'Alexandre dans les *Romans d'Alexandre* français," in *Alexandre*, pp. 303–19.

24. "And to that prince who marches with his troops, who lives by plundering, sacking and ransom, who controls what belongs to others, such generosity is essential; otherwise, his soldiers would not follow him. And with that which does not belong to you or to your subjects you can be a more liberal giver as was Cyrus, Caesar or Alexander, because spending what belongs to others does not detract from your reputation, rather it enhances it; only spending your own is what will hurt you." Niccolò Machiavelli, *The Prince*, ed. and trans. Mark Musa (New York: St Martin's Press, 1964), pp. 133–35.

25. See Piero Boitani, "L'aura e le ombre di Alessandro" in *Alessandro*, pp. 441–43.

26. Hugh (or Richard?) of Saint Victor, *Allegoriae in Vetus Testamentum* (*PL* CLXXV). See Dronke, *Alessandro*, p. li, and for other examples see Cary, pp. 118–42.

27. For the Vulgate *Alexandre*'s contrast to the texts with which it is frequently associated in literary history, the so-called *romans antiques* of *Thèbes*, *Enéas*, and *Troie*, see Aimé Petit, "Les romans antiques et Alexandre," in *Alexandre*, pp. 289–302.

28. See Emmanuèle Baumgartner, "L'Orient d'Alexandre," *Bien dire et bien aprandre* 6 (1988), p. 9, our translation.

29. Laurence Harf-Lancner, "La quête de l'immortalité: les fontaines merveilleuses du *Roman d'Alexandre* d'Alexandre de Paris," in *Sources et fontaines du Moyen Age à l'Age baroque* (Paris: Champion, 1998), p. 39, our translation.

30. For discussion of the name see Shigemi Sasaki, "'E si veira les bones, (…) / Que artus aveit faites en Orïent fichier'," in *Studi di storia della civiltà letteraria francese: Mélanges offerts à Lionello Sozzi* (Paris: Champion, 1996), pp. 1–20.

31. *Inferno* XXVI, in Dante Alighieri, *The Divine Comedy*, trans. Charles S. Singleton (Princeton: Princeton University Press, 1970): "dov' Ercule segnò li suoi riguardi

/ acciò che l'uom più oltre non si metta" (108–109) [where Hercules set out his marks, that no man should venture beyond them]; our translation.

32. For the parallels between Dante's Ulysses and Alexander, see D'Arco Silvio Avalle, *Modelli semiologici nella Commedia di Dante* (Milan: Bompiani, 1975), pp. 33–63.

33. Saint Bernard, "De Gradius humilitatis et superbiae," in Etienne Gilson, *La Théologie mystique de Saint Bernard* (Paris: J.Vrin, 1969), pp. 181–82, 85. See Sasaki, "'E si veira les bones...';" pp. 18–19.

34. See Baumgartner, "L'Orient d'Alexandre": "A la différence peut-être de l'autre monde celte, l'Orient d'Alexandre ne paraît ainsi prodiguer ses merveilles que pour mieux en montrer le caractère déceptif. Il ne s'offre que pour mieux se reprendre," (p. 13).

35. For the texts see *Prise*, pp. xlii–xlviii, xlix–lii, and 73–90.

36. For the relation of this text to the "horizontal" conception of a dialectic between this world and the Christian Otherworld, see Maria Luisa Meneghetti, "Cieli e terre nei secoli XI–XII: Orizzonti, percezioni, rapporti," in *Miscellanea del Centro di studi medioevali* (Milan: Università Cattolica del Sacro Cuore, 1998), pp. 184–85.

37. See Marylène Perez, "Alexandre le Grand dans l'Alexandréide," *Bien dire et bien aprandre* 6 (1988), pp. 73–76. Jean-Yves Tilliette argues that the hero of the Latin poem is essentially ambiguous and discloses the limitations of the character made popular by the *Roman d'Alexandre*; see "L'*Alexandréide* de Gautier de Châtillon: Enéide médiévale ou 'Virgile travesti'?" in *Alexandre*, pp. 275–86 (here p. 286).

38. Her vernacular corpus includes *MFRA II*; *RTC*; *Prosa*; Rutebeuf, *Dit d'Aristote*; Henri d'Andeli, *Lai d'Aristote*; and *Prise*.

39. See the *Book of Daniel* VIII, 5–8 and 11; the *Book of Maccabees* I, 1, 3–5.

40. VIII, 492–94: "ille cruentus/ Fatorum gladius, terrarum publica pestis."

41. See Pierre Briant, "Alexandre à Babylone: images grecques, images babyloniennes," in *Alexandre*, pp. 23–32.

42. See Catherine Croizy-Naquet, "Darius ou l'image du potentat perse dans le *Roman d'Alexandre*," in *Alexandre*, pp. 161–72 (here p. 164).

43. Gosman's corpus includes: *Prise*, from the second half of the thirteenth century; the three works—*Voeux* (1313–14), *Restor* (before 1338), and *Parfait* (before 1348)—comprising the so-called Paon Cycle; and two fifteenth-century prose compilations, the *Historia du bon roy Alixandre* by Jean Wauquelin (ca. 1448), and the anonymous *Fais et Conquestes du Noble roy Alexandre* (1450–70).

44. John L. Grigsby, "Courtesy in the *Voeux du Paon*," *Neuphilologische Mitteilungen* 86 (1985), p. 568.

45. See also Michelle Szkilnik, "Courtoisie et violence: Alexandre dans le *Cycle du Paon*," in *Alexandre*, pp. 321–39.

Chronology

356–323 B.C.	Alexander III, king of Macedon, called "the Great" on account of his conquest of Persia.

Major Works from Antiquity

ca. 40 A.D.	Quintus Curtius Rufus, *Historia Alexandri Magni*, an influential Latin history in ten volumes, the first two of which are lost.
1st century A.D.?	An apocryphal letter from Alexander to Aristotle concerning the marvels of India; may have originated in a Greek epistolary romance, a version of which figures in the Alpha version of the *Pseudo-Callisthenes*. Numerous Latin versions of the letter circulated independently. The *Epistola Alexandri Magni ad Aristotelem* was well known during the Middle Ages.
ca. 200 A.D.	The *Pseudo-Callisthenes*, or Greek Alexander romance, written in Alexandria and falsely attributed to the Greek historian and nephew of Aristotle. A seminal work for the medieval Alexander tradition, it was translated into numerous languages.
ca. 320–30 A.D.	Julius Valerius, *Res gestae Alexandri Macedonis*, a Latin translation of the *Pseudo-Callisthenes*.
9th century A.D.	The *Epitomè Julii Valerii*, an important abridgement of the *Res gestae* of Julius Valerius.
ca. 953 A.D.	Archpriest Leo of Naples, *Nativitas et victoria Alexandri Magni regis*, a Latin adaptation of the *Pseudo-Callisthenes*.
10th century A.D.	*Historia de Preliis*, an adaptation of the *Nativitas et victoria* of Archpriest Leo.

The Medieval French Tradition

ca. 1110–25	Fragment of a Franco-Provençal *Roman d'Alexandre* by Alberic de Pisançon, of which 105 octosyllabic verses

survive, in monorhymed *laisses*. Evokes the hero's birth
and education.

ca. 1155   Lamprecht, *Alexanderlied*, a Middle High German adaptation of Alberic's poem.

ca. 1160   The *Roman d'Alexandre* in decasyllabic laisses, adapted
from Alberic by a Poitevin poet, depicts the hero's *enfances*
and early exploits.

ca. 1170   Eustache, *Le Roman du Fuerre de Gadres*, recounts a raid
undertaken by Alexander's forces during the siege of Tyr.
This work has not survived in the original.

ca. 1170   Lambert le Tort, *Alexandre en Orient*, a lost dodecasyllabic
account of the Macedonian's adventures in India; draws
on the *Epitomè* of Julius Valerius and the *Epistola Alexandri
Magni*.

ca. 1170   The first eight laisses (159 verses) are all that survive of
a fragmentary *Mort Alixandre*, on the death of the hero
(ms. Arsenal 3472).

ca. 1175–80 Thomas de Kent, *Le Roman de toute Chevalerie* (over
12,000 verses) gives a synoptic account of the heroic
biography, elaborated in monorhyming dodecasyllabic
laisses; shows considerable independence from continental French antecedents.

ca. 1180   Jehan le Nevelon, *La Venjance Alixandre*, a continuation
on the avenging of Alexander's death.

ca. 1185   Alexandre de Paris (also known as Alexandre de Bernay),
Roman d'Alexandre. A composite synoptic romance of some
16,000 verses in monorhyming dodecasyllabic *laisses*, this
reworking of earlier Old French poems, known generally
as the "Vulgate" *Alexandre*, is comprised of four parts,
known as "branches": a twelve-syllable version of the
anonymous decasyllabic poem depicting the birth, childhood and youth of Alexander; an augmented rewriting of
the *Fuerre de Gadres* of Eustache; a vast remodeling of
Lambert le Tort's account of Alexander's oriental exploits;
and an expansive renovation of the *Mort Alixandre*.

1184–87   Gautier de Châtillon, *Alexandreïs*, a Latin epic based largely
on Quintus Curtius.

ca. 1191   Gui de Cambrai, *Le Vengement Alixandre*, another continuation detailing the vengeance exacted following the
death of the hero.

ca. 1213–14 The *Histoire ancienne jusqu'à César* contains a life of
Alexander reflecting the author's familiarity with the
Epitomè of Julius Valerius and the *Epistola Alexandri Magni*.

13th century	The prose *Roman d'Alexandre*, translated from the tenth-century Latin prose *Historia de Preliis*.
ca. 1250	The *Prise de Defur*, an anonymous interpolation of 1,654 alexandrines on the siege and capture of Defur incorporates several new episodes.
ca. 1260	The anonymous *Voyage d'Alexandre au Paradis terrestre* is an episodic interpolation of 503 alexandrine verses on the king's voyage to the earthly paradise.
ca. 1312	Jacques de Longuyon, *Les Voeux du paon*. The first of three works in the so-called "Paon Cycle," this interpolation in monorhyming alexandrine laisses augments the *matière* of the third branch of the Vulgate *Alexandre*.
before 1338	Jean le Court, Brisebarre, *Le Restor du paon*, a continuation of the *Voeux du paon*.
1340	*Le Parfait du paon*, by Jean de la Mote, the final poem in the Paon Cycle. Inserted into the *Prise de Defur*, it lies chronologically between the third and fourth branches of the Vulgate *Alexandre*.
before 1448	The *Histoire du bon roy Alixandre* by Jehan Wauquelin, a prose historical romance drawing on a verse version of the Vulgate *Alexandre* containing the *Fuerre de Gadres*, the *Prise de Defur*, the *Voeux du paon* and the *Restor du paon*, as well as on the prose *Alexandre*.
1450–70	*Les Fais et concquestes du noble roy Alexandre*, an anonymous prose reworking of the verse tradition.
1468	*Les Faits du grand Alexandre*, a prose translation of the *Alexandreïs* of Gautier de Châtillon, carried out by Vasque de Lucène under the patronage of the court of Burgundy.

1

The Prologue to the *Historia de Preliis*: A Pagan Model of Spiritual Struggle

Michel Zink

Is it permissible and is it profitable to read pagan authors? We know how insistently that question was raised during the patristic period. From this debate the Middle Ages retained in particular two illustrious passages from Saint Jerome and Saint Augustine, the former commenting on the regulations in Deuteronomy pertaining to the *captiva gentilis*, the latter justifying the *spoliatio Aegyptiorum*. Drawn from these was the notion that it was good to borrow from the knowledge of ancient letters that which is useful for deciphering the word of God. But for the Christian, can there be not only a useful tool for the study of the Scriptures, but even a direct moral profit to be gained from reading pagan authors and, through them, from a knowledge of the ancient world? Certain remarks of Saint Jerome suggest that this is possible. The idea is implicit, but indeed present, in the passage from Augustine on the *spoliatio Aegyptiorum*, and it is explicit in the *Confessions*. It underlies Cassiodorus's recommendation that monks copy the works of pagan antiquity—a counsel which rescued that literature for us. Later on it will be valorized through the didactic import of the *accessus ad auctores*.

The possibility and the conditions of this moral profit are expressed forcefully in the middle of the tenth century in the prologue to the *Historia de Preliis*, a translation of the Romance of Alexander by the Pseudo-Callisthenes, of which the Archpriest Leon had brought back a copy in 942 from Constantinople, where the Duke of Naples had sent him as an emissary. Whether this prologue, which survives in a very few manuscripts, is or is not by the Archpriest is of little consequence to our present concerns:

> Certamina vel victorias excellentium virorum infidelium ante
> adventum Christi, quamvis exstitissent pagani, bonum et utile est
> omnibus Christianis ad audiendum et intelligendum tam praelatis

21

quam subditis, videlicet saecularibus et spiritualibus viris, quia cunctos ad meliorem provocat actionem. Nam prelati, id est rectores, legendo et considerando quemadmodum praedicti pagani idolis servientes agebant se caste et fideliter atque in omnibus se inreprehensibiliter ostendebant, per eorum exempla bonorum operum ita acuant mentes suas, eo quod fideles et membra Christi esse videntur, ut multo magis meliores se illis demonstrent in castitate et iusticia atque pietate. Subiecti vero, id est milites sub milicia constituti, legendo vel audiendo talia certamina et operationes commilitum suorum, qui magis daemonibus quam Deo militabant, certent se prudentiores ostendere illis in omni opere bono, sicut decet militibus Christi. Nam dominis carnalibus pure et fideliter secundum praeceptum apostoli (1 Peter 2,13; cf. Romans 13,1–5, Titus 3,1) deserviant, Deo vero, creatori suo, tota mente ita decernt famulari custodiendo precepta eius, nulli umquam violentiam facientes aut aliena auferentes, sed in sua substantia abundantes, sicut precursor et baptista Christi, beatus Johannes, in Evangelio precepit (Luke 3,14), ne, quod absit, militando saeculo alienentur a militia caelesti. Licet namque et spirituales homines audire, quae et qualia certamina vel quam benignas operationes propter amorem saeculi in se habebant pagani ab initio usque ad adventum Christi, ut merendo considerent, quam sapientes et pios viros tunc possidebat diabolus excecando mentes illorum, ne suum agnoscerent creatorem et servirent creaturae potius quam creatori, et ideo intelligebant, quam iustum et necessarium fuit humano generi adventus Christi, quia secundum sacram scripturam, si nos non visitasset ex alto redemptor noster demonstrando se ipsum nobis viam salutis, per quam salvaremur, ut eum solum in trinitate adoraremus ipsumque verum creatorem omnium agnosceremus, funditus nos omnes in aeternum perieramus. Quapropter pura mente cum apostolo admirando proclamemus: "O altitudo sapientiae et scientiae Dei, quam incomprehensibilia sunt iudicia eius et investigales viae eieus" (Romans 11,33). Et iterum cum psalmista requirentes exclamemus: "Quis loquitur potentias Domini et auditas faciet omnes laudes eius?" (Psalms 106,2). Subaudis: nemo.[1]

(It is good and just that all Christians, those who command as well as those who obey, that is, laymen as well as ecclesiastics, listen and be able to understand [the story] of the battles and victories of the most eminent among the infidels who lived before the coming of Christ, pagans though they were, for everyone will find therein a means of bettering their conduct. In effect, those who command, the leaders, by reading and meditating on how these pagans, even though they worshiped idols, behaved in a chaste and upright manner and in every respect conducted themselves in ways beyond reproach, should by the example of their fine deeds sharpen their own conscience—always understood that they are among the faithful and the members of Christ—so as to show themselves very superior to these pagans in chastity, justice, and piety. As for the subordinates, the soldiers enrolled in the army, by reading and listening to accounts of the battles and the great deeds of their pagan companions at arms who more often fought in the army of demons than in that of God, they should fight in such a way as to show themselves more capable than their precursors of accomplishing all good actions, as befits the soldiers of God. They should in effect serve their wordly lords wholeheartedly and faithfully, according to the apostle's precept, and struggle to serve the true God, their Creator, with all their soul, respecting and observing His commandments, not committing violent acts or taking the possessions of others, but being content with what they have, as the blessed John, the precursor of Christ, he who baptized Him, prescribes in the Gospels, so that—God forbid!—making war in this world they not become separated from the celestial militia. Spiritual persons as well can hear the story and judge the quality of the combats engaged and the splendid acts of the pagans for the love of this world, from its origin unto the coming of Christ, in order to meditate usefully on the wisdom and piety of men whom the devil held in his power by blinding their spirits in order to prevent them from recognizing their Creator and to make them obey the creature rather than the Creator: they will also understand how just and necessary was the coming of Christ for mankind, since, according to Scripture, if our Redeemer had not come from on high to visit us and show us Himself the way of salvation by which we shall be saved, so that we adore Him alone and triune and recognize Him as the true Maker of all things, we would all be cast unto perdition for all eternity. For this, let us proclaim with a pure spirit in sharing the admiration of the Apostle: "O sublime wisdom and knowledge of God! How incomprehensible His judgments, how impenetrable His ways!" And with the psalmist let us add: "Who can tell of the mighty works of God, who can make all His praises heard?" Implied: no one.)

Do we assume that Archpriest Leon is recommending that Christians know the deeds—in this instance military actions—and not the literary works of pagan antiquity? *Certamina vel victorias*, that is what it is good and useful to know. Yet what does it mean here "to know"? To listen and to understand. The mediation of a story to which attention and intelligence are applied is supposed by *audiendum et intelligendum*. Implicit in the first sentence of this prologue is the slippage of the very meaning of the word *gesta*. The *Gesta Romanorum* is a book. What Leon brought back from Constantinople is a book; translating it, he made another book, of which this prologue is the insert. Farther along, it is to the act of reading as well that he invites both the *praelati* (*legendo et considerando*) and the *subjecti* (*legendo vel audiendo*).

In what way is such a reading profitable? The answer is given in the governing idea of the passage, which is the following: if the pagans, who had no attachments other than to this world, were servants of the devil who blinded them, and knew not God, were capable of such virtue, then Christians, who know and serve God, must be capable, each according to his station, to do far better. The reading of works that preserve the memory of the pagans' "combats or victories" is thus in service to that virtuous emulation.

What, then, is the nature of such emulation? It could be that which obtains, literally, between the great soldiers of antiquity, like Alexander, and the Christian warriors of the present time. That is what will shortly be offered, beginning with the *Historia de Preliis* itself, by the fictive personage of Alexander transformed into a chivalric model. In a sense, it is from this image that the idea of the Nine Worthies—the nine pagan, biblical, or Christian luminaries—will be spawned near the end of the Middle Ages. But such was not the idea of Archpriest Leon. According to his view, the heroic deeds of the pagans do not offer Christians a model of heroism, but of saintliness. He does not cite the exemplarity of pagan warriors for the benefit of Christian warriors—those Christians who are summoned to battle—but rather for the defender of the faith that every Christian should be. In other words, it is the Pauline metaphor of spiritual combat that legitimizes the interest in ancient battles. . . . It is therefore necessary, to profit from them, to apply them figuratively to the Christian life and thus to understand their true significance for a Christian: the *intelligendum* of the first sentence is thus not placed there by chance.

The most striking feature of this prologue is found elsewhere, however. On the contrary, there is nothing new about the allegory of struggle on behalf of the faith. Not only is it borrowed from Saint Paul, it also governs Christian exegesis of the historical books of the Old Testament. What is remarkable, on the other hand, is the fact that Leon bases his development on the description of a social hierarchy and the organization of society according to the military model, where clerics are officers and the laity simple soldiers. It is in terms of that hierarchy and organization that the example of pagan military virtues can be useful. At the same time, the military model used to describe Christian society is far from a pure metaphor.

For the leaders and the subordinates are the religious men and the laity: *tam praelatis quam subditis, videlicet saecularibus et spiritualibus viris*, expressions taken up again in *prelati, id est rectores . . . subjecti vero, id est milites sub milicia constituti*. The example of virtuous pagans must impel the spiritual leaders to rival them in chastity, justice, and piety, just as it should move the subordinate laymen to demonstrate their superiority to them in all good actions. Yet what follows in this advice to good Christian soldiers is addressed to real soldiers, because it reiterates the specific advice John the Baptist gives them in the Gospel of Luke. The spiritual leaders, to whom the author returns in closing, are urged to contemplate the example of the pagans: these wise and pious men, who were nonetheless blinded by the devil, allow us to understand the extent to which the advent of Christ was just and necessary and invite us to give thanks to the true God, Creator of all things, and to praise His works.

By considering the *praelati* as spiritual leaders and the *subditi* or *subjecti* either as laypersons subjected to spiritual leaders or as real soldiers, the Archpriest lays out his conceptualization of society, clerical as well as military, governed by religious leaders, while laymen are called metaphorically to be soldiers of Christ, yet also have fundamentally military occupations.

The ambiguity between the metaphor of combat used to depict the exemplary Christian life and the real struggles to which the Christian might be called had a long posterity in spiritual and literary contexts. It is thus not insignificant that it appears at the opening of a text that belongs to the prehistory of our romance of chivalry and adventure. To take an example from outside the domain of romance, it was to be deliberately maintained and developed as stylistic ornamentation and as an element in a demonstration by Saint Bernard in the *De laude novae militiae*. Let me recall the well-known opening of this treatise:

> Novum militiae genus ortum nuper auditur in terris, et in illa regione, quam olim in carne praesens visitavit Oriens ex alto, ut unde tunc in fortitudine manus suae tenebrarum principes exturbavit, inde et modo ipsorum satellites, filios diffidentiae. . . . Novum, invquam, militiae genus, et saeculis inexpertum, qua gemino pariter conflictu atque infatigabiliter decertatur, tum adversus carnem et sanguinem, tum contra spiritualia nequitiae in caelestibus. Et quidem ubi solis viribus corporis corporeo fortiter hosti resistitur, id quidem ego tam non judico mirum, quam nec rarum existimo. Sed et quando animi virtute vitiis sive daemoniis bellum indicitur, ne hoc quidem mirabile, etsi laudabile dixerim, cum plenus monachis cernatur mundus. Ceterum cum uterque homo suo quisque gladio potenter accingitur, suo cingulo nobiliter insignitur, quis hoc non aestimet omni admiratione dignissimum, quod adeo liquet esse insolitum? Impavidus profecto miles, et omni ex parte securus, qui ut corpus ferri, sic animum fidei lorica induitur. Utrisque nimirum munitus armis, nec daemonem timet, nec hominem. Nec vero mortem formidat, qui mori desiderat. Qui enim vel vivens, vel moriens metuat, cui vivere Christus est, et mori lucrum? Stat quidem fidenter libenterque pro Christo; sed magis cupit dissolvi et esse cum Christo: hoc enim melius.[2]

(It is said that a New Chivalry has just been born unto us, in the very
land where long ago the Word of God took on flesh; in these blessed
places where, with His powerful hand, He dispersed the princes of
darkness, the sword of the stalwart will soon finish exterminating the
last of their minions. By this I mean the infidels. . . . A New Chivalry
indeed, and such as the world has never known until now, destined
to lead, relentlessly, a double combat, against flesh and blood, and
against the spirits of darkness. That a man should consecrate all of his
bodily strength to the struggle against a corporeal enemy, that is no
rare occurrence, and I am hardly surprised by it; the same is true if
a man deploys the forces of his soul against vice and the seductions
of the demon, for the world is full of monks who wage this struggle;
but those for whom my admiration is truly ineffable are those heroes
of unheard-of audacity who, filled with courage, have girded themselves with the double baldric and the double-edged sword. The
knight who has in a single gesture clad his soul in the breastplate of
faith, and his body in arms of iron, is secure on all fronts and can
remain intrepid. Thus doubly armed, he fears neither man nor demon.
Far from fearing death, he desires it; Christ is his life, death his profit;
of what should he be afraid? He lives in confident surrender to God.
He could have but a single preference: to be freed from the bonds of
the flesh and complete his union with Christ.)

I could have ended this citation with *nec daemonem timet, nec hominem* (he
fears neither man nor demon), but that would not do justice to Saint Bernard.
For the magnificent cadence of his exordium shows that he is not taken in by
this literality of the combats of the faith: the familiar formulas inspired by Saint
Paul; the life in Christ for which the price of death is nothing; that union with
Christ to which every Christian for whom death is an advantage aspires—all
of this is valid for everyone, all of this is the vocation of every man, and not
just of the warrior-monks. Here is a case where the opening ambiguity, which
purports to promote the cause of the Templars, ultimately—in a reversal that
hints at the reservations of Saint Bernard—concludes by bringing their life
round to the universal model of the Christian life.

Of course this ambiguity between the metaphorical struggle of the
Christian life and the real battles of chivalric life was to loom especially large
in the *chansons de geste* and in vernacular romances. While offering no general
observations on that theme, I would simply recommend a rereading, in light
of the prologue to the *Historia de Preliis*, of the prologue of the *Conte du Graal*.
I do not do it here because everyone knows the latter text by heart and has
one's own ideas about it. It is quite apparent, however, that the Archpriest
Leon's prologue accords pertinence and a precise meaning to the parallel
between Philip of Flanders and Alexander the Great. In contrast, one perhaps

also senses in the prologue to Alexandre de Paris's romance a deliberate intention, almost a provocation, that carefully seeks to eradicate any allusion to Alexander's paganism and on the contrary presents him as one chosen by God.

As for the *Conte du Graal*, it is not by chance that Chrétien, at the beginning of a romance on Charity—for that is the subject of the romance—emphasizes that Philip of Flanders embodies the charity that was lacking in Alexander. For anyone who reads Leon in the meditative and spiritual frame of mind that was Chrétien's can see that the difference between Alexander and his Christian emulators lies in the fact that for the latter Charity is not just any Christian virtue; it is not even, we might say, just another theological virtue. It is the very nature of God (Saint John), and it is God present from within this world (Saint Paul: "When I was a child . . . I shall know as I am known"; the difference is between awaiting in faith and hope, and God already totally present in Charity). Nor is it by chance that Chrétien pretends—deliberately, of course—to confuse Saint John and Saint Paul, or rather brings them together in order to emphasize that they are saying the same thing. The emulation of ancient chivalry incites one to surpass it in God and God alone, that is, to live in Charity.

Notes

1. Cited from *Alessandro*, pp. 16–18.

2. *Tractatus de laude novae militiae*, 1–22, in *Sancti Bernardi Opera*, vol. 3, *Tractatus et opuscula*, ed. J. Leclerq and H. M. Rochais (Rome: Editiones Cistercienses, 1963), p. 214.

2

The Raid on Gaza in Alexandre de Paris's Romance

Emmanuèle Baumgartner

The episode known as *Fuerre de Gadres*, which occupies an important place in Branch II of Alexandre de Paris's version of the *Roman d'Alexandre*, is a well-known depiction of a cattle raid carried out by Alexander's army in the vicinity of an imaginary city in Palestine. According to tradition this city is located near Tyre, to which Alexander has laid siege. In Alexandre de Paris's version, however, it appears—geographical realities notwithstanding—to be confused with Gaza.[1] This episode of the *Alexandre* is not among those most highly esteemed nowadays: the interminable succession of repetitive skirmishes and the conventionally written *laisses* make it seem banal, in terms of both content and execution. The fact that Laurence Harf-Lancner leaves it out of her bilingual edition of Alexandre de Paris's version (*RA*) is suggestive. While that exclusion stems from editorial constraints, it also makes sense in terms of our modern tendency to read the *Roman d'Alexandre*—a text whose status is ambiguous, "aux frontières de l'épique et du romanesque," to echo the apt title of a recent study by Catherine Gaullier-Bougassas (*Frontières*)—exclusively for its "romanesque" qualities. Thus, rather than linger over the strictly epic passages, we seem more inclined to dwell on the family romance of a hero attempting to cope with the suspicion that he is a bastard, on Aristotle's education of his pupil, on evocations of the wonders of the East, or on the eulogies in Branch IV. Such a selective approach is not without justification; if, at the beginning of the twenty-first century, we may continue to read the *Roman d'Alexandre* and on occasion find pleasure in doing so, that reading must appeal to our own sensibility. The myth of the conqueror, which still haunted Napoleon, now seems obsolete. The fantastic vision of an Orient more terrifying than exotic is more likely to captivate the reader, who is enthralled even more by the precariousness of an heroic destiny onto which medieval authors merely projected their sober reflections on the vanity of worldly glory. But the literary historian's task, to the extent that this approach is still viable, is to attempt to understand why, during a certain period and for a certain audience, a type of text like the _chanson de geste_—the 'genre' to which, at least in formal terms, the _Roman d'Alexandre_ belongs—could please and interest its public, just as do, nowadays, the ritualized violence of Westerns and their larger-than-life dispensers of justice. The literary historian must also tease out Alexandre de Paris's likely esthetic objectives when in rewriting the first author, Eustache, he inserted into the latter's "riche istoire" (Br. I, v. 1)—into his "life" of Alexander (v. 62)—the epic text of _Fuerre de Gadres_, as well as the episode's implications concerning prowess and its foundations and the relationship between warriors, their leader, and those with whom they do battle. In sum, we must ask ourselves why this episode, which for us seems like such a disaster area in the text, was so successful in the Middle Ages, as is quite evident from the number of revivals and recastings of it that were produced.

Without going into undue detail, let us recall that the main source of _Fuerre de Gadres_ is the third version, interpolated, of the _Historia Preliis_, which was the point of departure for the lost version of _Fuerre_ composed by Eustache (whom Alexandre de Paris names at v. 1777). The scholarly editors of the _Roman d'Alexandre_, and more recently D. J. A. Ross,[2] have attempted to reconstruct this initially independent text, which Alexandre de Paris obviously revised and amplified extensively to make it an essential part of Branch II, which deals with Alexander's victories in the Near East, the conquest of Tyre, and the king's triumphant campaign against Darius. We should also recall that one version of the episode, which magnifies the role of Gadifer de Larris, is found in version β of the text, of which, in _laisses_ 317–40 of Branch III, the Val Daniel episode is a double; that the passage was interpolated into certain manuscripts of the _Roman de Toute Chevalerie_ by Thomas of Kent; and that there is also a Latin adaptation of Eustache in two manuscripts, of which one, examined by Ross, would seem to be complete. Finally, be it noted that the episode and especially the character of Gadifer were used again in the fourteenth century by the author of the _Perceforest,_ and that they play a fundamental role at the outset of that romance.[3] In that context, after the death of their father, the two sons of Gadifer become the protégés of Alexander, who gives one of them, Bétis (the future Perceforest), the kingdom of Scotland. In sum, _Fuerre de Gadres_ gave rise to nearly all of the avatars and modifications that a medieval text could undergo: after circulating autonomously, it was amplified and integrated into a larger ensemble; interpolated into another text; translated into Latin; it produced a double, and in the case of _Perceforest_, engendered the hero of a new text.

The episode's popularity during the Middle Ages is explained in part by its setting. The tropological patterns of thought prevalent during the period may, at the end of the twelfth century, have conditioned the public's interest in exploits that took place in the area conquered by the warriors of the First Crusade, notably the Valley of Jehosaphat (the Cedron Valley, east of Jerusalem) where the raid supposedly occurred and where, at the beginning of _La Chanson de Jérusalem_, a similar expedition was mounted by leaders of the Crusade.[4] Let us hasten to add, however—we shall return to this matter—that no trace of any religious dimension or crusading spirit is to be found in the version by Alexandre de Paris. We can thus more readily attribute the success of *Fuerre de Gadres* to the warlike quality of a passage capable of diverting the public's attention from a story that all too often strays from the epic dimension of its execution, so that the public (or at least its chivalric component) could at least find therein the kind of pleasure afforded by listening to *chansons de geste*.

The interest that the distinguished editors of the *Roman d'Alexandre* bring to this episode is less spontaneously motivated and perhaps more debatable. To follow them arduously through their labyrinthine search for the original text of Eustache is to realize how much their reasoning and reconstruction are attuned to degradations that Alexandre de Paris supposedly inflicted upon his source, and to showing how a text deteriorates as it undergoes successive reworkings.[5] It is of course legitimate, when the possibility presents itself, to attempt to reconstruct a source text, and the comparison, if it turns out to be possible—though is that really the case here?—may be fruitful. Yet can we simply assume that amplification is tantamount to degradation without thereby condemning virtually all texts produced during the Middle Ages? Without according undue attention to a pre-history of the *Fuerre de Gadres* that in any case remains quite obscure, it is undoubtedly more worthwhile to consider the extant—if not 'finished'—product offered by Alexandre de Paris, in order to see how the episode in Branch II functions and in terms of what criteria we might perceive the rewriting author's esthetic norms and ideological perspective.

As the editors of the *Roman d'Alexandre* note in an equally disapproving manner, Alexandre de Paris, in order to bring his compilation to completion, recycled everything available. He could thus not have failed to appropriate the *Fuerre* episode, which strengthened the text's epic dimension and offered him a way, using Eustache's model, to compose a kind of miniature *chanson de geste*. If we consider only *laisses* 1–108, the narrative structure is in fact both a closed entity and perfectly integrated into the larger ensemble comprised of the conquest of Tyre. It is during the siege of that city that Alexander decides to mount an expedition to the "val de Josafaille" (Br. II, L. 1) led by the peers, except for Clin and Ptolemy, under the command of Emenidus. Initially the Greeks have the upper hand, but with the arrival of the army of Betys of Gadres, coming to reinforce Balés of Tyre, Emenidus, realizing that his men are outnumbered, asks those of his entourage to seek help from Alexander. All of the warriors summoned, in a long series of parallel *laisses*, gallantly refuse to leave the battlefield. This includes a young unknown, poor and "désarmé," Corineüs, whose origins—he is the nephew of Emenidus—and background as a prisoner of Darius are disclosed (L. 39). After Aristé finally agrees to go for reinforcements, Alexander's arrival saves the day, despite the exploits of Gadifer the Egyptian, who eventually kills Emenidus. Betys of Gadres flees back to his city. After ravaging his lands, Alexander returns to lay siege to Tyre, which he finally overruns, then also takes Gadres (L. 108), before marching on Jerusalem.

As we can see from this brief summary, the episode, independent in Eustache's version, is well-integrated here into the rest of Branch II. On the one hand, the intervention of Betys of Gadres is linked with the siege of Tyre: he comes to the rescue of the city besieged by Alexander. On the other hand, the conquest of Gadres, which provides the episode's anticipated closure— though this denouement is an invention of Alexandre de Paris, since the account by Eustache ended, according to the editors of the text, at *laisse* 76— comes after the siege of Tyre and the famous episode of Alexander's "leap" (L. 84) and before the major battles with Darius.

The esthetic intent seems readily apparent here. Alexandre de Paris's version is, as numerous critics have emphasized, a compilation and rewriting of earlier texts.[6] Yet it is also—and these two aspects are no doubt related— a compilation of different modes of literary discourse that are more or less well-blended by the use of rhymed *laisses* and alexandrines. Hence an inter-section of the epic dimension with a problematic typical of romance, plus didactic and moral discourse, an encyclopedic intent, etc., about the only missing element being amatory discourse.[7] In this disparate ensemble, Branch II is the purest representative of an epic vein, and from that point of view *Fuerre*, as a complete *chanson de geste*, is exemplary. It is no doubt not by chance that its structure is reminiscent of the *Chanson de Roland*, which in many ways seems to be the operant model; it is already apparent in the episode where the Greek warriors refuse to go for help, a greatly amplified version of the debate between Roland and Oliver. We can also detect analogies between Alexander's return to the battlefield and the eventual conquest of Gadres, which would be the equivalent of Saragossa in the *Chanson de Roland*, and the second part of the *Roland*, which focuses on Charlemagne's return and victory. Moreover, in order to construct, or reconstruct, the Rolandian scenario from the text of Eustache, Alexandre de Paris has deftly implemented a vast arsenal of proper-ties that abound in the *chanson de geste*.[8] Nothing is overlooked: the frequent announcements (L. 67); the generous use of parallel *laisses* (e.g., the develop-ment beginning with L. 9, and parallel verses [vv. 655 and 692; 1799 and 1812]); the widespread recourse to stock motifs such as arming and the de-scription of arms; passages on the origins of warriors, as well as of their mounts (L. 70); the motif of the message to be delivered (L. 48); the motif of the besieged city; the *planctus* (L. 17 and 55) and the motif of bereavement (L. 18 and 25); the leader's exhortation on the battlefield (L. 45); the courtly motif of the sleeve fastened to the warrior's lance (L. 62). All are motifs gleaned from the conventional background formed by the multiple accounts of single com-bat and repeated evocations of skirmishes and pursuits.

This catalogue, by no means exhaustive, does not take account of the anomalies or displacements with regard to the canonic model. In the thick of the episode Alexandre de Paris is already developing the role of a figure inherited from Eustache: the pathetically equipped "pauvre saudoier" (L. 20, vv.

393, 809) who claims that his name is Corineüs (v. 850), a name no doubt inherited from Wace's *Brut*. In contrast with what transpires in the story—reconstructed from Eustache, of course—Emenidus, in order to convince the young man to go as messenger to Alexander, holds out the possibility of acquiring splendid arms in return for that service (L. 18 and 20). Yet twice he proudly refuses the offer; then, in the lengthy *laisse* 39, a kind of "romance" begins to take shape around the figure of the young warrior: he single-handedly conquers arms of great value and saves Emenidus who, as both men joyfully discover, is his uncle. The "romance" of Corineüs is above all an excellent example of amplification based on stock epic motifs. But the emphasis placed on poverty, which Corineüs overcomes alone, with bravura, while refusing to be in any way beholden to the king, compels a thorough reevaluation of the didactic and ideological dimension of *Fuerre de Gadres*, an episode that might initially have seemed a mere exercise in stylistics.

In the first place, it is surprising that in the *Roman d'Alexandre* one of the most effective epic passages, and one written with meticulous attention to detail, should be a cattle raid involving no mere scavengers but a military unit including all of the king's peers except Ptolemy and Clin. Moreover, ambiguity is apparent from the very outset: the object is to "querre la vitaille" (v. 27, seek provisions), then to "morir por la vitaille" (v. 69, die for provisions), and the expedition itself is labeled as "folie"(v. 67, madness). The emphasis is also on the heavy equipment of the knights "qui n'aloient mie en guise de berchiers" (v. 46, who weren't setting out equipped as shepherds), and the enterprise—a cattle-raid—seems meager indeed when compared to the magnitude of the losses sustained. It would no doubt be excessive, given our ignorance of the medieval reception of this type of text, to speak of mock-epic here, though a glance in that direction seems not entirely unjustified. Alexander's arrival on the battlefield clearly restores the epic and ideological norm. Not only does the conflict begin to favor the Greeks, culminating in their unscheduled capture of Gadres, but the peers' displays of heroism are restored to the prominence they deserve. Nonetheless, although they are extremely courageous, they can neither secure the victory nor compromise the superior prowess and authority of their leader. The significance of this is quite clear: the king remains the ultimate recourse.[9] Likewise in the *Roland*, even though Roland remained master of the battlefield and—at the expense of his own life, it is true—fended off the Sarrasins, only Charlemagne can avenge his nephew and the latter's companions.

Might we suspect, then, that this episode engages a subtle revision of epic values in general and of crusade values in particular? By its very repetition, in the emphatic, indeed swaggering, utterances to which it gives rise, the motif of successive refusals by potential messengers is a bit too reminiscent of the motif of excessive or outrageous vows, or "gabs" (the term in fact appears at v. 234). Not without irony, this motif also underlines the vainglory and rash prowess that propel Alexander's companions at this stage. To brandish dented and punctured armor in order to demonstrate one's valor, such is the requisite ideal that the Greeks voice interminably, in parallel *laisses* (L. 9, 10, 11, 12, 22) as well as in their fear, which comes across as truly pathetic, of becoming the objects of "male chançon" (vv. 380–83, derisive songs). Yet hardly anyone besides the "povre desarmé" (destitute warrior) might justifiably adopt the motif (L. 20) of pierced armor, and for a good reason: he has nothing better.

What the warriors' repeated refusal to carry the message reveals, or rather exposes, is the futile circularity of a kind of prowess that comes to nought because it is not predicated on any sort of transcendence. Unlike Roland and Oliver, Alexander's companions are engaged in no struggle in the name of God, nor for "Douce France," nor for their king, not even, fundamentally, for glory. The argument that in fact recurs insistently is that they must fight in order to merit the gifts in kind, the "honors" they have received from Alexander, and in order to obtain still others. This boils down to the fact that, beneath the brilliant veneer of epic writing in this passage, the questioning that lies at the heart of Alexandre de Paris's version already finds expression: that of whether a durable power base be founded on unlimited exercise of prowess and generosity, the systematic dispensation of wealth—the "conseil" or rule of government that Aristotle steadfastly proffers to his "pupil," but whose vanity and dangers the text here finally flushes out.

In this light, we can reread *laisse* 45 and Emenidus's astonishing exhortation to his companions at the most crucial moment of the battle, and compare his discourse with that, for example, of Hector to his men in the *Roman de Troie*, when he urges them to fight less for honor than in order to save their homeland and their families.[10] Emenidus is much more down-to-earth in his discourse:

> Lors s'escria en haut: "Deservons les saudees
> Que nos a Alixandres par maintes fois donees.
> Mal avroit emploié son vin et ses pevrees,
> Ses chars, ses venisons et fresches et salees,
> Ses riches dras de soie et ses porpres listees,
> Ses biaus henas d'argent et ses coupes dorees
> Et ses beles richeces qu'il nos a presentees,
> Se ci ne sont por lui nos proëces mostrees . . . (vv. 1022–29)

(Then he cried aloud: "Let us earn the rewards that Alexander has so often bestowed upon us. Poorly shall he have given his wine and preserves, his chariots, his fresh and salted venison, his lavish silk fabrics and his bordered crimsons, his handsome silver goblets and gilded vases, and all of the beautiful treasures he has presented us, if our prowess is not now made manifest for him . . .)

This exhortation echoes the "lament," also by Emenidus, in *laisse* 18, where he deplores the absence from the battlefield of the "frans rois debonaires qui tant nos seut amer" (v. 302, noble, gentle king who always esteems us so highly), that is, who bestows without counting them "pailes" (silks), gold, silver, and sumptuous gifts. He concludes by recommending that the warriors preserve, not their honor, but their "honors" (v. 1033), that is, the material goods that their leader has up until now lavished upon them.

Within this context one sees more clearly the function of the "povre desarmé," the exception he represents in the series of possible messengers, and the calling into question that he initiates. To the proposition that Emenidus makes him—to acquire splendid arms if he bears the message—he first replies that he does not wish to forego the opportunity to participate for the first time in an "estor plenier" (v. 433, major battle). He emphasizes above all that it is appropriate to send a messenger who is more "riche" than he, "qui mieus sache plaidier" (v. 431, who is better at argumentation). Whether we read "rich" according to its current meaning or as "powerful," the result is the same: only a messenger who is already affluent will be able to find the right words to deliver the message convincingly. As for the arms, he will win them for himself, stripping them from a magnificently equipped knight while also allowing himself the luxury of saving Emenidus. In contrast with the self-serving and ultimately ineffectual prowess of the peers we have here the gratuitous prowess of this self-made man, Cornineüs, about whom one can wager—he in fact dies shortly thereafter—that he will never owe a thing to Alexander. Unlike poor Sanson, who rushes into the fray out of gratitude to Alexander for having promised him the city of Tyre (vv. 282–83) and who at the hands of Betys de Gadres (L. 24), is the first to die.

We know how, at the end of Branch IV, Alexandre de Paris dwells at length on the exemplarity of a king able to blend prowess and generosity, the two virtues necessary for anyone who wishes to "bien tenir terre" (capably administer property): the conventional motif of largesse, in evidence throughout the text and evoked with special emphasis in the final *laisses* of that branch (L. 71 and 72, for example). On the other hand, perhaps the humble "soudoier" (mercenary) in Branch II, who is in fact a knight of noble birth, escapes from imprisonment in order to remind the public, at the outset of the king's conquests, of that other imperative: the gratuitous surge of prowess, that generosity of giving of oneself which cannot be bought with tangible presents, even by one whose name is Alexander.

The *Fuerre de Gadres* has often been compared with Crusade narratives, and even with possible sources in the *Historia Hierosolymitana* of Albert d'Aix and the *Chanson de Jérusalem* (*FG*, pp. 6–9). In the latter, Christian foragers finally rout a much larger Sarrasin army, thanks only to the miraculous intervention of Saint George and a number of other saints. Notably absent is the motif, which in the *Fuerre de Gadres* is crucial, of the warriors' successive refusals to go for help. In fact in the *Chanson* effectiveness in service of the Crusade is the top priority, not the quest for personal glory. If we juxtapose the two texts we can recognize the difference in tone, the *Chanson* being redolent of the miraculous and feeding on the hatred of the Sarrasins, evident in the wide variety of insults and off-color epithets addressed to them. It is normal that the text of Alexandre de Paris, and the *Roman d'Alexandre* in general, does not resound with the spirit of the Crusades: both sides are equally made up of pagans. Shortly thereafter, moreover, upon arriving in Jerusalem, Alexander sets a fine example of tolerance and recognition of the religion of the other. What remains truly remarkable, however, is the spirit of mutual respect that almost always prevails between the two sides and the place accorded the character of Gadifer the Egyptian, a prominence that increases in version β.[11]

Gadifer appears in the story in *laisse* 52, at the crucial moment when, just as the Greeks are losing the upper hand, Alexander has also just arrived on the battlefield, escorted by Ptolemy and Clin. The highly exotic mention of "Gadiffer de Laris ou croissent li paumier" (v. 1189, Gadifer from Laris, where the palm trees grow) immediately furnishes the pretext for a long portrait extolling the moral and martial virtues of the Egyptian, which are demonstrated forthwith in the rest of *laisse* 52. Specifically singled out for praise, moreover, is what is lacking among the Greeks: the art of retreating when necessary (vv. 1197–98). Then, from one *laisse* to the next, his praises are amplified. The courtly profile is underlined: he wears his lady's sleeve on his lance (L. 61).[12] In *laisse* 57, he sets a fine example of reserve and caution in response to the insults of Corineüs, whom he puts in his place, once again putting the common good before exacting vengeance upon the knight, whom he nonetheless eventually kills; and when he in turn succumbs to the blows of Emenidus (L. 62), the latter immediately acknowledges publicly his adversary's qualities and asks the Greeks to bury him on the battlefield. Might we not conclude from this splendid image of Gadifer that the total absence of crusading spirit and, indeed, of religious concern that typifies Alexandre de Paris's version facilitates the portrayal, at the end of the twelfth century, of an exemplary pagan, whose wisdom, moderation, and spirit of sacrifice contrast with the behavior of the presumptuous youths in Alexander's entourage?

One of the many problems raised by the *Roman d'Alexandre*, though perhaps it is a false problem, is the choice by the successive revisers of the epic form inaugurated by Alberic de Pisançon to compose a narrative that has so little in common, or so it seems to us, with the mental universe of the *chanson de geste*. The various authors do indeed recycle its motifs and mechanisms, yet they also elide the values that underlie them in the epic dimension. Do we therefore assume that inertia was a determining factor—that it was easier, moving from one version to another, merely to flesh out the epic *laisse* and verse, rather than starting from scratch, breaking the mold and adopting, for this "life" of Alexander, the octosyllabic couplet, the standard twelfth-century form of romance, historical narrative, and hagiography? Or must we conclude that the epic format ultimately seemed to be the best suited for celebrating and magnifying the "riche istoire" of the conqueror? Must we also suppose that by virtue of its relative elasticity, in the array of set formulae and "ready-to-wear" motifs it provides, the epic form offered greater ease of amplification, which is a marked tendency in stories about Alexander? Yet the fact that this form is finally only a frame that no adaptor ever dared break—beginning in the thirteenth century, writings about Alexander move directly from *laisse* to prose—in no way engages, if we take seriously the episode of *Fuerre de Gadres*, an epic worldview or the permanence of the values underlying the universe of the *chanson de geste*.

As a web of ruthless combats, the *Fuerre de Gadres* exposes their real motives and foregrounds the ostentatious pursuit of a futile kind of glory, while poorly concealing the heroes' desire to enrich themselves and ceaselessly acquire other possessions, as the story of the "povre desarmé" emphasizes. Brought to a happy conclusion by Alexander, the engagement demonstrates the companions' inability to triumph alone, unlike a Roland who unto death retains mastery of the battlefield. This text, indifferent to religious values, is among the few of this vintage to portray a pagan, Gadifer the Egyptian, in an ideal image whose greatness and merits Alexander himself acknowledges.

Thus, might we not suspect Alexandre de Paris of having undermined from within, even in this resolutely epic episode, the form and spirit of his ostensible model, and of having in some way forced to the point of caricature the mechanisms and motifs of the *chanson de geste*—in order to promote in passing other heroic models? Perhaps Gadifer, the hero of the just mean, of equilibrium and good sense, the courtly master of his speech and actions? Or Corineüs, the young warrior who on his own discovers the true measure of his prowess, without expecting other recompense for it . . . and in whom we might perhaps perceive the ancestor of another equally destitute, equally idealistic youth, Aymerillot in *La Légende des siècles*.

Notes

1. On this identification see *MFRA IV*, Index, pp. 106; 31–34.

2. D. J. A. Ross, "A New Manuscript of the Latin *Fuerre de Gadres* and the Text of *Roman d'Alexandre*, Branch II," *Journal of the Warburg and Courtauld Institute* 22 (1959), 211–53.

3. See Jane H. M. Taylor, *Le Roman de Perceforest, Première Partie* (Geneva: Droz, 1979), chapter XV et passim.

4. See *The Old French Crusade Cycle, vol. VI, La Chanson de Jérusalem*, ed. Nigel R. Thorp (Birmingham: The University of Alabama Press, 1992), *laisses* 1–17.

5. See in particular *MFRA IV*, pp. 22–25, 37–88 passim.

6. For a recent discussion see Gosman, *Légende*, pp. 11–67.

7. See Catherine Gaullier-Bougassas, "Alexandre et Candace dans le *Roman d'Alexandre* d'Alexandre de Paris et le *Roman de Toute Chevalerie* de Thomas de Kent," *Romania* 112 (1991), 18–44.

8. As Catherine Gaullier-Bougassas has clearly demonstrated; see *Frontières*, pp. 83–86.

9. On this point see Gosman, *Légende*, ch. X, "Les Compagnons," pp. 220–42.

10. See E. Baumgartner and F. Vielliard, *Benoît de Sainte-Maure, "Le Roman de Troie,"* édition bilingue (Paris: Librairie Générale Française, 1998), vv. 9629–80.

11. On this version and the evolution of the "Gadifer version" see *MFRA V*.

12. See Bénédicte Milland-Bove, "La manche et le cheval comme présents amoureux dans le *Roman d'Alexandre* d'Alexandre de Paris," *Cahiers de Recherches Médiévales (XIIIe-XVe siècles)* 4 (1997), 151–61.

3

Alexander's *Clergie*

Douglas Kelly

In Chrétien de Troyes's *Cligés*, we are reminded of the celebrated tradition of *chevalerie* and *clergie* as these passed from the Greece of Alexander the Great to Rome and then on again to settle, God willing permanently, in France (vv. 30–44). In the prologue to Chrétien's *Conte du graal*, the name of Alexander is explicitly linked to largesse, one of the virtues the Macedonian king acquired as a result of his education.[1] While the ideal education for aristocrats in the twelfth century seems to have included *chevalerie* and *clergie*,[2] Ernst Robert Curtius has cautioned against reading too much into the *conjointure* of the two in Chrétien's usage, noting that Chrétien's terms do not proclaim a twelfth-century humanism.[3] Recent work on *chevalerie* and its range of meanings in the twelfth century encourages us to look more closely at *clergie* too, to see what the word might have connoted to Chrétien's audiences when he linked the two terms.[4] Examination of the twelfth-century romances of Alexander by Alexandre de Paris and Thomas of Kent, each of which includes both domains in the account of the young noble's upbringing under the direction of Aristotle himself, may help us understand how knights and others understood and might have sought to emulate Alexander's *clergie*.

First a glance at *Athis et Prophilias*, a romance also attributed to Alexandre de Paris, will be instructive, as it too uses the *chevalerie-clergie* topos in the education of aristocrats destined to knighthood.[5] In both of its two versions,[6] young Roman noblemen are sent to Athens to learn *san et clergie* (*AetP* v. 202), while their Athenian peers go to Rome to learn *chevalerie*.[7] All therefore receive the same education, at what Chrétien's *Cligés* refers to as the ancient world's centers of the arts of warfare—the usual sense of *chevalerie* in the twelfth century (Burgess pp. 343–58)—and some form of learning. Erich Köhler has argued plausibly that the *Athis* adaptation of the traditional notion of *translatio imperii* to a *translation* of *chevalerie* is a peculiarly French phenomenon that locates the ideal among the nobility rather than in an imperial or royal figure (pp. 41–43). But what does the romance tell us about *translatio studii* as *clergie*?[8]

In fact very little: if the two heroes of *Athis et Prophilias* learned *san et clergie* in Athens, the content of their education is never set out in any detail. It seems to include law, but we hear none of the specifics, even from the Athenian legal experts themselves (vv. 6033–36). Certainly they do not study the martial arts: warfare and military prowess, as *chevalerie*, are Rome's educational prerogative in this romance. The narrator remarks that only those who had been to Rome knew the knightly skills and how to fight, and there were very few such young men left in Athens at that time (vv. 5915–20).

Even the Athenian Athis, who does become a conquering hero and skillful fighter, seems never to have studied *chevalerie* in Rome. But later, young Athenian nobles were absorbed by the study of *clergie*, so confident were they that their city was safe and that *chevalerie* was of little use to them (vv. 5905–10). However, Athis's study of *clergie* bears little fruit. Compare this with Albéric de Pisançon, who tells us that Alexander's masters taught him "totas arz" (v. 83):[9] ". . . Qui·l duystrunt beyn de dignitaz / Et de conseyl et de bontaz, / De sapientia et d'onestaz, / De fayr estorn et prodeltaz" (vv. 84–87, they taught about rank, counsel, and moral worth, of prudence and openness and warfare and prowess). Any qualities that Athis and Prophilias learned while studying in Athens are in no way evident in their conduct there: Athis gives up his wife in name only in order to assuage and finally heal the lovesickness of his Roman friend Prophilias; that friend actually consummates Athis's own marriage. Athis sinks into poverty and despair when dispossessed by his family for his remarkable act of friendship. Only later does Prophilias rehabilitate his friend, making it possible for Athis eventually to prove his mettle in combat, marry properly, and begin a brilliant chivalric career. But Prophilias himself has hardly been a model of moderation, given his passion for his friend's fiancée and wife and his deception in bedding down with her incognito.

To be sure, love in French romance is seldom governed by *san et clergie*, and *Athis et Prophilias* is no exception. The later version multiplies instances of the motif of amorous intrigues, adumbrated in the earlier Tours manuscript, adding adulteries to exchanged fiancées or wives and dwelling occasionally on the attraction older men and women feel for younger persons; broken promises and dubious wars proliferate.[10] None of this suggests the *san* taught and presumably learned in Athens, nor the utility of that *clergie* for the chivalric life; nor does it conform to ecclesiastical ethics for the aristocracy, which condemned such freedom in mores (Köhler pp. 48–49). Indeed, in the one instance where we see clerics in their pure, unchivalric species, they are the object of mockery. In the earlier Tours version of the romance, they sally forth in robes and high-heeled shoes to do battle with the Romans who are laying siege to Athens. "Mout furent bien a desconfire" (v. 5950, they were set for defeat), the narrator remarks wryly. When the Roman army advances on them, they beat a hasty retreat back into the city. They are routed: "Plus lor chëirent jus des botes / A ceuls que norri Aristotes, / Et d'esperons et de chapiaus / Et de chapes et de mantiaus / Qu'en ne vendroit en un marchié" (vv. 6007–11, Aristotle's students shed more boots, spurs and hats, capes and cloaks, than could be sold in a market.) The allusion to Aristotle, Alexander's own master, reminds us that the cleric on the battlefield is as laughable as the cleric in love in the *Lai d'Aristote*.[11] Despite their education, the traditional rivalry and suspicion of knight and cleric is very much in evidence in both versions of *Athis et Prophilias*.

The Tours version attributes the clerics' rout to their lack of experience in warfare (v. 6006), itself due to their exclusive devotion to *clergie*. After their ignominious defeat they return to their books, while the Romans march victoriously on to world conquest (vv. 6033–36, 6043–46; see Castellani, "*Athis,*" p. 151). There is no suggestion that Roman failure to study in Athens produced analogous defects; but we have seen that Athis's and Prophilias's *clergie* did not keep them from some foolish and potentially self-destructive actions that *clergie* in its moral dimension—Albéric's *dignitaz, conseyl, bontaz, sapientia,* and *onestaz*—might have helped them avoid.

How are these issues treated in Alexandre de Paris's *Roman d'Alexandre*? The twelfth-century romances tell us that Alexander acquired his education under Aristotle himself. According to Thomas of Kent, Aristotle "fu le plus sage, ceo seivent clerc et prestre, / Qe unqes fut el siecle for Jesu le celestre" (*RTC* vv. 456–57, was, as clerics and priests know, the wisest and most learned man who ever lived, except for the Lord Jesus); the *Roman d'Alexandre* also depicts him as first among "Les bons devineours" and the "Devins et sages clers" (*MFRA II*, br. I, vv. 271–73; cf. br. III, vv. 5159–60), and we may therefore regard Alexander as exemplary of the best and most desirable education. Aristotle has the young Macedonian learn both *chevalerie* and *clergie*, and, like the Romans, Alexander goes on to conquer the world. His enemy is the treacherous villain elevated to positions of power and authority but unfit for such an honorable rank—not the cleric, who, as we shall see, can occasionally be useful in his conquests.[12]

If the author of *Athis et Prophilias* and of the *Roman d'Alexandre* is the same person, another significant detail comes to the fore: his alleged ignorance of *clergie*. In lines that are, admittedly, somewhat opaque, the *Athis* author-narrator announces that he "Ne fu pas saiges de clergie, / Mes des auctors oï la vie; / Mout retint bien an son memoire" (*AetP* v. 9–11,[13] he was not knowledgeable regarding *clergie*, although he knew the life as related by the authoritative authors. He held it firmly in his memory). Does this reference to his *memoire* mean that he wrote from memory, or that he had the "life" set out for him, as in a written memorandum, as some variants suggest?[14] On the face of it, the first author of *Athis et Prophilias* has an incomplete education in *clergie*, although this may not have been perceived as a drawback by his chivalric audiences. This is not really different from Martin Gosman's evaluation of the author of the *Roman d'Alexandre*: "un homme instruit, un 'clerc' possédant une certaine érudition (entièrement ou partiellement scolaire) dont il profitait dès que les circonstances s'y prêtaient . . . versificateur malhabile."[15]

Alessandro Barbero has made some useful observations regarding the contrasting views of *clergie* among knights and clerics. The former often proclaim that "Nos vies ne s'acordent pas,"[16] an opinion which the *Athis* narrator seems to confirm by contrasting Roman *chevalerie* and Athenian *clergie* on the battlefield. In this context, then, Chrétien's juxtaposition of *chevalerie* and *clergie* is less a *bele conjointure* than a parting of the ways—a *disjointure* characteristic of an oxymoron. The two orders do not function in unison but have discrete roles, as in Adalbéron de Laon's famous schema outlining the separate tasks of *oratores, bellatores*, and *laboratores*.[17] The knight and the cleric represent separate and distinct orders in medieval society and romance. *Chevalerie* and *clergie* are, therefore, potentially less conjunctive than disjunctive, and sometimes even dysfunctional when conjoined (Barbero, p. 156).[18] The chivalric order does not usually condemn religious institutions per se, but rather clerics who are deemed cowardly and often more devoted to magic and the supernatural than to their religious duties. Although the knights are *bellatores*, romance clerics are rarely *oratores*. There is nothing here of that ideal philosopher-king that is evoked from time to time in contemporary Latin writing, most notably in John of Salisbury's *Policraticus*.[19]

Scholars have described Alexander's *clergie* in the context of his education, especially in the early romance versions of his life.[20] They have called attention to the perfunctory treatment of the truly clerical part of that education, the seven arts. For example, K. Sneyders de Vogel noted the imprecise allusions to the seven traditional arts of the trivium and quadrivium and the inclusion among the standard ones—geometry and astronomy as astrology—of mechanical and social arts like skill in arms, hunting, conversation with ladies, and singing and playing instruments (as distinguished from knowledge of the art of music), law and judgment, and languages other than Latin—a rather novel seven![21] Moreover, the arts of geometry and astronomy serve the entirely practical rather than theoretical ends of measuring heights and navigating at sea. On the other hand, Alexander also studied magic, an art usually ascribed to Nectanabus's instruction. In the twelfth-century Alexander romances, clerics frequently combine outward display of religious practices and fascination with the supernatural. Accordingly, along with his education in *clergie*, Alexander also learned necromancy, that is, the great secrets of nature apart from nature as a divine creation;[22] as we shall see, Alexander's world conquests include not only the world's kingdoms and empires, but also extend into the natural world.

Unlike Athis and Prophilias's careers, Alexander's offers some evidence of his acquired *san* and of his *clergie*. Although both Alexandre de Paris and Thomas of Kent describe Aristotle's instruction, including some liberal arts

(*MFRA II*, Br. I, vv. 335–42), the continental *Alexandre* is more circumspect as to both the arts' content and the rational development of Alexander's mind— *clergie* and *san* in the language of *Athis et Prophilias*. Alexander learns to read and write in Greek, Hebrew, Chaldean, and Latin—a wide-ranging grammar course. He is proficient in judging according to the principles of the arts of logic and rhetoric. Rhetoric is useful not only for persuasion, but also for judgment; this is deliberative rhetoric that is useful to the ruler in counsel. Alexander also learns quadrivial subjects: geography, meteorology, astronomy, and history (Br. II, vv. 5159–60). The Anglo-Norman *Alexandre* refers briefly to Alexander's acquisition of skill in the arts, but also of the social graces, hunting, horsemanship, gymnastics, and farming (*RTC* vv. 427–57). Alexandre de Paris adds what the young man learned from his alleged father, Nectanabus (Br. I, vv. 353–59): "Onques plus hardis rois de lui ne porta lance, / Par sa proëce a il sor tout le mont poissance; / Onques teus rois ne fu, s'en Dieu eüst creance. / Trop sot d'astronomie et plus de ningremance, / Assés sot de fisique, apris l'ot en s'enfance." (Br. III, vv. 5156–60; cf. IV, vv. 1152–53: No more courageous king ever bore lance. His prowess brought him dominion over the whole world. No such king ever was, had he had the true faith. He was learned in astronomy and even more so in necromancy; he was well grounded in the natural sciences, which he had learned in his youth.) Finally, he receives good counsel ("un bon chastïement," [Br. I, v. 343]: "Que ja serf de put ere n'et entour lui souvent, / Car maint home en sont mort et livré a torment, / Par losenge, par murtre, par enpoisonnement" (Br. I, vv. 344–46; cf. III, vv. 19–27 and 51–70: Do not allow low-born serfs to frequent him, for many die or suffer through their flattery, murder, and poisoning). This is, of course, a veiled warning to Alexander, but one which the denouement of both versions exemplifies and justifies. Although the young prince promises to heed this advice, vowing never to promote villeins in the administration of his realm, Alexander is poisoned by the *engins* and *enchantement* (Br. III, vv. 7786 and 7833) of his two villainous counselors, Divinuspater and Antipater. However, Divinuspater and Antipater are not really serfs, however villainous their mentality may be.[23] I shall return to this matter below.

But nature as well as nurture distinguish the young Alexander. The child is gifted. He learns more in seven years than another could in a hundred. Many are the wise and learned—"Li mestre des escolles, li bon clerc sapïent"—who come to make his acquaintance (Br. I, vv. 327–32) and marvel at his *clergie*. Among those who come to observe his precocious learning is Nectanabus, a man "d'engin . . . paréz" (v. 352, endowed with a deceptive mind), like Divinuspater and Antipater. He too becomes Alexander's master, building on Aristotle's teaching and extending it to the more dynamic features of astronomy and meteorology. His expertise in the obscure mysteries of the heavens derives from his unrivaled knowledge of necromancy (vv. 358–59). He understands the hidden movements of the heavens; he can also metamorphose appearances.

Thomas of Kent includes these features of Alexander's education in his romance, albeit in a different order and with different emphases. Nectanabus appears before Aristotle and we learn more about his lineage and biography. Like his counterpart in the continental *Alexandre*, Thomas's Nectanabus also excels in astronomy and necromancy. He is himself a shape-shifter, and uses this art effectively to seduce Alexander's mother (*RTC* vv. 257–79; cf. vv. 336–83). Thomas's description of Alexander's education includes preparation for knighthood as well as the trivium, quadrivium, and necromancy, which Nectanabus teaches him (*RTC* vv. 479–82). The Anglo-Norman Alexander rivals Tristan's accomplishments in most fields of aristocratic, chivalric, and clerical education. Thus, under Aristotle's mastery and with Nectanabus's contribution, "Bien siet a cheval e saveit de palestre, / De forest, de rivere, oisels gettre e pestre, / De lettrure e d'engin e de labur champestre, / Car li bons Aristotle fu sur trestoz son mestre" (*RTC* vv. 452–55: He knows how to ride a horse and do gymnastics; he is familiar with woods, rivers, and hunting with and raising birds; he knows how to read and write, how to think clearly and sharply, and how to administer farm work, for the worthy Aristotle was his foremost master.)

In both our later twelfth-century Alexander romances, then, the young hero-to-be is educated according to a model like that for young Romans and Athenians in *Athis et Prophilias*. But unlike that in *Athis*, here the brilliant education has a place in Alexander's life of conquest, although not so much as for Nectanabus who, according to Thomas of Kent, conquered more by magic than by arms while he ruled "Libya" (*RTC* vv. 50–63). To be sure, Nectanabus could not prevent the uprising that drove him into exile any more than Alexander could escape poison (*RTC* vv. 75–87). Moreover, Alexander kills his alleged father in a fit of anger—something the latter failed to prevent. As with the liberal arts, there are implicit levels of proficiency in knowledge of the magic arts.

Of Alexander's career after his education, one might say that he conquers as knight and as cleric.[24] Thus, the son inherits something from Nectanabus, his real or imaginary father. That is, he is indeed eager to conquer, but his conquests include the desire to dominate new and marvelous things, not just kings and empires. Accordingly, Alexander is not bent on violent conquest only. Those who are willing to accept his overtures to submission are treated like vassals and integrated into his military and administrative system: "Ne trueve fort cité qui tant soit bien muree / Dont il n'ait le treü, n'i estuet traire espee. / Trespasse le païs, ainc n'i ot contrestee" (*MFRA* II, Br. III, vv. 4935–37: He comes to no city that doesn't offer him tribute, no matter how well fortified it is; no sword had to be drawn. He moves through the country unopposed). However, those who offer resistence are violently subdued and often destroyed: "il ne trueve chastel ne cité qu'il ne fraigne / Ne nul home tant fort par armes ne destraigne; / Malvais orguel ne prise li rois une chastaigne,

/ A honte fait morir qui servir ne le daigne" (Br. III, vv. 5119–22: he comes upon neither castle nor city which he doesn't destroy, nor any man so strong that he doesn't subdue him by arms. The king has no esteem for enemy pride. He puts to shameful death anyone who does not deign to serve him). Although he kills the Babylonian emir who rejects his domination, he is measured in his violence: his men are not to kill the inhabitants of the country. Indeed, he says, "Se feütés m'estoit et plevie et juree, / Lor cités lor seroit de moi asseüree" (III, vv. 7087–88:[25] If they had pledged and sworn fealty to me I would have guaranteed the safety of their city).

The same conduct models what we may call Alexander's intellectual conquests. Here we move, as it were, from horizontal to vertical conquests. Like Nectanabus, Alexander wants to subjugate nature to his will. By confrontation with the new, the obscure, or the unknown, he carries out a two-pronged conquest of the universe—conquest that relies alternately on violent and peaceful means, just as it does in confrontation with rival realms and rulers. Thus, he ventures into India in pursuit of Porus and thence to the ends of the earth not only to conquer Porus's realm, but also to "prove and test all things" (Br. III, v. 2816; cf. v. 3720). India is full of marvels (vv. 994–96; cf. vv. 1177, 3277–78), and Alexander wants to see them all (vv. 1400, 2147). Accordingly, he confronts a human and animal world like that in medieval bestiaries. Part of the confrontation is imposed on him, as when "hippotames" eat his soldiers, armor and all, or later when hordes of thirst-maddened monsters and other beasts descend on the encamped army in search of water. Part is pleasant, as in the idyll with the flower maidens or the surprisingly compliant Amazons.[26] These encounters illustrate anew Alexander's two modes of conquest: either violent seizure and brutal destruction of those who refuse to submit, or peaceful integration into his domains in terms that are more feudal and even courtly than tyrannical. To see, for Alexander, is to confront and challenge to combat: "Car cil les escrïerent ques devoient garder / Q'il voient les mervelles des desers assembler" (III, vv. 2390–91: For they shouted out to be careful as they see the wonders of the desert gathering). Thus, to see marvels is to subject them to his domination, as with the Amazons: ". . . il veut veoir la terre ou n'a se femes non / Et qu'il la veut avoir en sa subjection" (vv. 7290–91, he wants to see the land inhabited only by women, and he wants to subdue it). By his conquests, Alexander is a king "qui tous dis fu de biens essamplaire" (v. 2715, who exemplified all good qualities). What are those *biens*? Porus has heard, and tells Alexander, that the Macedonian king is in quest of "proëce, segnorie et barnage" (v. 2230; cf. v. 2766). These broad attributes fall traditionally in the realm of *chevalerie*, not *clergie*; but *clergie* can also call for *proëce* and *segnorie* in Alexander's case.

Alexander confronts, and even seeks out, strange and violent inhuman or superhuman beings and places elsewhere than on the surface of the earth in far-off India. His undersea voyage and his flight contribute to his knowledge acquired in youth,[27] practically enhancing the conventional learning he acquired under Aristotle as well as the supernatural knowledge dispensed by Nectanabus. However, knowledge and conquest coalesce in these adventures, for seeing the monsters of India and undersea usually requires or at least entails some reference to combat.[28] The marvelous but combative beasts and places on earth have their counterparts underwater and even in the heavens. Let us look therefore at these seemingly more scientific conquests to see what Alexander hopes to gain from such adventures.

The undersea voyage begins after Alexander overthrows Darius and sets out into the Eastern wildernesses. He looks forward to new conquests; since he has conquered most of the earth, he now wants to plunge into the sea. "Assés ai par la terre et venu et alé, / De ciaus de la mer voil savoir la verité, / Ja mais ne finerai si l'avrai esprové." (Br. III, vv. 396–98: I have come and gone over many regions of the earth. I want now to know the truth about the inhabitants of the sea; I will not stop until I have put it to the test of personal experience). In a vessel made of unbreakable glass, he is lowered into the sea with two young companions. What does he discover? *Sens*—not *sens de clergie*, but *sens de chevalerie*: ". . . molt i ai apris sens de chevalerie, / Comment guerre doit estre en bataille establie / Aucune fois par force et autre par voisdie, / Car force vaut molt peu s'engiens ne li aïe" (vv. 529–32, I learned much about knighthood down there: how combat must be carried out, sometimes by brute force, at other times by wit. For brute force is of little avail if it is not aided by a sharp mind).[29] This is obvious to him when he observes the big fish eating the smaller ones (vv. 445–48). He learned a lot, he says, from the big fish: defend yourself well. That is the way it is in this world: the big triumph, the small always suffer. The spectacle amuses Alexander immensely: "si s'en rist volentiers" (v. 476)—insight, no doubt, into the sense of humor among the high and mighty! (See Ménard, pp. 436 and 443.) Alexander is, after all, a big fish since swallowing Darius.

But Alexander also attributes this impulse among the big fish to avarice. Avarice takes from the poor and gives to the rich—hardly his own spirit of largesse. This uniqueness in Alexander's chivalric mentality—largesse as a manifestation of his *sens de chevalerie* again, not *de clergie*—sets him apart not only from the clerics who taught him to practice largesse, but from his own vassals too. His barons had counseled against the submarine dive because, if he were lost on the expedition, they would then either separate and disband or be destroyed by their enemies.[30] But Alexander reserves the right not to listen to counselors, manifesting a disinterest in law, the subject which was so prized among the Athenian clerics in *Athis et Prophilias*. "Por noient . . . en avés tant parlé," he exclaims in rejecting his barons' advice, "Car por tout l'or du mont ne seroit trestorné" (Br. III, vv. 403–404: Your long speeches are useless; I won't let you change my mind for all the gold in the world). Thus, Alexander's achievement of the exploit confirms that no ruler need always heed his barons' counsel when he knows better. Catherine Gaullier-Bougassas has perhaps best expressed this impulse to unique excellence: "L'image du roi qu'ils (Alexander de Paris and Thomas of Kent) ont pourtant voulu modeler sur les valeurs politiques du XIIᵉ siècle s'efface ... devant celle d'un individu singulier qui cherche à réaliser ses désirs personnels au lieu de promouvoir l'intérêt de sa communauté. Il suit un parcours initiatique qui le confronte à sa propre identité, à ses origines et au destin que des puissances supérieures lui ont fixé, et qui le transforme profondément, en faisant ressortir les ambiguïtés, les zones d'ombre de son personnage" (*Frontières*, p. 22). Provided Alexander has the *sens de chevalerie*, he needn't be like the villein who sends his dogs on ahead of him where he himself is afraid to venture alone or first.

> Mais li rois est molt fols et peu fait a proisier
> Qui toutes ses besoignes fera par conseillier—
> Puis qu'il a tant de sens qu'il se sache targier—
> Et a autrui s'atent; bien le puis afichier
> Que il n'est mie rois ne ne vaut un denier,
> Ains est espoëntaus q'on seut en champ drecier
> Qant li vilains en veut les oisiaus manecier,
> Il ne set ne ne puet ne traire ne lancier. (Br. III, vv. 550–57)³¹

(But that king is a great fool and deserves little respect if his tasks are dictated by the advice of others—given that he has enough intelligence to defend himself—and relies on others to tell him how to act. I can indeed claim that he is no king at all and is unworthy of the honor; he is rather a scarecrow like those which the villein sets up in the field to frighten away the birds; he is incapable of using his own weapons against them.)

Whereupon Alexander cuts short the discussion, ordering a meal so that he can go to rest!
Yet even a monarch can err by venturing too far.

> Or aproisme li tans, li termes est venus
> Que Babilone iert prise et li palais rendus
> Ou il sera destruis et ses grans los perdus.
> Conseus de nisun home n'en pot estre creüs;
> Par nul de ses barons ne pot estre tenus,
> Por aler a sa mort est par matin meüs. (Br. III, vv. 4868–73)

(Now draws near and comes the time and term in which Babylon will be taken and the palace surrendered in which he will be destroyed and his great fame lost. No counsel is of any avail, none of his barons can keep him back; he sets out in the morning for his death.)

His attitude is no different when he decides to leave the earth to explore the heavens, just before he captures Babylon. The exploit is carried out with the same marvelous ingenuity as the undersea voyage: "Comment i monterés? Dites l'engignement" (v. 4980, how will you go up there? Tell us the trick). Again brushing aside his barons' anxiety, he harnesses seven or eight griffons which he has attracted with pieces of fresh meat. Seating himself in a kind of carriage, Alexander attaches more meat to his spearhead and holds it out in front of the griffons; in pursuit of the unattainable meat, they bear him aloft. He directs their movements by aiming the lance so as to steer them in the direction he wants, whether up or down or to the side.

Why does Alexander do this? Initially, he wants to see the heavens, from the mountains up to the firmament. He also wishes to fly over the whole world to survey his conquests. Finally, he wants to find out how clouds hold water (vv. 4969–75). He achieves the first two goals, passing through different spheres in the geocentric universe and surveying the earth (Br. III, vv. 5046–61), but there is no mention of his actually performing the one truly clerical task of discovering how clouds hold water: he hastens past the clouds, with no word about his observations. "Fait ot bone jornee" (he had a good day), remarks the narrator (v. 5061). But Alexander is no Icarus. When the celestial fire threatens to melt or inflame his carriage, he points his lance downward and returns safely to earth.

Alexander's flight is, like his underwater plunge, a test, in both senses of the word—an experiment and a trial. "Hui ai veü as ieus que j'ai molt desirré, / Car tout ai ensaié et tout ai mesuré" (Br. III, vv. 5083–84: Today I have seen with my own eyes what I have longed to see: I have tested and measured all things). But he is testing more as an athlete tests himself than as a scholar, saying nothing about his scientific curiosity even when he passes by rain clouds on his way up to the burning heavens. What Alexander wants is that people marvel at his unique excellence, and that means at his marvelous, superhuman exploits. That is why he puts himself to the test on land, in the sea, and in the air, even confronting the celestial fire. It is as if he wants to conquer all four elements.[32] Undersea he learns how to conquer (vv. 4987–90). In the skies he sees all that he has conquered: "Le mont si com il est et de lonc et de lé / Si com je l'ai veü l'ai je tout conquesté" (vv. 5085–86, I have seen the full length and breadth of the world, and as I have seen it I have conquered it). All, that is, except for Babylon. He therefore returns to earth and sets out forthwith to lay siege to that city.

Let me try to illustrate Alexander's motivation by considering another of his superhuman exploits, one that retained its fascination as marvelous achievement in the later Middle Ages: the hero's fabulous leap onto the walls of Tyre.[33] He besieged the city for some time, but encountered formidable opposition there and elsewhere—notably, in the *Fuerre de Gadres* foraging expedition[34] and against the constructions he raised for the siege but which his opponents destroyed. In his desire for vengeance, Alexander falls back on his knowledge of military engineering and of astronomy, and more specifically the tides. He has several military constructions built, including an amphibious "berfroi" (Br. II, v. 1913) which the rising tide will transport right up to the walls of Tyre. Alexander will occupy it alone, or, as he puts it more precisely: "En celui n'avra home fors Damedieu et moi, / Ne ja plus n'i avrai fors armes et conroi" (Br. II, vv. 1916–17: no one will occupy it except me and the Lord God, and I will have nothing more with me than my arms and equipment). Like his venture into the heavens, so his leap into the thin air from tower to wall is a solitary achievement. One is reminded of the duel that decides the fate of the war against Nicholas despite the latter's gigantic size (Br. I, vv. 1514–19).

We note, then, how *clergie*—practical *clergie* as engineering—serves Alexander's *chevalerie*. After killing the Duke of Gadres, who is defending Tyre, Alexander executes his marvelous leap. "Oés" exclaims the author, "dont se porpense li rois de grant vertu: / Ja fera hardement a tous jors menteü, / Dont parleront encore li grant et li menu" (Br. II, v. 1961–63. Listen to what the valiant king has in mind: he will perform an act of courage that will never be forgotten, and that great and small will talk about). Alexander springs from his tower, fully armed, onto Tyre's walls in full view of all. Dumbfounded at his prowess and stunned for a long moment, the defenders are unable to react. In the meantime, Alexander siezes the initiative; rushing into the city and placing himself squarely in front of a great tree in order to protect his back, he holds off all those who finally come to their senses and attack him. His own knights quickly break down the now undefended main gate and rescue their king; they then proceed to massacre all those who do not surrender.

In all of these adventures, Alexander evinces a desire to conquer by extraordinary feats, followed by the pleasure of overseeing what he has achieved by conquest. Overcoming natural obstacles with an intelligence superior to that even of his high counselors, his *sens de chevalerie* demonstrates a truly unique excellence (at least, in his authors' eyes). To know, see, and test the world is thus a form of chivalric conquest, not of clerical inquest. It derives from the *san de chevalerie*, far removed from the *san de clergie* that would seek to know and comprehend the world that, for Alexander, seems to exist only for him to conquer it. He evinces, for example, no detectable interest in the laws of his realm, the subject that engrossed young Athenians in *Athis* and apparently kept them from learning the martial arts in Rome. Nor does one hear a moralistic reading of his life like that in the *Alexandreis*; its author Gautier de Châtillon, unlike Alexandre de Paris, is "saiges de clergie," and he evaluates Alexander's life accordingly.[35] There is enough in the French poems to conclude that, like the big fish he admires devouring the smaller ones, Alexander intends to be the biggest fish of all and devour the whole world by and for his own *chevalerie*. In his eyes, this is an admirable task worthy of his unique excellence.

To be sure, Alexander does sometimes rely on clerics or clerical types—old men, religious men, or an occasional devil (but no legal experts)—to achieve his goals and avoid becoming himself a victim. Therefore, conquest may require appealing to those who know marvels and their secrets. When Alexander wishes to know his fate he calls on an Egyptian whose fame rests on his knowledge of fortune and oracles, combining the functions of "devin" and "clers" (Br. III, vv. 6073, 6077). This is, as it were, a promotion of the commonplace idea of the cleric in the Alexander romances and elsewhere: just as the house clerk reads for the king,[36] so the higher orders of the clergy practice magic, prophesy the future, and interpret dreams.

Of course, as we have seen, Alexander himself has been trained in necromancy, and his order of intelligence can rise above that of his counselors. Since he knew "escripture" and "letres" in four languages (Br. I, vv. 335–36; Br. III, vv. 2852 and 2856–57), his use of clerics to read for him is only a convenience. He knows how to speak several languages and interpret signs too (Br. III, vv. 3582–84). But his knowledge of necromancy and, especially, of prophecy has obvious limits. He is very much afraid of death whenever he feels truly threatened, and strange and marvelous places frighten him for this reason—for example, the Val Périlleux, where his *clergie* is admired, but by the devil (Baumgartner, "Orient," p. 14).[37] Alexander's attitude toward clerics in matters like these contrasts strikingly with that toward his baronial counselors. Those clerics in-the-know become essential. This is especially true in India and beyond, as when he comes to the two automats:

> . . . li pas est contredis.
> Desor aus ot deus briés, que uns clers ot escris,
> Qui les fait par augure deffendre au passeïs.
> Alixandres descent du destrier arrabis
> Et monte sor le pont si s'est outre escuellis.
> Quant vit les deus enfans qui ont les mals saisis,
> Il se retraist arriere, qu'il cuide estre peris. (Br. III, vv. 3398–404)

> (The passage is prohibited. Above them were two inscriptions which a cleric had written; they stated that magic forbade them passage. Alexander dismounts from his Arabian charger, goes onto the bridge and over it. When he sees the two young men who had taken up their hammers, he pulls back in fear for his life.)

There is also deep mistrust of clerical guides. Guides are suspect anyway since they can and do collaborate with Alexander's enemies rather than with him, despite generous promises of reward for their services (Br. III, vv. 1004–16). Still, they can be necessary, as Alexander realizes after having killed some for their treachery (cf. vv. 1105–6, 1136–41, and 1467–79). Later, another cleric, or more specifically an "astrenomïens" (v. 2988), gives him information about the three enchanted fountains at the end of the world, and still another closes a passage using magic (vv. 3399–400). Clerics as magicians constructed the Fountain of Youth: "Ensi com l'orent fait enchanteor letré" (v. 3641, as the learned magicians had made it). They can also prophesy: one announces Alexander's death (vv. 3784–810). The relation that Barbero notes between magic and religion in the minds of the knightly aristocracy (pp. 166–70) is a factor in Alexandre de Paris's conception of *clergie*, and that conception defines Alexander's own learning. This supports Barbero's view of knights' uncertain distinction between magic and religion as well as their suspicion and mistrust of clerics, especially, in Alexander's world, of clerics who were not beholden to the Christian God—a kind of cleric they could also find in the other *romans d'antiquité*.[38]

The results of this inquiry into Alexander's *clergie* are less important in themselves than in their implications for our understanding of the notion of *clergie* in romances. To be sure, Alexander romances, whose versification and style often seem closer to the *chansons de geste* than to contemporary romances, cannot be expected to favor clerical ideals or their realization even in a figure as exceptionally well-educated as Alexander. Moreover, as we have seen, Alexandre de Paris may confess his own incomplete education in the arts that form the tradition usually associated with *clergie*. However, given the analogies identified above between the twelfth-century knight's conception of and attitude towards *clergie*, which the Alexander romances seem to mirror, may we not ask whether the intended audiences of most high-medieval romances did not share those opinions? Did the *clergie* that even a Chrétien de Troyes evokes not have much in common with that exemplified and ridiculed in *Athis et Prophilias*, or mirrored in the education of a number of characters like Thessala in *Cligés* who have learned necromancy, an art of which they–like Nectanabus—make practical use (*Cligés* vv. 2984–90; cf., for example, vv. 6638–42)? Even Erec in *Erec et Enide* relies on fairy craft to make the coronation robe that literally wraps him in the quadrivium. Lip service to *clergie* might entertain, like nature programs on television, but in the last analysis rarely offers much more, perhaps because it was not desired by most vernacular audiences. In the last analysis, *chevalerie*, not *clergie*, prevails as an ideal in the Alexander romances, no doubt because the knight finds, vis-à-vis the cleric, that "Nos vies ne s'acordent pas."

Notes

1. *Cligés*, ed. Stewart Gregory and Claude Luttrell (Cambridge: Brewer, 1993), vv. 193–217 (lesson given by Alexandre the emperor of Constantinople to his son Alixandre when the latter embarks for Arthur's court; Alexander the Great is named in v. 6679); *Le roman de Perceval ou Le Conte du graal*, ed. Keith Busby (Tübingen: Niemeyer, 1993), vv. 14–15 and 57–59.

2. See Gaullier-Bougassas, *Frontières*, pp. 302–30; cf. Erich Köhler, *Ideal und Wirklichkeit in der höfischen Epik: Studien zur Form der frühen Artus- und Graldichtung* (Tübingen: Niemeyer, 1970), chap. 2.

3. Ernst Robert Curtius, *Europäische Literatur und lateinisches Mittelalter*, 2nd ed. (Bern: Francke, 1954), pp. 388–89.

4. See most recently Glyn S. Burgess, "The Term 'Chevalerie' in Twelfth-Century French," in *Medieval Codicology, Iconography, Literature, and Translation: Studies for Keith Val Sinclair*, ed. Peter Rolfe Monks and D. D. R. Owen (Leiden: Brill, 1994), pp. 343–58; and Jean Flori, *L'essor de la chevalerie xie–xiie siècles* (Geneva: Droz, 1986). Cf. Martin Gosman, "Le *Roman de toute chevalerie* et le public visé: la légende au service de la royauté," *Neophilologus* 72 (1988), 337–38; Gosman, "Le *Roman d'Alexandre* et les 'juvenes': une approche socio-historique," *Neophilologus* 66 (1982), 330–32; *Frontières*, pp. 308–30; and Gosman, "*Touzjor vesquirent d'armes, itel fu lor labor.* l'aventure épique dans le *Roman d'Alexandre*," in *De l'aventure épique à l'aventure romanesque: mélanges offerts à André de Mandach*, ed. Jacques Chocheyras (Bern: P. Lang, 1997), pp. 85–98.

5. I use the term "topos" in its common medieval sense as a place common to any kind of person, thing, or action and susceptible of amplification in conformity with the author's intention. As such, topoi are sources of original invention. For example, the seven liberal arts, as topoi, can be variously defined and described, as K. Sneyders de Vogel's examples from early Alexander romances show in "L'éducation d'Alexandre le Grand," *Neophilologus* 28 (1943), 161–71.

6. The romance has received little attention, and these matters of dating and attribution are still uncertain. Wendelin Foerster dates it before *Cligés* but does not accept the attribution to Alexandre de Paris in "Randglossen zum Athisroman (Athis und Cligés)," *Zeitschrift für romanische Philologie* 36 (1912), 731–33 and 735; Alessandro Vitale-Brovarone dates it in the second half of the twelfth century in "Un nuovo frammento del Romanz d'Athis et Prophilias," *Atti dell' Accademia delle Scienze di Torino. II: Classe di scienze morali, storiche e filologiche* 111 (1977), 332 n. 8 (the text of this mid-thirteenth-century manuscript is the long version; cf. pp. 335–36); Alfred Adler assumes the attribution to Alexandre de Paris and the earlier date in "Höfische Romanen neben und nach Chrétien: Bilder und sinngebende Nebenbilder," in *Le roman jusqu'à la fin du XIIIe siècle: partie historique*, vol. 4 of the *Gründriß der romanischen Literaturen des Mittelalters* (Heidelberg: Winter, 1978), p. 21; Martin Gosman questions the attribution because of the later date he assigns to *Athis* in *Légende*, p. 128.

7. Unless otherwise indicated, all references are to the earlier version in the Tours manuscript. On the differences between the two versions, see Marie-Madeleine Castellani, "*Athis et Prophilias*: histoire de Rome ou histoire d'Athènes?" in *Entre fiction et histoire: Troie et Rome au moyen âge*, ed. Emmanuèle Baumgartner and Laurence Harf-Lancner (Paris: Presses de la Sorbonne Nouvelle, 1997), pp. 147–60.

8. According to Herbert Grundmann, *studium* as such did not join the ideals of *sacerdotium* and *regnum* before the thirteenth century. See his "Sacerdotium—Regnum—Studium: zur Wertung der Wissenschaft im 13. Jahrhundert," *Archiv für Kulturgeschichte* 34 (1952), 5–21. Does this mean that *clergie* in Chrétien's twelfth-century *translatio* connoted ecclesiastical functions rather than education? On the range of meanings

covered by *sens de clergie* in French romances, see my *The Art of Medieval French Romance* (Madison: University of Wisconsin Press, 1992), pp. 117–18.

9. AdeP = Albéric de Pisançon, *Alexandre*, in *MFRA* III, pp. 37–42. Albéric does not include necromancy in Alexander's curriculum.

10. On these additions, that amplify motifs found in the earlier Tours version, see Castellani, "*Athis.*"

11. See Philippe Ménard, *Le rire et le sourire dans le roman courtois en France au moyen âge (1150–1250)* (Geneva: Droz, 1969), pp. 176–77.

12. I use "villein" to refer to medieval social orders beneath the nobility and "villain" to refer to a moral or social type, whatever his or her social status. On the ambiguous status of Divinuspater and Antipater, see Gosman, "Alexandre le Grand et le statut de la noblesse ou le plaidoyer pour la permanence: prolégomènes à l'histoire d'une légende," in *Non nova, sed nove: mélanges de civilisation médiévale dédiés à Willem Nooman*, ed. Martin Gosman and Jaap van Os (Groningen: Bouma, 1984), pp. 85–86.

13. On these lines and the mysterious "vie" found in all manuscripts of the later version of *Athis*, see Kelly, p. 117. The passage is missing in the Tours manuscript due to a missing folio, but was probably in the original version, since, as Hilka, the editor, points out (p. xlix), the later version branches off from Tours only at v. 2609. See also Castellani, "Version longue—version brève: l'exemple d'*Athis et Prophilias*," *Bien dire et bien aprandre* 14 (1996), 110.

14. B. N. fr. 793 (= ms. B) and London B. L. Add. 16441 (= ms. L) read: "Ne fu pas saiges de clergie / Mes des auctors oï la vie / Mout retint bien *lonc sa memore* / Si nos reconte d'une estoire / De .II. Citez. . . ." B. N. fr. 375 (= ms. A) replaces "oï" by "savoit" and reads v. 11 as follows: "ml't mostre selonc sa memore." *Memoire* may refer to a written memorandum which the author turned into verse. For examples of such memoranda as a stage in romance composition, see Kelly, pp. 75–78 and 100–103. Still, there is evidence that anyone, including knights, might be a storyteller; see W. P. Gerritsen, "Een avond in Ardres: over middeleeuwse verhaalkunst," in *Grote Lijnen: syntheses over Middelnederlandse letterkunde* (Amsterdam: Prometheus, 1995), pp. 157–72.

15. Gosman, "Les derniers jours d'Alexandre dans le *Roman d'Alexandre:* fin d'une vie 'exemplaire,' " in *AGMA*, p. 174.

16. Alessandro Barbero, *L'aristocrazia nella società francese del medioevo: analisi delle fonti letterarie (secoli X–XIII)* (Bologna: Cappelli, 1987), p. 142; quote from Benoît de Sainte-Maure's *Le Roman de Troie*, ed. Léopold Constans, Société des Anciens Textes Français (Paris: Firmin Didot, 1904–12), v. 4008. Cf. Martin Gosman, "La genèse du *Roman d'Alexandre*: quelques aspects," *Bien dire et bien aprandre* 6 (1988), 27, and his "Le *Roman d'Alexandre* et ses versions du XIIᵉ siècle: une réécriture permanente," *Bien dire et bien aprandre* 13 (1996), 7–23.

17. Georges Duby, *Les trois ordres ou l'imaginaire du féodalisme* (Paris: Gallimard, 1978); cf. Köhler, pp. 61–62 esp. n. 2 and Gosman, "*Roman d'Alexandre*," pp. 328–29.

18. The antagonism between the two is more pronounced in *chansons de geste* than in romance, but the Alexander romances are on the borderline between these two

kinds of French writing in the twelfth century; see Ménard, pp. 80–81 and 175–78. This issue surfaces in other vernacular works from this period and after; see, for example, *Le clerc au moyen âge, Senefiance* 37 (Aix-en-Provence: CUER MA, 1995), esp. Christine Ferlampin-Acher, "Grandeur et décadence du clerc Estienne dans *Artus de Bretagne*," (165–95), and Gérard Gouiran, "'Car tu es cavalliers e clers' (*Flamenca*, v. 1899): Guilhem, ou le chevalier parfait" (197–214).

19. See *Frontières*, pp. 302–303.

20. Wilhelm Hertz, "Aristoteles in den Alexander-Dichtungen des Mittelalters," in his *Gesammelte Abhandlungen*, ed. Friedrich von der Leyen (Stuttgart: Cotta, 1905), pp. 1–33; K. Sneyders de Vogel; Penny Simons, "Theme and Variations: The Education of the Hero in the *Roman d'Alexandre*," *Neophilologus* 78 (1994), 195–208; *Frontières*, pp. 302–41. Cf. Mariantonia Liborio, "Alessandro e la conoscenza," in *Alessandro*, pp. 115–19.

21. Sneyders de Vogel bases his interpretation on Albéric de Pisançon's version and its rewriting in the Venice ms., ms. L, and Lamprecht (pp. 168–71).

22. Magic as a clerical art does not appear in Albéric but apparently surfaces first in the Venice ms. (Sneyders de Vogel, p. 167). On figures like Nectanabus in romance, see *Frontières*, pp. 168–69.

23. On the ambiguous status of these traitors between villainy and nobility, see Gosman, "Genèse," pp. 42–43.

24. This reconfirms Carey's judgment that conquest is the single constant theme in these works; see Part B, chap. 4. See also Udo Schöning, *Thebenroman-Eneasroman-Trojaroman: Studien zur Rezeption der Antike in der französischen Literatur des 12. Jahrhunderts* (Tübingen: Niemeyer, 1991), pp. 20 and 40–42; and Aimé Petit, *L'anachronisme dans les romans antiques du xiiᵉ siècle*, diss. Lille III (Lille: Atelier National de Reproduction des thèses—Université de Lille III, 1985), pp. 315–17. On Alexander as trickster like Nectanabus, see Liborio, p. 117.

25. Similar passages: *MFRA* I, vv. 1718–90 (Aristotle tricks Alexander into lifting the siege of Athens), II, vv. 2415–21, and III, vv. 2123–44.

26. Cf. Ménard, "Femmes séduisantes et femmes malfaisantes: les filles-fleurs de la forêt et les créatures des eaux dans le *Roman d'Alexandre*," *Bien dire et bien aprandre* 7 (1989), 5–17. On marvels in general in the Alexander romances, see Harf-Lancner, pp. 53–57. The *RTC* is especially rich in marvelous beasts.

27. "Fu d'astronomie sa pense enluminee, / Que de toutes estoiles connut la compassee" (*MFRA* I, vv. 76–77: he was very knowledgeable about astronomy, for he knew the movements of all the stars); see also *MFRA* III, vv. 984–97, 2145–48, 2947–49, 2975–76, 3185–204, 3415–21, 3523–44, and 3715–27.

28. See Emmanuèle Baumgartner, "L'Orient d'Alexandre," *Bien dire et bien aprandre* 6 (1988), 10; Harf-Lancner, pp. 48–51.

29. See Catherine Gaullier-Bougassas, "La réécriture inventive d'une même séquence: quelques versions du voyage d'Alexandre sous la mer," *Bien dire et bien aprandre* 14 (1996), 11–12.

30. *MFRA* III, vv. 399–402. Cf. Gosman, "Derniers jours," pp. 179–83; Gosman, "Alexandre le Grand," pp. 81–86; Gosman, "*Roman de toute chevalerie*," pp. 335–43 (with differences between it and the continental *Alexandre*); Gosman, "*Roman d'Alexandre*," pp. 328–39; and *Frontières*, part II, chap. 4.

31. On Alexander's reaction, see *MFRA* III, *laisses* 26–28, and *Frontières*, pp. 330–38.

32. Alexander tried to enter the Earthly Paradise only in a later interpolation; on these interpolations see Gosman, "Le *Roman d'Alexandre*: les interpolations du XIIIᵉ siècle," in *Le roman antique au moyen âge*, ed. Danielle Buschinger (Göppingen: Kümmerle, 1992), pp. 61–72.

33. See, for example, Jean Renart, *Le roman de la rose ou de Guillaume de Dole*, ed. Félix Lecoy (Paris: Champion, 1962), vv. 5320–23.

34. See Emmanuèle Baumgartner's essay in this volume.

35. Carey, pp. 191–92 and 193–95; Marylène Perez, "Le personnage d'Alexandre le Grand dans l'*Alexandréide*," *Bien dire et bien aprandre* 7 (1989), esp. 19–21. Cf. Alexandre Cizek, "Considérations sur la réception du thème d'Alexandre le Grand au moyen âge," in *Littérature et société au moyen âge*, ed. Danielle Buschinger (Paris: Champion, 1978), pp. 201–30.

36. Cf. Jean-Guy Gouttebroze, "Entre les historiographes d'expression latine et les jongleurs, le clerc lisant," in *Le clerc au moyen âge*, pp. 215–30.

37. *MFRA* III, vv. 2716–18, 2799–2801, 2824–25; cf. III, vv. 3864–77.

38. Gaullier-Bougassas, *Frontières*, pp. 167–68. On *poète* in this sense in the *Roman de Troie*, see Baumgartner, "*Ecrire, disent-ils*: à propos de Wace et de Benoît de Sainte-Maure," in *Figures de l'écrivain au moyen âge*, ed. Danielle Buschinger (Göppingen: Kümmerle, 1991), p. 46.

4

Alexander and Aristotle in the French Alexander Romances

Catherine Gaullier-Bougassas

Since the twelfth century, many authors of "mirrors of princes" and of political commentary cite the example of Alexander to illustrate their encomia of scholarly monarchs and to show the beneficial effect of learned culture on the exercise of power.[1] But if medieval clerics know that Aristotle was the Greek king's preceptor, they have at hand no precise information about the contents of his teaching and of the relationship between the two men, and modern historians are still in large measure confronted with this "void" in the story.[2] In the historical Latin works available in the twelfth century—those of Quintus Curtius, Justin, and Orosius—Aristotle almost never appears. Certainly the references to Alexander's assassination of Aristotle's nephew and disciple Callisthenes may recall his ties with the Greek king; but while they indicate that Alexander eliminated Callisthenes because he refused to prostrate himself before the ruler, they disclose nothing about Aristotle's reaction. They suggest, nonetheless, the likely beginning of a conflict; above all, they cast light on the limits of the influence of the philosopher's teaching, while inflating the portrait of the conqueror.[3]

Until the fifteenth century—before the rediscovery of Plutarch—only the Latin translations of the Pseudo-Callisthenes offer a detailed account of Alexander's childhood. But they too most often merely mention Aristotle.[4] To him they prefer Nectanabus, the astronomer and Egyptian king who, in the dual role of father and preceptor, seems to determine the king's future. Without ever adopting the intractability of a master seeking to inculcate laws and impose prohibitions, Nectanabus gives the impression of inspiring in his son his own hunger for learning and the illusion that man can acquire absolute mastery of the universe. With his astrological and magic practices, he is much more fascinating to the authors than what they were able to know of Aristotle.

Nonetheless these Latin texts, following the account of the childhood of the prince, evoke a few exchanges of letters between the king and the philosopher, who remained in Greece with Olympias. Alexander informs him of his successes, without receiving advice and even less instruction from him, to the point that he seems to achieve full independence and retain only a bond of friendship with Aristotle. The longest and most famous letter, the *Letter from Alexander to Aristotle on the Marvels of India*, shows the profit drawn by the king from his instruction and his passion for the observation of cosmic phenomena and the strange fauna and human inhabitants of the Orient. It thus reflects a sort of reversal of roles, with the student completing the teacher's lessons through his scientific exploration and even tending to take his place. Its prologue is never, to our knowledge, taken up in the French adaptations of the twelfth and thirteenth centuries. One reason for this is perhaps that the hero is implicated in the prolongation of Aristotle's writings on physics, which were becoming known yet also arousing much resistance, and would soon be censored.[5] As for the letter that, according to the *Historia de Preliis*, the philosopher addressed to the king before his death, it shows just how much the teacher defers to the authority of his former pupil, when Aristotle develops a panegyric that assimilates Alexander to a god.[6] These Latin texts thus confine the philosopher to a very secondary role and deprive him of all authority over the king: not only is he surpassed by a child prodigy who astounds him, but he is from the outset rivaled and virtually eclipsed by the unsettling Nectanabus.

Authors like Thomas of Kent (1175) or the adapter of the prose *Roman d'Alexandre* (first half of the thirteenth century) who remain faithful to these Latin texts also attribute only a minor influence to Aristotle. On the other hand, those who deny any filiation between Alexander and Nectanabus and explicitly conceive their works as mirrors of princes emphasize the philosopher's authority in order to enhance the king's prestige. In the twelfth century, in the works of Gautier de Châtillon and Alexandre de Paris, Alexander thus becomes one of the literary heroes who best embodies the ideal union of *clergie*, royalty, and chivalry. The specificity of the French Vulgate of the *Roman d'Alexandre* is that while celebrating Aristotle, it surrounds his portrait with ambiguities, to which we shall return.[7] They can perhaps be interpreted as so many hidden connections between Aristotle and the Nectanabus of the Latin texts. It is as if, in the rewriting by Alexandre de Paris, Aristotle were meant to subvert the figure of the magician and relegate him to oblivion, but without the author attempting—or being able—fully to achieve that end.

One of the first authors to insist on Aristotle's teaching, a few years before Alexandre de Paris, is Gautier de Châtillon. Without retracing the childhood of the conqueror, his *Alexandreis* begins with a long sermon by Aristotle to the young prince (Book I, vv. 82–155). The philosopher appears as an austere old man who works on his *Logic* and wields an absolute authority over his pupil. Although he has long forbidden Alexander to respond to Darius's attacks, he suddenly urges him to take up arms and teaches him how to realize his ambitions. His principal role then becomes to support the conquest of

Persia: after holding forth on the great royal virtues, he counsels Alexander on military strategy. His conception of largesse differs from that attributed to him by Lambert le Tort and Alexandre de Paris, to the extent that he commits the king to rewarding not only the nobles but also all those who distinguish themselves by their personal qualities. It is this aspect that Rutebeuf sets out to develop when he adapts this discourse in his *Dit d'Aristote*, identifying himself implicitly with the men of merit yet humbly born who serve kings and expect rewards from them.[8] In addition to Rutebeuf's poem, the success of this passage of the *Alexandreis* is attested by the existence of several other adaptations. Some of these circulated independently; one was incorporated, in the fifteenth century, into one of the manuscripts of the *Histoire du bon roi Alexandre* by Jean Wauquelin.[9]

In this political lesson by Aristotle the influence of the *Secretum Secretorum* has often been discerned. We know in fact that the latter presents itself as a response by the philosopher to a question by Alexander about the treatment to be accorded the Persians, and it is true that the discourse that the Latin epic attributes to the philosopher may evoke certain passages of the encyclopedia.[10] The themes it develops, however, are also so commonplace in twelfth-century political discourse that it remains difficult to prove the existence of direct borrowings from the Latin text, especially since the chronology of the different translations of the latter seems to oppose it.[11] Despite its great success from the end of the thirteenth century onward, moreover, the *Secretum Secretorum* had little influence on the medieval accounts of the life of Alexander. The reason may be simply that it contributes virtually nothing to the portrait of the Greek king, who is merely the dedicatee of the work. The only anecdote it introduces, that of the malicious young Indian woman, was never taken up, to the best of our knowledge, in the *romans d'Alexandre*.[12] In the fifteenth century Jean Wauquelin does cite the *Secret of Secrets* under its Latin title, but, in the interest of the coherence of his narrative, he merely refers his readers to it.[13]

Whatever the sources of Aristotle's discourse in the *Alexandreis*, Gautier de Châtillon gives the philosopher the unambiguous role of a master above all suspicion. His authority supports Alexander's politics, but must not overshadow it. Thus Aristotle intervenes only twice, and fades into the background behind the young king from the time of his coronation. It is Alexandre de Paris who, after Lambert le Tort, lends a greater density to the character of the philosopher, especially in that he depicts the childhood of Alexander. In keeping with the ambiguity that characterizes his version, his portrait of Aristotle seems to oscillate between the image of a virtuous master and that of an accomplice in the Greek king's desire for total power.

According to Alexandre de Paris, Aristotle is Alexander's only preceptor before the arrival of Nectanabus; he initiates him into all the arts and thus forms his mind. He teaches him the sacred languages, the natural sciences (especially astronomy), then rhetoric, logic and politics:

Aristotes d'Athaines l'aprist honestement;
Celui manda Phelippes trestout premierement.
Il li mostre escripture et li vallés l'entent,
Greu, ebreu et caldeu et latin ensement
Et toute la nature de la mer et du vent
Et le cours des estoiles et le compassement
Et si com li planete hurtent au firmament
Et la vie du siecle, qanq'a lui en apent,
Et conoistre raison et savoir jugement,
Si com restorique en fait devisement;
Que ja sers de put aire n'ait entor lui sovent,
Et en aprés li mostre un bon chastïement:
Car maint home en sont mort et livré a torment,
Par losenge et par murdre, par enpoisonement. (*MFRA II*, Br. I,
    vv. 333–46)

(Aristotle of Athens educated him nobly; he is the first master Philip
had chosen for him. He has him read the texts, and the young man
understands quickly; he teaches him Greek, Hebrew, Chaldean, and
Latin, and all that is known of the sea and the wind, the course of
the stars and its measure, how the planets oppose the movement of
the firmament, and life in this world in all its forms. He teaches him
to use his reason and judgment, as rhetoric sets forth. Finally he gives
him a wise counsel: never to surround himself with serfs, with lowborn men, for many have suffered death, torture, slander, assassination,
and poisoning at their hands.)

At least until the Persian campaigns, Aristotle directs Alexander in the exercise
of power and his projects of conquest. It is also the knowledge of natural
sciences received from Aristotle that seems to incite Alexander to the observation of the natural phenomena of the Orient, even if Alexandre de Paris does
not emphasize this point, preferring instead, like Gautier de Châtillon, to
emphasize the philosopher's ethical and political teaching. The explanation is
perhaps that Aristotle's authority must not directly support the exploration of
virgin territory reserved for the gods, which might appear as sacrilege. The
idea of scientific curiosity detached from the desire to exalt divine creation
would also risk too strong a recall of Nectanabus. While Nectanabus in the
earlier texts represents the pleasure principle, encouraging the belief that man
can transgress all laws and that the powers of reason are infinite (*MFRA II*, Br.
III, ll. 2–3),[14] the basic function assigned by Alexandre de Paris to Aristotle
seems on the contrary to be to impose limits on his pupil's desire for power
and incite him to undertake just and wise enterprises, in conformity with the

values of the twelfth century. His virtue is opposed to the subversive curiosity of Nectanabus, and he undergoes a partial process of Christianization.

As a spokesman, at least in appearance, for an aristocratic conception of royalty, Aristotle inculcates in Alexander, as the foundation of royal authority, the absolute preference to be accorded the nobility, and the example of Darius serves to prove the wisdom of excluding the common people in favor of the nobly born as the king's counsellors and companions. The political precept that is presented as the culmination of his teaching is the duty scornfully to reject the low born and the serf.[15] One could further speculate that the insistence on this topos of twelfth-century literature does not merely derive from political discourse but may also be implicitly directed against Nectanabus, a man of inferior status according to Alexandre de Paris.

Finally, Aristotle stands in for the king in the making of two important decisions. He presides over the organization of his army, advising him to choose twelve peers, twelve equals (Br. I, l. 31).[16] With the creation of this institution, which of course recalls the model of Charlemagne, one might at first think that he is inciting the king to share the royal prerogatives, to be wary of too personal and too absolute a power. Alexander, in an attitude of perfect obedience and blind confidence, then directs him to name the twelve men. Then Aristotle accompanies him to the Orient and, as in the *Alexandreis*, urges him to conquer Persia (Br. III, ll. 2–3). It is there that Alexandre de Paris fully exploits his authority to obliterate the image of the greedy and bloodthirsty conqueror found in many historical texts, and to legitimize his expansionist politics. The philosopher endorses the conflict with Darius as a just war, one that is to allow Greece to regain its full sovereignty and then bring justice, civilization, and prosperity to the Persians by ridding them of their tyrant. The conquest of Persia is, according to him, a divine mission, inasmuch as Alexander is to rush to the aid of the humble populace unjustly crushed by the serfs that Darius had preferred to the nobility:

> Dayres a fait en Gresce grans persecucions,
> Molt en a avoir pris et or et raençons,
> Or est tans du vengier, chauce tes esperons,
> Car heent le de mort toutes ses regions
> Por ce q'a mis sor aus sergans issi felons,
> Des noaus de sa terre, des fieus a ses garçons.
> Cil n'ont cure de Dieu ne de ses orisons,
> Ciaus qui ne se raiembent getent en lor prisons,
> Li avoirs de la terre est tous lor abandons.
> Li pueples prie a Dieu et fait aflictions
> Q'ançois viegne seur aus male confusions
> Q'il ne soient vengié du roi et des gloutons. (Br. III, l.2, vv. 28–39)

("Darius has persecuted Greece; he has taken its riches and its gold as ransom. Now the time has come for vengeance: put on your spurs! In all his lands he inspires nothing but mortal hate, for he has set treacherous servants over them, the dregs of the land, the sons of his knaves. They care nothing for prayers addressed to God: they throw those who do not pay into prison; all the wealth of the country is abandoned to them. The people pray to God and protest that they would rather suffer dreadful consequences than fail to be avenged of the king and these wretched men.")

Up to this point Aristotle seems to be the true strategist of Greece. Indeed, Alexandre de Paris exploits the Athenian episode to show that any attempt at independence, and even more at rebellion, on the part of his pupil is doomed to failure in the face of the wisdom of such a master (Br. I, ll. 78–82).[17] For the Latin account of the negotiations with Demosthenes he substitutes a version much less favorable to the Greek king, in that it glorifies Aristotle at his expense. This is the legend of the ruse devised by the philosopher to prevent Alexander from destroying Athens: learning that his pupil has sworn to do the opposite of whatever he might recommend to him, Aristotle vigorously enjoins him to raze the city. Alexandre de Paris here celebrates the victory of both *clergie* and a political ideal hostile to royalty over the greed and authoritarianism of the young king. He also proves that the master retains enough authority to oppose the aberrations of his pupil and set him back on the right course.

If this image of an Alexander submissive to the philosopher dominates until the Persian campaigns, thereafter Aristotle disappears from the account of the exploration of India, precisely from the moment when Alexandre de Paris reveals and implicitly condemns the sacrilegious desire of the conqueror to take the place of the gods. We may at first think that he did not wish to compromise the philosopher in adventures not in keeping with the duties of a king, or relate a confrontation between him and his former pupil that would unduly discredit the latter. The only mention of Aristotle that he introduces appears when he recounts that the oracle of the trees of the Sun and the Moon proclaim the eternal glory of the philosopher, as if he were trying at that point to indicate that Aristotle's teaching was not responsible for the premature disappearance of Alexander (Br. III, l. 213, vv. 3825–26).

Finally, nonetheless, and with no explanation whatever, the author describes the philosopher's presence before the king's mortal remains in Babylon (Br. IV, l. 51). He has just referred to Alexander's violation of the major precept taught him by Aristotle, never to be generous with serfs, and he attempts to impose this explanation of the king's death in place of those already suggested. Thus would Alexander prove once again, in disobeying the teaching of his master, the pertinence of that teaching, as in the example of Darius. But at this moment Aristotle does not reproach him for the favors he has lavished on

Antipater and Divinuspater, and no longer offers any moralizing discourse. The reason is not simply the very reductive character of this final interpretation. What is at work is a transformation undergone by the philosopher, one which seems to call into question his stature as *maître de sagesse*.

Alexandre de Paris, taking his cue no doubt from Gautier de Châtillon, now describes Aristotle as an old man whose physical weakness and untidiness are the consequences of a philosopher's life. Like an ascetic, a cynic or, for the medieval mind, a hermit, he nourishes himself on bread and water, seeks solitude, and his unkempt appearance reflects his scorn for worldly things:

> Bien fu de philosophe ses fais et ses abis,
> Ne lui chaloit de soi, tous estoit enhermis;
> Barbë ot longe et lee et le poil retortis
> Et le chief deslavé et velus les sorcis;
> De pain et d'eaue vit, ne quiert autres pertris;
> Onques n'issi d'Ataines uns seus clers si soutis. (Br. IV, l. 51,
>   1020–25)

> (His life and habits were certainly those of a philosopher: he took no care for himself, and was always reclusive; he had a long, wide beard and tangled hair, an unwashed head, bushy eyebrows; he lived on bread and water, and sought no other food. Never did such a subtle mind come from Athens!)

But behind this apparent celebration, an ironic attitude on the part of the author is apparent. In fact Aristotle is no longer occupied with writing his *Logic* in Greece, and above all he does not lead the solitary life the narrator pretends to give him, because he is henceforth assumed to have accompanied the king on his Oriental journey. On the contrary: he is much involved in the world and in worldly affairs, in an expedition, moreover, that is not only extraordinary but also sacrilegious—an expedition of which he approves, as is evident immediately afterward in his panegyric of the Greek king. Alexandre de Paris in effect chooses to suggest that Aristotle loses his reason to the point of assuming all the excesses of his pupil. He does not hesitate to revolt against the gods and divinize Alexander, before being interrupted by his companions—who accuse him of blasphemy—and fainting:

> "Alixandre, de toi nos ont li dieu traïs;
> Se tu peüsses vivre seul dis ans acomplis,
> Tu fuisses dieus en terre aourés et servis,
> Et te feïsons temples, auteus et crucifis.
> Ahi! Dieus, molt par es envious et faillis,
> Qui les malvais espargnes et les bons nos ocis."

Or deïst ja mervelles qant il fu acuellis,
Qant doi autre gramaire, Varo et Egesis,
Li senerent de loins que trop iert esbahis,
Qant il des dieus mesdist, trop est de sens maris.
Ja chaïst jus pasmés, tous est esvanuïs,
Qant Litonas l'aert et l'estraint vers son pis. (Br. IV, l. 51, 1064–75)

("Alexander, the gods have betrayed us in taking you from us: if you could have lived only ten years more, you would have been adored and served like a god on earth; we would make temples for you, and altars, and crucifixes. Alas! God, how envious and cruel you are to spare the wicked and kill the good!" He would have spoken even more astonishing things, but he was interrupted when two other grammarians, Varro and Egesis, signaled to him from afar that he was too carried away and was taking leave of his senses to speak ill of the gods. Then he fainted, and would have fallen if Litonas had not come to his aid and restrained him.)

This all takes place as if the wise man were becoming a sycophant, a courtier, so subject to his former student that he places him above all laws, even those of the gods—as if the master were absorbed by his former disciple.[18]

The heroic grandeur of Alexander could certainly justify excessive praise, especially from his companions, whose sorrow might excuse their state of mental distraction; but to show Aristotle, in spite of his status as philosopher, reacting like the peers, and with an even greater degree of immoderation and weakness, can be seen as calling into question the moral authority that he was supposed to incarnate, even as a symbolic destruction of his role of authoritarian master. All the more so since Alexandre de Paris must have recalled the well-known episode of Alexander's assassination of Callisthenes, who had opposed the deification of the Greek king in the name of philosophy. It could thus seem surprising that Aristotle would wish to adore the king as a god and to erect temples to him. Certainly Alexandre de Paris could have found some seeds of this discourse in the final letter that the *Historia de Preliis* attributes to Aristotle (see pp. 242–43 of the edition), but it is he who added the blasphemy and the revolt against the gods. The letter as it stands, moreover, is never incorporated into the other *romans d'Alexandre*, undoubtedly an indication that Aristotle's deification of the Greek king would no longer appear as a reaction fully worthy of a philosopher, even for the clerics who praised the king without reservation. Thus, in the thirteenth century, the author of the prose *Roman d'Alexandre* adapts it while changing its content. Here Aristotle, instead of making Alexander the equal of a god, seeks to bring him back to humility, reminding him of all that he owes to God and his men's devotion, and then instructs him to reward the latter (*Prosa*, pp. 242–44). He thus regains the authority and wisdom of a master, and it is this version that Jean Wauquelin prefers in the fifteenth century.[19]

In the Vulgate of Alexandre de Paris, the final intervention of Aristotle perhaps reflects a criticism of the vanity of pagan philosophy, all the more since the author later invokes Alexander's status as a man of pagan antiquity in order to explain his failings (br. IV, l. 74, v. 1679). Might we perhaps also see in it an implicit attack on the greater diffusion of Aristotle's writings in the Parisian schools where Alexandre de Paris may have studied? Nothing allows us, of course, to affirm this with certainty. One can simply point out that the introduction of ambiguities into the portrait of the philosopher coincides with progress in the knowledge of Aristotelian philosophy and the increase in resistance to it. The *Lai d'Aristote* by Henri d'Andeli, from the beginning of the thirteenth century, also shows, although in a very different context, how Aristotle, again described as a weakened and ugly old man, has lost his wisdom and his authority over Alexander. Here Aristotle sternly reproaches Alexander for his infatuation with a young Indian woman and for having neglected his political duties for her. Out of spite, the young woman decides to seduce the old philosopher in order to ridicule him and put an end to his influence; she succeeds so easily that Aristotle accepts to be ridden by her before Alexander, then himself regrets that his *clergie* had not enabled him to resist the urging of his senses.[20] This short account is only indirectly inscribed in the later accounts of Alexander's life, since the scene it sketches, although famous early on, is not introduced into them. The thematics of love, like the involvement of the text and its author in the Parisian University disputes and also in the debates of cleric versus knight, no doubt remained too remote from the spirit of the Vulgate of Alexandre de Paris and of the cycle constructed from it. But despite the very marked satiric value of the burlesque image of Aristotle ridden by the Indian woman, the critique of the philosopher is perhaps equally profound in Branch IV of the *Roman d'Alexandre*. In effect, Alexandre de Paris introduces no comic tonality, but accuses the philosopher of impiety and makes this denunciation resonate with that of Alexander's pride.

Finally, instead of seeing in the end of the *Roman d'Alexandre* a distant reflection—possible but hypothetical—of resistance to Aristotelian philosophy, we may better question the logic of the portrait of Aristotle within the work itself, and the work of intertextuality that gave rise to it. If the role of the philosopher seems at first constructed as an inversion of that of the astronomer Nectanabus of the Latin texts, the *Roman d'Alexandre* at the same time often suggests connections between the two men, connections that are gradually reinforced, until finally, upon the king's death, Aristotle perhaps merges symbolically with the figure of the enchanter that he was originally supposed to conceal.

By equating Alexander with a god, even though after his death, Aristotle in fact lends him an aura of the omnipotence that Nectanabus, according to

the translations of the Pseudo-Callisthenes, had inspired in him from his childhood. His last words may be compared with the prophecy that Nectanabus
pronounces when he chooses the most favorable moment for the birth of his
son: that he will acquire absolute power, comparable to that of a god.[21] In
addition, Alexandre de Paris depicts Aristotle intervening at the beginning of
the king's life to predict a glorious destiny for him. In this text it occurs not
at Alexander's birth but in his early childhood, when the philosopher is substituted for the seer Antiphon as one of the interpreters of the dream of the
egg and the serpent (Br. I, l. 9-14). His explanation that glorifies Alexander,
accepted by Philip of Macedonia because it accords with his own desires,
seems very partisan and reductive, all the more so since the author then places
it into competition with those of two other seers. It conceals several literal
elements of the dream under the cosmic symbolism of the egg: neither the
negative image of the serpent that represents Alexander, nor the reasons for his
early disappearance or his desire to return into the eggshell are explained.
According to one of the manuscripts, Aristotle even attempts to deny the
literal properties of the dream by introducing a doubt about the king's death
upon his return to Greece:

> "Oiés, segnor, fait il, une raison certaine.
> Li oés dont il parolent n'est mie chose vaine,
> Le monde senefie et la mer et l'araine,
> Et li moieus dedens est terre de gent plaine;
> Del serpent qui'n issoit vos di par sainte Elaine
> Que ce est Alixandres qui souffrira grant paine
> Et iert sires du mont, ma parole en iert saine,
> Et si home aprés lui le tendront en demaine,
> Puis torra mors ou vis en tere mascedaine,
> Si com fist li serpens qui vint a sa chievaine." (MS B, Br. I, l.14,
>   312–21)

> ("Hear for certain, lords," says he, "The egg they speak of is not a
> trivial thing. It signifies the world, with the sea and the sand, and the
> yolk in its midst is the land inhabited by men. The serpent that comes
> forth from it, I say by Saint Helen, is indeed Alexander, who will
> suffer greatly and will be, I confirm, the master of the world, which
> his men will still rule after him. Then he will return, dead or alive,
> into Macedonia, just as the serpent returns into its retreat.")

His role is thus from the outset to celebrate the young prince without reservation and to serve his interests, even if by means of manipulating the signs
of divine will. Not only does the author perhaps recall that the Greek philosopher wrote a treatise on the interpretation of dreams; he also implicitly likens

him to Nectanabus, who is also expert in the interpretation and even the production of dreams, and also a herald of the king's triumphs.

If Alexandre de Paris denies any bond of filiation between Alexander and Nectanabus and accentuates the influence of the philosopher, it is nonetheless surprising to note that later, when retracing Alexander's education, he nearly places the teachings of the two learned men into competition. Both are in effect assigned to teach Alexander astronomy, without any reason for the doubling of instruction in this science ever being made explicit (Br. I, ll. 15, 16, vv. 337–39, 354–57). The Greek philosopher thus seems to represent the serious side, while Nectanabus draws it toward the dark side of magic. If Alexandre de Paris uses the philosopher to correct the suspect influence of the Oriental, he does not completely eliminate the latter, and perhaps seeks to set up a play of mirrors between the two men. When Alexander later begins his celestial ascent or expresses his curiosity about the natural phenomena of the Orient, it is not apparent which master's lessons are brought to fruition.

The Athenian episode also pursues, in roundabout ways, the comparison of Aristotle with Nectanabus. In his description of the Greek city, Alexandre de Paris includes a pillar allegedly erected by Plato, with a lamp always lit at its summit. This edifice could have evoked the lighthouse of Alexandria (Br. I, l. 78, vv. 1695–1702). Athens, Aristotle's city, is therefore implicitly associated with the Egyptian city which, despite its having been founded by Alexander, is represented in many manuscripts of the *Historia de Preliis* as the city of Nectanabus.[22] The ingenuity and sense of humor that the episode attributes to Aristotle also recall the astrologer of the Latin texts more than they agree with the portrait of the philosopher as master of ethics and politics offered elsewhere by Alexandre de Paris. It is not with sermons, in the name of the ethical and political principles he has taught him, that Aristotle exacts obedience from his pupil. Only a ruse stops Alexander in his project of destruction, and the Greek king pronounces himself taken by surprise and *enchanté* by his teacher:

> Quant l'entent Alixandres, si a le vis troublé,
> Ses deux poins fiert ensemble si a le chief craulé,
> Et dist a soi meïsmes, "Malement ai erré,
> La vile est de moi cuite, tuit sont asseüré;
> Au savoir Aristote ai malement gardé.
> Mes maistres m'a souspris et bien m'a enchanté." (Br. I, l.82, vv.
>   1780–85)

(At these words Alexander, his face troubled, wrings his hands and shakes his head: "I was wrong," he says to himself, "the city is let off, they need not worry! I did not hold to the wisdom of Aristotle; my master surprised and overcame me as if by magic!")

The unexpected choice of the verb *"enchanter"* perhaps signals here again the hidden presence, behind Aristotle, of the magician Nectanabus. We note too that Jean Wauquelin, in casting the romance in prose, seems to have been troubled by this sequence. He changes its meaning by suppressing both the evocation of the lighthouse and the ruse of Aristotle: according to him, the master easily talks his pupil into sparing the city. Now nothing at all about his attitude is evocative of Nectanabus, and there is nothing to condemn Alexander (BN fr. 9342, f. 20–21 verso).

In the *Roman d'Alexandre*, moreover, it is while they are in Athens that the philosopher first directs Alexander's ambitions toward the Orient. He does not yet seek to legitimize them, but he shows no concern for the ravages that the conquests will inflict and that the narrator announces without indulgence. A whole network of elements raises the question as to whether the support that he later lends Alexander does not provide the pretext for an expansionist politics devoid of any ethical objective. One wonders whether the ideal that he professes later dissimulates the extent to which he incites the king merely to satisfy his excessive thirst for power. The differences among his various political discourses would seem to support this view. In effect, Alexandre de Paris does not make Aristotle's fine speech about the Persian people who call upon God for aid against the tyrant oppressor fully convincing, for nowhere else does he recommend that the king respect religious law or concern himself with the people. On the contrary, he evokes the latter only in his expression of scorn for serfs. Everything thus leads us to believe that he exhorted Alexander to surround himself with twelve peers less in order to invite him to share power than out of a simple concern for military effectiveness. And when the story progressively demonstrates that Alexander, far from considering his peers as equals, succumbs to the temptation of authoritarianism, the author never prompts the philosopher to invervene to call him to order.

More than a master, Aristotle is perhaps from the beginning an accomplice. To be sure, he does not proceed as openly as the astrologer of the Latin texts, and most of the time he attempts to give the king's conquests the honorable appearance of an effort to civilize the Orient; but like Nectanabus, he serves above all Alexander's inordinate desire for power.

But why would Alexandre de Paris have brought the image of the Greek philosopher closer to that of the Oriental magician? How are we to explain these hidden connections resulting from the author's work of rewriting, and from the "dialogue" that he establishes with the Latin translations of the Pseudo-Callisthenes? Our hypothesis is that the veiled presence of the Easterner behind Aristotle could be paralleled with the latent reemergence in the East of the king's illegitimacy, as well as with the progressive revelation, also in the East, of his sacrilegious pride.[23] Just as the question of Alexander's illegitimate origins and then of the role of Nectanabus never completely disappear, and just as the glorification of Alexander is often contradicted by a story that heightens the flaws in his character, so does Alexandre de Paris construct a double image of Aristotle: he gives him the semblance of a *maître* of ethics and politics who replaces the magician in order to set limits for Alexander but, at the same time, he tends to contest this authority by suggesting that his attitude recalls Nectanabus's immoderation.

This double image is specific to Alexandre de Paris's account; it appears neither in the *Alexandreis* nor in the prose *Roman d'Alexandre*. Nor does Jean de Wauquelin retain it in his prose account. Only the *Prise de Defur* and the *Voyage d'Alexandre au Paradis terrestre* prolong it, once they are integrated into the Vulgate of Alexandre de Paris in the manuscript tradition (see *Prise*). Like the *Faits des Romains*, these two accounts cause the philosopher to intervene in the legend of the Greek king's voyage to the Earthly Paradise, and they offer two different rewritings of his discovery of a marvelous stone or apple just before his arrival in Babylon. Aristotle, substituted for the pious Jew of the Latin text, metamorphoses into a pre-Christian sage to whom the divinity entrusts the delicate mission of explaining to the king a sign that in the Latin source announces both the divine condemnation of his greed and the imminence of his death. The philosopher proceeds to weigh the enigmatic object and reveals its *senefiance*, according to a logic that differs in each text.[24]

In the *Prise de Defur* (ll. 57–58), Aristotle bluntly explains to his pupil that the eye engraved on the stone sets before him an image of his own insatiable gaze. He severely denounces the excessiveness of his greed and his will to power, and warns him against the torments of Hell (11. 1580–92). As for the author of the *Voyage d'Alexandre au Paradis terrestre* (11. 8–16), his adaptation suggests on the contrary that Aristotle does not perfectly fulfill his mission, as if he were still halfway between a pre-Christian monotheism and paganism. The confusion attributed to him seems to signify that he is divided between the duty imposed upon him by the divinity and his affection for his pupil, and perhaps also that he is reluctant to acknowledge the limited influence of his teaching as revealed by Alexander's failure to observe it. Far from adopting the critical point of view of a moralist, he seeks to exculpate the Greek king. The complex speech that he begins blends celebration of royal grandeur with an incomplete and biased explanation of the sign of divine condemnation. Not only does he first reduce the meaning of the apple to a *memento mori*; he also counters immediately that Alexander will overcome death through the immortality that the memory of his glory and largesse will afford him (l. 12). Then he holds forth in general against pride and greed, but pretends to consider that it does not apply to Alexander (l. 13). Finally, after further praises, the explication that he gives of the king's imminent death is not at all that of a punishment and seems to reflect his own reaction against divine will, but in roundabout ways, without the blasphemy of the version of Alexandre de Paris. He suggests in effect that the gods are jealously drawing Alexander into their midst in order to profit from his grandeur, to such an extent that he transforms his death into the apotheosis and immortalization of which the king had dreamed (l. 14, vv. 282–84). When, at his student's request, he proceeds to weigh the fruit, he continues to refuse to castigate Alexander's pride and conceals the divine condemnation (l. 15). Here too he plays the role of an accomplice who prefers to glorify the prince rather than show him God's judgment, as if he were a prisoner of his adherence to paganism.

In the end, the splendid image of the union of prince and philosopher, projected in numerous didactic texts that cite the example of Alexander and Aristotle, does not consistently inform the literary accounts of Alexander's life. Certainly their authors, in introducing the Greek philosopher, use him, at least at first, to celebrate the king and at the same time to boast of the influence of clerics—their own influence—on rulers. But either they accord Aristotle only a restricted role, and thus tend to minimize the influence of his teaching, or else they play with his prestigious authority and surround it with ambiguity. Alexandre de Paris thus presents him by blending celebration and critical equivocation, and this is found also, in another form, in his portrait of Alexander. Thereafter, thanks to the rediscovery of Plutarch in the second half of the fifteenth century (in 1468) Vasque de Lucène provides further details of the contents of the instruction the philosopher provided Alexander.[25] He thus shows the limits of the influence of this education on the king, notably when he includes a historic fact that the French *romans d'Alexandre* always carefully "ignore": Callisthenes's opposition to Alexander's desire to make himself the equal of a god, and the consequent assassination of the philosopher.

Notes

1. The clerics of the court of Henry II Plantagenet, who promote this ideal of the learned prince and who incessantly repeat that an uneducated king is a crowned ass, almost always include Alexander in their list of cultivated rulers, along with Caesar and Charlemagne. See notably Jean of Salisbury, *Policraticus*, ed. K. S. B. Keats-Rohan (Turnhout: Brepols, 1993), ch. IV, Book IV, cap. 6; Denis Fouchelat and C. Brucker, ed. and trans., *Tyrans, Princes et Prêtres* (*Le Moyen Français* 1987), p. 66; Giraldus Cambrensis, *Topographia Hibernica*, ed. J.-M. Boivin, in *L'Irlande au Moyen Age: Giraud de Barry et la Topographia Hibernica* (Paris: Champion, 1993), pp. 266–78; and in the *De Principis Instructione Liber*, and Pierre de Blois, *Lettres*. For studies and citations see R. R. Bezzola, *Les Origines et la Formation de la Littérature courtoise en Occident (500–1200)* (Paris: Champion, 1944–63), Part III, pp. 1–87.

2. See esp. P. Briant, *Alexandre le Grand* (Paris: Presses Universitaires de France, 1977), pp. 5–6; P. Faure, *Alexandre le Grand* (Paris: Fayard, 1985), pp. 34–35, 105–6; idem., *La vie quotidienne des armées d'Alexandre* (Paris: Hachette, 1982), pp. 145–59.

3. Quintus-Curtius, *Histoire d'Alexandre*, ed. and trans. H. Bardon (Paris: Les Belles Lettres, 1948), Book VIII, 5–13 to 8–22; Justinian, *Abrégé des Histoires Philippiques*

de Trogue Pompée, trans. E. Chambry and L. Thély-Chambry (Paris: Classiques Garnier, 1936), Book XII, ch. VII, 1–2; Orosius, *Histoires contre les Païens*, ed. and trans. M. P. Arnaud-Lindet (Paris: Les Belles Lettres, 1990), Vol. I, Book III, 18, 10 on the murder of Callisthenes. Plutarch's *Life of Alexander*, which deals with these matters extensively, was not rediscovered until the second half of the fifteenth century; see *Vie d'Alexandre*, ed. and trans. F. Flacelière and E. Chambry (Paris: Les Belles Lettres, 1975, trans. repr. in Editions Autrement 1993), pp. 25–27 on Alexander's teachings and 77–82 on the assassination of Callisthenes; the translation of *Sur la Fortune et la Vertu d'Alexandre* is included (pp. 109–69).

4. *Julii Valerii Epitome*, ed. J. Zacher (Halle, 1867), pp. 16, 55; *Historia de Preliis Alexandri Magni*, in *Prosa*, pp. 35, 139–40, 242–43, 253.

5. *Epistola Alexandri ad Aristotelem de miraculis Indiae*, ed. W. Walther Boer (Meisenheim am Glan: A. Hain, 1973), trans. G. Bounoure and B. Serret in the *Roman d'Alexandre du Pseudo-Callisthène* (Paris: Les Belles Lettres, 1992), appendix I, pp. 123–46. For the reception of Aristotle in the Middle Ages, see Fernand Van Steenberghen, *Aristote en Occident. Les origines de l'aristotélisme parisien* (Louvain: Editions de l'Institut Supérieur de Philosophie, 1946).

6. *Historia de Preliis*, pp. 242–43.

7. On the relations between Alexander and Aristotle in the eastern and western *romans d'Alexandre*, see the pioneering study of W. Hertz, "Aristoteles in den Alexander-Dichtunger des Mittelalters," *Gesammelte Abhandlungen* (1905), 1–155. See also my *Frontières*, esp. pp. 288–89. On iconography: C. Raynaud, "Aristote dans les enluminures du XIIIe au XVe siècle," in *Mythes, cultures et sociétés, XIIIe–XVe siècles* (Paris: Le Léopard d'Or, 1995), pp. 201–31.

8. For the *Dit d'Aristote*, see the editions in Rutebeuf, *Oeuvres complètes* by Edmond Faral and Julia Bastin (Paris: Picard, 1969), and Michel Zink (Paris: Classiques Garnier, 1989); also *Poèmes de l'Infortune et autres poèmes*, ed. Jean Dufournet (Paris: Gallimard, 1986).

9. See H. Christensen, *Das Alexanderlied Walters von Châtillon* (Halle: Verlag der Buchhandlung des Waisenhauses, 1905), pp. 129–35; P. Meyer, "Notice d'un ms. Messin (Montpellier 164 et Libri 96)," *Romania* 15 (1886), 169–70; R. Wisbey, "Die Aristotelesrede bei Walter de Châtillon und Rudolf von Ems," *Zeitschrift für deutsches Altertum* 85 (1954–55), 304–11; Raffaele de Cesare, "Volgarizzamenti antico-francesi dei 'Praecepta Aristotelis ad Alexandrem,'" *Miscellanea del centro di studi medievali* 2 (1958), 35–123. For Jean Wauquelin we have consulted ms. fr. 9342 of the Bibliothèque Nationale de France. The text is partially translated by O. Collet in *Splendeurs de la cour de Bourgogne*, ed. D. Régnier-Bohler (Paris: Laffont, 1995), pp. 483–564. The text of ms. 456 of the collection Dutuit du Petit Palais, the only ms. to include an adaptation of the precepts of Aristotle, is edited by S. Hériché (thesis, Sorbonne, 1997).

10. On the *Secretum Secretorum* see J. Monfrin, "Sur les sources du *Secret des Secrets* de Jofroi de Waterford et Servais Copale," in *Mélanges de linguistique romane et de philologie médiévale offerts à M. Maurice Delbouille* (Gembloux: Duculot, 1964), II, pp. 509–

30; idem, "La place du *Secret des Secrets* dans la littérature française médiévale," in *Pseudo-Aristotle. The Secret of Secrets, Sources and Influences*, ed. W. F. Ryan and C. B. Schmitt (London: Warburg Institute, 1982), pp. 73–113; M. Grignaschi, "La diffusion du *Secretum Secretorum (Sirr al-'asrâr)* dans l'Europe occidentale," *Archives d'Histoire doctrinale et littéraire du Moyen Age* 47 (1980), 7–70. *Le Secré des Secrez* of Pierre d'Abernun is edited by O. A. Beckerledgge (Oxford: Anglo-Norman Text Society, 1944).

11. In the twelfth century, the first Latin translation of Jean of Seville includes only the advice on hygiene from the Arabic treatise; see H. Suchier, ed., in *Denkmäler provenzalischer Literatur und Sprache* (Halle: Max Niemeyer Verlag, 1883), pp. 473–80. Unless earlier texts have been lost, a more complete Latin translation and a large diffusion of the text giving rise to French translations did not appear until the first half of the thirteenth century. See Roger Bacon's translation, ed. Robert Steele, *Opera hactenus inedita Rogeri Baconi*, fasc. V, *Secretum Secretorum* (Oxford: Oxford University Press, 1920).

12. See Wilhelm Hertz, "Die Sage vom Giftmädchen," *Gesammelte Abhandlungen* (Stuttgart and Berlin: Cotta, 1905), pp. 156–209.

13. Ms. BNF fr. 9342, ch. 5; trans. O. Collet, ch. 5, p. 493.

14. On Nectabus see my *Frontières* and also "Nectanabus et la singularité d'Alexandre dans les *Romans d'Alexandre* français," in *Alexandre*, pp. 303–19.

15. In lending to Aristotle such a "livre de sarmons" (Br. III, l. 2), Alexandre de Paris perhaps alludes to the *Secret des Secrets* but does not seem directly inspired by that encyclopedia, which in any case does not develop such an aristocratic ideal and sets forth another conception of largesse. He appropriates instead a political ideal already prevalent in the twelfth century in vernacular texts. Comparisons could be more readily established with the *Livre des Manières* of Etienne de Fougères or with the "sermons," also composed in Alexandrine *laisses*, of Guichard de Beaulieu and Thibaut de Marly.

16. In rewriting this episode, Alexandre de Paris reinforces the decision-making role of the philosopher. In the earlier version of the Venice manuscript, it is Clin and Ptolemy who advise Alexander to select twelve "compagnons, qui buen chivaler soient e vassal aduré" (l. 77, v. 818). Aristotle then appears in the list of the twelve peers (l. 78). The Venice version is edited in *MFRA I*.

17. In the earlier texts it is another philosopher who intervenes. In the *Historia de Preliis*, it is the philosopher Anaximenes (par. 44, p. 88).

18. Aristotle also calls for the Greek king to be avenged. Guy de Cambrai, in his *Vengement Alexandre*, relates his participation in the combats of the punitive expedition against Antipater; see Bateman Edwards, ed. (Princeton: Princeton University Press, 1928).

19. Already in the twelfth century, Thomas of Kent replaced this intervention by Aristotle with the discourse of a group of anonymous philosophers, that he borrowed from the *Disciplina clericalis* of Petrus Alfonsi, no doubt because this discourse, bearing on the vanity of earthly power and wealth, fits far better with the medieval conception of wisdom (l. 544).

20. See *Le Lai d'Aristote* of Henri d'Andeli, ed. Maurice Delbouille (Paris: Les Belles Lettres, 1951).

21. See esp. *Historia de Preliis*, paras. 5–9. One may also consult Thomas of Kent's version (I, 9, vv. 209–17; l. 14, 17).

22. For the frontispieces of the manuscripts of the *Historia de Preliis,* that present Alexandria as Nectanabus's city, see D. J. A. Ross, "Nectanabus in his palace: a problem of Alexander iconography," *Journal of the Warburg and Courtauld Institutes* 15 (1952), 67–87. The version of the *Epitome* in the Legnica manuscript also attributes to the magician the construction of a tower that quite precisely recalls the lighthouse of Alexandria as it is described in the Latin treatises on the marvels of the world: a tower constructed on four enormous glass crabs, with a magic mirror on its summit; see A. Hilka, "Studien zum Alexandersage, die Leignitzer *Historia Alexandri Magni,*" *Romanische Forschungen* 29 (1911), 16.

23. We know that the oracles of the trees of the Sun and the Moon reveal to him his mother's adultery and announce that she will be condemned by an ignominious death (Br. III, l. 213). For detailed analysis, see my *Frontières*, pp. 343–519.

24. We recall that this object has the marvelous quality of being so heavy that it proves impossible to weigh it, except when it is covered with dust, when it becomes extremely light as if by enchantment. It thus signifies, first, the total power enjoyed by Alexander during his life and, secondly, the destruction of his power in death.

25. The *Faits du Grand Alexandre* by Vasque de Lucène is partially translated by O. Collet in *Splendeurs de la cour de Bourgogne* cit., pp. 565–627. It is primarily an adaptation of Quintus-Curtius, but the author, faced with the disappearance of the first books of this text, then takes his lead from Plutarch's *Life of Alexander*, which he knows through the Italian translation of Guarino da Verona. On Aristotle's education of Alexander see Book I, ch. VII, pp. 575–76, and on the murder of Callisthenes, Book I, ch. XII (trans. p. 579) and Book VII, ch. XI–XVIII (pp. 605–8).

5

Alexander's *Gabs*

François Suard

Several times in the romance by Alexandre de Paris, the Macedonian conqueror uses his wit to overcome his adversaries. Two are notable: before his second battle against Porus, he visits the enemy camp in disguise and spreads false information destined for his adversary; later, before the expedition against Babylon, he impersonates Antigonus, one of his peers, in order to return the wife of queen Candace's son Candeolus, and later visits the queen herself under this assumed identity. Both episodes are found in the Pseudo-Callisthenes and in Julius Valerius, but the medieval text differs from the models in its treatment.[1] What, then, is the meaning and what is the function attributed by the medieval author to such maneuvers, which have different contexts and—since Porus is completely taken in by Alexander, while Candace recognizes him immediately—differing degrees of success? It seems that we are confronted here with a side of the conqueror marked by knowledge and cleverness, one that complements the more evident image of military prowess and power. The inevitable ambiguity resulting from disguise, however, has its impact on our interpretation of the medieval hero: all things considered, we are invited to read these passages as *exempla*, deliberately enigmatic passages from which a profitable lesson may be drawn.

Let us look first at Alexander's visit, disguised as a chamberlain, to Porus's camp. The Pseudo-Callisthenes includes two visits to an adversary's camp by the hero in disguise. In the Greek text he first goes to Darius's camp after having received in a dream the order of the god Ammon, who appears to him in the attributes of Hermes (II, 13–14)—wearing the chlamys, the caduceus, the wand—and topped off with a Macedonian cap. The hero dons the costume in which the god has appeared to him, and Darius invites him to his feast. During the meal, Alexander packs into his garment all the cups he can lay his hands on and explains to Darius that, since Alexander "whenever he offers a dinner to his officers and bodyguards, makes gifts of cups," he thought Darius would do the same. At the end, the conqueror is recognized by one of Darius's envoys, but the Persian ruler is too drunk to notice, and Alexander escapes with his cups. This first episode is not, at least directly, used by the author of the *RA*. Later Alexander visits Porus. The first version of this second sequence, closer to the medieval romance, derives no doubt from the *Letter from Alexander to Aristotle* (*RA* pp. 133–34); the second, more concise, account is found in book III of version L, its content so different from the first that it could not be the source of the *RA*.

The *Letter from Alexander* recounts that after crossing the desert Alexander arrives at the place where Porus has assembled his army. The Indian, curious to know more about Alexander, offers to let him replenish his supplies. The Macedonian puts on a disguise and presents himself as an ordinary procurer of wine and food, explaining that his master, "like a man of a certain age . . . is warming himself in his tent by the fire."[2] Porus is delighted to learn that he will do battle against an old man, and gives the pseudo chamberlain an insulting letter for Alexander. Back in his own camp, Alexander laughs at the "barbarian's proud and fatal thoughtlessness."[3]

The *RA* takes up the essential elements of this short account, which it develops and endows with a meaning in keeping with its own conception of the hero. The opening is similar: Alexander, under the same conditions in both texts, decides to disguise himself and proceed to the enemy camp; he goes on an unusual mount, a mare with an indescribable coat: "N'estoit noire ne blanche; ne vos sai deviser / De quel poil ert la beste, onques ne sot ambler" (III, 1536–37: It was neither black nor white; I am unable to tell you what its color was, and it could not amble). This grotesque mount, which obviously prompts negative comparison with Alexander's admirable Bucephalus, shows the writer's vivid imagination; nothing of the kind is found in the model. This nag does exactly as it pleases: it goes backward instead of forward, and when spurred shows its rebellious nature, rearing up and jumping from side to side and kicking. To Porus, who stops the animal, the hero presents himself as Alexander's chamberlain, charged by him with acquiring cakes and wine, and wax to make candles to light the meal. Porus asks him to be his messenger to the Macedonian and questions him about his master. Here again, the *RA* alters the model, because the pseudo chamberlain initially presents himself as Alexander's intimate, jocular companion, which Porus can hardly interpret correctly: "Il n'a si privé home ne chambrelenc ne qeu; / Assés, qant je me veul, me gap a lui e geu" (III, 1567–68: No chamberlain or cook is nearer to him than I, and when I choose to I joke and banter with him). The French romance also follows this with greater emphasis on the alleged decrepitude of Alexander, who is then described as a feeble old man, chilled to the bone and obliged to wear two coats in high summer, although his ardent desire for conquest is insatiable. The latter allegation, absent from the model,[4] will later play an important part in the French romance.

What lesson may one draw up to this point? It is clear that the medieval author understands this scene as a *gab*, as Alexander himself identifies it to his companions:[5] "Por Porron escharnir me sui mis en tapin" (III, 1605: I disguised myself to make a mockery of Porrus), and his men fully appreciate the joke played on the enemy: "Grans gas en font entr'aus, assés s'en sont joué / De Porrun le roi d'Ynde que il avoit gabé, / De lui se vont gabant deci q'au maistré tré" (III, 1639–41: They guffaw and joke among themselves about Porus whom he had fooled; they make fun of him, all the way to the royal tent). On this point, the ancient text and the new agree: the point is to ridicule the enemy and exalt Alexander, who has risked his life alone in his enemy's camp and fooled him into believing in the existence of a shivering old Alexander.

But the story in the *RA* does not stop there. After Porus is defeated, it returns to the theme, central in the work, of Alexander's largesse, emphasizing the enemy's error in believing the accusations of avarice made against him— which Alexander himself had supported during his incognito visit. In fact Porus is utterly confounded when he discovers his adversary's generosity, which the Persians' lies had concealed: "Assés me fu mandé par briés et par message / Q'ainsi te demenoit fors avarisse et rage" (III, 2224–25: I was often informed by letters and messengers that you were ruled thus by greed and rage). Alexander's generosity toward his defeated adversary and the very lengthy lesson he gives him about covetousness thus appear as an indirect response to the scene of the *gab*; the hero appears to be a paragon of largesse, who thus wins the hearts of his soldiers: "Ses com m'aiment mi home par ma grant largeté? / De ma volonté faire se sont tous jors pené" (III, 2244–45: Do you know how my men love me for my generosity? They always strive to carry out my will). Thus the scene of the *gab* is not only a kind of oxymoron, immediately clear to the reader, who is amused to find his hero disfigured in Porus's eyes alone; it also shows in an unexpected way the coherence of Alexander's portrait, with the constant reminder of his generosity.

Also possible is a double reading of the longer *gab* scene (III, 4429–4864), which occurs after the conquest of India and prior to that of Babylon. Again disguise is involved: Alexander assumes—first in his own camp, then in that of foreigners—the identity of one of his companions, Antigonus, to come to the assistance of the wife of a son of queen Candace, then to visit the queen herself. She is not fooled by his disguise, however, and gives herself to him. This complex passage, which has been studied by Catherine Gaullier for the relations between Alexander and Candace,[6] also merits examination in terms of the function of the *gab*.

In the Pseudo-Callisthenes and Julius Valerius, the adventure begins with an exchange of letters between Alexander and Candace. The king requests presents or a meeting; Candace sends a substantial tribute, but also a painter who surreptitiously does a lifelike portrait of the conqueror, which Candace then conceals from everyone. Soon thereafter, the wife of her son Candeolus is abducted, and he decides to call upon Alexander for help. He is welcomed by Ptolemy as Alexander sleeps: when the king learns of the request he passes himself off as Antigonus, head of the royal bodyguards. He advises Ptolemy, to whom he confers the royal insignia, to grant the request, then takes charge of the successful rescue mission. To reward the pseudo Antigonus, Candeolus escorts him to queen Candace. In a private interview, the queen shows him the portrait, and thus gives him to understand that she has seen through his disguise. Alexander regrets not having his sword, to kill first the queen and then himself, but Candace guarantees him her protection. Reassured, he succeeds in calming the quarrel that has arisen between Candeolus, indebted to him, and another of the queen's sons, the son-in-law of Porus, who wants to destroy Alexander's envoy through hatred for the master. When he departs, Alexander receives rich presents from Candace.

In the *RA* the episode begins as the queen's passion for Alexander awakens. Omitted is the exchange of letters found in the model text, with emphasis placed instead on the volatile love inspired by the conqueror's reputation: "Candace la roïne oï la renomee, / tant l'ama en son cuer a poi n'en est desvee" (III, 4435–36: Queen Candace got wind of his renown; such love for him was born in her heart that she almost lost her reason). The gifts are in response not to any request from Alexander but to her own passion. As for the conqueror, he appears to promise only aid, even though Candace's messengers assure her on their return of his intense love: "Li message revienent, la novele ont contee / Que li rois Alixandres l'a tant fort aamee / Plus que nisune feme qui de mere soit nee" (III, 4449–51: The messengers return with the news that King Alexander has come to love her more than any other woman in the world).

As Catherine Gaullier has shown, the *RA* develops the signs of Candace's passion: the sending of more gifts and, without the king's knowledge, the painting of a very close likeness of the hero. This image at once becomes a love object, on which the lady lavishes her affection: "Sovent baise l'ymage, acole et vait entor; / Tel travail a la dame ne puet avoir gregnor" (III, 4484–85: She often kisses the portrait, grasps and embraces it; her suffering for love could not be greater). The difference from the model is notable, for there the queen is not enamored of the conqueror: she answers him nobly, refusing, in *JV*, to visit him and enjoining him, as in the Pseudo-Callisthenes, not to mock the color of her skin.[7] In this context the secret portrait of Alexander can appear only as a device for the eventual demonstration of feminine superiority, not an acquisition prompted by love that serves initially to fuel her passion.

In *RA* there ensues, with no transition, the abduction of Candeolus's wife (III, 4486–513). Seeking help from Alexander, the unfortunate husband hastens toward the Macedonian's tent (III, 4510), before which stands an *aucube*, an elegant low tent of ornate blue silk, its entrance gilded. Ptolemy, one of Alexander's peers, stands there with naked sword, flanked by knights. Hence a misunderstanding: because of the crown, Candeolus presumes he is in the presence of Alexander and salutes Ptolemy as king. In regal fashion, Ptolemy asks why he has come. After hearing Candeolus's tale of woe, he pretends to convene his council, passing Alexander off as Antigonus.

The romance gives a different version of this crucial misunderstanding, which leads to a different sense of Alexander's attitude. In the Pseudo-Callisthenes too, Ptolemy is immediately mistaken for Alexander (p. 138, l. 7); but it is when he wakes the latter to report Candeolus's request for aid that the king endorses the deception by giving his companion both his diadem and a robe worthy of a king, then by assuming the identity of Antigonus, who will be summoned to the royal council. Alexander is in charge of the action here, whereas in the *RA* Ptolemy makes the first move, proposing to his master a sort of challenge that the king at once accepts; and the advice favorable to Candeolus that Alexander gives about the case betrays an interest—absent in the model—in Candace: compassion for the son should, he avers, be stirred "por amor sa mere" (III, 4542). Accordingly, Ptolemy suggests that Alexander himself deliver the aid to the queen and not return until the matter is settled.

Here, unlike the case of the *gab* on Porus, it is the peer Ptolemy who usurps Alexander's identity with the king's implicit consent by entering into the game. What do we find here? A *gab*, obviously, of which Candeolus is the victim—his credulity is mocked—or rather the beneficiary, since Alexander in person comes to his aid by returning his wife to him. But why such a game?

This scene in the *RA* attributes to Ptolemy a sort of authority over Alexander that is lacking in the model. It is amply justified in the medieval romance by the fact that this peer has been extravagantly rewarded—first among all the king's companions—after the victory over Nicolas (I, 1452–53). But we may also imagine a sort of complicity between the two youths, with the companion perhaps intuiting, from the moment when the pseudo Antigonus alludes to Candace's interests, that an amatory adventure is imminent: "Or sai bien ou ce pent" (I know very well where that is leading), he says,[8] perhaps anticipating the excursion to see Candace that Alexander will soon undertake.

But it seems too that there is an additional nuance, in the king's demonstration of his aptitude to take up the most unexpected challenges. The series of scenes that follow is in fact presented as a succession of adventures not chosen but freely accepted, which parallel in a comic mode the heroic or painful adventures of the Val Périlleux or the prophetic trees.

Charged by Ptolemy with rescuing Candeolus's wife, the pseudo Antigonus immediately gives orders: he needs a guide, whom Candeolus will request from his mother. Hence, perhaps, an opportunity for a first, indirect, contact with Candace, who will perceive in this request the competence of the Macedonian warriors. Then, in the name of Alexander, he commands the abductor to return his prey. The abductor scorns Alexander, and thereby seals his own fate: "il comperra ancui ce qu'il dira par ire" (he will soon pay for what he says in anger, 4631). The pseudo Antigonus has assembled his war machines, and the abductor (the duke of Palatine in the *RA*) is frightened and ready to come to terms—to return Candeolus's wife, to give hostages—but in vain. He will be hanged from one of the pillars of his city's gate. Here again, we find contrast with the model, in which the inhabitants of the besieged city return the abducted spouse to Alexander and kill the offender; in the *RA* the conqueror, disguised as Antigonus while avenging the insults to Alexander, acts with his traditional valor and brutality, controling the events from beginning to end.

But the game is not over, and the comedy continues to be played out between Alexander and Ptolemy, companions in ruse. The latter speaks haughtily to his supposed vassal: has he carried out his task properly? Their dialogue, absent from the model, shows first the vassal's confidence in the valor of his master and underscores, with Alexander's reply, the extent of his victory as well as the fundamental theme of his generosity. The city's defenses have been destroyed, he says, and "Cestui rendi sa feme tout a sa volonté, / Les prisons et la proie et canqu'i ot trové, / Ainc n'en reting denree, ains li ai tout doné" (III, 4692–94: I returned his wife to him as he desired, as well as the prisoners and the booty I found; I kept nothing for myself, but gave it all away).

The final moment of the play between Alexander and Ptolemy in the *RA* is not the least interesting. In *JV*, Candeolus asks Alexander (presumed to be Ptolemy) to accompany him to see Candace, and the hero replies that he must first submit the request to the king—who will accept, we may be sure. In the medieval romance, Ptolemy-Alexander sends Candeolus back to his mother, declaring that he would be happy to meet her, but when Candeolus then invites him to present himself to her, with promises of great rewards, the peer cleverly reserves the place for his master. Impossible to take such a lady by surprise, he says, for "Amor de riche dame molt tost se change et mue, / Teus cuide qu'ele l'aint nel prise une laitue" (III, 4705–6: the love of a powerful woman quickly changes: one who thinks himself loved by her may in fact not be esteemed at all). A messenger must be sent to prepare the visit, and who better than the one who had avenged Candeolus and returned his wife to him? Here Ptolemy cleverly eludes the possible consequences of the usurpation of identity to which he has until now lent his hand. For in fact it is the king himself—still in disguise—who is to visit Candace, both because of the lady's rank and because of the possible nature of the ensuing encounter. Here Ptolemy, panegyrist of the exploits of his master, once again serves as go-between, engaging him in a new adventure.

This adventure begins, as in the model, with misunderstanding and disguise. To the queen, Candeolus offers naive words of praise for the man he takes to be Antigonus. He is not exceptional in stature, but powerful: "Nel despisiés vos pas por ce s'il est petis; / Espaulles a bien faites et les membres fornis" (III, 4748–49: Do not scorn him because of his small stature; his shoulders are broad and his limbs are powerful)—thus establishing that the hero's worth is not due to an extraordinary size that would place him above his companions.

Thereafter, it is the queen who at least in part leads the game. For the first time, the hero's ruse is recognized, because the lady's ruse has preceded it. Candace immediately recalls the portrait she had commissioned, and recognizes Alexander, confirming the identification by leading him into the room where she keeps the portrait. She reveals what she knows to Alexander, at the same time presenting herself as the woman who loves him: why then continue to conceal his identity from her?

The hero's response is brutal, a violent threat against Candace, as in the model: "Quant je laissai m'espee, moult par fis grant folie; / Se je la tenisse ore, n'en portissiés la vie" (III, 4778–79: I was foolish to come without my sword; if I had it now, you would lose your life). Does he fear finding himself in a place where his life is in danger, since Candace's younger son, married to the daughter of Porus whom Alexander has killed, cannot fail to be his enemy? Is this spite at having been unmasked by a woman? The hero is far from indulging the lady who speaks to him of love, and here the *RA* closely follows its model: in *JV* Alexander declares to Candace that after having killed her, he would have accompanied her in death (p. 146, ll. 26–28), in order that no stain obscure his great deeds of the past.

The lady must demonstrate her subtlety first of all, then her loyalty. Subtlety, in that she is able to make him forget her triumph over him through an ingenious ploy: she reminds him that while he is indeed Alexander, his disguise is fully effective with all except the woman who loves him and humiliates herself before him. This may be a subtle echo of the famous *logion*, familiar from his response to Darius's propositions of peace, according to which there is but one Alexander, and his acts cannot be understood by others: "Se fuisse Perdicas, ne lairai ne vos die, / Ja eüsse otroié molt tost ceste partie, / Mais je sui Alixandres si ne le ferai mie" (II, 2668–70: If I were Perdicas, I shall not fail to tell you, I would have endorsed this arrangement at once, but I am Alexander, and I shall not do it). Now again there is only one Alexander, but for one woman who declares her love for him: "Moi soies Alixandres si que nel sache nus, / Et a trestous les autres soies Antigonus" (III, 4791–92: Be Alexander with me in secret, and be Antigonus for all the rest). The formula is found in the model, but utilized in a very different perspective: there Candace first triumphs by calling by his real name the pseudo-messenger who praises the marvels of her palace, then following with a warning about the need for prudence in a place where dangers abound.[9]

In both texts the scene continues with the risk to which Alexander is subject because of Candace's younger son. It is dramatized in the medieval romance, where the young man soon recognizes Alexander, whereas in the model he attacks him as the Macedonian's envoy. The *RA* thus returns to the motif of the unsuccessful disguise, perhaps to create an effect of symmetry, in that a clairvoyant Candace will reduce another clairvoyant to silence. Showing great loyalty, she loudly counters her son's words using any means at her command. The man before their eyes, she tells him, could not pretend to be the master of the world: "Ainc sous le monde Dieu n'avint tele aventure / Que Dieus a itel home donast du mont la cure" (III, 4818–19: Never in the created world did God give the charge of all the universe to a man such as this one)— a means of reintroducing the opposition between the appearance of the hero and his true worth, but also a touch of irony because she knows well that such is in fact the power of Alexander.

Candace's son, although apparently convinced by his mother's arguments, nonetheless wants to kill the man he holds at his mercy because of his hatred for Alexander. The lady strikes the young man, who leaves the scene. The hero then yields to her love, and their farewells are those of two accomplices: Candace gives the pseudo-messenger presents for his master, and declares that she feels too unwell to be able to receive Alexander—a visit now obviously useless—while Alexander thanks the lady, in a veiled but nonetheless quite precise manner, for the precious gift she has given him.

This ending of the episode is totally different from that in the model, where, as Catherine Gaullier has shown, there is no amorous relation between Alexander and Candace, who declares as he takes his leave that she wishes him to consider himself one of her sons.[10] But the way in which Alexander avoids the danger represented by Candace's younger son is changed. In the model, the queen asks Alexander to exercise his renowned cleverness to avoid a fratricidal war between her sons, one of whom defends the pseudo Antigonus while the other attacks him (*JV* p. 148, ll. 17–19). The hero proposes that the two brothers be generous toward him, in order to attract Alexander into their midst and put him to death as they see fit. Candace praises this ingenuity, which functions on two levels: a false promise that averts the danger, but also a play with identity and temporality. There is no need to await Alexander, since he is already there.

Thus, at the end of the episode in the Pseudo-Callisthenes, Alexander retains the honor of the victory. Candace's strategem of the portrait has momentarily neutralized the hero's ploy in assuming his disguise, but at the scene's end she needs Alexander, and the assistance he renders gives him once more the advantage, as the queen acknowledges in observing that she now believes his supremacy to be due more to his famous wisdom than to military force (p. 149, ll. 8–10). In the *RA* the winner seems to be Candace, who controls the action from beginning to end; defending Alexander against her younger son, she finally leads the hero to accept her love. Alexander pardons the offending young man because of the affection he now feels for the mother: "Se il m'avoit pis dit et fait honte gregnor, / Tout seroit pardoné, dame, por vostre amor" (III, 4838–39: If he had said and done even worse to me, all would be pardoned, lady, for love of you). Then he accepts union with the lady, and their love is celebrated by the narrator: "Grant joie font ensemble par bien et par amor" (III, 4842: They share a moment of happiness inspired by empathy and love). But the scene also ends on an exchange of wit between the two partners, which eliminates any sense of a loss of merit on Alexander's part. The *dit de losengeor* with which the hero takes his leave—"S'Alixandres mes sires vous avoit a oissor, / Mieus avroit esploitié que tuit si ancissor" (III, 4858–59: If my master Alexander had you for his wife, he would have achieved more than all of his ancestors)—expresses his gratitude for the lady's gift of herself,[11] even as it presents that gift as the object of a desire yet to be satisfied, since the fortunate lover is not, in this artificial discourse, Alexander; and the queen, his equal in subtlety, declares that she feels no desire to receive the Macedonian, confirming through this coded utterance how well-satisfied she is with the man who is before her. Thus, in a context that associates *gabs* and courtly exchanges, the *RA* demonstrates in a manner different from that of the model that the hero is not inferior to Candace, since the two are united, through love, and also through their fine wit.

The two passages examined here, while apparently secondary in the work as a whole because they lack either the military element or the *merveilleux*, are nonetheless rich in suggestions about Alexandre de Paris's conception of his work and of his hero. They confirm the presence, here as in the model, of a comic vein that recalls the importance of *sens* (I, 58), associating guile and mastery of language with prowess. The hero does not always win in this game—Candace's ruse precedes Alexander's—but even his failure or partial success glorifies the knowledge generally attributed to him, thus permitting a more complex reading of his heroic itinerary.

Before the city of Athens, we know, the cleverness of Aristotle triumphs over that of Alexander, and thus saves the city. When the hero, aware of his master's friendship for the Athenians, swears not to obey him—"Sor sa loi lor jura et par foi lor afie / Que ja n'en fera riens q'Aristotes li die" (I, 1732–33: He swore on his faith and his honor that he would do nothing that Aristotle told him)—Aristotle advises that Alexander set fire to the city and destroy it. Alexander can only acknowledge Aristotle's superior tactic, since his own vow of disobedience now dictates that he spare the city: "Au savoir Aristote ai malement gardé. / Mes maistres m'a souspris et bien m'a enchanté" (I, 1784–85: I was powerless against Aristotle's cleverness. My master took me in and enchanted me). The lesson is clear: the disciple cannot surpass his master. But this is not merely a necessary recall to humility; with this *exemplum* the author of the *RA* also explains the conqueror's itinerary, and perhaps the responsibility of a third party. The advice to sack Athens, even before it is formulated, has been presented as the origin of Alexander's conquests and destructions: "Et a dit tel parole dont le roi a pesé, / Dont puis furent maint regne essillié et gasté"

(I, 1772–73: He spoke words that the king regretted, and which subsequently caused the ruin and devastation of many a country), which confirms the vow the hero had made to himself: "Alixandres chevauche et a forment juré / Ja mais ne finera en trestout son aé / Desi que il avra tout le mont conquesté / Et de par toutes terres l'avront segnor clamé" (1787–90: As Alexander rides he swears to himself that he will never stop until he has conquered the whole world and been recognized as lord of all the earth). Thus we are shown the intrinsic ambiguity of an event: on the one hand, thanks to Aristotle, Athens is saved; on the other, also because of Aristotle, his pupil Alexander is propelled toward universal conquest, and his personal responsibility is thus diminished.

It is the same ambiguity that we found in the double reading of the objects sent by Darius to Alexander. For the Persian ruler, the *semblances* sent to Alexander—"Un frain, une pelote, une verge de lis, / Et un escrin d'argent ou avoit ens or mis" (I, 1907–8: a bridle, a ball, a sorb branch, and a silver coffer containing gold)—were to call him back to humility and the fear of those more powerful than he: the ball is the emblem of the child still engaged in play; the bridle and the branch are reminders of a necessary obedience that is acquired by punishments; the full coffer would seem to display the absolute superiority of Darius, revealed here in his wealth.[12] Alexander, we know, alters the significance of these objects, in a sense very close to that of the Pseudo-Callisthenes: the ball is the world, offered up to the hero's conquest; the branches signify victory over his enemies, the bridle widespread submission to him; the coffer full of gold represents the superiority of his warriors and their love for him (vv. 2149–62)—a possible allusion to his constant gifts to them, evidence of the largesse that gains his men's affection. In spite of the closeness of the formulas, however, we note the greater coherence of the medieval romance, especially for the last of these items. Whereas the Pseudo-Callisthenes interprets the coffer as the tribute that Darius will pay to Alexander, remaining within the military context that opposes the two pretenders to sovereignty, the *RA* expands the theme of conquest to that of generosity and the affection consequent upon bestowal of the gift.

We may perhaps interpret in a comparable perspective the episode of the Amazons, which is treated in a way quite different from its model in the Pseudo-Callisthenes (Book III, 25–30, pp. 108–17). In the Greek text, Alexander notifies the Amazons of his intention to visit their land; in response, they describe their bellicose ways and warn him that they will encamp on their boundaries. Alexander demands that they send him messengers, who will receive rewards and leave at the end of a year, to be succeeded by others. The Amazons accept and acknowledge Alexander's supremacy; but if one of the messengers loses her virginity, she is to remain with the Macedonians! The *RA* blends this episode with the rest of the work in treating it in a courtly manner.[13]

The point of departure is the end of the conquest of Babylon, the foreseen goal of the hero's itinerary. Samson, a Saracen who has survived the battle, hears Alexander declare that he is now lord of all the world, and points out to him that the kingdom of the Amazons remains to be conquered. The hero decides to claim their tribute, and approaches their land. One of the Amazons alerts the queen to this insatiable conqueror's imminent attack: "Tant par est, ç'oï dire, d'avarise provés / Que de tout l'or du mont ne seroit assasés" (III, 7390–91: I have heard that he is so greedy that all the gold in the world would not satisfy him). Thus it is gold and extravagant gifts that the queen prepares to send him, but the rest of the account will show that she has been misinformed: it is not greed that guides Alexander. Floré and Beauté, the queen's courtly Amazon ambassadors, beguile two of the Macedonians, who request and obtain their love, but their beauty and valor are equally effective upon Alexander, who accepts the queen's offer to submit to him and re-nounces the tribute he might have expected from her. Now that his "segnorage" is acknowledged, he announces that "Por la vostre biauté et por le vasselage, / Devant tous mes barons pardonrai le chevage" (III, 7621–22: Because of your beauty and your valor, I renounce the tribute in the presence of all my barons).

Thus, Alexander is innocent of the accusation of greed, as he had been earlier in the case of Porus; but the queen, who has succeeded in avoiding the risk of destruction of her land, is not totally victorious in the confrontation, and this gives rise to another sort of *gab* by the hero, realized through his enamored warriors or, better, through the power of love, to which even the invincible Amazons must submit. Lord of a court where love is present, Alexander in effect holds captive—though with their full accord—the beautiful Amazons sent by the queen: "Or vos dirai noveles: Floré avés perdue / Et Biauté sa compaigne, car amors l'a vaincue" (III, 7679–80: I have news for you: you have lost Floré and her companion Beauté, for Love has conquered them). We are far removed from the perspective of the Pseudo-Callisthenes, where copulation is inevitable for the perpetuation of the race, yet also a source of exclusion.[14] No doubt Floré and Beauté will remain with the Greeks, but voluntarily, and within a legitimate union whose source is the power of love. The queen reacts with chagrin, proof that she had expected to resolve the affair by her gifts. The complex lesson of this disappointment is that Alexander cannot be trapped by exploiting a cupidity that in fact he does not possess: it is his own worth, to which we may associate love's power embodied by his two peers, that imposes his law—a courtly law, that adds a refined touch to the conqueror's glory.

The two scenes of *gab*, complemented by convergent passages, furnish useful information. Linked to the comic element in the work, they attest first of all to a form of supremacy in Alexander in addition to that of his military force: the mastery of ruse (*engien*) and the derision of his adversaries. In this they recall classical epic traits. An essential form of knowledge is put into practice here, and when Alexander seeks to compete with someone stronger than he in this arena—his master Aristotle, or a woman—he risks being re-minded, at his expense, of an fundamental rule. More generally, this form of knowledge invites us to think about the ambiguity of meaning, about the discrepancy between appearance and reality, and about the polysemous nature of signs; in this sense the *RA*, like the work that served as its model, offers the reader a lesson "qu'a gent laie doive auques portifier" (I, 31: that should be of profit to lay people).

Yet the medieval romance harmonizes these didactic components within its own narrative perspective and makes of Alexander an enduring example of largesse and courtliness. The episode involving Porus offers a caution against greed, as does the assistance given to Candeolus, since the hero abandons all of his conquests. But the courtly perspective also comes through in the development of the episodes involving the Amazons and Candace: love triumphs, as does cleverness in the latter case, which associates the two lovers through their mastery of elegant speech in such a way that there is neither winner nor loser.

Notes

1. *Pseudo-Callisthène. Le Roman d'Alexandre*, trans. G. Bounoure and Blandine Serret (Paris: Les Belles Lettres, 1992); Julius Valerius, *Res gestae Alexandri Macedonis*, ed. B. Kuebler (Leipzig: Teubner, 1888), here abbreviated as *JV*; *RA*.

2. *RA* p. 133; see also *JV* p. 203, ll. 9–11.

3. *RA* p. 92. The hero indicates that he seeks to buy provisions; in reality, he wants to observe Porus's wild animals, who inspire fear in him. The Indian asks for news of Alexander, and the hero replies that he is well and wants to see Porus. The latter makes a comparison between Alexander and the wild beasts he will use against him, charging the disguised hero to transmit this image; Alexander replies that the Macedonian, as son of a god, is already informed.

4. In the *JV* Porus asks only why Alexander does not then consider his age (p. 203, ll. 13–14).

5. In *JV*, Alexander tells his mother that after having read Porus's threatening letter he broke into hearty laughter (p. 203, l. 22).

6. Catherine Gaullier, "Alexandre et Candace dans le *Roman d'Alexandre* d'Alexandre de Paris et le *Roman de toute chevalerie* de Thomas de Kent," *Romania* 112 (1991), 18–44; see also *Frontières*, pp. 405–13.

7. "Nec nos aestimes ex colore, quippe cui animi liberalis species intuenda est, non satis corporis forma praejudicat" (p. 136, ll. 18–20: Do not judge us by our color, for it is the image of a generous spirit that is to be observed, and not what the body makes visible).

8. The formula is also present in the Arsenal and Venice manuscripts.

9. "Vera mihi dixisti haec, Alexander mi" (You have spoken the truth, my Alexander: *JV*, p. 145, l. 25); "Quare esto Antigonus apud illos, cum mihi soli Alexander habeare" (Then be Antigonus for the others, and Alexander for me alone: p. 147, ll. 10–11).

10. "Utinam, Alexander mi, te quoque velles ad numerum mihi addere filiorum!" (Would to heaven, my Alexander, that you wish to count yourself among my sons!: p. 149, ll. 5–6).

11. My interpretation differs here from that of Gaullier-Bougassas (*Frontières*, p. 409). Alexander does not lie to Candace, who has sought not to marry him but to know his love in order to conceive an heir by him. In my reading the *dit de losengeor* is not that of a liar but that of a skilled flatterer.

12. ". . . et l'escrin plain d'or mier / por ce que il se doit vers lui humelïer" (and the coffer full of gold, because he must humble himself before Darius, 1920–21).

13. See Aimé Petit, "Le traitement courtois du thème des Amazones d'après trois romans antiques: *Enéas*, *Troie* et *Alexandre*," *Le Moyen Age* 89 (1983), 63–84.

14. See III, 26: "Celles d'entre nous qui veulent être déflorées restent auprès des hommes. Et toutes les filles qu'elles peuvent mettre au monde passent chez nous à l'âge de sept ans" (those women among us who wish to lose their virginity remain with the men. And all the daughters they bear come to us at the age of seven).

6

"Mout est proz e vassaus"/"Mout es corteis": *Vasselage* and Courtesy in the *Roman d'Alexandre*

Rupert T. Pickens

In the introduction to her reedition and translation of the Vulgate *Roman d'Alexandre* by Alexandre de Paris, Laurence Harf-Lancner cogently and insightfully discusses the romance's fundamental ambiguity.[1] The Vulgate text is indeed subtended by a number of antitheses: ancient and modern, Oriental and Western, pagan and Christian, unknown and known, legitimacy and bastardy, largesse and hubris, epic and romance. Such polarity is exemplified in an abundance of passages where texts and quasi-verbal artifacts are presented as objects of scrutiny from various perspectives, and the meanings ascribed to them shift as one is superseded by another; related to these episodes are portrayals of masking, deception, and dissimulation.

A case in point is the gifts sent to Alexander by Darius when the young king is poised to invade Persia (*MFRA* II, Br. I, *laisse* 88): a bridle, a ball, a rod of service-tree wood, and a box filled with gold. Alexandre de Paris calls these objects *samblances* (vv. 1906, 1910)—symbols, emblems, allegories, that is, things that signify something else.[2] Darius endows the objects with meanings that are specified in a written message. He sends Alexander the rod because he is a frivolous adolescent who needs to be taught a lesson; the ball is a child's toy for him to amuse himself with; the bridle is a necessary restraint; the box of gold is a sign that Alexander should humble himself before Darius, his rightful overlord whom he should strive to serve and obey (vv. 1910–24). But Alexander proffers other readings, contrary readings, the accuracy of which the Vulgate text subsequently bears out. The ball shows that Alexander will conquer the world; the rod, that he will beat those who stand against him; the bridle, that all will hold their lands from him; the gold, that his men will be raised higher than any others and that they will always remain loyal to him (vv. 2152–58).

Later, after Alexander's first victory over him, Darius sends the young king another gift: a mule loaded with fine poppy seed grain, along with the message that Darius commands two-to-three-times as many men as there are seeds in the load. Alexander takes up a pennyweight's worth of the seeds and swallows them. "Are Darius and his knights so sweet and tasty?" he asks. "Then they will be easy to destroy in battle. Because Greeks are hard and fierce when they fight, no one can withstand their steel." Alexander counters with a gift of his own: a glove filled with pepper. This *alegorie* signifies that, "just as this little bit of pepper is harder to swallow than poppy seeds," so Alexander's knights, who are like lions, are stronger in battle than those commanded by Darius, who are as easy to defeat as defenseless cattle (see Br. II, *laisses* 113–17).[3]

In these and many similar instances, conflicting readings are implicated in different ways of construing *vasselage* and *cortoisie*. In contriving his *semblance*, Darius behaves "que preus et que cortois" (Br. II, v. 2468: like a man endowed with prowess and *cortoisie*), while Alexander responds "a loi de bon princier" (v. 2511, in the manner of a noble prince), that is, with a display of qualities we shall regard as constituting *vasselage*. My purpose in the present study is to explore the relationships between such "courtesy" and such *vasselage* in the Old French Alexander romances: the decasyllabic romance and the Vulgate text of Alexandre de Paris.

As Glyn S. Burgess has demonstrated, *vasselage* and *cortoisie* are the two *mots-témoins*—overarching, defining principles—of French culture of the noble court in the twelfth century.[4] In some texts more or less contemporary with the earliest Alexander romances—the Oxford *Roland*, the *Couronnement de Louis*, the *Charroi de Nîmes*—, the terms are virtually synonymous. As designators of cultural values, they stand together in opposition to *vilenie*, that which is excluded from the court. In other texts, like the Arthurian section of Wace's *Brut*, *vasselage* and *cortoisie* appear to be in polar opposition;[5] in light of their synonymy elsewhere, therefore, they constitute a basis for the kinds of ambiguity that are characteristic of the Alexandre de Paris romance as a whole. In such texts, both *vasselage* and *cortoisie*, as distinct values, are opposed to *vilenie* and are untainted by it. In still other texts, such as the earlier romances of Chrétien de Troyes, *vasselage* is neither opposed to nor synonymous with *cortoisie*, but is subsumed in a form of *cortoisie* strongly identified with women and also defined negatively by *vilenie*.[6]

When we find the adjectives *vassal* and *cortois* and their derivatives *vasselage* and *cortoisie* in the same text, how do we distinguish among synonymy, opposition, and subordination? It is essential to examine the context in which the words occur, in terms both of particular loci and of the trajectory of the text as a whole. In a recent series of semantic studies devoted to early *chansons de geste*, to Wace's *Brut*, and to Chrétien de Troyes, I have drawn upon Burgess's work, as well as that of Karl D. Uitti and Michelle A. Freeman,[7] in an attempt to understand what it means to be *cortois*—to be "courtly," "courteous"—in the French-speaking world of the twelfth century.[8] While Old French *cortois*, which means etymologically "belonging to the court," is commonly translated, without nuance, as *courtois* in modern French and as "courteous" or "courtly" in English, what "belonging to the court" actually signifies in the Middle Ages is not a constant, but a cultural phenomenon determined by different societies in specific times and places (see Uitti and Freeman, esp. pp. 102–19). English "courteous" and "courtly," no less than modern French *courtois*, suggest a refinement in manners, speech, and feelings—especially involving *fin'amors*—that evokes certain texts written after 1150. But such modern terms as *courtois* and "courteous" often prove totally inadequate in denoting the *cortois*, for example in the early *chanson de geste*, which values steadfast faithfulness to an overlord in word and in deed, on the battlefield as in the feudal court.

Epic *vasselage* is exemplified in the Oxford *Roland* by Roland, Oliver, Thierry, and certain of Charles's advisors, all of whom are described as *cortois* or as speaking *cortoisement* while fighting or while arguing in court. Whether or not these heroes' speech is elegant or refined is beside the point; they are *cortois* not because of how they speak, but because of what they have to say. Theirs are *paroles haltes* (1097, lofty words): "Rollant est proz e Oliver est sage:/ Ambedui unt merveillus vasselage . . ." (1093–94, Roland is worthy and Oliver is wise: both possess wonderful *vasselage*).[9] *Vasselage* embraces physical and moral prowess; it implies *sagesse*, that is, experience, a sense of what is right, and intelligence. *Vasselage* also encompasses valorous perseverance in support of one's cause (Roland and Oliver will fight to the death), as well as nobility (they are *bon*, 1095–97), and lofty speech (their words are equal to their deeds). Above all, when they speak *cortoisement* elsewhere in the poem, Thierry's words express his steadfast devotion to his king and to his justice (3823), while Roland urges his companions to uphold their king in battle and to destroy his enemies (1164).

Thus the *mot-témoin vasselage* expresses, as its etymology suggests, the duties of good vassals and the physical and intellectual attributes they employ in the service of their lord and king. But it is clear from the texts that kings also incarnate *vasselage* and perform *vasselage*. Alexander arms himself "a guise de vassal" (Br. III, v. 3997: like a good warrior) and he is "espris de vasselage" (Br. II, v. 2806: aflame with *vasselage*), which drives him to his conquest. It is not primarily a question of the duties and services that kings owe their vassals, although reciprocity is certainly part of the equation. More importantly, the king's *vasselage* signals the interests of the realm; it also signals the physical and moral qualities that inspire *vasselage* in others. The kind of "romance courtesy" in opposition to *vasselage* that I have described as concerned with refined feelings and behavior is implied in a passage from the Arthurian section of Wace's *Brut*, where the narrator remarks that the knights and ladies of Arthur's court, and even the peasants in his kingdom, surpass in *cortoisie* the nobility of any other realm. The keynotes, however, are fashion and the granting of amorous favors by "dames cortoises."[10] To win their ladies' favors, moreover, knights must demonstrate their chivalric prowess three times. Tests of knighthood come in games, not on the battlefield, for this is the time of the *pax arthuriana*, when knights grow soft.[11]

In the decasyllabic Alexander romance, the term *cortois* appears to be conservative in its usage, that is, *cortoisie* is synonymous with *vasselage*.[12] The word first occurs after the youthful Alexander proclaims to his father that he intends to be knighted. He is strong, he is young, he is vigorous—"Asez soi forz et soi jovnes e freis" (Arsenal §17, 169)—and he promises that after he receives his arms, he will defend his father's kingdom against Darius, otherwise it will fall into ruin. Philip responds, "Dit avez que corteis" (§17, 174), which can mean nothing other than "You have spoken like a man of *vasselage*."[13] Another, more elaborate example pertains to the two formulaic expressions included in my title: "Molt est proz e vassaus" (Arsenal §55, 531) and "Molt es cortois" (§58, 560).[14] As Alexander leads his army against Darius's vassal, King Nicholas of Caesarea, Darius's nephew Samson arrives in the Greek encampment. Samson first appears as a "corteis pelerin" (§52, 505: *cortois* pilgrim), a remarkable description that recalls an episode in the *Couronnement de Louis*.[15] Samson's counterpart in the *Couronnement* is *cortois* not because he is noble or strong in battle, but because his words condemn the rebellious traitors and praise William, defender of the Carolingian cause.

Samson is initially perceived to be a "pilgrim"[16] because he carries a staff of apple wood and, more to the point, to be *cortois* because he looks like a "noble youth" with his golden locks and his silk gown (§52, 505–09), signs of strength and wealth. His *cortoisie* is then more clearly defined in a broader context. Speaking to Alexander, whose identity he does not know, Samson names himself and establishes his royal birth. He further declares that he has avenged an act of treason committed against his father, and he is fleeing to King Philip for protection with the hope that Prince Alexander will equip him to move against Darius, who implicitly condones the treachery. In words that echo the classic definition of *vasselage* in the Oxford *Roland*, Alexander recognizes by Samson's words that he is "Molt . . . proz e vassaus" (§55, 531: most worthy and *vassal*).

Samson has just come from Caesarea, where King Nicholas is raising an army to invade Greece. If he is given a horse and riding gear, he says, he will go to Caesarea and bring back news of the traitor's preparations for war. Alexander declares that he will indeed send him as his messenger. But Samson will not serve a man he does not know: "Conoistrai vos premier" (§57, 560: "First I will know who you are"). By these exchanges, Alexander recognizes that Samson is "Molt . . . cortois" (§58, 561). In the parallel observations, "Molt est proz e vassaus" and "Molt es cortois," Alexandre assesses Samson's character as his speech reveals his sense of honor, his determination to fight, his rejection of a traitorous regime in Persia, and his declarations of loyalty to the Greek king. *Vassal* and *cortois* are synonymous. When Alexander names himself, Samson praises God that he has found his rightful lord (§59, 753–74).

Samson's *cortoisie* suits him to be a messenger, for the attributes of *vasselage* are also those of ambassadors who represent their lord's interests in an enemy's court.[17] Indeed, when Samson and his companions deliver Alexander's message to the traitor Nicholas, they are "corteis mesager" (§68, 665) as much for their loyalty to Alexander as for Samson's stinging rebuke at Nicholas's disrespect for Alexander: "Fool of a king," he says, "you can threaten all you want: your threats are not worth a penny to me. When you see Alexander of the fierce demeanor, you will fear him more than the lark fears the hawk. The day will come when he will avenge himself against you, and he will take your crown of pure gold away from you" (§68, 658–63).

The decasyllabic romance provides two other noteworthy examples. One involves Queen Olympias as the only woman in this version to be associated with *cortoisie*; I shall come back to her when discussing a parallel passage in the Vulgate text. In the second example I find the only evidence in the decasyllabic romance that *cortoisie* is concerned with wit and elegance. When a messenger from Nicholas of Caesarea delivers his challenge to King Philip, Alexander begs his father to send him against him (Arsenal §46). The king rises and addresses the messenger *corteisement*:

> . . . Corteisement a dit au mesager:
> "Amis, dist il, pensez de l'espleiter,
> Per tei voldrai a Nicolas nuncer
> Que ors li vol Al'x. envïer;
> Unc ne reçut si corteis mesager.
> Ensemble lui irunt mi chivaler;
> Se il de lui ne me poënt venger,
> Ja mais vers mei n'enn ost uns repairer." (§47, 457–64)

(He told the messenger *cortoisement*, "Friend, you've got to hurry back. Through you I want to inform Nicholas that now I intend to send Alexander to him. Never has he received such a *cortois* messenger. My knights will ride with him. If they fail to avenge me against him, may not one of them dare come back to me alive.")

At first glance the two occurrences of *cortois*, in the adverb and in the expression *corteis mesager*, appear conventional; certainly the latter relates to the commonplace, as exemplified by Samson, of the messenger who displays *vasselage* in his speech. But the "message" that Alexander is to deliver to Nicholas is not verbal, but military—and the prince and the knights who come with him are expected, if necessary, to fight to the death in upholding Philip's interests. This is *vasselage* in its strictest and starkest sense. The adverb *corteisement* also denotes a way of expressing *vasselage*, but Philip's message unexpectedly centers on the wordplay to which the adverb calls particular attention: *corteisement, corteis mesager*.

Corteisement refers to the content of Philip's speech, but it also describes how the message is constructed as wordplay. In fact, Philip's joke is an early instance in French of *facetia*, a manner of witty speech.[18] The Latin *facetia* has more elevated meanings than either modern French *facétie* or English *facetiousness*. As Stephen Jaeger has shown, Latin texts from as early as the mid-eleventh century mention the elegance of *facetia* and speaking *facete* in various noble and ecclesiastical courts, but references do not occur in French until a hundred years later.[19] Wace, writing in 1155, translates Geoffrey of Monmouth's adverb *facete* as *curteisement* and the adjective *facetae*, "women who speak *facete*," as *curteises*. Such, in fact, are the ladies in Arthur's court who require their suitors to prove themselves before earning their favors (Jaeger, p. 199; Pickens, "*Vasselage* épique," pp. 174–77).

The *mot-témoin cortois* and its derivatives occur with extraordinarily high frequency in the decasyllabic romance. In the 785 verses preceding the Lambert le Tort prologue in the Arsenal manuscript, *cortois* and *cortoisement* are found ten times, for an average of once for every eighty lines. Thus the decasyllabic romance is far more concerned with the *cortois* than any of sixty or so narratives for which Burgess provides data ("Étude sur le terme *cortois*," pp. 206–8), including the *Lais* of Marie de France. By contrast, the Alexandre de Paris text is more typical of that corpus as a whole. In its nearly 16,000 verses, I count twenty-five occurrences of *cortois*, or one for every 640 lines. The density in Alexandre de Paris is greater than in either the *Roman de Troie* or the *Roman d'Eneas*, but less by half than in the *Roman de Thèbes*. More to the point, *cortois* and its derivatives occur eight times less frequently in Alexandre de Paris than in the decasyllabic romance.

And yet the values of *vasselage* and *cortoisie* permeate nearly every *laisse*. Alexandre de Paris accomplishes this feat by multiplying and endlessly repeating the secondary terms and their synonyms that gravitate around the two *mots-témoins*. A particularly rich example is found in Porus's confession to Alexandre:

> "Sire, ce dist Porrus, en ce oi grant damage:
> Quant Dayres fu ocis sor Gangis el rivage,
> Assés me fu mandé par briés et par message
> Q'ainsi te demenoit fors avarisse et rage.
> Onques si *nobles* hom n'issi de ton *lignage*;
> Se seüsse si bien ta vie et ton *corage*,
> Ja de toute ma guerre ne fust percie targe,
> En pais sans contredit t'alasse faire *homage*.
> Tu vas querant *proëce*, *segnorie* et *barnage*;
> Qui la te contendra molt fera grant folage,
> Nel puet garir chastiaus ne fors cités marage
> Que tu nel sieues tant que tu li fais damage.
> Ce que tu as conquis par force et par *barnage*
> Dones tu volentiers, n'en fais nului salvage;
> *Humilités* te vaint et fait rendre ton gage.

Onques si *larges* hom ne fu de nul *parage*,
Plus as tu hui doné et moi et mon *lignage*
Que ne se raembroit l'amiraus de Cartage."
(Br. III, vv. 2222–39, my emphasis)

("My lord," said Porus, "I heard much slander about you: When Darius
was killed on the banks of the Ganges, I got word many times, in letters
and by messenger, that excessive greed and madness drove you to it.
Never was such a noble man as you born to your family. If I had
known your way of life and your heart as I do now, never would a
single shield have been splintered in any war started by me, for without
hesitation I would have gone in peace to pay you homage. You go in
search of prowess, lordship, and noble valor. Anyone is unwise to contest against you: no castle or fortress built by the sea can withstand your
efforts to destroy it. All that you have won by force and by skill in battle
you willingly give away, and you rebuff no one; humility overcomes
you and you surrender to it. Never did such a generous man come
from any noble stock, and today you have given me and my kin more
than the emir of Carthage would have to ransom himself.")

This passage exemplifies the Vulgate romance's ambiguity by offering
two readings of the same "text," that is, Alexander, one of which is proved false
and the other eminently true. Porus had been informed that Alexander was
driven by greed and madness, that is, by *vilenie*. Recent experience, however,
confirms just the opposite. Alexander is a noble man of high birth, a lord to
whom he could have sworn fealty because he seeks after prowess, lordship, and
valor in warfare. These qualities are the flowering in the mature conqueror of
the virtues apparent in his younger days in Branch I, when Alexander was
already regarded as "preux et de bon escïent" (v. 326, worthy and very thought-
ful), and when his companions praised "sa grant cortoisie, / Son sens et sa
prouece et sa chevalerie" (vv. 2428–29, his great *cortoisie*, his intelligence, his
prowess, and his military skills).
　We recognize in Porus's confession that other quality that marks
Alexander's exemplary *cortoisie* in a very special way: his legendary largesse.
These new qualities—new to conventional *vasselage* in their extraordinary
intensity—are likewise evident from Alexander's youngest years:

Molt fu preus Alixandres qant ot passé dis ans;
De par toutes les terres a mandé les enfans,
Les fieus as gentieus homes et tous les plus vaillans;
Assés en poi de terme en ot aveuc lui tans
Com s'il eüst la terre a quatorze amirans.
Largement lor donoit et faisoit lor talans. (Br. I, vv. 369–74)

(Alexander showed great worthiness when he was just over ten years old. From every land he summoned the most valiant sons of noble men. In little time at all he gathered with him as many as if he owned the land of fourteen emirs. He gave liberally to them and did as they wished.)

Here "prowess" is defined as giving generously to the boys he has gathered and doing all he can to please them.[20]

Throughout the romance of Alexandre de Paris, *cortoisie*-as-*vasselage* is typically connoted by terms suggesting the conventional qualities as well as the new quality of generosity that gravitate around the *mots-témoins*. Several passages are noteworthy, however, for particularly dense concentrations of the term *cortois* and its derivatives, and these merit close scrutiny. One is the celebrated Gadifer de Larris episode in the *Fuerre de Gadres* section (Br. II, *laisses* 52–62). Another is the series of parallel *plaintes* on the death of Alexander in Branch IV, *laisses* 34–75.

In Branch IV, *cortoisie* is defined in reference both to Alexander's largesse and in more conventional terms:

    1. In the peer Aridés's allegory, where the accent is on liberality:

"Que porrons devenir qant proëce est hui morte?
Cortoisie et largesce, serree est vostre porte;
Ja mais ne sera hom qui la clef en destorte.
Or poons nos bien dire que largetés avorte,
Ne puet mais remanoir que doners ne resorte . . ." (vv. 862–66)

("What can become of us now that Prowess has died today? Courtesy and Largesse, your door is shut; never again will anyone be able to turn its key. Now we can say with certainty that Liberality has aborted, and it will not be long before Munificence fades away . . .")

    2. In the apostrophe of Perdicas, who is described as *cortois* because he is "sans losengerie" (v. 1138, without deceit); here largesse and *cortoisie* are set against cowardice:

"Alixandre, biaus sire, bons rois sans couardie,
Fontaine de largesce et puis de cortoisie,
Comblés d'ensegnement et res de vilonie . . ." (vv. 1151–53)

("Alexander, dear lord, noble king without cowardice, fount of largesse and wellspring of courtesy, brimming with learning and untouched by dishonor")

    3. And in a remark by the narrator which, in its epic formulation, brings us back to the romance's antithetical underpinnings:

Se il fust crestïens, ainc tels rois ne fu nes,
Si cortois ne si larges, si sages, si menbrés,
Si cremus en bataille, ne d'armes redoutés. (vv. 1556–58)

(If he had been a Christian, no king like him would ever have been
born, or one so courteous or so openhanded, so intelligent, so far-
seeing, so dreaded in battle or fearsome at arms.)

These tributes to Alexander's *cortoisie* in the concluding branch echo earlier
circumstances, when his men believe that he is dying of shock and they
"regretent le roy et sa grant cortoisie, / Son sens et sa prouece et sa chevalerie"
(Br. I, vv. 2428–29: mourn for the king and his great courtesy, his intelligence, his prowess, and his skills at knighthood), when Alexander "li preus
et li cortois" storms the Robber Baron's stronghold (v. 2315), or when
Alexander offers to sacrifice himself in the Perilous Valley (Br. III, vv. 2621–
28; 2719–29).

The *cortois* Gadifer de Larris is a loyal vassal of Betis de Gadres, the lord
of Tyre. He is remarkable because he organizes his men's retreat as they flee
before Alexander's conquering forces, yet at the most opportune moments he
turns about to face and defeat his enemies. His men suffer no harm in the
retreat until he is finally overcome and killed by Emenidus, whom he unhorsed twice earlier in the day (Br. II, *laisse* 52). Gadifer plays in the *Roman
d'Alexandre* the role of the noble Saracen of the *chanson de geste*, but in the
Vulgate text his significance lies especially in the fact that he is in many ways
Alexander's double. He is *vassal* (Br. II, v. 1418); "Por son lige segnor est entrés
en grant paine" (v. 1400, he has suffered great distress for the sake of his liege
lord); he is "Li gentieus chevaliers a la chiere certaine" (v. 1422, The noble
knight with the confident demeanor); he is "preus et ses chevaus bons" (v.
1428, he has knightly prowess and his horse is strong [like Bucephalus]), and
in all the kingdom of Egypt there is no better knight (v. 1191); he is "plains
de grant vasselage" (v. 1484, full of great *vasselage*), a man of stalwart heart (v.
1486); "Ou que il vit le bien, sel vaut molt avancier / Et vilains paroles et lais
dis abaissier" (vv. 1202–3, he seeks to promote things that are worthy wherever
he finds them and to strike down unworthy speech and destructive words).
Alexandre de Paris's narrator further remarks that "He was so valiant and his
horse was so strong that he would have gotten away without any harm, we
believe, had he chosen to flee with Betis's other knights, but he protected his
companions just like a wild animal keeping its young safe from a wolf; he
knew that he was their only defense, and he was right, for if he were to be
killed or captured, their protection would be gone" (vv. 1427–33). This is why
he keeps turning to fight. Such are the heroic qualities that give definition to
his *cortoisie*: he is "larges et cortois" (v. 1201), like Alexander, and after his death
his Greek enemies mourn for "lui et sa cortoisie / Et la tres grant proëce qu'il

avoit acuellie" (vv. 1524–25, for him and his *cortoisie* and the very great prowess
that he had attained).

On one occasion Gadifer confronts a Greek form of *cortoisie* that is
seriously flawed. The narrator remarks that Gadifer's heroic retreat is worthy
of being exalted in history books ("en oevre d'estoire," v. 1355); no one could
blame him for it, no one except some "musart de maudire auguisiés / Et de
folie plus que de sens enpraigniés" (vv. 1353–54, a dimwit keen to slander and
more imbued with folly than with good sense). At once a Greek knight,
Corineus, begins taunting him: "*Vassal*,[21] turn back around. Why do you dishonor yourself? It is unworthy of you to go off and leave your men behind.
Today you have tested us many times at close range, but now it seems to me
that you have cooled down, and your reputation suffers when you run away.
You have no right to the sleeve you are wearing" (vv. 1358–63). These are
precisely the kind of "vilaines paroles et lais dis" (v. 1203, unworthy speech and
destructive words) that Gadifer, like Chrétien de Troyes's patron Philip of
Flanders, seeks to root out.[22]

Despite Corineus's "dis orgelleus" (arrogant speech), and despite the fact
that he is "molt outrecuidés" (most presumptuous, vv. 1366, 1378), Alexandre
de Paris's narrator remarks that he is "*cortois et preus* . . . / Et chevaliers molt
bons et molt bien afaitiés;/ Se tant ne parlast d'armes, trop fust bien enseigniés"
(vv. 1375–77, *cortois* and full of prowess . . . and a very stalwart knight and
highly accomplished; if he did not speak so much about fighting, he would
have been very well trained). As though to correct the contradiction in attrib-
uting, albeit with an attenuating disclaimer, *cortoisie*—even *cortoisie-as-vasselage*—
to an overweening and unperceptive knight, Alexandre de Paris has Gadifer
comment, after bringing Corineus down with a lethal blow, that "you would
have been a man of great worth if you had not been arrogant" (v. 1391).

However wonderful they are, these examples involving Alexander and
his "Saracen" counterpart Gadifer de Larris do little to elaborate possibilities
already evident in the decasyllabic romance or to expand the identification of
cortoisie and *vasselage* beyond the embellishment of endowing *vasselage* with
extraordinary largesse. Other passages in the Vulgate incorporate *facetiae* with
the stereotypical *messager courtois*—Darius's *samblances* (Br. II, *laisse* 113), for
example, and the verbal game that Aristotle plays *cortoisement* with his pupil (Br.
I, v. 1755) when, as the Athenians' ambassador, he lays the groundwork for his
famous verbal trick.[23]

But what of "romance courtesy"? The relationship between *vasselage* and
courtoisie may be regarded in a theoretical perspective recently articulated by
Simon Gaunt.[24] Texts in which the terms are synonymous uphold the values
of male homosocial bonding associated with feudalism (cf. Gaunt, pp. 22–70).
Texts in which *vasselage* is opposed by a different mode of *cortoisie* acknowledge
that women have the power to limit male bonding. Texts, finally, in which
vasselage is subordinated to that new mode of *cortoisie* both grant women the

power to limit male bonding and seek to undercut that power (cf. Gaunt, pp. 71–121). What, then, of those dimensions of *cortoisie*, apparently absent in the decasyllabic romance, that empower women to limit and even to undo the homosocial bonding inherent in *vasselage*? The *mot-témoin cortois* and its derivatives occur with significant frequency in five sections involving women who are the most important female characters in the Vulgate. Not in their order of appearance, they are, first, the women of Darius's court: his mother, his wife, and his daughter Roxane; second, the Amazons; third, Candace; fourth, Olympias; and last, Roxane as Alexander's wife.[25]

When Alexander captures the women in Darius's court, "D'une chose fist bien et que cortois provés" (Br. II, v. 3000: with respect to one thing he behaved honorably and like a man who was *cortois* tried and true): he entrusts the women for safekeeping to certain of his vassals who keep them away from men (vv. 2991–3004). Although Alexander eventually makes Darius's mother ruler of Susa (*laisse* 147), and although he is later wed to Darius's daughter (who is not even named here), Alexander's *cortoisie* is not an honor that is extended primarily to these ladies, but an act of largesse designed to benefit Darius alone. Alexander avoids shaming Darius, not the ladies: "He commends the ladies to two of his fiefholders, and each of them has pledged and sworn to him that never will any man on earth get so intimate with them that Darius might be shamed or dishonored by him" (vv. 3001–4). Alexander's gestures, in particular his eventual promise to marry Roxane, convince Darius that he is a worthy enemy—"Molt es humeles guerriers et feeus enemis" (v. 3032, you are a very humble warrior and a trustworthy enemy)—with whom he can reach a truce. This episode once more exemplifies *cortoisie-as-vasselage*; it is an honor—a courtesy (cf. Uitti and Freeman, pp. 118–19)—that Alexander extends to the ladies, or rather to Darius, and not a quality the ladies possess in their own right.

Elsewhere women are themselves endowed with *cortoisie*, and they operate in an environment imbued with *cortoisie*; it is they who introduce into the Vulgate text the new association of *cortoisie* with refined behavior and feelings and with *fin'amors* that had first emerged, in French literature, in the Arthurian section of the *Roman de Brut*. The Amazons (Br. III, *laisses* 425–50), who are the last nation to be subdued by Alexander, embody a wide range of characteristics that exemplify both *vasselage* and the new *cortoisie*.[26] They are "de grans valors" (v. 7273, of great valor), there are no knights anywhere better than they are at fighting in battles or at tournaments (vv. 7274–75); they are of distinguished lineage and they know how to "faire vasselage" (v. 7260, to practice *vasselage*). That they are also "preus" (vv. 7238, 7258) and "sage[s]" (vv. 7351, 7392) constitutes a rich and ironic ambiguity. On the one hand, *proëce* and *sagesse* are among the classic constituents of male homosocial *vasselage*, while the Amazons are joined by female homosocial bonding. On the other hand, when applied to women, the terms usually denote more passive qualities such as virtuous modesty and appropriate manners and behavior.

Two maidens, expressively named Floré and Beauté, are emissaries from the Amazon queen. Accordingly, when they visit Alexander, they are perceived as "cortoise[s]" (vv. 7483, 7619) no doubt because they are *vassales*, as faithful bearers of their queen's words, and also because they know how to address others in an appropriate way. Like Samson in the decasyllabic romance, they fall within the tradition of the "cortois messager." But the Amazons' "courtesy" also embraces a wider variety of physical and moral traits that are conventional in courtly romance and lyric texts. As Alexander observes, "vostre dame est molt sage, / Qui si beles puceles tramet en son message, / Cortoises et proisies et de molt bel aage, / Et si semblés molt bien femes de haut parage" (vv. 7617–20, "Your lady is very astute when she sends such beautiful maidens on her errand, maidens who are *cortoises*, praiseworthy, and at a lovely age, and you look like women of noble birth"). Thanks to the maidens' *biauté* as well as their *vasselage* (v. 7621), Alexander exonerates the Amazons from paying him tribute. Finally, it is their manners, their artistic skills, and their beauty, no less than their *vasselage*, that immediately cause two of Alexander's peers, Aristé and Cliçon, to fall in love with them and desire to marry them. They are accomplished singers who know the courtly repertoire—they sing together a lay of Narcissus—, and it is the sound of their "vois de seraine" (v. 7472, mermaid voices) that first attracts the Greek knights.

Queen Candace is also "cortoise et sage" (v. 4607), and she is attended by a knight, "cortois et avenant" (v. 4577, *cortois* and attractive), who appropriately serves as her messenger to Alexander.[27] We might infer that these descriptive expressions connote conventional *vasselage*, were it not for the fact that Candace behaves very much like a romance heroine—the lady in Marie de France's *Milun*, for example—who suffers from *amor de lonh* and loses her reason after she hears Alexander's praises sung. She loves him for his *vasselage*, but her love manifests itself as an extreme form of *fin'amors* when the only means she has to satisfy her passion is to contemplate Alexander's portrait. Alexander in his turn, like Milun, is seduced by the lady who loves him. The episode (Br. III, ll. 246–270) turns to farce as Alexander and his peer Antigonus exchange identities and as Alexander's identity is revealed by his portrait when he visits Candace as Antigonus.[28] The ensuing visit ends in a half day's exuberant lovemaking. For his part, Alexander certainly enjoys Candace, but he does not love her as she loves him.

Alexander's mother, Olympias, is the first woman in the Vulgate to be described as *cortoise*. The attribute dates from the decasyllabic romance, where she is introduced into the text as she bows to her son "corteisement" (*laisse* 18, v. 181) and then runs to embrace him and shower him with kisses. That she is *cortoise* may simply mean, as Martin Gosman has suggested, that she knows how to behave in court, as befits the etymological meaning of the term.[29] However, her subsequent words are spoken, I would argue, under the sign of that same *cortoisie*. She tells Alexander that he was auspiciously born (*laisse* 19, v. 187): he will tame Bucephalus, he will rule his father's kingdom, it is time for him to be knighted, and his prowess and other noble qualities (v. 192) will soon be manifested. Her speech betokens the *cortoisie-as-vasselage* that dominates the decasyllabic romance.

In the Alexandre de Paris text, Olympias's *cortoisie* is imbued with other qualities. At the poem's opening she is described as "belle et gente et eschevie" (Br. I, v. 149: beautiful, noble, accomplished), the daughter of a powerful king. She is also "preus" (v. 153). But her *proëce*, like her *cortoisie*, is subject to very specific definition because, like the two Amazon maidens, she is skilled in music (vv. 154–56). Significantly, Olympias is also implicitly associated with the Amazons by juxtaposition at the end of Branch III where, at the conclusion of the Amazon episode, Alexander receives a letter from his mother warning him of Antipater and Divinuspater's treachery.

The description of Olympias at the beginning of the Vulgate continues with a telling comment: ". . . Cil iert prives de li, si ne s'en couvroit mie, / Qui par armes queroit pris de chevalerie, / Et li donoit biaus dons, car de biens iert garnie . . ." (Br. I, vv. 157–59, any man was her intimate friend—and she did not try to hide it—who in the exercise of arms sought distinction in knighthood, and she bestowed him with handsome gifts, for she was wealthy.) These lines are richly ambiguous. On the one hand, foreshadowing her son's largesse, she generously rewards acts of *vasselage*. On the other hand, like the *dames cortoises* in the Arthurian section of Wace's *Brut*, she openly bestows her favors on knights who display their prowess in tests of chivalric skill: intimacy with *privés* can be sexual as well as social (as in Br. II, vv. 3001–4). One Olympias is wholly *vassale*, the other is subject to a destructive form of *cortoisie*.

Displays of romance courtesy are sporadic intrusions into a text dominated by homosocial *cortoisie-as-vasselage*, a text where Alexander's ambition is driven by *vasselage* and his virtues and his aptitudes, even his largesse, are defined by that *vasselage*. The Amazons, Olympias, and even Candace—women who perhaps embody another mode of *cortoisie* with which the readers of the Vulgate are just as familiar—are likewise susceptible to definition also in terms of *vasselage*. In light of the Vulgate text's fundamental polarity and its essential ambiguity, what emerges in such a reading is that, while romance courtesy may appear to be inconsequential to the values of *vasselage*—for example, Candace's love for Alexander—, it may actually threaten to undermine those values.

The Amazons' ambivalence is unconditional. As female counterparts of Alexander and his men, they are warriors who embody homosocial *vasselage*. At the same time, they are compelled to reproduce, and once a year they hold a festival on the borders of their kingdom where they meet male knights. Their mating involves courtly talk recalling the love games in Wace's depiction of Arthurian *cortoisie*: "La parolent d'amors et de chevalerie / Et font lor volentés trestout par drüerie" (Br. III, vv. 7244–45: There they speak of love and knighthood and satisfy their desires in lovemaking.) Among the children born from these unions, the girls are kept and raised by the Amazons, while the boys are expelled: not slaughtered, as in classical myth, but sent back across the border to their fathers (vv. 7246–49).

From the standpoint of the male knights, then, courtly dalliance with Amazons offers no threat to their *vasselage*: as lineage—*lignage, parage*—is an essential value, it is guaranteed to the knights by the return of their sons. From the women's standpoint, their *vasselage* is assured by maintaining female lineage through their daughters. Danger comes to the Amazon community, however, when Floré and Biauté yield to the temptations offered by romance courtesy and cross a forbidden boundary: they fall in love with men with whom normally they might only have mated, and they end up marrying them. When their queen rides away from the Greek encampment in a huff because she is angry that Alexander has allowed them to marry, Floré and Biauté implicitly stay behind in Alexander's realm with their husbands. By contrast, Aristé and Cliçon's *vasselage* is unthreatened: they have their wives with them to assure their lineage. In all events, Floré and Biauté are so insignificant in the grander scheme of Alexandre de Paris that they are never mentioned again.

As we have seen, Alexandre de Paris deliberately injects ambivalence into his description of Olympias, in order, as scholars claim (see Harf-Lancner, *RA*, pp. 82–83, n. 16), to acquit her of the charge of adultery that has dogged her throughout history and to establish thereby the legitimacy of Alexander's birth. Indeed, the narrator steadfastly supports the reading that is favorable to Olympias's character (Br. I, vv. 174–84), but at the same time he subverts her cause by providing the contrary explanation that is the basis of her detractors' slander (vv. 166–76).

Candace is Olympias's double because she is a queen who acts on behalf of her son. At Porus's urging, Candace marries her youngest son to his daughter (Br. III, *laisse* 31). It is this son who later precipitates his mother's unhoped-for meeting with Alexander when his young wife is kidnapped and he solicits the Greeks' help in recovering her. More significantly, Candace is the double of Olympias as slanderers perceive her. Just as any knight who proves his worth in battle can be Olympias's *privés*, so Candace is introduced into the Vulgate text as the *privee* of King Porus (Br. III, v. 617), and the precedent of Olympias helps define Candace's relationship with her "intimate friend." Similarly, Candace's complicated involvement with Alexander gives elaborate definition to Olympias's alleged behavior with her own *privés*.

What is at stake is nothing less than Alexander's own *vasselage*—the legitimacy of his lineage that is his claim to Macedonia. Alexandre de Paris's narrator defends Olympias, but the question of Alexander's legitimacy continues to haunt the hero. The unfavorable reading of Olympias's *cortoisie* is the reason why King Philip repudiates her and marries a certain Cleopatra (Br. I, *laisses* 83–84), and it is the basis for Porus's revolt against Alexander (Br. III, vv. 4166–68).

Olympias and Candace are singled out for special attention in the Vulgate. Olympias is the first woman to appear, and it is in reference to her that the word *cortois* is first recorded; Candace is remarkable in the Lambert le Tort prologue (Br. III, *laisse* 1) because she is the only woman mentioned in its synopsis and more especially because three of the prologue's fifteen lines are devoted to episodes involving her (vv. 8–10), while Darius and Porus have one apiece (vv. 2–3). Roxane, however, is gradually insinuated into the text over the course of several branches; in a sense, therefore, she constitutes a stronger strand in the text's fabric.

By contrast, there is little that is ambivalent in Roxane's *cortoisie*. As she benefits indirectly from Alexander's *cortoisie*-as-largesse, Roxane is introduced in a series of brief references, where she is not even named. Each of the succeeding allusions—there are five within a hundred lines—is slightly more elaborate than the one preceding it. In Branch II, when Darius is wounded by Alexander and his troops flee, Alexander captures Darius's mother, his wife, and "sa fille au cler vis, qui iert gente pucele" (v. 2971, his daughter of the shining face who was a noble maiden). The women are mentioned again in the next two *laisses* (vv. 2981–83, 2997–98), with emphasis the third time on the "grans biautés" of both mother and daughter. The fourth reference, in the same context, summarizes the others: ". . . vostre fille est bele et si a molt cler le vis" (v. 3026, your daughter is beautiful and her face fairly shines), while the fifth amplifies: "sa fille estoit bele et ot cler le viaire, / Sa coulour samble rose et soleil qui esclaire" (vv. 3069–70, his daughter was beautiful and her face was bright. Her color was like a rose and the shining sun). In like fashion, she appears somewhat later, early in Branch III, in a pair of *laisses similaires* in which the dying Darius offers her in marriage to Alexander (vv. 272–73, 294–96). Finally, in Branch IV, the description of Roxane attains unprecedented elaboration as she is named. At Alexander's coronation,

> Sa mollier Rosenés, qui tant avoit biautés,
> Fu aveuc coronee et ses cors atornés,
> Cors de si bele dame ne sera ja mais nés.
> Qui veïst son viaire, com il iert colorés!
> De blanc et de vermeil estoit entremellés,
> Et li cors avenans et li cuers esmerés.
> Sous ciel n'a si dur home, tant soit vilains provés,
> S'il esgardast la dame, ne fust d'amors navrés,
> Tant iert de bones teches ses cors enluminés. (vv. 68–76)

(His wife Roxane, who was so beautiful, was crowned and robed with him. Never again will such a beautiful woman's body be born. If only you had seen her face, how it was colored! It was white and red mixed together, and her body was attractive and her heart pure. Under heaven there is no man so hard, no matter how uncourtly he proves to be, who would not be wounded by love if he looked at the lady, she shone with so many noble qualities.)

A grant joie en menerent le roi Mascedonés.
Qui donques reveïst sa mollier Rosenés,
Ainsi com li baron l'en menerent aprés!
Ne fu si bele dame des le tans Moÿsés.
Sa corone soustienent Leone et Filotés,
Desus tinrent un paile Caulus et Aristés,
Que li chaus ne li arde le vis ne le palés. (vv. 104–11)

(With great rejoicing they led the Macedonian king away. If only you had seen his wife Roxane then, how the noblemen led her away after him! There had not been such a beautiful lady since the time of Moses. Leone and Filote held up her crown, Caulus and Aristé held a silken canopy over her so that the sun did not burn her face and neck.)

Roxane's heartrending beauty, so great that even an uncourtly *vilain* would be moved by it, is indeed a value that pertains to *cortoisie*, but it is in this regard only that Roxane is as ambiguous a figure as the other women. Hers is not the kind of *cortoisie* exemplified by Candace or by the adulterous Olympias, or that to which Floré and Biauté fall subject. When at last Roxane speaks *cortoisement*, it is to lament her dead husband: ". . . Les proëces du roi cortoisement retrait: / 'Ha! sire, rois des rois, qui tant chastel as frait, / Tant mur et tante tor as torné a garait! / Envers orgelleus home ne feïs malvais plait, / Et qui te vaut servir nel preïs a forfait . . ." (vv. 904–08, with *cortoisie* she enumerates the king's acts of prowess: "Ah, my lord, king of kings, who has brought down so many castles and turned so many walls and towers into plowed earth! You never took up a cowardly cause with anyone arrogant, and you did not treat as a criminal anyone who wanted to serve you.") To complete her fifteen-line eulogy, she extols Alexander's world conquest as well as his largesse, and she bewails the despair of knights who now face financial ruin and the loss felt by all other men (vv. 909–15). Only in closing, as she faints and fades from the history, does she take three lines to express her personal grief (vv. 916–18). Earlier, as Alexander lies dying, Roxane discloses to him that she is pregnant (vv. 198–201). These are her first words recorded by Alexandre de Paris, who thereby underscores the crucial fact that Roxane has assured the continuation of Alexander's line. Her concerns are those of *vasselage*: she is its instrument as well as its *porte-parole*. Ethically, her *cortoisie* is the match of her husband's *vasselage*.

To conclude, I would like to return to the broader topic of the ambiguous texts that Alexandre de Paris inscribes in his romance and recall Darius's *semblance* of the poppy seed. As we have seen, Alexander swallows a pennyweight's worth of the seeds. "Are Darius and his knights so sweet and tasty?" he asks. The text is actually more subtle and more complex than my quick summary has made it out to be. What Alexander really says is, "'Ceste chose est molt simple et molt fait a proisier. / Est Dayres ausi humles et il et si guerrier?'" (Br.

II, vv. 2508–9: This thing [the mouthful of seeds] is very *simple* and deserves to be highly prized. Are Darius and his warriors just as *humle*)? The question is directed to Darius's messenger, and the story turns on ambiguous meanings of the words Alexander chooses, *simple* and *humle*. *Simple* has a variety of meanings ranging from negative—"simpleminded" and "soft"—to positive— "pleasant" and "straightforward." *Humle* is similarly ambiguous, with senses ranging from negative—"base," "lowborn"—to positive—"modest," "unassuming," and "sweet natured."[30] Darius's messenger assumes the positive, noble register of both terms, all the more so as *simple* is coupled with "molt fait a proisier" (it deserves to be highly praised, or highly valued), and he answers that Darius and all his knights are indeed as Alexander has said (v. 2510).[31] Yet Alexander's response assumes the terms' other meanings (Darius and his men are soft, they are inferior): / "Dont sont il en bataille a destruire legier. / A ce que li Grieu sont en estor sur et fier, / Ja ne porrés garir encontre lor acier . . ." (vv. 2512–14, Then they will be easy to destroy in battle. Because Greeks are hard and fierce when they fight, no one can withstand their steel). Alexander behaves similarly with the lowborn assassins of Darius. Pretending that he is grateful to them, he promises to reward then by telling them that "they shall wear bracelets on their arms and medallions about their necks. I shall raise them higher, no matter whom that grieves, than any man in my entourage, no matter how praiseworthy he is, and they shall be wonders for wise men and fools to behold" (Br. III, vv. 319–22). When the villains confess, expecting great riches, they find shackles around their arms, a noose about their necks, and a gallows to exalt them above Alexander's men.

Another example is the prophetic dream Alexander has when he is five years old (Br. I, vv. 255–62). He sees himself about to eat an egg that no one else wants, but it rolls out of his hand, drops to the floor, and breaks in half. Out comes a snake that crawls around his bed three times, and then goes back to the eggshell, which becomes its tomb, for it dies as it goes back in. Such a dream is prophetic, and it is a text that requires interpretation. Different readings are provided by three wise men. In one reading, the snake represents a prideful conqueror who is on the verge of making a vast conquest when he turns about and loses his strength (*laisse* 12). In another, the snake represents a foolhardy conqueror who sets out to subdue lands by brute force, but when he is forsaken by those on whom he depends, he will return home in a wretched state (*laisse* 13). In the last reading, which is Aristotle's, the eggshell represents the world and the yoke within is the dry land and all its inhabitants. The snake is Alexander who, after many trials, will be lord of the world, and his men will rule over it after him. He will come back to Macedonia dead or alive (*laisse* 14).

Yet another variant is provided by Alexander's perhaps hubristic undersea voyage (Br. III, *laisses* 18–28).[32] The descent in the bathosphere is meant to be the conquest of another world, a world of the unknown. More importantly, Alexander observes the natural habitat and the natural habits of the creatures of the deep, and he learns lessons of immense value to him. Like one steeped in the tradition of the Physiologus, he reads nature like another kind of text requiring interpretation. He watches the hierarchy of fish, observing how every fish is swallowed by a bigger fish, and concludes that the world beneath the sea has a feudal order like the one he knows on land—indeed, that the feudal order is natural (vv. 444–48, 465–75, 481–89). Then he discovers how some sea creatures lay traps to trick their prey, and he sees military applications for their tactics (vv. 453–64)—this he calls "sens de chevalerie" (v. 529). Also, like a reader of the Physiologus, he discovers a moral level of meaning: the cycle of fish devouring fish represents the triumph of cupidity in the world. Finally, the experience instills in him the resolve to pursue his conquest through India to the edges of the earth (vv. 515–20). In short, he knows both how to accomplish his mission and what its moral and political purpose is:

> ". . . molt i ai apris sens de chevalerie,
> Comment guerre doit estre en bataille establie
> Aucune fois par force et autre par voisdie,
> Car force vaut molt peu s'engiens ne li aïe.
> Ne sai noient de roi puis qu'il fait couardie,
> Mais soit larges et preus et ait chiere hardie.
> Tholomé, ce covient, la letre le vos crie,
> Ja parole de roi ne doit estre faillie.
> Sachiés que mainte terre est sovent apovrie
> Par malvais avoué qu'en a la segnorie . . ." (vv. 529–38)

("I have learned a great deal there about the art of knighthood, how war must be pursued in fighting sometimes with might and at other times with cunning, for might is worth very little unless it is aided by ingenuity. I am not interested in a king once he behaves like a coward, but a king should be generous and demonstrate prowess and have a confident look. Ptolemy, it is fitting—and written authority proclaims it to you—that never should the word of a king be broken. And know well that many a land has been impoverished by an evil ruler who has lordship over it.")

In each of these examples, as in many similar incidents throughout the Vulgate, one reading of a text is superseded by another that acclaims the values of *vasselage*. Hot, hard-to-swallow Greek pepper that connotes *vasselage* supplants soft, base, easy-to-consume Persian poppy seed. Lowborn criminals receive the rewards of Alexander's just retribution and not power and riches. Failure of weak and foolish rulers gives way to world conquest by Alexander. Alexander perceives *vasselage* in terms of the natural order and comprehends that *vasselage* is not only the means of conquest, but indeed its purpose. In inscribing Olympias's text and its divergent readings as the first in a great, exemplary series, Alexandre de Paris establishes the sense of the reading exercise by exploiting the very ambivalence of the *cortois* in texts written after 1150 or so. In his world, nevertheless, it is not the courtesy of Candace that conquers all, but *cortoisie-as-vasselage*. A key to understanding the cultural history of France at the end of the twelfth century lies in determining whether Alexandre de Paris's vision proves to be outmoded, or whether he and likeminded writers succeed in reinvigorating a conservative ethos.

Notes

1. *RA*, Introduction. I cite throughout from *MFRA* II; translations are my own.

2. According to Harf-Lancner, *senefiance* is the "fil directeur" of Alexandre de Paris's romance. See "De la biographie au roman d'Alexandre: Alexandre de Paris et l'art de la conjointure," in *The Medieval Opus: Rewriting and Transmission in the French Tradition*, ed. Douglas Kelly (Amsterdam and Atlanta: Rodopi, 1996), pp. 59–74, esp. pp. 68–69.

3. We recall that the glove is, in synecdoche, the emblem of its owner. Another episode (1: §§121–123), the Enchanted Mountain, exemplifies the Vulgate text's fundamental polarity in another way. "When a cowardly man began climbing, he immediately grew bold; the very worst in the world was stirred with courage. Similarly, the worthy man grew craven and faint-hearted in deeds and in words; the very best is a fool there and a churl" (Br. I, vv. 2525–29); "And the cowards went about encouraging the noble, and they said to the worthy men: 'You are all weaklings. We are the ones who will conquer the world from here to the Orient' " (vv. 2549–51).

4. Glyn S. Burgess, *Contribution à l'étude du vocabulaire pré-courtois* (Geneva: Droz, 1970), esp. ch. 2–3, and "Étude sur le terme *cortois* dans le français du XIIᵉ siècle," *Travaux de Linguistique et de Philologie* 31 (1993), 195–209.

5. Rupert T. Pickens, "*Vasselage* épique et courtoisie romanesque dans le *Roman de Brut*," in *De l'aventure épique à l'aventure romanesque: mélanges offerts à André de Mandach*, ed. Jacques Chocheyras (Bern: Peter Lang, 1997), pp. 165–86.

6. Pickens, "Courtesy and *Vasselage* in Chrétien de Troyes's *Conte del Graal*," in *Echoes of the Epic: Studies in Honor of Gerard J. Brault*, ed. David P. and Mary Jane Schenck (Birmingham, AL: Summa, 1998), pp. 189–221.

7. Karl D. Uitti, with Michelle A. Freeman, *Chrétien de Troyes Revisited* (New York: Twayne, 1995), esp. pp. 102–23.

8. Pickens, "*Vasselage* épique" and "Courtesy and *Vasselage*"; also "Arthur's Channel Crossing: Courtesy and the Demonic in Geoffrey of Monmouth and Wace's *Brut*," *Arthuriana* 7.3 (Fall 1997), pp. 3–19, and "Le Sens du terme *cortois* dans les premiers poèmes du Cycle de Guillaume d'Orange," forthcoming.

9. The text and translation are from *The Song of Roland: An Analytical Edition*, ed. Gerard J. Brault, vol. 2 (University Park and London: Pennsylvania State University Press, 1978).

10. *Le Roman de Brut de Wace*, ed. Ivor Arnold, 2 vols. (Paris: Société des Anciens Textes Français, 1940), vol. 2, vv. 10503–16; translations are my own.

11. As Cador complains in his defense of warfare and *vasselage*: "Uisdive met hume en peresce,/ Uisdive amenuse prüesce,/ Uisdive esmuet les lecheries,/ Uisdive esprent lé drüeries" (vv. 10743–46, Idleness makes men lazy, idleness impairs prowess, idleness provokes debaucheries, idleness kindles love affairs).

12. *MFRA* 1; cf. the *Alexandre décasyllabique* in *MFRA* 3, pp. 61–100; translations my own.

13. On the education of Alexander, see Penny Simons, "Theme and Variations: The Education of the Hero in the *Roman d'Alexandre*," *Neophilologus* 78 (1994), 195–208.

14. The *est* in the first statement is meant as a second-person. Cf. the variant *estes* (Venice §54, 530), also *es* in the "Archetype" (§57, 561 [vol. 3, p. 89]).

15. *Les Rédactions en vers du Couronnement de Louis*, ed. Yvan G. Lepage (Paris and Geneva: Droz, 1978), Rédaction *AB*, pp. 1437–68.

16. As Olivier Naudeau argues, *pelerin* here means "foreigner," "traveler from far away," in "La Langue de l'*Alexandre décasyllabique*," *Revue de Linguistique Romane* 58 (1993), 433–59, esp. p. 450 (# 19), whereas the pilgrim in the *Couronnement* has been to St. Martin's at Tours (thus he is, in Naudeau's terms, a pilgrim "in the Christian sense").

17. On the "messager cortois," see Jacques Merceron, *Le Message et sa fiction: la communication par messager dans la littérature française des XIIe et XIIIe siècles* (Berkeley: University of California Press, 1998), pp. 79–81.

18. The Venice manuscript manifests *cortoisement* in the way of describing how Philip speaks, but bears the variant *aspra soudaier* (cruel warrior) for *corteis mesager* (Venice §46, 454). In the Venice text, there is no witty wordplay, therefore no *facetia* because the ambiguity is resolved; the sense of *cortoisement* thus reverts to the strict meaning of "with a display of *vasselage*."

19. C. Stephen Jaeger, *The Origins of Courtliness: Civilizing Trends and the Formation of Courtly Ideals 939–1210* (Philadelphia: University of Pennsylvania Press, 1985), pp. 155–68.

20. What Alexander knows of the ethical and political dimensions of *vasselage* he learns from Aristotle (Br. III, vv. 16–48, 49–80); thus Alexander's *sagesse* is rooted in *clergie* as well as *chevalerie*. Aristotle's lessons are to be compared with Charlemagne's advice to the young Louis in the *Couronnement de Louis* (Rédaction *AB*, 72–86, 150–59, 166–214).

21. As a challenge addressed to an enemy in battle, the noun *vassal* is considered an insult.

22. "Li cuens est tex que il n'escote / Vilain gap ne parole estote, / Et s'il ot mal dire d'autrui, / Qui que il soit, ce poise lui" (*Li Contes del Graal*, 21–23: The count does not harken to wicked gossip or prideful words, and if he hears evil spoken of another, no matter whom, it grieves him). Chrétien de Troyes, *The Story of the Grail (Li Contes del Graal), or Perceval*, ed. Rupert T. Pickens, trans. William W. Kibler (New York and London: Garland, 1990). In a gesture to the conventions of *fin'amors* to which Alexandre de Paris does not allude in an altogether noble register, "En son bras [Gadifers] ot lacie une manche s'amie, / Qui n'estoit mie garce ne povrement norrie, / Mais riche damoisele, fille au roi d'Aumarie" (Br. II, vv. 1499–1501: He had tied on his arm a sleeve belonging to his lady friend, who was not a low-born wench raised in poverty, but a rich maiden, the daughter of the king of Mahdia [in Tunisia]). See Gosman, *Légende*, p. 240. Corineus's discourteous taunt acknowledges the implications of Gadifer's gesture.

23. Other examples of the *mesager cortois* include Br. III, vv. 1625, 4577, 5333, 7619.

24. Simon Gaunt, *Gender and Genre in Old French Literature* (Cambridge: Cambridge University Press, 1995).

25. See Gosman, "L'Élément féminin dans le *Roman d'Alexandre*: Olympias et Candace," in *Court and Poet: Selected Proceedings of the Third Congress of the International Courtly Literature Society (Liverpool 1980)*, ed. Glyn S. Burgess (Trowbridge, Wilts.: Francis Cairns, 1981), pp. 167–76, and *Légende*, pp. 243–65.

26. See Aimé Petit, "Le Traitement courtois du thème des Amazones d'après trois romans antiques: *Enéas, Trois* et *Alexandre*," *Le Moyen Age* 89 (1983), 63–84, esp. pp. 69–70, 76–82; also Gosman, *Légende*, pp. 258–62.

27. See Gaullier-Bougassas, "Alexandre et Candace dans le *Roman d'Alexandre* d'Alexandre de Paris et le *Roman de toute chevalerie* de Thomas de Kent," *Romania* 112 (1991), 18–44, esp. pp. 37–38; also Gosman, *Légende*, pp. 253–58.

28. The *fabliau*-like situation appropriately echoes the tone of Alexandre de Paris's reference to Gadifer's lady friend (see n. 22).

29. Gosman, "L'Élément féminin," p. 171; on Olympias, see also Gosman, *Légende*, pp. 248–53, and Gaullier-Bougassas, *Frontières*, pp. 347–69.

30. We recall that, according to Porus (Br. III, v. 2236), Alexander's virtue of being "humble"—his *humilités*—is the very basis of his largesse; therefore, it is a quality of one who embodies *vasselage*. Darius likewise links Alexander's *humilités* with another aspect of *vasselage*, his trustworthiness (Br. II, v. 3032).

31. "Oil, fet il, mes sire et tuit si chevalier." I have corrected an error in punctuation in the Armstrong edition which is reproduced by Harf-Lancner.

32. For Harf-Lancner, Alexander's undersea voyage and his griffin flight, "vertical conquests" that frame the Indian adventures and the discovery of the Orient, are "emblématiques de la soif de connaître et de la démesure du héros" ("De la Biographie au roman d'Alexandre," p. 64; see also pp. 63, 69–72).

7

"A paine a on bon arbre de malvaise raïs": Counsel for Kings in the *Roman d'Alexandre*

William W. Kibler

Over the centuries Alexander has been nearly everything for everybody. Each succeeding culture, as it gained identity and self-consciousness, projected onto the legend of the great Macedonian its own aspirations, values, and manners. In the Hebrew tradition, he is a preacher and prophet; Christian exegetes emphasize his faithful obedience to God; for the Persians he can be either the arch-Satan, for destroying the altars of the Zoroastrian religion, or the true king of Persia, son of Darius rather than of Philip of Macedonia; for the Greeks, he is a demigod; for modern historians he is alternately an adventurer, a ruthless conqueror, a visionary, or a monster not unlike Hitler.[1] Is it any wonder, then, that the Middle Ages made of him a paragon of kingship and chivalry, a model for king and noble alike? This is clearly recognized by Laurence Harf-Lancner in the excellent introduction to her translation of the medieval French *Roman d'Alexandre*: "Alexandre donne d'abord une image de la royauté idéale . . . [L]e *Roman d'Alexandre* entend surtout proposer un modèle de gouvernement, un «miroir du prince» comme ceux qui fleurissent tout au long du Moyen Age" (*RA*, pp. 44–45).

Alexandre de Paris's version of the *Roman d'Alexandre*, composed sometime after 1180 and during the reign of Philip II Augustus, proclaims its didactic purpose in its opening lines:

> Qui vers de riche istoire veut entendre et oïr,
> Por prendre bon example de prouece acueillir,
> De connoistre reison d'amer et de haïr,
> De ses amis garder et chierement tenir,
> Des anemis grever, c'on n'en puisse eslargir,
> Des ledures vengier et des biens fes merir,
> De haster quant leus est et a terme soffrir,
> Oëz dont le premier bonnement a loisir. (I, 1–8)[2]

> (He who wishes to hear verses rich in history,
> to find therein a splendid example of prowess,
> to learn what to love and what to hate,
> how to keep one's friends and cherish them,
> to destroy one's enemies inexorably. . . .
> to avenge wrongs and reward good actions,
> to act quickly if need be, or temporize,
> listen then to the beginning of my tale.)

The lesson, although composed by a cleric, is aimed, like that of most other vernacular texts of this period, at the principal audience for this literature, the aristocracy, as the closing *laisses* of the fourth and final Branch make clear:

> Segnor, ceste raison devroient cil oïr
> Qui sont de haut parage et ont terre a baillir. . . . (IV, 1630–31)
> Ci doivent prendre essample li prince et li baron . . . (IV, 1668)
> Li rois qui son roiaume veut par droit governer
> Et li prince et li duc qui terre ont a garder
> Et cil qui par proëce veulent riens conquester,
> Cil devroient la vie d'Alixandre escouter. (IV, 1675–78)
> (My lords, those who are of high lineage
> And have land to rule should pay heed to my tale . . .
> Princes and barons should take example here . . .
> The king who wishes to govern his kingdom justly
> And the princes and dukes who have land to protect,
> And those who wish by valor to conquer anything,
> Should all listen to the life of Alexander.)

The *Roman* provides, thus, a mirror for princes. It suggests patterns of action and behavior, of reward and punishment, of friendships and enmities, appropriate to the ruling class. The lessons of *prouesse* and *largesse*, of courage and valor in the face of great odds, of fidelity to one's cause and one's men, of generosity to one's faithful followers, are all lessons that could be culled from any *chanson de geste* or *roman antique*; what sets Alexandre de Paris's poem apart is its insistence that a noble ruler not rely upon the counsel of lowborn men. This theme—which has been identified by Alfred Foulet, Martin Gosman[3] and Laurence Harf-Lancner, among others—is closely linked to another which, while latent in earlier versions of the romance, only comes to dominance in Alexandre's *remaniement*: I mean, the condemnation of a money economy and concomitant praise of the traditional role of largesse. Indeed, it may well be that Alexandre de Paris saw in these themes a way to give unity and direction to his entire compilation. Alexander's lessons at the beginnings of Branches I and III draw heavily on these themes; and in Branch IV Alexander, like Darius at the beginning of Branch III, will die at the hands of evil, lowborn plotters (*MFRA* VI, pp. 6–7).

What I would like to suggest is that the repeated attacks in Alexandre's poem upon money, and unworthy advisors who work for money, stem from an identifiable cultural context that has come to preoccupy the highest levels of the aristocracy in the latter decades of the twelfth century, at precisely the time when Alexandre de Paris was composing his version of Alexander of Macedonia's story. This preoccupation may have been first introduced into the Alexander legend by Lambert le Tort's *Alexandre en Orient*, composed in the 1170s, but it is Alexandre de Paris's version that brings it to special prominence. That Lambert, from Châteaudun on the edge of the Beauce, and Alexandre de Paris both flourished in the *mouvance* of the Capetian kings of France, whereas earlier writers who treated the Alexander materials were from outside the royal domain, is perhaps not entirely coincidental. My method, therefore, will be first to trace the rise of these themes through a comparison of Alexandre's poem with its immediate predecessors, and second, to evoke the historical context that might account for a special insistence upon them.

The Vulgate version of the *Roman d'Alexandre* composed by Alexandre de Paris in the last decades of the twelfth century is a skillful combination of several earlier texts, which the author/*remanieur* incorporated into his rework-ing of the story into dodecasyllabic *laisses*. Alexandre de Paris refers on several occasions to earlier texts and poets, and says in his prologue that his intent is to update Alexander's story: "D'Alixandre vos voeil l'istoire rafreschir" (I, 11). The success of his *remaniement*, which seems to be the first to introduce Alexander to the Paris region (AdeP II, p. xi), was such that the earlier texts he drew upon were, for the most part, lost to us. The earliest treatment of the Alexander legend in French is that by Albéric de Pisançon, writing in the half-Provençal, half-Franco-Provençal dialect of the southern Dauphiné in the first third of the twelfth century; Albéric's text, which apparently treated only Alexander's *enfances* (or youthful exploits), is preserved by a fragment of 105 octosyllabic lines.[4] Around 1160 another Poitevin adapted Albéric's poem into decasyllabic *laisses*; again, only the *enfances* were treated. The decasyllabic *enfances* were joined in the 1170's to a new dodecasyllabic *Alexandre en Orient* by Lam-bert le Tort and an anonymous *Mort Alixandre* to form a version known today as the archetype or amalgam.[5] This version is reflected variously by three manu-scripts, Arsenal 3472 (*A*), Venice Museo civico, VI, 665 (*B*), and B.N. 789 (*L*).[6] Finally, sometime after 1180, Alexandre de Paris unified all these earlier texts into a single harmonious composition often referred to as the "Vulgate Alexander."

What remains of the *Alexandre décasyllabique*, preserved only in the Ar-senal and Venice manuscripts, recounts in about 800 ten-syllable lines a version of Alexander's *enfances* up to the defeat and death of King Nicholas of Caesarea. The decasyllabic portion of the Arsenal manuscript (*laisses* 1–76), which is closer to the archetype than Venice,[7] is followed immediately by a folio added in the fourteenth century by an Italian scribe,[8] presumably to replace the lost or mutilated outside folio of quire 2. This folio comprises the end of *laisses* 76 and 77 in decasyllables, plus *laisse* 78 and the first three lines of *laisse* 79, in dodecasyllables. *Laisses* 78–79 correspond to the first two *laisses* of Alexandre de Paris's Branch III. However, Aristotle's lesson in *laisses* 2–3 of Branch III is missing in Arsenal, which continues with the Death of Darius episode (corresponding to *laisses* 8-17 of Alexandre de Paris's Branch III), before rejoining Alexandre de Paris's version for the remainder of Branches III and IV. New material introduced by Alexandre de Paris can be most easily isolated in the *enfances* section and at the juncture of the decasyllabic and dodecasyllabic texts, i.e., at the transition from his Branch I to Branch III. A comparison of Alexandre de Paris's Vulgate version with what we can surmise to have been the earlier stages of the work allows us to isolate important themes afforded special prominence by Alexandre de Paris.

The Arsenal manuscript begins with an eight-line prologue of the most banal type: "C[h]ançon voil faire per rime e per lioine / Del rei F[e]lip lo rei de Macedoine . . ." (A, 1–2: I wish to make a song that's richly rhymed / about King Philip of Macedonia); to which Venice adds eleven lines concerning the poem's reputed source, before both segue into the heavenly signs heralding Alexander's birth and the accompanying births of thirty sons of counts who would serve Alexander well. The heavenly signs are found early in Alexandre de Paris's poem as well (vv. 22–29), but he adds an additional two hundred lines of prologue before reaching the thirty sons of counts in *laisse* 8. Alexandre rehearses here *topoi* found in countless *chanson de geste* and romance prologues: the literary superiority of his work to that of his predecessors, references to a written source, and an assertion of the didactic purpose of his poem, to which we have already alluded.[9] None of these *topoi* appear in the Arsenal or Venice texts, but it is only the latter that is of special interest here. Alexandre insists repeatedly on his hero's exceptional largesse, for it is this quality, along with his *prouesse* and *sagesse*, that will distinguish him from lesser men and make him a worthy model for princes:

> Mes ne soit mie avers, s'aneur veut essaucier,
> Car ainc par averté ne puet riens gaagnier;
> Qui trop croit en tresor trop a le cuer lanier,
> Ne puet conquerre aneur ne terre justicier. (I, 52–55)
> (Be not miserly, if you wish to win honor,
> For one can gain nothing by avarice;
> He who clings to money has a coward's heart,
> And will never win lands or honor.)

This condemnation of avarice functions as an important leitmotiv in Alexandre's poem, serving to distinguish his hero from the "mauvés seigneurs [qui] ne

donnoit vaillant une denree / Ne seul tant que montast une pomme paree . . ."
(I, 97–99: wicked lord who wouldn't give a penny, not even as much as a
rotten apple).

Alexander's generosity is the main theme of the Vulgate's *laisses* 5 and 6,
while *laisse* 7 repeats the story from Arsenal and Venice that Alexander refused
to suckle a non-noble breast. *Laisses* 9–14, which can be designated "Alexander's
broken-egg dream," are apparently original with Alexandre de Paris. The five-
year-old child dreams he witnesses a serpent slither forth from a broken egg,
circle his bed three times, then return to the eggshell to die. Two sages provide
false interpretations of the dream, which only Aristotle of Athens, who will
become Alexander's principal teacher in the dodecasyllabic poem, can interpret
properly. The episode has no equivalent in Arsenal or Venice, and apparently
replaces one in the Latin sources in which Alexander observes a prodigy, which
is interpreted by a single master. Aristotle's appearance here early in Alexandre
de Paris's poem is perhaps inspired by the celebrated *Epistola Alexandri ad
Aristotelem de mirabilibus Indiae.*

Laisse 15 outlines the course of study proposed by Aristotle and concludes with lines central to our theme:

> Et en aprés li moustre un bon chastïement,
> Que ja serf de put ere n'et entour lui souvent,
> Car maint home en sont mort et livré a torment,
> Par losenge, par murtre, par enpoisonnement.
> Li mestres li enseigne et li varlés aprent;
> Il en jure le ciel et quanqu'a lui apent
> Que ja nus sers par lui n'avra essaucement. (I, 343–349)
> (Afterwards [Aristotle] gives him a good warning:
> Let him never surround himself with lowborn serfs,
> For their flattery, murders, and poisonings
> Have tortured and killed many a man.
> The master instructs and the youth learns;
> He swears by the heavens and all above
> That he will never bring a serf to power.)

In *laisse* 17 we learn that by the age of ten Alexander is already attracting a
retinue of noble and valiant youths through his exceptional generosity; the end
of this *laisse* again highlights the twin themes we have identified, largesse and
the necessity to seek and heed only the advice of noble-born counselors:

> Largement leur [to his retinue] donoit et fezoit lor talens:
> Chevaus et muls d'Espaigne et palefroiz amblans,
> Tirés et dras de soie et pailes aufriquans.
> Ses ostieus resambloit foire de marcheans,

Tant avoit entour lui de petis et de grans.
Ne prenoit pas conseil aus honnis recreans,
Mes a ses gentils hommes, a touz les mieus vaillans,
A ceus qui mieus resamblent hardis et conbatans.
La parole est bien voire et si est connoissans
Que li bons fet le bien et si est conseillans;
Ja de male racine n'ert abres bien portans. (I, 374–384)
(He gave generously to his men, as much as they desired:
Horses and Spanish mules and smooth-stepping palfreys,
Silk cloths from Tyre and rich African fabrics.
His lodgings looked like a merchant fair—
There were so many nobles, great and small.
He did not take advice from shameful cowards,
But only from the most valiant of his noble companions,
Those who were the boldest and most bellicose.
The adage is quite true and sensible which says
That the good man does good and listens to good counsel;
A good tree does not grow from poor rootstock.)

Laisses 18–22 recount the taming of Bucephelus in terms similar to those in the archetype represented by Arsenal and Venice (*laisses* 9–16),[10] although in the latter he is aged fifteen when he tames his horse, rather than ten. This enables the archetype then to move directly to the knighting of the fifteen-year-old Alexander by Philip, his father, whereas the dodecasyllabic version requires an additional *laisse* to age him from ten to thirteen years and five months (I, 503). This new *laisse*, number 23, is an occasion for Alexandre de Paris to provide additional praise of his hero and namesake's exceptional largesse, which attracts to him all the "damoisiaus de pris . . . [et] fuiz aus nobles hommes de par tout le païs" (I, 499–500: worthy young men and sons of nobles from throughout the land). Philip's barons approach their king and assure him that he can retire now and leave his country's fate in Alexander's hands, for he will defeat its enemies, lavishly reward its barons, and destroy the social-climbing *nouveaux riches*:

Cestui plet conperront li cuvert riche assis
Qui les frans chevaliers ont fez povres mendis
Et ont les granz tresors et les chiers pailles bis
Dont li regnes de Grece est vestus et porpris. (I, 518–21)
(The skinflints sitting on their riches,
Who have reduced the brave knights to begging
And hold the mighty treasures and rich silk cloths
That should embellish the noble Greeks, will pay dearly for this.)

Following this advice, Alexandre de Paris's redaction cuts straight to the dubbing ceremony and ensuing festivities, reducing these to a single *laisse* (25) where Arsenal and Venice drew them out into nearly thirty (17-44). Both redactions then recount the challenge to Philip by King Nicholas of Caesarea, and Alexander's haughty reply. In both versions Alexander next summons his men, but with a most telling difference. In the archetype, he leaps upon the dais and exhorts them to follow, and in no time at all 200,000 answer his call. In Alexandre de Paris's poem, the new king of Greece opens his treasury and lavishly pays his troops even before they set forth. More significantly yet, he appropriates the wealth of the usurers and *nouveaux riches* for his cause:

> De ce fist Alixandres que gentilz et que fiers,
> Que frans roys debonneres, que nobles chevaliers:
> Quant ot par les contrees mandé les sodoiers,
> Par le congié son pere a pris les usuriers,
> Les sers de put afere, les felons pautonniers,
> Qui les tresors avoient et les mons de deniers
> Qu'il lessoient moisir a muis et a sestiers;
> Touz les a departiz aus povres chevaliers,
> Aus povres bacheliers qui il estoit mestiers . . . (I, 645–653)
> (Alexander acted in a grand and bold manner,
> Like a worthy king and noble knight:
> When he had summoned his soldiers throughout the lands,
> With his father's leave he seized the usurers,
> The lowborn serfs, the slimebags,
> With their treasures and the heaps of coins
> They left molding in their crates and barrels.
> He distributed it all to the poor knights,
> To the impoverished youths who needed it.)

There follows yet another lesson by Aristotle on the political benefits of largesse (I, 673–84). Both versions continue with the departure of Alexander's army, the encounter with Darius's nephew Samson, and the latter's emissariat to King Nicholas. But again Alexandre de Paris adds a telling detail: Samson praises Alexander for refusing to heed the advice of lowborn men, unlike his uncle Darius:

> "[Alixandres] n'est mie roys Daires o le cuer pautonnier.
> Qui d'un serf racheté a fet son conseillier
> Ja devant Alixandre n'oseroit aprochier.
> S'uns li disoit losenge por nului empirier,
> Li roys le feroit pendre ou tout vif escorchier." (I, 834-38)

(Alexander is no King Darius with his faint heart.
Anyone who made a ransomed serf his counselor
Would never dare approach Alexander.
If one lied to him to bring down another,
The king would have him hanged or flayed alive.)

The dodecasyllabic redaction next treats us to a lengthy battle of nearly 750 lines (*laisses* 38–72), apparently original with Alexandre de Paris, for Arsenal and Venice dispose of the combat between Alexander and Nicholas in a single *laisse* (archetype 75) before rejoining in their next *laisse* Alexandre de Paris's Vulgate version near the opening of Branch III, the pursuit of Darius. Alexandre de Paris, meanwhile, completes his first Branch by drawing upon various sources—a B★ redaction of the amalgam for *laisses* 73–104, Quintus Curtius's *Epitome Julii Valerii* and the *Historia de Preliis* for *laisses* 105–28, and finally Eustache's *Fuerre de Gadres* for *laisses* 129–57 (*MFRA* III, p. 25). *Laisses* 75–128 are new, transitional material attributable to Alexandre de Paris (AdeP, p. xvi), and they return briefly to the theme of the evil servant in the story of Philip's momentary repudiation of his wife Olympias on the advice of his wicked seneschal, "Jonas [li] cuivers" (I, 1843). Philip is recalled to his duty by his son Alexander, who chastizes him that: "Mout par fet grant folie hom de vostre escïent, / Qu'est venuz en eage et a guerpi jouvent, / Qui lesse sa moillier pour dit de fole gent" (I, 1868–70: "A man of your wisdom and your age, who has left his youth behind, behaves most foolishly to repudiate his wife on the words of foolish people.")

Branch II constitutes the *Fuerre de Gadres*, drawing extensively on Eustache's earlier poem. *Laisses* 110–49 provide original linking material to Branch III, which is based on a now-lost poem by Lambert le Tort that recounted Alexander's expedition to the East. This *Alixandre en Orient*, assigned to the 1170s, is recognized as part of the archetype out of which Alexandre de Paris developed his Vulgate version, and contains in its opening *laisses* thematic material that may have inspired Alexandre de Paris to stress in Branch I the importance of traditional largesse and the concomitant dangers of raising the lowborn to positions of prominence. However, since Lambert's work was absorbed without independent traces into Alexandre's *remaniement*, we can no longer determine whether the development of the theme of unworthy servants in what is now Branch III of Alexandre's poem is due to Lambert, or whether it was added, modified, or elaborated by Alexandre in his reworking of his predecessor's poem. This theme appears with particular insistence in the second and third *laisses* of Branch III, which may in fact not be by Lambert, as we shall suggest below.

The first seven *laisses* of Alexandre de Paris's Branch III afford a transition from Branch II, which is not in the archetype, to the material taken from Lambert's *Alexandre en Orient*, which constitutes the core material of Branch

III. Alexandre's *laisse* 1 is an invocation, "Or entendés, segnor . . ." (Listen, lords . . .) imitating material from Lambert le Tort's prologue as it is reflected in Arsenal and Venice, though in slightly different form and circumstances; *laisses* 2 and 3 contain Aristotle's advice to Alexander; while *laisses* 4–7[11] provide the essential transitional material.

Laisses 2 and 3, which develop the parallel themes of avarice versus largesse, noble versus lowborn servants, faithful versus traitorous service in Aristotle's advice to Alexander, are interpolated quite abruptly into the poem, between the invocation and transition *laisses*. But Alfred Foulet presumes, due partly to their presence in the Venice manuscript and the evidence of erasures in Arsenal and partly to their development of themes that recur in *laisses* 8–17, that they go back to Lambert and the archetype: "Despite their abruptness, it seems legitimate to assume that stanzas 2–3 go back to Lambert le Tort . . ."[12] Foulet's reluctance here to pronounce definitively (as he does repeatedly elsewhere) opens the possibility, at the least, that the material was original with Alexandre de Paris, rather than Lambert, and was copied later into the Arsenal and Venice versions—just as the *Fuerre de Gadres*, for example, was interpolated into the archetype in the Venice manuscript. The tenor of Aristotle's advice here is consonant with concerns we have already found to be dominant in Alexandre de Paris's redaction of Branch I, and may well have been introduced by Alexandre to link his earlier revision of Branch I to Lambert's material. This argument is somewhat strengthened, too, by the material condition of the Arsenal manuscript, which omits most of *laisses* 2–5 at this point.[13]

After encouraging Alexander to show largesse especially to "les povres chevaliers" (poor knights; III, 22), Aristotle urges his ward to take up arms against Darius, whose subjects all hate him for having placed baseborn masters over them: "Car heent le de mort toutes ses regions / Por ce q'a mis sor aus sergans issi felons, / Des noaus de sa terre, des fieus a ses garçons" (III, 31–33: For all his lands hate him mortally because he has placed such wicked servants over them, the worst of his land, the sons of his knaves). Aristotle continues his advice in the following *laisse* in what is the most sustained treatment of the theme of lowborn advisers, including the bit of proverbial wisdom—attributed here to Solomon—that furnishes the title of this paper:

> "Ja cuivers losengiers ne soit par vos oïs.
> Se tu ne crois tes sers, ja ne seras honis;
> Ja sers ne sera bons qui sovent n'est aflis,
> Au tierc an ou au quart soit ses avoirs partis.
> Li sages Salemons le dist en ses escris:
> A paine a on bon arbre de malvaise raïs.
> Nule riens n'est si male comme sers enrichis;
> Qant il a son segnor tous ses avoirs froïs
> Portés en autre terre, et de sous lui fuïs,

L'avoir, se li sers muert, a cil qui'n est saisis;
Ja n'en avra ses sires vaillant une pertris.
Par ses malvais sergans est princes malbaillis,
Qui tolent les avoirs as grans et as petis,
Par coi il est de Dieu et du pueple haïs;
Li pechiés l'en remaint, cil en est enrichis,
Et s'il veut de l'avoir, bien en est escondis.
Assés voit on de ciaus qu'ont lor segnors traïs,
Ques ont empoisounés ou as coutiaus murdris;
Ton conseil ne lor di ne en aus ne t'afis." (III, 52–70)
("May a flattering knave never have your ear.
If you don't believe your serfs, you'll never come to shame;
No serf will come to good unless regularly called to account:
Confiscate his wealth every third or fourth year.
Wise Salomon said in his writings:
A good tree does not grow from poor rootstock.
Nothing is so bad as a rich serf:
When he has stolen all his lord's goods,
Carried them to another land and buried them,
At his death they belong to whoever recovers them;
His lord will never see any of it again.
A prince is ill served by his wicked servant,
Who steals goods from rich and poor alike.
The lord is despised by God and his people;
He comes out the loser and his servant is enriched;
If he wants his share, his servant puts him off.
You see many servants who betray their lords,
Who poison or stab them to death;
Do not confide in them or tell them your secrets.")

As Foulet has pointed out, a striking feature of the account of Darius's demise in *laisses* 8–17 is that there is no battle between himself and Alexander. The Persian monarch assembles an army as large as Alexander's, but his men refuse to fight for a king who has oppressed them at the behest of his inner circle of lesser men (*MFRA* VI, p. 6):

Mais por ce fu vaincus et ses regnes conquis
Qu'es fieus de ses garçons estoit ses consaus mis
Q'avoit fait de sa terre seneschaus et baillis,
Donees gentieus femes et es honors asis.
Cil li ont tous ses homes afolés et malmis,
Les vilains confondus et les borgois aquis,
Les povres chevaliers ciaus ont tenus si vis

Q'assés sont plus dolent que se il fuissent pris . . . (III, 172–79)
(But he was defeated and his kingdom conquered
Because he confided in the sons of his knaves,
Made them senechals and baillifs of his land,
Gave them noble wives and bestowed fiefs upon them.
These lowborns oppressed and tormented all his people,
Crushed the peasants, overwhelmed the city dwellers,
And brought low the poor knights,
Who are more wretched than if they'd been taken prisoner . . .)

Finally, as he lies dying, Darius himself warns Alexander not to place his confidence in baseborn serfs:

"Ne vos chaut vos cuivers essaucier ne chierir,
Ja de riens ne jorrés qu'il vos puissent tolir
Et tous jors vos vauront engegnier et traïr.
Li mien, qui me devoient honorer et servir,
A dolor me font vivre et ma vie fenir." (III, 300–305)
("You must not raise up or cherish your churls,
Whatever you have they'll steal
And will seek constantly to deceive and betray you.
My knaves, who should have honored and served me,
Have caused me to live and die in misery.")

By now it has become abundantly clear that Alexandre de Paris has introduced or elaborated in his redaction of the *Roman d'Alexandre* a number of passages either criticizing Darius for having placed his trust in lowborn advisers or urging Alexander to avoid doing so. This theme is a particularly timely one for its period, and it seems no coincidence to me that Alexandre de Paris, who is the first to introduce the Alexander legend to the Paris region, appears to have been particularly obsessed by it. While I agree with Martin Gosman that there is no "flaming gun" that would allow us to associate Alexandre's poem with the court of Philip II Augustus (*Légende*, p. 187), it does not seem unreasonable to me to see in it the reflection of ideas that were current among the upper aristocracy of that period; ideas, indeed, that they unsuccessfully hoped the king would adopt. The lesson here, then, is really one that would appeal to the displaced aristocracy rather than to the king himself, who had already chosen the opposite path.

This theme of baseborn men being elevated by royal patronage to positions of prestige is not unique to Lambert and Alexandre de Paris, for it figures prominently as well in several contemporary romances, notably *Partonopeu de Blois*, Jean Renart's *Roman de la Rose ou Guillaume de Dole*, and Adenet le Roi's *Cléomadès*. In *Partonopeu*, the theme of the *fils a vilain* raised to positions of honor and power occurs in the depiction of Anchises as a "fils a d'iable" who betrays King Priam, who had raised him from serfdom to a position of authority; in praise of King Clovis for promoting destitute but deserving nobles rather than hiring mercenaries; and in the Sonegur episode, where a baseborn advisor costs the Viking king the loyalty of his best barons. In *Guillaume de Dole*, the emperor Conrad is lauded for excluding lowborn advisors, who abuse their power and alienate noble vassals from their king (Lecoy ed., vv. 575-86). *Cléomadès* likewise develops the subject of persons of base extraction raised through royal favor to positions of inappropriate prominence. From only a slightly different angle, Catherine Croizy-Naquet shows in this volume how the portrait of Julius Caesar in the *Faits des Romains* serves to denounce the politics of Philip II Augustus, who is actually mentioned in the text and appears as an avatar of Caesar. "A travers César," she writes, "l'auteur [des *Faits des Romains]* pourrait vouloir dénoncer l'absolutisme royal et le rôle secondaire réservé à l'aristocratie du Nord de la France."[14] As Lionel Friedman has observed, this is in fact a constant political attitude of the aristocracy throughout the Capetian period, and can be found as early as the reign of Robert II the Pious (972-1031).[15] However, it appears to come to special prominence in the later-twelfth and early-thirteenth centuries, when the rising monied class and the favors accorded them within the king's curia became an increasingly unpleasant reality for the traditional aristocracy.

The twelfth century was a time of profound institutional changes in the government and monarchy of France, which recent studies by Eric Bournazel and John Baldwin have brilliantly traced.[16] Following over a century in which the Capetian ruler was elected by the barons, essentially *primus inter pares*, the principle of monarchical succession from father to son was successfully established during this period. Concomitantly, the notion of the crown as separate from the person of the monarch was beginning to be argued. But most profoundly, the very institutions of government, the counsel and *curia regis*, were being profoundly altered. Beginning in the early twelfth century, in the reign of Philip I, the monarchy slowly began assembling a group of advisors who were separate from the magnates of the kingdom. These latter were still vying actively with the king for effective control of the land and could not be trusted to give impartial advice or to sustain the policies of the monarchy. To replace them in the *curia* the Capetian rulers promoted, first, impoverished knights (*milites*) from the lower aristocracy, who thereby depended solely upon the king for their position and livelihoods; and, second, beginnning late in the reign of Louis VII—that is, in the 1170s, at precisely the time of Lambert's *Alexandre en Orient*—untitled, unlanded clerics (*légistes*) trained at the University of Paris.

The crisis and its eventual resolution came, however, during the reign of Philip II Augustus. His coronation on 1 November 1179 at the age of fifteen, with his father fast approaching death, was attended by the most important prelates and magnates of the realm, notably Count Philip of Flanders and representatives of the various branches of the powerful Champagne family, such as the archbishop of Reims, Guillaume aux Blanches Mains, who asserted his exclusive right to perform the ceremony (Baldwin, p. 6). All were seeking to gain control over the youthful monarch to advance their own agendas and assure their own preeminence. Although the magnates had deserted the royal court at the beginning of the century, Louis VII brought them back into the government in the second half of his reign, and they remained a significant force in the early years of Philip II's own reign. Nonetheless, with some help from Henri II Plantagenêt, Philip was able to stand firm against these powerful French magnates in the first decade of his reign, and then in the second he began to turn the tide against them. According to John Baldwin, the decade of the 1190s, following the unsuccessful Third Crusade, "witnessed transformations in both personnel and institutions that rendered it the decisive *tournant* of Philip's reign, indeed of early Capetian history" (p. 101).

Most of the magnates close to the crown at the beginning of Philip's reign, inherited in many cases from his father, were dead by the 1190s. While occasionally still present on important occasions, the great barons no longer filled significant administrative roles. For these the king preferred his own men, chosen for the most part from among the knightly class, but also including bourgeois and persons of lower birth (see Baldwin, ch. 6). Among the closest of Philip's counselors throughout his reign was a certain Brother Guérin, who eventually rose to be bishop of Senlis and was richly endowed with properties by his grateful king. Guérin served in the royal chancery, compiling records for the reign; he presided regularly over the Norman exchequer; he was the arbiter of numerous ecclesiastical disputes; he handled accounts for the king, and he played a prominent role in Philip's signal victory at Bouvines. No counselor was more trusted or closer to the king in the last thirty years of Philip's reign, yet Guérin was almost certainly of humble origins. And he was not alone. All of Philip's closest advisers after 1190 were of low or humble origin; after the fall of Philip of Flanders in the early years of the reign, the great magnates were effectively excluded from the *curia regis* and exercised no significant political influence.

Chroniclers of the reign, writing for the most part at non-royal courts, often reflect the magnates' contempt for Philip's closest advisers. A telling instance is recorded by the anonymous chronicler of Béthune and cited by John Baldwin:

> In both versions of [his] chronicle, [the anonymous chronicler of Béthune] relates that when the king deliberated on a project for invading England, he called together his trusted counsellors, Brother Guérin, Barthélemy de Roye, and Henri Clément. These three summoned a fourth . . . most likely Gautier the Young. In the chronicler's brief portraits

of the three who were named one can sense a tinge of hostility on the part of a vernacular writer articulating the high aristocracy's disdain for the inner circle of lesser men. Brother Guérin, the Anonymous declares, was a Hospitaler who spoke well but was too clever and dominant over the king. Although he had become bishop of Senlis, he was of low birth (*de basses gens*). Henri the Marshal was a small knight (*petit chevalier*), but because he had served the king well in war, he had been rewarded with the great fief of Argentan in Normandy. Barthélemy de Roye, a 'great knight' (*gran chevalier*), was also much favored in the king's *conseil*. Avoiding the term *prud'homme*, which normally denoted aristocratic approval, the chronicler makes pointed reference to Guérin's low birth and to Henri's lesser station, which rendered their promotions and rewards all the more remarkable.[17]

This battle for control of the king's council, won eventually by the lowborn *légistes*, was at its height in the 1170s and 1180s, at the end of the reign of Louis VII and the beginning of that of his son Philip II Augustus, and, not coincidentally, at precisely the time Lambert and Alexandre de Paris were composing their versions of the Alexander legend. It seems to me highly probable that in stressing traditional forms of largesse and reliance upon the advice of the magnates of the realm, Lambert, and especially Alexandre de Paris, were weighing in heavily on the side of the traditional aristocracy. The *chanson de geste*, the form chosen by the Alexander poets, is a conservative genre that promotes inherited values; its primary audience was the embattled aristocracy who saw their role in society being slowly eroded by the lesser nobility and, worse, the upstart bourgeoisie and clerkly classes. But where the *chansons de geste*—most notably those of the Rebellious Vassal cycle—denigrated or obfuscated the role of the king in favor of the barons, the *Roman d'Alexandre* sought instead to provide a model of ideal kingship, in the hope, perhaps, that Louis VII and Philip II would prefer sugar to gall.

Notes

1. See the Introduction by Richard Stoneman to *The Greek Alexander Romance* (Harmondsworth: Penguin, 1991), pp. 2–4.

2. This and all subsequent quotations are taken from *MFRA II*; references are to Branch number followed by line numbers. Translations are my own.

3. See Gosman, *Légende*, esp. his third chapter, "Le filigrane idéologique."

4. *MFRA III*, pp. 3, 37–60.

5. A reconstruction of the archetype for the first 785 lines of the decasyllabic version of Branch I is in *MFRA III*, pp. 61–100.

6. *MFRA III*, p. 8; cf. *RA*, p. 20. Manuscript *L* (B.N. 789) gives a unique version of Branch I, *laisses* 1–36, which combines elements borrowed from both Alexandre de Paris and the *Alexandre décasyllabique* with much original material; the 860 lines of the Vulgate's Branch I, 1–36 are expanded to 2037. The first 72 *laisses* of *L* are published in *MFRA III*, pp. 101–54.

7. Venice includes the *Fuerre de Gadres* episode (which is Branch II of the Vulgate) and an original passage (*laisses* 569–74) relating the punishment accorded Alexander's assassins, neither of which was in the archetype.

8. Paul Meyer, *Romania* 11 (1882), p. 249 and Milan La Du, commentary on the Arsenal MS in *MFRA I*, p. 362.

9. See *RA*, p. 79N.

10. For simplicity's sake, *laisse* numbers for the Venice and Arsenal text are taken from the reconstruction of the decasyllabic archetype by Lucien Foulet in *MFRA III*.

11. These four *laisses* are found in *A* as well as in Alexandre de Paris, but their absence in *B* suggests that they were taken by the scribe of this section of *A* from an Alexandre de Paris manuscript, rather than from the archetype.

12. *MFRA VI*, p. 5. Mentions of the defeat of Darius along the banks of the Ganges River (III, 45 & 79) are apparently inspired by the Latin *Epistola Alexandri ad Aristotelem* preserved in the A version of Pseudo-Callisthenes and which, it must be remembered, was purportedly addressed to Aristotle by Alexander. The Latin text narrates Alexander's adventures in India, dwelling on the odd creatures he encountered there, but does not take up the twin themes that interest us.

13. See the discussion in *MFRA I*, pp. 344ff and the plates of these folios after p. xvi.

14. I would like to thank the author for generously providing me with a prepublication copy of her paper.

15. Lionel J. Friedman, "Jean Renart and an Attribute of Rulers," *Modern Language Notes* 71 (1956), 426–30. I am grateful to Matilda Tomaryn Bruckner for bringing Friedman's article as well as the presence of this theme in *Partonopeu* and *Guillaume de Dole* to my attention. More especially, I appreciate her sending me a prepublication copy of "Romancing History and Rewriting the Game of Fiction: Jean Renart's *Rose* Through the Looking Glass of *Partonopeu de Blois*," in which she discusses the presence of the theme of lowborn counselors in these works as well as in the *Roman d'Alexandre*. *Partonopeu* is roughly contemporaneous with Alexandre de Paris's text, while *Guillaume de Dole* is about a generation later and *Cléomadès* dates from the late thirteenth century.

16. Eric Bournazel, *Le gouvernement capétien au XIIᵉ siècle: 1108–1180. Structures sociales et mutations institutionnelles* (Paris: Presses Universitaires de France, 1975); John W. Baldwin, *The Government of Philip Augustus: Foundations of French Royal Power in the Middle Ages* (Berkeley: University of California Press, 1986).

17. Anonymous of Béthune, *Histoire des ducs,* 120; *Chronique des rois*, 764. Cited in Baldwin, p. 123.

8

Giving Fiefs and Honor: Largesse, Avarice, and the Problem of "Feudalism" in Alexander's Testament

Stephen D. White

When, in Branch IV of the Vulgate *Roman d'Alexandre*, Alexander realizes that he is dying (Br. IV, v. 253), he lies down on a gold bed covered with silk and makes a generous gift of land to each of the twelve peers, whom Aristotle had previously chosen to be the king's principal companions (Br. I, v. 668–95) and whom Alexander himself had previously promised to reward in this way (Br. I, vv. 1388–92).[1] Each of you, Alexander now tells the peers, will have a reward (*guerredon*) for your services (*servises*) (Br. IV, v. 285); each will have "land and fief and *casamentum*" (*terre et fié et chasement*: Br. IV, v. 287).[2] To the first peer, Ptolemy, he gives Egypt and, along with it, Cleopatra as a wife; and to Philipperideus, Cleopatra's son by Alexander's father Philip, Alexander gives the land of Esclavonia, which he later gives as well to two other peers. To a second peer, called Clin, Alexander gives all of Persia. Emenidus of Arcage gets the gift of Nubia. Alexander then gives greater India to Aristé, Syria to Antiochus, Cilicia to Antigonus and Caesarea to Filote. To Licanor he gives Alenie and Esclavonia as well. His gift to Festion consists of Hungary and the kingdom of Ansor. For a third time, Alexander makes a gift of Esclavonia, this time to Leoine, who also receives Venice. Finally, he gives Carthage to Aridès and Greater Armenia to Caulus of Macedonia. Having now given *casamenta* to all twelve peers, Alexander orders the last eleven of them to become the men of the first, Ptolemy, and to receive their lands from him and become his tenants. Receiving them as his men, Ptolemy undertakes, in effect, to warrant Alexander's gifts to them by promising that they will not lose any of their lands as long as he lives;[3] the peers respond, in turn, that they will provide Ptolemy with aid. Alexander dies a little later, and in eulogizing him (Br. IV, vv. 642–1366), the peers and Aristotle praise him primarily for his generous giving and view his death as a victory for largesse over avarice (Br. IV, vv. 664–66, 749, 864–66, 1282, 1311).[4] According to Licanor, addressing his dead lord: "Your great largesse could never be equalled./ For even before you had acquired wealth by conquest,/ You had already given it away or promised to give it away./ Well were the twelve peers rewarded for their service (*servise*);/ Each had for it [i.e., their service] a crown of gold"(Br. IV, vv.1305–9).

The question of why, in a poem written in the late twelfth century A.D., a king who died in the fourth century B.C. should be represented as rewarding his men with lands that are clearly identified as "fiefs" is more difficult to answer than one might think.[5] The most obvious answer, which is implicit in the remarks of a recent commentator on Alexandre de Paris's poem, is simply that in the episode just considered, as in other parts of the poem, this poet, like the authors of other romances of antiquity, anachronistically modelled antiquity on "the realities" of twelfth-century "feudal society," where, it is assumed, feudal lords rewarded their men's services with fiefs.[6] This way of relating Alexander's imaginary gifts of "fiefs" to the so-called "realities" of twelfth-century feudal society will not, however, satisfy many recent writers on the history of feudal society and feudalism. Some of these historians now dismiss "the fief" as a postmedieval construct that medievalists should abandon (Reynolds, p. 2).[7] Others, in discussing twelfth-century feudal society, continue to employ what I refer to in this paper as the contractual model of feudalism. In this model the term "fief" does not refer, as it generally does in our poem, to land that a lord gives to someone who is already his man in return for the man's past service. Rather it is applied to land that the lord gives to someone who becomes his man, just before the man receives the fief under the terms of a feudal contract or contract of vassalage specifying the future service in return for which the man will hold the fief from his lord.[8] Whichever of these opposing positions on the fief we adopt, the argument that Alexander's gifts of fiefs were simply modeled on "feudal realities" collapses, in one case because feudal realities were radically misrepresented in the poem, and in the other because there were no feudal realities for the poem to represent or misrepresent. However, by severing, in one way or another, all connection between Alexander's imaginary gifts of fiefs and twelfth-century practice (feudal or not), each of the historical arguments about feudalism just mentioned also rules out, for one reason or another, the possibility of explaining why Alexander's gifts to the peers are represented as they are in the Vulgate *Alexandre*. Because proponents of the contractual model of feudalism have sometimes maintained that, centuries before the time when this poem was composed, Carolingian lords gave so-called benefices or fiefs to their men out of generosity and in recognition of their men's loyal services (Ganshof, pp. 11, 50), these scholars could argue that although the form of fief-giving practiced in our poem by Alexander was *not* modelled on twelfth-century realities, it was based on an accurate tradition about how fief-giving among the Franks had been practiced centuries before. This argument, however, leaves us with the problems of explaining how a largely accurate image of an archaic, Carolingian form of fief-giving had been transmitted over a period of several centuries, why the image was so often used by Alexandre de Paris (not to mention other twelfth-century writers), and, above all, what meaning this particular image of the fief as a reward for service could have had in a society where, in practice, the fief was understood in entirely different terms.

These problems begin to look soluble, however, if we start our discussion of them by rejecting two traditional assumptions of writers on feudalism: first, that only a single, contractual model of feudalism can capture the many different forms of fief-giving that were, in fact, practiced in France during the central Middle Ages, as Fredric L. Cheyette shows with particular clarity in a forthcoming study of Occitan fiefs;[9] and, second, that by 1000 if not earlier, the image of fiefs as rewards for service had lost all practical significance and lived on only in poetic representations of what were self-evidently archaic or imaginary fief-giving practices. We can then abandon, as well, the assumption underlying one part of Susan Reynolds's critique of feudalism: that because the contractual model of feudalism just mentioned is easy to deconstruct into a variety of different practices and, more specifically, because the medieval term "fief" was not consistently used as a univocal, technical legal term, fiefs and fief-giving, even when they are explicitly represented as such in both legal and literary texts, are not worth investigating as evidence about medieval legal culture.[10] Finally, we can then take account of the fact that because terms such as "fief," "casamentum," "honor," and "land" all carried multiple meanings, some of them consistent with modern historical usage and others not, fiefs and fief-giving could be—and were—represented in different and sometimes conflicting ways both in documents of the kind that Cheyette, for example, analyzes and in literary texts, including the Roman d'Alexandre, where Alexander's fief-giving, as we shall see, is contrasted with the fief-giving that bad, avaricious lords use as a kind of bribery or extortion.[11]

Because Alexander's last gifts of fiefs are *not* represented as feoffments governed by feudal contracts but *are*, in fact, depicted in terms virtually identical to the ones that historical texts had, on occasion, used to represent fief-giving for several centuries down through the time of our poem's composition,[12] we do not need to choose between treating Alexander's imaginary gifts as the products of poetic invention or arguing that they were simply modelled on the so-called "realities" of feudal practice. As represented through the use of a malleable feudal discourse that metaphorically posited a social relationship between lord and man that was mediated by land, fief-giving could itself take multiple forms, take on different meanings even when it took the same form, and be represented in multiple ways. In this chapter I explore the hypothesis that by celebrating Alexander's gifts of fiefs as examples of his largesse and by contrasting them with pejoratively constructed images of the bribe-like gifts of avaricious lords such as Darius, Alexandre de Paris's poem draws on a complex feudal discourse that had been in existence for several centuries or more.[13] By selectively using this discourse, the Roman d'Alexandre presents images of fief-giving that can help us to understand, first, what Pierre Bourdieu has called "the gift as experienced, or at least, as supposed to be experienced," and, second, the gift as it was not supposed to be experienced but must often have been experienced, particularly by the least-empowered recipients of a lord's gifts.

As we might have expected, instead of either directly reflecting the so-called "realities" of inherently ambiguous feudal practice or departing from practice totally, the poem shows, by deploying one form of feudal discourse, how fief-giving was mystified as largesse and, in Bourdieu's terms, misrecognized, as it had to be misrecognized in order for it to be put into practice and construed as honorable for both giver and recipient.[14] In a less obvious way, the poem also shows, by using an alternative form of feudal discourse, how the dishonorable use of fief-giving as a form of bribery or extortion was both acknowledged and yet explained away as the expression of the avarice of bad lords. In representing fiefs and fief-giving, the Vulgate *Alexandre* obviously did not describe ordinary legal practice realistically, any more than other Old French narrative poems did when, for example, they represented appeals of treason decided by judicial duels.[15] Instead, the text presents contrasting images of good and bad styles of gift-giving, including fief-giving, and integrates each image into a different model of lordship: a model of good, generous lordship, embodied in Alexander, and a contrasting model of bad, avaricious lordship, embodied in lords such as Darius. Nevertheless, in representing fiefs and fief-giving through the use of terms such as "fief," "*casamentum*," "inheritance," "seisin," "enfeoff," "giving," and "giving back," the poem draws on a feudal discourse in terms of which the ordinary, as well as the extraordinary, practice of fief-giving was constructed.

The finding that the late twelfth-century Vulgate *Alexandre* draws on a well-established feudal discourse to create a meaningful and unmistakably feudal landscape for Alexander's empire is particularly noteworthy not only because it is incompatible with the conventional theory that centuries earlier fiefs had ceased to be considered, for all practical purposes, as rewards for services, but also because the finding is hard to reconcile with the revisionist history of medieval French property rights that Susan Reynolds presents as a radical alternative to the conventional story of how twelfth- and thirteenth-century feudal tenure gradually developed out of feudal practices dating back to the period before 1100. Emphasizing the differences between twelfth- and thirteenth-century land law, Reynolds first argues that "the properties of French nobles [were not] called fiefs before the thirteenth century, except in contexts where the word had a quite different meaning" from the one it acquired after 1200 (p. 274). Proposing a new way of explaining when and how an idea of feudal tenure took shape before 1200, she argues that, to the extent that feudal tenure existed at all in twelfth-century France, it was, in that period, only in the process of being imposed by rulers and lawyers on nobles, whose property rights before 1100 had been so full and so free of any superior claims that they must have been closer to those of the modern freeholder than to those of feudal tenants in the contractual model of feudalism (p. 73). Even after 1100, she implies, feudal tenure and thus feudal discourse must both have been seen by nobles as devices by which their rights in land were restricted by rulers.

Although the arguments that Reynolds uses to support this hypothesis have the virtue of revealing fatal flaws in the contractual model, the hypothesis takes no account of significant continuity in the history of feudal discourse over the course of the eleventh and twelfth centuries. Because her argument does not consider how fief-giving is represented as a form of patronage in twelfth-century texts, including Old French poems such as the Vulgate *Alexandre*, where the fief can hardly be dismissed as "a postmedieval construct" and needs to be explained as a medieval concept with a history that began well before 1100, Reynolds is in no position to compare twelfth-century feudal discourse with earlier forms of feudal discourse. A preliminary comparison of this kind suggests that however much Alexander's imaginary gifts of fiefs may differ from the feoffments of later French law, the fiefs he gives are still depicted in most instances as rewards for service and, as such, are virtually identical to fiefs mentioned not only in twelfth-century *chansons de geste,* such as *Raoul de Cambrai* and *Le charroi de Nîmes,* and in twelfth-century historical writing, but also in texts as old as the early eleventh-century Conventum of Hugh of Lusignan and the almost contemporaneous letter of Fulbert of Chartres on fidelity.[16] If so, then a form of feudal discourse that shows fiefs being exchanged for service should not be interpreted, as Reynolds proposes to do, as something that twelfth-century rulers and their agents created and imposed so as to restrict the property rights of nobles who, before 1100, had understood those rights in terms of an entirely different discourse.

Freely drawing on feudal discourse, *Le roman d'Alexandre* represents Alexander's gifts to the twelve peers as gifts of fiefs partly by emphasizing certain formalities that the king observes in making them. In several cases the poem shows him making his gift by means of the traditional gesture of giving his gage (Br. IV, vv. 306, 365, 503) to a kneeling donee (Br. IV, vv. 365, 410, 481, 503). The witnessing of several gifts is specifically noted as well. With the Macedonians watching, Alexander "enfeoffs" (*fievé*) Caulus with Greater Macedonia (Br. IV, v. 515). As Filote kneels by the foot of the bed on which the king reclines, Alexander, again with the Macedonians watching, invests (*revest*) him with Caesarea (Br. IV, v. 410–11). The king himself repeatedly represents his gifts as parts of honorable exchanges of land for service (Br. IV, vv. 394, 399–400, 418–20, 475, 507–8) and is praised, after his death, for having honored his men with gifts (Br. IV, vv. 706–7, 785, 807–8, 1421). After giving Cilicia to Antigonus, the king undertakes to give him other lands "because you have been of such great good service (*service*) to me" (Br. IV, v. 393). He gives land to Filote "because you have served (*servi*) me so very well" (Br. IV, v. 409).

His gifts are routinely identified as rewards (*merite*) (Br. IV, vv. 295–97) or countergifts (*guerredons*) (Br. IV, vv. 420–21, 456). Alexander tells Licanor that "you have served me so well . . . that in my lifetime you shall have a countergift (*guerredon*) for [doing so]" (Br. IV, vv. 420–21). He says that because of what Festion has done for him, he owes him a countergift (*guerredon*) and will give him land (Br. IV, vv. 456–57). After announcing that "the day for Caulus to be rewarded (*guerredonê*)" has come (Br. IV, v. 509; see also 327–29) and then giving him Macedonia, Alexander tells him: "You have always served (*servi*) me with good will and I, I believe, have given you a very rich gift" (Br. IV, vv. 512–13). Addressing all twelve peers, Alexander says: "You have always done more than I have asked of you; I wish to recompense (*guerredoner*) all of you for your services (*services*)" (Br. IV, vv. 472–73). Confirming what the poem has already shown about the peers' participation in Alexander's army, the king explicitly identifies as military the services in return for which he makes his gifts to them (Br. IV, vv. 473, 509). Explaining his gift to Antigonus, Alexander says that he was "the noblest *chevalier*" and had "always served him well" (Br. IV, vv. 393–94); Licanor, he says, was known for his "*chevalerie*" and had used his sword to do good service, for which a great fief would be his reward (Br. IV, vv. 418–23). The rich fief given Caulus is a reward for fighting alongside his lord (Br. V, vv. 507–9).

While sometimes emphasizing the intangible dimensions of fiefs by representing them as "honors," the poem draws attention to the practical legal significance of Alexander's gifts of fiefs by showing that he "invests" (Br. IV, v. 411), "enfeoffs" (Br. IV, v. 515), and "seises" (Br. IV, v. 516) his men with land and "houses" them by giving them *casamenta* (Br. IV, vv. 321, 516, 517). The poem also shows that the land Alexander gives is "quit" of obligations and counterclaims (Br. IV, vv. 306, 326, 409, 511), is supposed to be held "without dispute" (*sans tençon*) (Br. IV, v. 326), and should pass as an "inheritance" (*hiretage*) to the donee's heirs (Br. IV, vv. 364, 498, 510). Several of Alexander's gifts, moreover, explicitly convey power over his fief's leading inhabitants, including kings, dukes, castellans, and knights, who are to do homage to the donee, fight under his banner, acknowledge his lordship, and show him honor (Br. IV, vv. 322–26, 359–60, 428–30, 457–58). By giving land to a peer, Alexander makes him a lord whose men's relationships to him are closely analogous to the peer's own relationship with Alexander. By making gifts of this kind to all twelve peers, Alexander provides them with fiefs, which could also be represented as honors, *casamenta*, or, simply, lands.

The feudal discourse used in representing Alexander's last gifts also appears in earlier episodes. Having promised to make a gift to Aristé with his glove (Br. III, v. 4118), Alexander later uses his glove to invest him with land taken from Porus (Br. III, vv. 4074–78, 4117–18). Darius contends that Alexander's father Philip should serve him because he holds land from him and is his liegeman (Br. I, vv. 1896–97). After Samson, disinherited by Darius, becomes Alexander's liegeman and undertakes to serve him, Alexander, on the understanding that he can conquer Samson's lost inheritance, renders the inheritance to Samson and undertakes to give him land of his own if Samson serves him; Samson then becomes Alexander's man (Br. I, vv. 724–51). Alexander expands Antiochus's "fief" with "the honor of Bagdad" (Br. IV, v. 1205). Antipater, the lord of Sidon, is condemned for giving Alexander poor "service" for his "land" (Br. III, vv. 7730–32) and for betraying a lord who had given him "rich fiefs" (Br. IV, v. 1049). Alexander's takeover of the Amazon kingdom provides a more extended illustration of how the poem constructs a feudal landscape. The queen offers to place her kingdom in Alexander's charge, hold it from him, and provide him with ten thousand female soldiers in time of war. Accepting the offer, Alexander says that when the queen has done him homage, he will, with his barons' consent, give her fief and inheritance back to her (Br. III, vv. 7669–72). Kneeling before Alexander, the queen does homage to him and reiterates her promise to aid him. Although angered by the news that Alexander has arranged marriages between two of his men and two of her women, she does not contest her new lord's claim to exercise this kind of power in her fief (Br. III, vv. 7678–84). In representing a so-called *fief de reprise*,[17] rather than a fief given as a reward for service, this episode shows how Alexander's fief-giving practices could take different forms.

Although Alexandre de Paris's poem often represents Alexander's gifts of land as gifts of fiefs, most of these feoffments differ significantly from ones that appear in the contractual model of feudalism.[18] Whereas in this model the lord gives his man a fief in return for future services, while the man does homage to the lord and swears fealty to him at the time of the gift, Alexander usually gives fiefs in return for *past* services, not *future* ones, to men, who, at the time of the gift, do *not* do homage or swear fealty to him, though they have presumably done both previously. Instead of initiating exchanges of land for future service, as feoffments do in the contractual model, Alexander's gifts of fiefs are literally "countergifts" (*guerredons*), which he uses to reciprocate gifts of service previously made to him. Because Alexander's gifts of fiefs extend preexisting relationships, rather than inaugurate new ones, and because they are rewards for services that his donees have already performed, the fiefs he gives to them cannot possibly serve the instrumental, economic function of providing them with what F. L. Ganshof once called "the means of furnishing [a] lord with the [future] services required by the contract of vassalage" (p. 106). Instead of constituting what Marc Bloch saw as the vassal's "pay," the fiefs that Alexander gives to his men are both rewards for their honorable services and tokens of their honor.[19]

In *Le roman d'Alexandre* fief-giving is also represented as a form of largesse, which the poem treats as an essential attribute of a good lord. As practiced by Alexander, fief-giving, like other forms of gift-giving, manifests the generosity of a lord whose ability to honor his men by rewarding them with fiefs and other forms of wealth depends on his ability to acquire land and movable wealth, with their aid, through conquest. As practiced by Darius and by other avaricious lords with whom Alexander is repeatedly contrasted, fief-giving, along with other forms of gift-giving, is a kind of bribery, which bad lords, who are, almost by definition, unable to conquer new lands or defend their own territories, use to buy services from their lowborn, ill-chosen underlings or to extort them from nobles. Each of these two contrasting images of fief-giving is thus integrated into a different model of lordship. In each model, the same kinds of people—the lord, his magnates, his knights, and his serfs—and the same forms of wealth—land and movable prestige-wealth—are associated through the mediation of two contrasting processes, namely giving and taking.[20] On the one hand, because the good lord is generous, he can secure the support of both magnates and knights for the purpose of conquering and plundering the territories of his enemies, whose wealth he can then use to honor and reward his men, thereby preparing the way for further conquests and more gift-giving. On the other hand, because the bad lord displays his avaricious nature by hiding his wealth from his nobles, keeping his poor knights poor, and making gifts only for the purpose of extracting specific services from bribable underlings, he cannot retain the loyalty of his men, conquer new territory, or defend his own land. The bad lord acquires additional wealth only by taxing, oppressing, and disinheriting his own nobles.

Because, in *Le roman d'Alexandre*, the interdependency of generosity and conquest is openly acknowledged, Alexander appears in a favorable light when he proposes to conquer territory so that he can make gifts to Samson, to Ptolemy, to the other peers, and to his poorest knights. He is also praised for giving the peers what he had taken from Saracens (Br. IV, vv. 668–70), for killing Nicolas and giving his own men Nicolas's land (Br. IV, vv. 831–43), for freely giving away what he had conquered (Br. III, vv. 2234–35), and for being such a great conqueror that he can make his men possessors of other people's wealth (Br. I, vv. 2103–4). Had he lived, his mourners say, he would have conquered the whole world and given away all its wealth (Br. IV, vv. 910–11). In an anecdote about Alexander told by the thirteenth-century writer Philippe de Navarre, the interdepency of largesse and conquest is explained more clearly when Alexander says: "I desire to conquer everything and to give everything away so generously that I shall retain nothing except the lordship and the honor; and I wish to be avaricious only in keeping for myself honor, the love of my people, and the love of all those who serve me. And for the sake of this, I will possess the lordship of the world; and whatever I can conquer and possess I shall give *to those through whom I conquered it*."[21]

By specifying in this way the proper beneficiaries of Alexander's gifts, this speech brings out more explicitly than does Alexandre de Paris's poem that instead of practising indiscriminate, disinterested, or charitable generosity, Alexander uses a distinctive form of largesse: he gives and gives generously mainly to the nobles who serve him in war, and rarely if ever gives much to anyone else. Indeed, as *Le roman d'Alexandre* clearly reveals, anyone who is not a beneficiary of his largesse is likely to be a victim of his plundering. Not only does he exclude serfs from his presence (Br. I, vv. 226–27, 232); with his father's permission, he also divests them, as well as usurers and felons, of their property so that he can give land to poor bachelors (Br. I, vv. 648–57). Whereas Darius gives honors and even noble wives to lowborn men (Br. III, 175), Alexander follows the advice of Aristotle, who tells him that there is nothing worse than a rich serf, that a serf will never be good unless he is punished, and that every three or four years, Alexander should simply seize the serf's hoarded wealth (Br. III, vv. 49–50).[22]

Within his own social class, by contrast, Alexander practices largesse that is free, spontaneous, uncalculated, openhanded, and seemingly disinterested. Since Alexander freely, publicly, and joyously gives fiefs, as well as other prestigious gifts, to reward his men, and since his men freely and joyously love, honor, and loyally serve Alexander, there seems to be a connection between, on the one hand, each individual gift of a fief that Alexander makes to a man and, on the other, the services that the man performs for Alexander. But that connection is repressed or euphemized as much as possible.[23] Because Alexander both promises and gives his men many gifts of many different kinds,[24] individual gifts of fiefs easily get lost in the never-ending flow of lordly largesse. Instead of hiding his wealth, as avaricious lords do, Alexander distributes it freely (Br. I, vv. 205–16), giving away as much land as he has (Br. I, vv. 514–21) and promising to give away more when he conquers it (Br. I, vv. 646–47). Whereas avaricious lords never give until they know exactly what they will receive in return for their gifts (Br. I, vv. 95–100), Alexander keeps no clerk with him to record his gifts and calculate their value (Br. I, vv. 514–21); nor do his men calculate the extent of their services to him (Br. III, vv. 2687, 4703), and they receive rewards (*guerredons*) greater than the services they have performed (BR. IV, v. 1392).

In these ways, the economic role of the fief, the practical value of the man's services, the exchange value of the fief, and the role of fief-giving as an instrument for extracting service are all concealed as much as possible. Since fief-giving, as Alexander practices it, is a form of largesse that honors both donor and donee, the question of what, precisely, is exchanged for what when he gives away a fief remains open. In fact, the question is never even raised in the poem, except in cases where an avaricious lord such as Darius disinherits his man[25] or where a treasonous man fails to serve his lord.[26] Although it is clearly understood that each of Alexander's men will continue to serve him after receiving a gift from him, that gift, to the extent that it is associated with the man's service at all, is represented as a reward for past service, not as pay for future service, which, it is further understood, the man performs in the expectation of gifts of fiefs. In short, the lord's gift of a fief in return for service is not openly acknowledged for what, in one sense, it is, namely an essential part of the ongoing process of maintaining a lord's following.[27] If we can assume on the basis of other evidence that it is shameful for a lord to buy his man's services and shameful for his man to sell them, then the closer the parties come to calculating and acknowledging a precise, quantifiable connection between gift and service and a clear relationship between the value of each, the less honorable and noble the gift of a fief will be. If largesse is to serve its multiple purposes, the lord and the man, to adapt Bourdieu's formulation, "must not be entirely unaware of the truth of their exchanges . . . , while at the same time they must refuse to know and above all to recognize it" (Bourdieu, p. 6).

The truth of exchanges of fiefs for services between a lord and his men includes several troubling possibilities that do not arise in Alexander's realm but become realities in the territory of any lord who does not expand his domains. First, when the lord does not have enough land to reward all his followers, he may find it necessary to reward some of them at the expense of others.[28] Second, the lord's need to use land to reward some of his men will conflict with the claims of other men to hold their lands heritably. Third, because every lord must sooner or later secure from his gifts a return that his men will not necessarily offer spontaneously, he must sooner or later extort services from some of them, thereby turning his previous gifts to them into what some will now see as bribes. In *Le roman d'Alexandre* these contradictions and conflicts, when they are acknowledged at all, are simply blamed on the avarice of bad lords such as Darius, whose style of giving is sharply contrasted with Alexander's. Instead of scrupulously rewarding the past services of loyal *fidèles*, saving poor knights from poverty, and giving generously for the sake of giving, the avaricious lord, as Alexander explains to Porus, oppresses his nobles with inquests and taxes (Br. IV, vv. 2206–95). Instead of gaining the political support from nobles that he needs to conquer new territory and defend the territory he already has, Darius, for example, gives "honors" and noblewomen to lowborn men, who oppress his serfs, burghers, and poor knights and shame the nobles so that eventually the king has no one to support him (Br. III, vv. 172–81). Refusing to support a "bad lord" (*malvais segnor*), the nobles leave the task of defending Darius to the serfs whom he has enriched (Br. III, v. 188). They would be fools, they say, to remain with a lord who has disinherited and abased them in order to raise their inferiors above them (Br. III, vv. 240–43). Instead of showing love to the wellborn, Darius raises his serfs (*culverts*) above his nobles (Br. III, vv. 255–56).

What distinguishes an avaricious lord such as Darius from a generous lord is not that he gives away nothing at all, but rather that he makes gifts of the wrong kind in the wrong way to the wrong people and thus establishes, through giving, the wrong kinds of relationships with donees. Instead of giving spontaneously, joyously, and without calculation, he gives only when he must do so in order to achieve his own ends. His gifts look like payments or bribes, rather than gifts; the relations they establish are, in F.G. Bailey's terms, purely "transactional," not "moral," in that they entail only balanced exchanges of finite wealth for specific services, which must be immediately rendered in full.[29] Whereas the generous lord has no clerks to write down his gifts and calculate their value, the avaricious lord needs such people because, for him, gift giving involves calculation, which, in turn, involves computing and comparing the respective values of his own gifts and of the returns he expects from them. He never makes even the smallest gift unless he knows what kind of countergift he will get in return (Br. I, vv. 98–100). When Darius summons Porus to help him against Alexander, he offers to pay him and his men and promises to give him Alexander's armor and horse; when he summons his own men to help him defend himself against Alexander, he cannot count on their support and therefore threatens those who do not answer the summons with dire punishments (Br. III, vv. 202–10, 166–68). In both cases Darius is represented unfavorably for trying to buy or extort service that a generous lord's men would provide eagerly and spontaneously. On other occasions he tries to secure service or tribute improperly by claiming, in effect, that he has already paid for it with the gift of a fief. By demanding services and/or tribute from Philip and Alexander on the grounds that they hold land from him, he is, in effect, claiming that because he has given them lands, they are now in his debt (Br. I, vv. 1895–1904, 2084–2188).

Bad as avaricious lords are made out to be in the *Roman d'Alexandre*, the forms of fief-giving that they practice can be seen, not only as indicators of bad lordship, but also as commonplace, quasi-legitimate patronage strategies that in historical practice, lords of finite territories ordinarily used and had to use to maintain authority over nobles with virtually infinite appetites for honor. As Marc Bloch saw, the bad lord of twelfth-century Old French literature is just a caricature of ordinary lords in real life. "The good master," Bloch observed, "is he who keeps in mind the maxim which one of the *chansons* numbers among Charlemagne's lessons to his successor: 'Take care not to deprive the orphan child of his fief.' But how many lords were—or had to be—good masters?" (p. 196). Leaving aside Alexander, how many lords could afford to be good lords all the time? In lordships that did not continuously expand, as Alexander's kingdom did, practices that are stigmatized as marks of bad lordship—promising fiefs without giving them, giving fiefs without warranting them, disinheriting minors, marrying heiresses and widows to underlings, patronizing lowborn men, and buying political support with gifts and promises of gifts— could also be seen by the bad lord's friends as legitimate methods of conserving or distributing resources that he needed to honor his friends at the expense of their enemies.[30] From an outside-observer's perspective, the same practices look like necessary elements of a patronage system in distributing honor in a

lordship where honor is a limited good and where, given the intense competition for honor among a lord's men, the lord, in the absence of opportunities
for conquering new territory, could maintain his own power only by disseis-
ing, disinheriting, and dishonoring some of his men and giving their honors
to others. Other forms of bad fief-giving, notably rewarding lowborn people,
can be seen as securing necessary political support or, even more favorably, as
rewarding mere knights, whose poverty gave them claims on a lord's largesse.

By starkly contrasting the generous lord, who scrupulously avoids such
practices, with the avaricious lord, who uses them constantly, the *Roman
d'Alexandre* misrepresents and conceals as much as possible the various forms
of fief-giving and fief-taking that lords routinely used and had to use merely
to maintain honor. In the same way, by contrasting the well-rewarded nobles
and knights of the generous Alexander with the oppressed, disinherited nobles
of the avaricious Darius and with the same king's servile, bribable underlings,
the poem radically simplifies the political experiences of men patronized by
lords. The execution of this ideological strategy involved the deployment of
two contrasting images of fief-giving, one associated with generous lords such
as Alexander and the other with avaricious lords such as Darius. In one image
the fief looked like an honorable reward for honorable service; in the other
the fief looked like a bribe.[31] By simplifying and moralizing the politics of fief-
giving, *Le roman d'Alexandre* reproduced and mystified but failed to resolve a
fundamental underlying ambiguity in fief-giving, which could never, of course,
be distinguished clearly and conclusively from bribery.

Notes

1. In the text and notes, references in parentheses are to branch and verse
numbers in *RA*; translations mine.

2. On the term *"casamentum"* as a rough equivalent of the term "fief," see *Mediae
Latinitatis Lexicon Minus*, ed. J. F. Niermeyer (Leiden: Brill, 1976), s.v. For doubts about
whether the term had any consistent meaning, see Susan Reynolds, *Fiefs and Vassals: The
Medieval Evidence Reconsidered* (Oxford: Clarendon, 1994), pp. 119–20.

3. On warranty see Paul R. Hyams, "Warranty and Good Lordship in Twelfth-
Century England," *Law and History Review* 5 (1987), 437–503. On warranty in a *chanson
de geste*, see Stephen D. White, "The Language of Inheritance in *Raoul de Cambrai*:
Alternative Models of Fief-holding," in *Law and Government in the Middle Ages: Essays
in Honour of Sir James Holt*, ed. George Garnett and John Hudson (Cambridge: Cambridge University Press, 1994), 173–97 (here 181–82).

4. For praise of largesse, which is often accompanied by explicit condemnations
of avarice or covetousness, see, e.g., *Lancelot do Lac: The Non-cyclic Old French Prose
Romance*, ed. Elspeth Kennedy (Oxford: Oxford University Press, 1980), vol. 1, pp. 288,
l.19 to p. 289, l.12, which also appears in *Lancelot: roman en prose du XIIIe siècle*, ed.

Alexandre Micha, 9 vols. (Geneva: Droz, 1978–82) vol. 8, XLIXa.28–30 (pp. 21–23); *L'Histoire de Guillaume le Marechal*, ed. Paul Meyer, 3 vols. (Paris, 1891–1901), ll. 2679–712, 4297–319; Raoul de Houdenc, *Le roman des eles*, in *Le roman des eles, by Raoul de Houdenc and The Anonymous Ordene de la chevalerie*, ed. Keith Busby (Amsterdam: Utrecht Publications in General and Comparative Literature 17, 1983), ll. 150–266; Richard W. Kaeuper and Elspeth Kennedy, *The Book of Chivalry of Geoffrey de Charny: Text, Context, and Translation* (Philadelphia: University of Pennsylvania Press, 1996), p. 143. In "The Politics of Gift-exchange. Or, Feudalism Revisited," in *Medieval Transformations*, ed. Esther Cohen and Mayke de Jong (Leiden: Brill, forthcoming), I compare the passage from the Prose *Lancelot* with a discussion of William Rufus's prodigality in William of Malmesbury, *De Gestis Regum Anglorum Libri Quinque*, ed. William Stubbs, 2 vols., Rolls Series no. 90, vol. 2 (London, 1887–89), cc. 313–16 (pp. 226–27). On William Rufus's practice of taking from the English so that he could give to knights and strangers, see *The Ecclesiastical History of Orderic Vitalis*, ed. and trans. Marjorie Chibnall, 6 vols. (Oxford: Clarendon Press, 1969–80), vol. 5, book 10, chap. 2 (pp. 200–3); on William the Conqueror's lack of generosity, see Orderic, *Ecclesiastical History*, vol. 2, Book 4 (pp. 312–15).

5. In the Pseudo-Callisthenes' account of Alexander's last moments, Alexander gives no fiefs and, instead, appoints rulers of territories in his empire and bequeaths land to various people. See *The Greek Alexander Romance*, trans. Richard Stoneman (Harmondsworth, Middlesex: Penguin, 1991), pp. 152–55.

6. *RA*, pp. 5–58 (here p. 41).

7. For comments on Reynolds' critique of feudalism see Dominique Barthélemy, "La théorie féodale à l'épreuve de l'anthropologie (note critique)," *Annales HSS*, mars–avril 1997, no. 2, 321–41. See also reviews by Fredric L. Cheyette in *Speculum* 71 (1996), 998–1005; Paul R. Hyams in *Journal of Interdisciplinary History* 27(1997), 655–62; Stephen D. White in *Law and History Review* 15 (1997), 349–55.

8. For the model see F.L. Ganshof, *Feudalism*, trans. Philip Grierson, 3rd ed. (New York: Harper, 1964) and, for a more recent statement, Paul Ourliac and Jean-Louis Gazzaniga, *Histoire du droit privé français de l'An mil au Code civil* (Paris: Albin Michel, 1985), pp. 220–22. For a critique of the model, see Stephen D. White, "Service for Fiefs or Fiefs for Service: The Politics of Reciprocity," in *Négocier le don*, ed. Gadi Algazi et al. (forthcoming). For recent works that invoke the contractual model, see, e.g., Constance Brittain Bouchard, '*Strong of Body, Brave and Noble': Chivalry and Society in Medieval France* (Ithaca: Cornell University Press, 1998), pp. 35–46; and Catherine Vincent, *Introduction à l'histoire de l'occident médiéval* (Paris: Livre de Poche, 1995), pp. 65–66.

9. Fredric L. Cheyette, *Ermengard of Narbonne and the World of the Troubadours* (Ithaca: Cornell University Press, 2001), chapters 10-13.

10. Reynolds insists that "we cannot understand medieval society and its property relations if we see it through [postmedieval] spectacles. Yet every time we think of fiefs and vassals we do just that" (*Fiefs and Vassals*, p. 3). Reynolds has much more to say about how we are not to think of medieval fiefs than about how we should think of them.

11. On alternative models of the fief and fief-giving, see White, "Discourse of Inheritance"; idem, "La politique de la fidélité: Hugues de Lusignan et Guillaume d'Aquitaine," in *Georges Duby: L'Ecriture de l'histoire*, ed. Claudie Duhamel-Amado and Guy Lobrichon (Brussels: De Boeck, 1996), pp. 223–30; and Barthélemy, "La théorie féodale."

12. On fiefs as rewards for service see White, "La politique de la fidélité"; idem, "Stratégie rhétorique dans la *Conventio* de Hugues de Lusignan," in *Mélanges offerts à Georges Duby*, 4 vols. (Publications de l'Université de Provence: Aix-en-Provence, 1993), vol. 2, *Le tenancier, le fidèle et le citoyen*, pp. 147–57.

13. On feudal discourse see White, "Discourse of Inheritance"; "La politique de la fidélité"; and "Stratégie rhétorique." The "discourse of fiefs" is discussed from a different perspective in Jean-Pierre Poly, "La crise, la paysannerie libre et la féodalité," in Eric Bournazel and Jean-Pierre Poly, eds., *Les féodalités* (Paris: Presses Universitaires de France, 1998) at, e.g., p. 112.

14. On misrecognition and gifts see Pierre Bourdieu, *Outline of a Theory of Practice*, trans. Richard Nice (Cambridge: Cambridge University Press, 1977), p. 6.

15. The notion that judicial procedures were represented realistically in romances is contested in Stephen D. White, "Imaginary Justice: The End of the Ordeal and the Survival of the Duel," *Medieval Perspectives* 13 (1998), 32–55; and "Liars, Bunglers, and Lawyers in Old French Literature: Lying, Mispleading, and Legal Artifice in Imaginary Treason Trials," in *Medieval History in the Comic Mode*, ed. Laura Blanchard (forthcoming).

16. See my articles cited above in nn. 3, 8, and 11.

17. On this kind of fief, see Ganshof, *Feudalism*, pp. 121–23; Reynolds, *Fiefs and Vassals*, esp. 260–63.

18. Alexander's gifts usually differ as well from the feoffments that form one element of the "ritual of vassalage," as analyzed by Jacques Le Goff in "The Symbolic Ritual of Vassalage," in idem, *Time, Work, and Culture in the Middle Ages*, trans. Arthur Goldhammer (Chicago: University of Chicago Press, 1980), 237–87 (here p. 249).

19. Marc Bloch, *Feudal Society*, trans. L.A. Manyon (Chicago: University of Chicago Press, 1961), p. 175: "the grant of a fief was the pay of a commended individual." What was expressed in terms such as fief, according to Bloch, was "basically an economic concept. By fief was meant a property granted . . . against an obligation to do something" (p. 167).

20. One list of the things Alexander gives away includes not only duchies and kingdoms, but also birds, dogs, cloaks with fur collars, silver goblets, gold cups, horses that are strong and beautiful, and mules with fine harnesses.

21. *Les Quatre âges de l'homme: Traité moral de Philippe de Navarre*, ed. Marcel de Fréville (Paris: Firmin Didot, 1888), c. 70 (p. 41). Translation my own. My emphasis.

22. For Aristotle's entire speech see Br. III, vv. 16–87. For Darius's fall, which is blamed largely on his disposition to give to serfs, see Br. III, vv. 163–347.

23. The men to whom Alexander gives fiefs rarely do him homage on swear fealty to him. The same goes for enfeoffed men in other stories. For a rare example, see Jehan Bodel, *La chanson des Saisnes*, ed. Annette Brasseur (Geneva: Droz, 1989), vol. 1, vv. 1149–61, which Ganshof cited from an earlier edition in *Feudalism*, pp. 125–26.

24. References to gifts in *Le roman d'Alexandre* include: Br. I, vv. 157–65, 703–43, 1057–59, 1078, 1084, 1452–53, 1475–76, 1633–93, 1858, 2280, 2295, 2507–14, 2631–58, 2670–71; Br. III, vv. 899, 4118, 4132, 5988–98, 7634–45; Br. IV vv. 121, 141–42, 942, 1047–49, 1139, 1164, 1204–11, 1216, 1389, 4074, 4078, 4112–14, 4385.

25. See Br. III, vv. 240–43. The question is also raised in *Raoul de Cambrai* (see White, "Discourse of Inheritance") and in *Le charroi de Nîmes* (see White, "Stratégie rhétorique").

26. As in the case of Antipater (Br. III, vv. 7730–32).

27. If the gift of a fief is to honor both lord and man, it must be misrecognized or euphemized as a love token of the kind that Philippe de Navarre mentions in a story about a king of Jerusalem and a rich man of his. Refusing a gift that the king gave him, the rich man said, "Lord, you give me too much, give to others." The king replied to him, "Take my gift, because it seems to me that from a new gift there comes new love or new remembrance of love" (*Les Quatre âges de l'homme*, c. 71 [p. 41]).

28. In fact, the mere expectation that some will be rewarded at the expense of others intensifies envy and competition among the lord's men.

29. F. G. Bailey, *Stratagems and Spoils: A Social Anthropology of Politics* (Oxford: Blackwell, 1969), p. 48.

30. See White, "Discourse of Inheritance."

31. See Bourdieu, *Outline*, pp. 190–97.

9

Take the World by Prose:
Modes of Possession in the *Roman d'Alexandre*

Michelle R. Warren

The late twentieth century has taken shape as an era of transnational consolidation coupled with ethnic fragmentation. In this politically and economically contentious world, literary criticism turns frequently to representations of coercive contact—between ethnic groups, nations, economies, genders, etc.—and a growing body of research is grappling with the theoretical and practical repercussions of such contact. While much of this research concerns the modern period of colonial expansion, the origins of nationalism, and the fractious dynamics of postcolonial and transnational societies, a portion is increasingly being generated from medieval studies. As medievalists (mostly in the United States) have sought their place in this new critical terrain, they have both theorized and demonstrated the portability of post(-)colonial paradigms while rigorously maintaining their historicism.[1] In light of these studies, the story of Alexander the Great clearly deserves a prominent place among historical representations of imperial desire and colonial ambition.

Within the Alexandrian corpus, the thirteenth-century French prose *Roman d'Alexandre* (edited in *Prosa*) extends the story's colonizing mode furthest. Translated from the tenth-century Latin prose *Historia de Preliis*, this version turns aside from the chivalric and courtly themes that dominate twelfth-century verse narratives as well as later narratives in both verse and prose.[2] Whereas Alexandre de Paris, for example, blames Alexander's death on his unwise promotion of non-noble followers, the prose redactor never mentions the dangers of social mobility and attributes the animosity of Alexander's assassins to political resistance. Likewise, whereas the dangers of Alexander's own *démesure* dominate verse narratives,[3] the prose redactor turns outrageous intentions (e.g., Alexander's taming of the horse Bucephalus) into casual accidents. Formal differences between twelfth-century verse and thirteenth-century prose, then, coincide with a shift in the representation of sociopolitical values: as the

prose *Alexandre* narrates the geographic, genealogical, and ethnographic domains of Alexander's conquests, it manifests an expansionist ideology devoid of
courtly concerns. I will argue that these representations of imperial desire are
in fact uniquely at home in the realm of prose.

My approach to Alexander's imperialism has been shaped by contemporary studies of colonial and post(-)colonial representations.[4] The methods and
theories of postcolonial studies are multiple, and not always mutually compatible at all levels. Nonetheless, most studies attend to relations of unequal power
and the coercive dynamics that sustain them.[5] Postcolonial analysis often
problematizes the relations among central and peripheral positions (political,
geographical, philosophical, etc.), and thus foregrounds the dynamics of edges—
the literal and figural boundaries between spaces, peoples, languages, times, and
ideas. By focusing on the limits of difference and resemblance, postcolonial
studies situate paradox, ambivalence, and irony in relation to cultural representations. The shifting boundaries of resemblance—and their narrative traces—
reveal shifting patterns of domination. Lines of difference are policed by force,
as colonial powers violently reshape the boundaries between what belongs to
the empire and what does not—in terms of territory, human populations, and
knowledge itself. Expansionism, in other words, forcefully reconfigures the
relationships between what belongs together (through resemblance) and what
does not (through difference).[6]

Alexander's story is fundamentally an imperial one, structured by the
progress of territorial conquest. As he moves across foreign landscapes, he
repeatedly encounters civilizations and hybrid beings who destabilize the difference between the familiar and the foreign. In the prose *Alexandre*, he often
reacts violently when confronted with hints of resemblance; at other times, he
lets differences remain curious anomalies. In both cases, his encounters with
indigenous peoples stabilize difference, offering the reader intractable images
of successful imperial hegemony. The redactor in fact frequently modifies the
Latin source in order to underscore Alexander's absolute difference and his
rejection of resemblance. In the end, Alexander attempts to stave off the
proliferation of likenesses by installing replicas of his own imperial body in the
civic centers of his empire.

Alexander is thus portrayed as the confident possessor of lands and
peoples, only faintly shadowed by destructive semblance. The narrator's complicity in this portrait militates against the ambivalence that often accompanies
post-colonial representation. The prose *Alexandre* ultimately exposes the pro-
ductivity of rejecting difference as well as the sterility of near-resemblance, in
a dual vision that maintains focus on the incomparable feats of Alexander
himself—a model to be admired but not imitated.[7] This failure of semblance
is ideologically flexible, capable of engaging the imagination of a range of
readers, from the royalist to the rebellious. Empire, then, is available to the

imagination of prose-literate readers, even while it may remain unavailable to them in the political sphere. Marvelously, the prose *Alexandre* purveys this dualistic vision of empire with an utter lack of ambivalence, coolly calculating the mechanisms of imperial fantasy.

Territory furnishes the material level of expansionism, and the prose *Alexandre* allies historiography with righteous possession from the beginning. The narrative opens by recounting the history of Macedonia before Alexander: "La terre de Macedone fu premierement apellee Emache" (The land of Macedonia was first called Emache).[8] *Terre* occupies iconically the first position of the first sentence, the immovable site that sustains a continuous genealogy of noble possession (Emache was the first king to raise the reputation of knights). The territorial pedagogy that begins here in the prologue continues throughout the narrative, as the narrator collaborates with Alexander's imperialist project by systematically teaching the contours of his possessions. As Alexander conquers lands beyond Macedonia, the narrator simultaneously hands historical knowledge to the reader by identifying the names of places and peoples; as he crosses into India, the narrator reports only his arrivals and departures, thereby taking possession of space (for both Alexander and the reader) through an intensive colonial pedagogy of naming and narration.

Meanwhile, Alexander himself acquires land through battle and the almost magical force of his own penetrating gaze. Well advanced on this imperial itinerary, for example, he takes possession of the land and people ("prist la gent") beyond Hercules's Frontier. He displaces potential resemblance with Hercules with a new difference: he has gone further. The very fact that people live beyond the Frontier testifies to Hercules's incomplete dominion. After extensive travels on the far side of the Frontier, Alexander encounters Hercules's Columns, which mark the edge of the physical land. Beyond these limits of land and empire (now joined as one by Alexander's new conquests), the differences that structure imperial progress dissolve: the sea seems to join sky ("la mer Oceane qui joint au ciel par samblant"). The dissolution seems all the more pervasive when Alexander spies an island *beyond* the shore where he *sees* people speaking Greek. Here, at the end of difference, Alexander encounters his own people. Yet he cannot actually reach them: the men who try to cross to the island are eaten by large fish (pp. 225–26). In the aquatic border, lethal fish impede the encounter with sameness, with the self. Alexander's situation suggests that the desire for new origins drives expansion, yet precludes the return to origins. The conqueror cannot touch the ultimate object of desire, only deploy an imperial gaze that imagines possession. In this moment, then, the narrator offers dominion to all who can read through Alexander's eyes, and see themselves reflected from beyond the end of the world.

The possessive power of the imperial gaze becomes explicit as Alexander returns from the edge and makes his way back to Babylon. Along the way, he conceives the idea of a flight into the sky when he climbs a tall mountain that "seems" to join the sky. By looking down on the land, Alexander aims to possess it in a single, encompassing gaze.[9] Although he could not cross the water that joined the sky, he now flies there, losing physical contact with the land. Alexander goes so high "qu'il li sambloit que toute la terre fust aussi come unes aires en coi l'en met les blés, et la mers li sambloit aussi [tortue] com une colevre environ la terre" (that it seemed to him that all the land was like a container in which one puts wheat, and the sea seemed to him twisted like a serpent around the land, p. 230). The image of the planet as *aires* (field, container, or threshing floor[10]) reduces it to a truly possessable scale, encompassed by the limited length of a serpent.

In flight, Alexander rules the world in the imaginative mode Mary Louise Pratt calls "monarch-of-all-I-see."[11] Describing this landscape, the narrator adopts Alexander's imperial eyes. Upon Alexander's return, his men recognize overtly the flight's possessive performance: "Long live king Alexander, lord of the whole world, of the sky and the sea as well as the land" (p. 231). As of this moment, Alexander has constituted his full imperial power—but only as a memory, preserved in narrative and recoverable through the reading of history.[12] As with the Greeks at the end of the world, possession resides in Alexander's imagination, and in that of the reader who has seen through his eyes.

As if the Macedonians' declaration of Alexander's possession of sky, land, and sea inspired him to take this last domain, Alexander immediately prepares for submarine exploration. In the sea, he finds "diverses samblances" of fish: "He saw also many marvels that, because they are not believable to men, he did not want to reveal to anyone" (p. 232). From here, the French prose redactor adds to the Latin source, reporting that Alexander did reveal that he found fish in the "samblance" of men and women who walk along the ocean bottom and live off of other species just like men do on land. The discovery of anthropomorphic *semblance* at the bottom of the sea returns once again to the colonial paradigm of indigenous resemblance. Alexander possesses this almost-same through an imperial gaze that engenders a submarine ethnography. When his men reproach him for endangering himself in such perilous fieldwork, he counters that he has gained so much (*gaaignié*) that he will govern more wisely, for he has seen that force is worth little without craft (*engin*, pp. 232-33).[13] The conquering vocabulary (*gaaignié, force, engin*) allies this lesson with imperial desire and the techniques of its success. Moreover, since the reader does not see all that Alexander saw, the narrative exposes readers' similarly possessive desire for prose description.[14]

Subsequent to his scopophilic triumph, Alexander returns to Babylon. Having defined the basis of viable rule as total conquest (pp. 55, 139-40), he now seals his triumph semiotically: he replaces Hercules's monuments with two columns of his own, sculpted in his own image ("Il coulombes en sanblance de roi") and installed in Babylon and Persia. Each is twenty-five feet tall, "and he had written on them all the work, the victories and the battles, that he had had" (p. 244, the verse tradition offers no corresponding monuments). Here, Alexander becomes his own imperial biographer—presumably, in prose: the summary of his deeds implicitly gathers together his prose letters to Darius, Porus, Olympia, and Aristotle. We might even imagine Alexander as editor of his own collected works, proffering an anthology of the empire to all who enter his cities. After all of his battles against difference and denials of resemblance, he produces in these figures his own monumental semblances as figures of empire. These commemorative twins, emblematically occupying the imperial capitals and inscribed with imperial history, hold the place of genealogical reproduction: Alexander resembles only himself. The perfectly twinned phalluses withhold the production of difference: signs of imperial sterility, they forestall the future by suspending the empire in a perennial past and making imperial history available to all who can read Greek (or Latin or French).

Twinning himself in stone, Alexander bypasses genealogy in favor of historiography. Indeed, throughout the narrative he consistently and violently defies genealogical resemblance. In fact, all of his genealogical relations—to his father, his mother, and his own progeny—are troubled by irregular filiation. First of all, he has three fathers: Nectanabus the Egyptian, Amon the god, and Philip the Macedonian. As biological son of both Nectanabus and Amon (so it seems), Alexander embodies an Egyptian fusion of mortal and immortal. Philip, by contrast, can claim paternity only circumstantially (the French redactor implicitly ratifies his claim by systematically substituting *Philip* for *Amon* in the formulaic salutations of Alexander's letters). Although the narrator never comments on the relative legitimacy of Alexander's three fathers, Philip himself remains troubled by the acute problem of dissemblance: Alexander, bearing the name of Philip's previous son, disturbs filial patterns because he has what the narrator calls "sa propre semblance" (p. 29). Looking like himself, Alexander bears no traces of genealogical resemblance (the usual basis of dynastic continuity) to any of his fathers.

Philip's desire for genealogical semblance nearly leads to infanticide (pp. 42–43), while Alexander's desire for difference leads to patricide when he kills Nectanabus for claiming paternity (p. 31). Alexander's very face presents dissemblance, as his eyes are two different colors (p. 29). Through his dissimilar eyes, he purveys an imperial gaze that derives its authority from difference, rendering his vision unique and ultimately only partially available to even the most imaginative reader.

When confronted with his own image as an adult, Alexander feels an attack on the very basis of his identity and power. Tellingly, this image is constructed by Candace, who resembles Alexander's mother Olympia—and therefore presumably Alexander himself to some degree. Candace, queen of Tradiaque, tries first to avoid Alexander by refusing to join him for sacrifices to Amon (p. 208). Along with this message, she sends a painter to make a sculpture of Alexander (p. 209). No passion-filled courtly dame, as in the verse tradition, Candace is a savvy rebel to the empire who uses the statue to recognize the conqueror should he arrive—as he eventually does. Even though he disguises himself as a messenger, Candace calls him by name and explains her knowledge by showing him the sculpture. Alexander immediately pales in the face of this proof that the native has superior knowledge; Candace adds to his humiliation by pointing out that after all of his exploits he has finally fallen at the hands of a "foible feme" (feeble woman, p. 216). Alexander becomes suddenly angry when he realizes that he does not have his sword: "Since you have betrayed me, by my will, I would kill first you and then myself" (p. 217). These homicidal and suicidal impulses derive directly from his encounter with semblance, which has the power to overturn imperial disguises; Candace's ploy, and his violent reaction, vividly portray the degree to which his power rests on the maintenance of difference.

The culmination of Alexander's imperial progress returns to the troubled genealogical dynamics that shadow him from before his birth. Immediately after the description of the twin columns, the narrative turns to the description of a hybrid child-beast, claimed by a Babylonian woman to be Alexander's child. The upper body of the child looks human but seems dead (it has "samblance morte"); below the navel it has "forme de plusiors bestes qui s'entrecombatoient" (the form of several beasts who fought among themselves, pp. 244–45). This child of imperial desire incarnates colonial hybridity, literally fusing the noble conqueror with the monstrous native. Moreover, Alexander's astronomer (in an explanation not found in the Latin source) interprets the child-beast as a sign of Alexander's impending disinheritance. Rather than embodying dynastic continuity, the child-beast represents fatal discontinuity— and disruptive multiplicity in place of a stable passage of dominion, for the astronomer also predicts that the beasts represent Alexander's men who will fight among themselves after his death (pp. 245–46). The hybrid infant, like Alexander's twin columns, embodies the sterile products of imperial desire. In this case, the product may be fictional, since the narrator only reports the mother's *claim* of Alexander's paternity; it belongs nonetheless to history.

The French redactor disturbs genealogical order further by revising the terms of Alexander's will. If Roxanne has a male child, he is to be emperor of everything after Alexander, and the Macedonians may give him "tel non com il vodront" (whatever name they wish); if she has a girl, the Macedonians may elect whatever king they wish (p. 253).[15] Even this indeterminate ordering of succession is disrupted by the revelation after Alexander's death that he and Roxanne do have a child, named Hercules; through him Alexander crosses a genealogical frontier just as he did the territorial frontiers of the child's name-sake. Yet this Hercules is poised to die in prison: the rebellious barons first murder Olympia, then incarcerate Hercules and Roxanne (p. 267). Although named for Alexander's most successful predecessor, this Hercules (the living potential for the empire's unlimited extension into the future) never even makes it out of the city. None of Alexander's "progeny," then, continues his imperial performance—not the phallic columns of history, not the hybrid child-beast, not Hercules II. They all embody partial resemblances that fatally compromise the imperial future, exposing the political instability of reproductive desire, whether it focuses on resemblance or difference, genealogy or historiography. The narrative thus reveals the sterility of possessive fantasies founded on genealogical discourse.

These genealogical dynamics are replicated in Alexander's dealings with various groups outside his family. As he progresses across India, he encounters numerous beings who challenge the stability of cultural difference, and thus the foundations of empire. All have representational histories covering the entire Middle Ages; many derive ultimately from Pliny's *Naturales Historia*.[16] Each presents Alexander with a unique configuration of the familiar and the foreign. He first encounters the radically "other" in the guise of the "similar" when he meets cannibals.[17] Cannibals embody a trope of colonial ambivalence par excellence: they are humans "like us" who nonetheless engage in practices of intolerable difference, practices themselves predicated on the literal assimilation of resemblance.[18] The French redactor abbreviates the detailed Latin ethnography, leaving out the practice of eating malformed babies but clearly maintaining the fact that these people eat their dead (pp. 140–41). Alexander fears that the cannibals will attract imitators (that is, that difference will turn into resemblance), and so he gathers them together and takes them to a place between two mountains. He prays to God to bring the mountains together; they come within twelve feet of each other, and Alexander makes a gate that cannot be broken or burned. Although the gate and the mountains enclose the cannibals, they themselves are not destroyed. This act of enclosure is the culmination of a triumphant process of occupation, while also performing the terrors that linger just below the colonized surface: behind the gates, the cannibals continue their strangely seductive practices—and may in fact find their way out one day.

Alexander's second dramatic encounter with troubling semblance is with the Amazons, warriors like him who happen also to be women. When he demands their submission, Queen Calistidra defends herself with an ethnography of her land and people. She advises Alexander not to engage her culture of gendered difference, which effectively regulates the separation of men and women, and warns further that he can gain no honor from defeating women while she can gain much from defeating the most powerful man in the world (p. 157). Although Alexander first laughs, and then threatens war, in the end he invites the Amazons to a meeting for peace.

As soon as Calistidra decides to pay the tribute that Alexander demands, the French narrative expands the encounter significantly from the Latin source. In negotiating the Amazons' relatively autonomous submission, the messenger Flor casts Calistidra in the role of a courtly *dame*: "ele le [le treü] vous envoie de par nous tel com dame (le) doit envoiier a chevalier c'est a savoir l'anel de son doi" (she sends it [the tribute] to you through us, just as a lady must send it to a knight, that is to say the ring from her finger). The gift of the ring and the reference to customary relations between *dame* and *chevalier* suggest a courtly exchange, as does the beginning of Alexander's reply: "We thank your queen for the good will she has toward us, by which we receive her in our love and in our company, and as for the tribute that she sends us, we consider ourselves paid" (p. 159). Alexander's shift back to the discourse of legal subordination at the end highlights the courtly performance as performance: the reconciliation only occurs because, in contrast to her defiant ethnography, Calistidra now accepts the role of *dame* in a courtly game that allows Alexander to dominate. The encounter with the troublingly similar "other" is resolved when she assimilates the conqueror's logic and performs her "proper" gender role. When she herself is subsequently constrained to appear in person before Alexander, she and her entourage reestablish their vital and "improper" difference: Alexander's men marvel at their beauty, but even more at their superior equestrian skills (p. 160).[19]

Alexander's exchanges with the Bragmanni (*Brachmannians*) also test the limits of difference. His correspondence with this ascetic race was widely used in the Middle Ages to represent an Eastern critique of worldly Christians, and often appeared as an autonomous letter collection (Friedman, pp. 164–70). The French redactor, however, excises all of the correspondence criticizing Alexander's conquests. As a result, the exchange turns into a criticism of the Bragmanni's isolationism, which redounds to the honor of Alexander's expansionism. King Dindymus's (Lindimus) letter states that the Bragmanni's life is pure and without sin. Alexander's reply likens the Bragmanni's cultural values to imprisonment, and mocks the idea that prisoners can be happy. He says that what the Bragmanni consider natural, his own people reserve for the guilty, and he concludes: "it seems to me that your life is not all pleasant, but is punishment and discomfort" (pp. 199–200). Alexander has this conclusion (or possibly the entire exchange) engraved on a column of marble, a memorial to the morality of conquest and the immorality of isolationism: "Then Alexander commanded that a column of marble be raised in that place, and he had written on it the letters told above so that they would be in the memory of those who would come after him" (p. 201). The inscription is all the more remarkable because the Latin text represents the stone as a general mark of Alexandrian exploration, reporting that it is inscribed with the slogan: "Ego Alexander perveni usque huc" (I Alexander came as far as this, p. 201). The French prose *Alexandre* thus collocates expansionism and historiography, displacing an icon of possession with an epistolary justification of expansionist ideology.

Throughout India, the narrator demonstrates Alexander's conquering possessiveness through an extended colonial ethnography of the hybrid species that populate the newly domestic terrain. Each new being is described in terms of its partial resemblance to known entities. Faced with this confusingly strange yet faintly familiar world, Alexander reacts with either curiosity or violence. In the nonviolent mode, he proceeds as an ethnographic tourist, a colonial collector of narrative and biological specimens. When he meets anthropomorphs, for example, like the women with horns and beards down to their breasts, or those with hair down to the ground and feet like horses (pp. 178–80), he interrogates them in Indian about their lifestyles and customs. In the case of the civilized Ginosofites (*Gymnosophisti*, or "Going-Nakeds"), Alexander asks explicitly if he can observe their customs (p. 184). Elsewhere, the anthropomorphs do not speak, but are described in details that nonetheless offer the reader an intriguing glimpse of alien cultures, like the beautiful women who wear ugly clothes and arms made of silver and gold, or the hairy female amphibians, or the twelve-foot-tall women with large teeth who are covered in fur like camels (pp. 175–79). When Alexander later discovers six-foot-tall, gold-colored people on an island, he is not satisfied with narrative but instead captures thirty to take back as living specimens (pp. 236–37).[20] In each of these cases, he is content to marvel at cultural differences. He takes possession (either literally or figuratively) without assimilating, performing imperial annexations that leave the indigenous cultures largely undisturbed. Since most of these cultures are comprised solely of women, cultural difference translates into gendered difference, underscoring the potential for intercourse and the production of hybridity that Alexander and his male army repeatedly refuse.[21]

Elsewhere, when faced with hybridity, Alexander turns into an ethnographic aggressor, a colonial exterminator. These encounters begin with descriptions that read like biological collages; they purvey absolute differences by enumerating partial resemblances. There is, for example, an animal similar to a hippopotamus except that it has feet like a crocodile, a back like a stag, and moves more slowly than a snail (pp. 175–76).[22] Each time, whether it is a matter of serpents with emeralds in their heads or six-foot ants, Alexander and his army attack and kill. In fact, the French text systematically adds this destructive resolution to the Latin source, which usually only describes the animals. Alexander reserves his most virulent attack for a captured wild man, whom he orders burned after determining that he has no sense despite his resemblance to humans.[23] If hybrid beasts represent ambivalence, as F. N. M. Diekstra has suggested in relation to Latin bestiaries,[24] then Alexander acts to destroy embodiments of dual and multiple perspective. This Indian bestiary (destroyed as it is revealed) is not moralized or allegorized, like comparable compendia of animals from the twelfth and thirteenth centuries.[25] The narrative of battle takes the place of moralized glosses, and the methods of description are empirical instead of allegorical; they mobilize familiar realities to convey strange ones. Alexander's ethnographic tourism brings all of these hybrid creatures into contact with the known and under the jurisdiction of his empire through description.

Alexander's domain does have epistemological limits, however. He fails notably, for example, to master time in repeated efforts to see the future.

Preoccupied with his death from the beginning (p. 60), he has two opportunities to learn of it: from the trees at the House of the Sun (pp. 203–7) and from the god Cesagnotis (pp. 220–21). Yet he never acquires specific knowledge of the future; he recognizes instead that Fortune governs his imperial destiny.[26] The narrator, by contrast, manifestly penetrates the temporal barriers that elude Alexander, transgressing the differences between past and future. In the prologue, the narrator casts historiography as a science governed by the seven liberal arts, which provide temporal mastery: "ramenbrant des chozes passees, esploitant des presentes et porveant de celles qui sont a avenir" (remembering things past, exploiting those present, and foreseeing those that are to come, p. 8). The liberal arts dominate time just as Alexander dominates space, making historiography an imperial science. The narrator subsequently performs both remembrance and prophecy by precisely dating Alexander's death: whereas the Latin text says that the poisoning takes place "quadam die" (one day), the French text says that it occurred the day of the crowning, "which is to say, on the day of Holy Cross, which is the fourteenth day of September, in the year of Adam four thousand and nine hundred" (p. 249). Alexander's death thus follows at a precise temporal distance from the creation of humanity, while simultaneously engaging the Christian future: September 14 will not become "Holy Cross Day" until after the advent of Christ. With these retrospective temporal calculations, the narrator masters tropes of time. His representation of Alexander's several failures at such mastery identifies the difference between Alexander's imperial desire and his own historiographic achievements. Successful imperial projects take time, literally and figuratively, as they encompass durable memory; the prose *Alexandre* demonstrates that such projects only succeed in narrative.

Translation also performs Alexander's limits and the narrator's mastery. For Alexander, languages remain distinct. The narrator specifies that he speaks the Indian language of his new subjects, or uses interpreters who speak it to communicate with them. What's more, the prophetic trees speak alternately in Indian and Greek, as if the two were interchangeable (p. 205). In these moments, the preservation of linguistic difference suggests that Alexander's imperial possession remains partial. The narrator, by contrast, effects a translation and revision of the Latin *Historia de Preliis* that completely appropriates its authority for French. The prose project takes possession of ancient history, substituting French for the historic language of Roman imperialism. Once again, Alexander's own deployments of language within the narrative testify to his failure to possess in the same discursive mode. Since translation takes possession of discursive terrain, it demonstrates once again that historiographical expansionism surpasses realistic possibilities.

If the path of relentless expansionism is common to all versions of Alexander's story (rendered in more or less courtly terms across the centuries), the lesson of colonial possession is particularly at home in the prose medium.

In form and function, the prose *Alexandre* purveys a unique conjunction of possessive maneuvers—maneuvers specifically unavailable to most readers in social and political reality. The text shares in the possessive modalities of French prose translation in general at the beginning of the thirteenth century. Indeed, the earliest date for the work has been set at 1206 because part of the epilogue is taken directly from the *Histoire ancienne jusqu'à César*, translated for Roger of Lille before 1206;[27] the *Histoire ancienne* itself draws occasionally from the verse *Alexandre* (Ross, "The History," pp. 190–91, 200, 209–10, 212–16). Although the regional and social origins of the prose *Alexandre* remain unknown, I think it is fruitful to view it as an adoption and transformation of Greek imperial history analogous to the contemporary reception of Roman history.

In both the *Histoire ancienne* and the *Alexandre*, French takes over ancient imperial history—perhaps for the imaginative benefit of aristocratic patrons and readers (as Gabrielle Spiegel argues for the *Histoire ancienne*[28]), perhaps for some less clearly defined purpose. In both cases, this taking occurs in prose. The form is significant because, like imperialist expansion, prose confronts limits and then passes over them. As a self-referential mode that encompasses irreconcilable differences, prose offers rich terrain for imaginative modes of possession. Indeed, Jeffrey Kittay and Wlad Godzich argue in *The Emergence of Prose* that the prose medium took shape in direct opposition to the consolidation of French royal power at the turn of the thirteenth century.[29] That is, they link the medium itself with the social goals Spiegel discerns in the earliest prose translations. Although Kittay and Godzich occasionally paint with broad and even superficial strokes, their essay provocatively suggests the possibility that *prosaics* can be theorized as legitimately as poetics.

Prose's ability to constitute a self-referential textual domain derives from two characteristic strategies: the destabilization of the narrative voice, and the use of conjunctive syntax. For Kittay and Godzich, the absence of the jongleur's voice de-centers the narrative, divorcing it from the stable reference of oral performance (pp. 17–18).[30] The prose *Alexandre* first manifests this strategy in the account of Alexander's birth, where the narrator juxtaposes the conflicting accounts of Orosius and Vinchens without assigning priority to either one (pp. 5–6). By withholding the narrative "I" that usually judges the relative viability of historical accounts, the redactor places all reports on equal ground, so that the narrative of Alexander's genealogy encompasses the boundary between multiple sources. This is an endlessly extendable process of composition that can take possession of all known historical accounts through the multiplication of the most potent conjunction, *et*. Later, when the narrative "I" does intervene, it does so only to refer to its own act of narration in phrases such as "com je vous conte" (pp. 163, 201, 202). Moreover, whereas in the verse *Alexandre* messengers generally deliver messages orally (like jongleurs), here epistolary exchanges position the reader in multiple and conflicting relations to a shifting narrative "I" as different interlocutors speak in the first person.

Alexander himself narrates his conquests (the *estoire* itself, later inscribed on his marble bodies) to Olympia and Aristotle in letters (pp. 106, 139, 242). His voice thus encompasses the voice of the *estoire*, while also representing only one of many subject positions demanded of the prose-literate reader. This conflation encloses history within a self-referential universe.

Conjunctions likewise occupy new space in the discursive terrain of history. *Et, puis, apres,* and *tandis que,* for example, extend the narrative to encompass cultural differences without imposing hierarchical epistemologies. Of *tandis que,* Kittay and Godzich conclude that "conjunction and disjunction work formally together: they are both seams" (p. 124). In contrast to verse parataxis, prose sentences develop an extended vocabulary of such seams, which join while separating. This dual function directs all reference toward the narrative space itself, again foreclosing disruptions from outside. The prose *Alexandre* commonly manifests seams of conjunction with *puis* and *apres* as the redactor extends the narrative to reflect Alexander's territorial gains. The redactor encloses the seams between the Latin source and new French material within the speech of the *estoire* itself: "Mais atant se taist l'estoire dou roy Pausania et retorne a Alixandre qui estoit en Hermenie. Or dist l'estoire que . . ." (But at this point the *estoire* falls silent about king Pausania and returns to Alexander, who was in Armenia. Now the *estoire* says that . . . ; p. 50). The boundary between existing narrative and new historical territory is constituted by this claim to silence (*atant se taist*) which enables new speech (*or dist*). The *estoire* thus includes its own enabling silence as a past event, fully integrated into the narrated future on the seam that takes no time (*or*). In the literally blank space between past silence and future speech (the space before the *or*), history takes new places. Elsewhere, less obvious seams displace compact Latin conjunctions, as phrases like "Interea Alexander scripsit . . ." (Meanwhile Alexander wrote . . .) become, "When Alexander knew that everyone in the world was obeying him like a lord, then he sent his letters . . ." (p. 242). These expansions fill in the space of disjunction with the performance of conjunction, ensuring that the seams in fact take up space. These kinds of narrative sutures witness the crossing of boundaries, as the redactor writes history in the interstices of the Latin source. They ultimately enclose history within a singularly self-referential domain.

Conjunctions and the destabilization of narrative subjectivity both contribute to the totalizing effects of prose, that is, to the ways in which it seems to possess time and place absolutely while occluding the autonomous existence of alternate histories. Kittay and Godzich observe that because prose is not tied to performance, discursive authority lies within the text itself, not outside it (pp. 34, 53–58). Prose furnishes the desirable landscape of expansionist imagination by remapping the boundaries of identification: "the preexisting opposition between what is our territory (the inside, the true) and what is not (the foreign, the untrue) is remapped to allow what is ours to be either historical or fictional" (p. 183). They conclude dramatically: "Prose, able to carry its deixis from within itself, can give us the world" (p. 209). Steve Nimis has used this conclusion to explain the heterogeneity of ancient Greek novels,[31] while others have reached compatible conclusions by different routes: Michèle Perret speaks of self-generating texts that seem "always already there" (p. 175), and Emmanuèle Baumgartner of "totalitarian" prose.[32] Prose's ability to encompass differences culminates in a hegemonic structure, a vision without borders.[33] Prose thus creates its own autonomy, and can unmoor history from the political structures it sustains. Prose's totalizing effects, which can claim endless tracts of epistemological space, enable readers to cast themselves within an ever-expanding universe whatever the real state of their territorial possessions.

Encounters with the totalizing, marginless world of prose demand a new kind of literacy from the reader. Prose's ability to cross cultural borders links the medium to expansionist ideologies, since each border crossing provides the reader with new territorial possessions: "With the emergence of prose, virgin territory becomes that which can be explored" (Kittay and Godzich, p. 125). Thus prose literacy may be described in terms that resonate with the transience associated with colonial subjectivity: "the reader is to unmoor himself or herself from a single or singular perspective and travel the road of positionality" (p. 124); there is thus no "master subject" in prose, no single governing consciousness to impose limits (pp. 126, 130). Strikingly, Kittay and Godzich refer to a reader "armed" with this kind of literacy (p. 126), as if the act of reading prose could aggressively challenge authority. The prose-literate reader thus forcefully occupies a succession of disconnected positions, whose cumulative effects purvey the possessive ethos of colonialist expansion.

The prose *Alexandre* takes possession of new narrative territory most dramatically in the conclusion. Where the Latin text ends with a portrait of Alexander and a list of the twelve cities he founded, the French expands Tholomeus's speech and quotes the writing he inscribed on Alexander's tomb:[34] "Chi gist Alixandres, rois de Macedone, qui par fer ne pot estre vaincus, mais l'ochist le venim, en l'an dou coumencement dou monde IIII m et IX cens as XV jours de septembre" (p. 260: Here lies Alexander, king of Macedonia, who could not be vanquished by iron, but rather venom killed him, in the year four thousand nine hundred since the beginning of the world on the fifteenth day of September.) The epitaph is not, however, the epilogue: in prose, such monuments and their inscriptions cannot contain the limits of history. The narrative continues with the battles waged by Alexander's original companions; the narrator notes that after fourteen years none of them remained alive. Crossing over the border of the Latin source, the redactor summarizes their wars using the text of the *Histoire ancienne*. Importing this text, he annexes the Roman imperial future to the Greek imperial past. In the seam between these two histories, the narrator speaks at length: "Then it happened that all those whom you have heard named here before disputed amongst themselves after the death of Alexander, as you will soon be able to hear and understand, because of their felon hearts and their great envy. And so I will tell you first of all why the discord happened, on account of which they fought amongst themselves, and the great hatred that was never satisfied. And all this was because of a letter that king Alexander had made . . ." (p. 262). As the sentence goes on and on, it encompasses much of the preceding narrative as well as the events to come, once again enclosing narration within its own referential bounds. The plurality of temporal and spatial perspectives underscores narrative possession of all imaginable historical territory. History is thus not contained in the life of a single hero, but represents an expanding universe, capable of crossing new boundaries with the addition of a single conjunction.

Once these battles have been narrated, the narrator begins to enumerate the dead. At this moment, he recognizes that the story will never reach its limit: "But it would be too long a thing to say and recount the ambushes that they inflicted on each other and the manner of the battles and mêlées, such that so many good knights, worthy and hardy, were killed and conquered by force, so at this point I will leave my speech . . ." (p. 268). The final "leaving" (*lairai*) of speech (*parolle*) takes place in the future, a prophecy of silence to come that will arbitrarily hold the place of future narrative, beyond which there is no present and no past (*or dist l'estoire*). Moreover, the promise of silence is contained within the material space of the book itself (*atant*), localizing the voice of history within the literal written space of narrative. The narrator's choice to leave off speaking thus becomes arbitrary rather than necessary: he abandons a task that has no end, in a clear example of what Kent Hieatt called the "imperialism of the artificer."[35] Indeed, the narrative could go on and on—through the events of the *Histoire ancienne* and beyond: there is no end to the story of the postimperial. Conclusion is all the more aggressive within prose, since ending itself goes against the grain of the medium's expansive relation to limits.[36]

The potentially endless chain of expansive substitutions afforded by prose literacy has the capacity to disrupt hegemonic discourse—hence the medium's attractiveness as a mode of aristocratic resistance (Kittay and Godzich, p. 207). Yet this same endless chain can also subsume resistance itself: no boundary is off limits. The project of the prose *Alexandre*, initiated in the same period as the *Histoire ancienne* and carried on into the late thirteenth century, thus rests uneasily between resistance and hegemony. By its very form, it takes imaginative possession of a global geography and a vast ethnographic catalogue. Yet its strident discursive forms, confident possessors of imperial history, can sustain authoritative desires from almost any social quarter.[37] Alexander himself embodies the pitfalls of expansionism. Like the prose medium, he encounters and possesses new territories as he pursues his conquests. And like prose, he must negotiate new relationships between the strange and the familiar—between differences and resemblances. Alexandrian prose aggressively encompasses imperial violence. And while the narrative as a whole offers imperial paradigms in descriptions of territory, genealogy, and ethnicity, Alexander's own reactions to difference constitute an aggressive imperial subjectivity. The similarity between Alexander and the *Alexandre* thus indicates that the expansionist ideology mobilized in his history is uniquely at home in prose historiography, especially since Alexandrian verse offers courtly resolutions and overlooks differences. Unlike prose, however, Alexander's expansionist potential is ultimately limited. This difference between the historical conqueror and the conquering subjectivity offered to the reader by the prose narrator keeps the fantasy of domination available to all readers, even those who possess nothing. From the fragmented and discontinuous subjectivity made available through prose literacy, anything is possible.[38]

Notes

1. E.g., Kathleen Biddick, *The Shock of Medievalism* (Durham: Duke University Press, 1998); Kathleen Davis, "National Writing in the Ninth Century: A Reminder for Postcolonial Thinking about the Nation," *Journal of Medieval and Early Modern Studies* 28 (1998), 611–37; Patricia Clare Ingham, "Marking Time: Branwen, Daughter of Llyr and the Colonial Refrain," in Jeffrey Jerome Cohen, ed., *The Postcolonial Middle Ages* (New York: St. Martin's Press, 2000), pp. 173–91.

2. Martin Gosman summarizes the relationship between the French and Latin texts, as well as courtly themes across the centuries: "Le *Roman d'Alexandre en prose*: un remaniement typique," *Neophilologus* 69 (1985), 332–41; "Alexandre le Grand et le statut de la noblesse ou le plaidoyer pour la permanence: prolégomènes à l'histoire d'une légende," in *Non Nova, Sed Nove: mélanges de civilisation médiévale dédiés à Willem Noomen*, ed. Martin Gosman and Jaap van Os (Groningen: Bouma's Boekhuis, 1984), pp. 81–93; "Le roman d'Alexandre et les 'juvenes': une approche socio-historique," *Neophilologus* 66 (1982), 328–39.

3. Laurence Harf-Lancner, "De la biographie au roman d'Alexandre: Alexandre de Paris et l'art de la conjointure," in *The Medieval Opus: Imitation, Rewriting, and Transmission in the French Tradition*, ed. Douglas Kelly (Amsterdam: Rodopi, 1996), pp. 59–74 (here pp. 70–73).

4. I use "post-colonial" to signal a chronological relation to a specific colonial past, and "postcolonial" to refer to concepts not attached to specific historical relations.

5. Robert Young introduces post(-)colonial criticism cogently in *Colonial Desire: Hybridity in Theory, Culture, and Race* (London: Routledge, 1995).

6. I discuss relations among medieval and postcolonial studies more extensively in "Making Contact: Postcolonial Perspectives through Geoffrey of Monmouth's *Historia regum Britanniae*," *Arthuriana* 8 (1998), 115–34.

7. Gosman reaches a similar conclusion by a different route in "Le *Roman*," pp. 339–40.

8. *Prosa*, p. 1. The edition presents the *Historia de Preliis* and the *Roman d'Alexandre* in parallel columns; English translations are my own.

9. Alexander's quest for knowledge presages the organized science of the modern imperial state, where scientific inquiry seeks to master the depths of nature; see Amy Boesky, "Bacon's *New Atlantis* and the Laboratory of Prose," in *The Project of Prose in Early Modern Europe and the New World*, ed. Elizabeth Fowler and Roland Greene (Cambridge: Cambridge University Press, 1997), pp. 138–53; James Romm, "Alexander Biologist: Oriental Monstrosities and the *Epistola Alexandri ad Aristotelem*," in *Discovering New Worlds: Essays on Medieval Exploration and Imagination*, ed. Scott D. Weston (New York: Garland, 1991), pp. 16–30.

10. David J. A. Ross, "The History of Macedon in the *Histoire ancienne jusqu'à César*," *Classica et Mediaevalia* 24 (1963), 181–231 (here p. 230).

11. Mary Louise Pratt, *Imperial Eyes: Travel Writing and Transculturation* (London: Routledge, 1992), pp. 204–5.

12. Gosman, by contrast, portrays Alexander's possession of "only" narrative as a sign of failure ("Le *Roman*," p. 338).

13. In the verse *Roman d'Alexandre*, Alexander observes the small fish defeated and moralizes about human greed like the Latin bestiary tradition: see *MFRA II*, p. 154, ll. 506–11; Willene B. Clark, "Zoology in the Medieval Latin Bestiary," in *Man and Nature in the Middle Ages*, ed. Susan J. Ridyard and Robert G. Benson (Sewanee, Tenn: University of the South Press, 1995), pp. 223–45 (here p. 231). Like the prose *Alexandre*, Brunetto Latini's thirteenth-century French prose bestiary avoids moralization; see *Li livres dou Tresor*, ed. P. Chabaille (Paris: Imprimerie Impériale, 1863), pp. 182–83.

14. In the verse *Alexandre*, the two vertical voyages frame Alexander's horizontal expansions (Harf-Lancner, "De la biographie," p. 64). Their collocation in the prose *Alexandre* presents the quest for knowledge as the culmination of colonial ambition.

15. In the Latin source, Roxanne is to receive half of Macedonia if she has a male child; she is to rule herself if a girl is born (pp. 253–54). I discuss the imperial abdication implicit in "tel roi com il vodront" in "Marmiadoise of Greece: The Force of Ancient History in the *Estoire de Merlin*," *Romance Languages Annual* 9 (1997), 141–48.

16. John Block Friedman, *The Monstrous Races in Medieval Art and Thought* (Cambridge: Harvard University Press, 1981).

17. The episode is usually associated with Gog, Magog, and the Hebrew tribes. However, the Spanish *Libro de Alexandre* also refers to cannibals; see Ian Michael, "Typological Problems in Medieval Alexander Literature: The Enclosure of Gog and Magog," in *The Medieval Alexander Legend and Romance Epic: Essays in Honour of David J. A. Ross*, ed. Peter Noble, Lucie Polak, and Claire Isoz (Millwood, NY: Kraus, 1982), pp. 131–48 (here pp. 140–43).

18. W. Arens, *The Man-Eating Myth: Anthropology and Anthropophagy* (New York: Oxford University Press, 1979); Maggie Kilgour, *From Communion to Cannibalism: An Anatomy of Metaphors of Incorporation* (Princeton: Princeton University Press, 1990).

19. Once again, the difference from the Vulgate *Alexandre* could not be more radical: there, the episode culminates with Flor's marriage to one of Alexander's men (*MFRA II*, p. 316, ll. 7678–82).

20. Friedman remarks of this and similar episodes in the Alexandrian tradition that "the naturalist's voice joins that of the colonialist" (p. 145).

21. In the verse *Alexandre*, by contrast, encounters with indigenous women often lead to courtly engagements (e.g., *MFRA*, pp. 221–22).

22. Clark notes a similar strategy in the illustration of unfamiliar animals, like the crocodile itself, in Latin bestiaries (pp. 236, 241).

23. "Sense" is determined by watching the man's reaction to a naked girl who is placed in his enclosure (pp. 202–3): meaning and hybrid intercourse again coincide.

24. "Such a one is ambivalent and inconstant in all his ways": "The Physiologus, the Bestiaries and Medieval Animal Lore," *Neophilologus* 69 (1985), 142–55 (here p. 148).

25. See Clark; Florence McCulloch, *Mediaeval Latin and French Bestiaries* (Chapel Hill: University of North Carolina Press, 1960); Debra Hassig, *Medieval Bestiaries: Text, Image, Ideology* (Cambridge: Cambridge University Press, 1995).

26. Alexander quotes Fortune to Nicolas, as a reminder that the great are soon brought low, and vice versa (p. 38); when Alexander is poisoned, the narrator notes that Fortune will not let Alexander stay atop the wheel for long (pp. 248–49); in his testament, Alexander discourses on Fortune at length (pp. 252–53).

27. David J. A. Ross, "Some Notes on the Old French Alexander Romance in Prose," *French Studies* 6 (1952), 135–47 (here pp. 146–47); Renate Blumenfeld-Kosinski, "Moralization and History: Verse and Prose in the *Histoire ancienne jusqu'à César* (in BN fr. 20125)," *Zeitschrift für romanische Philologie* 97 (1982), 41–46 (here p. 44).

28. *Romancing the Past: The Rise of Vernacular Prose Historiography in Thirteenth-Century France* (Berkeley: University of California Press, 1993), pp. 97, 116, 225, 317.

29. Jeffrey Kittay and Wlad Godzich, *The Emergence of Prose: An Essay in Prosaics* (Minneapolis: University of Minnesota Press, 1987), pp. 3–13, 179. I discuss further implications of prose in *History on the Edge: Excalibur and the Borders of Britain, 1100–1300* (Minneapolis: University of Minnesota Press, 2000), pp. 173–76.

30. See also Michèle Perret, "De l'espace romanesque à la matérialité du livre: l'espace énonciatif des premiers romans en prose," *Poétique* 50 (1982), 173–82.

31. "The Prosaics of the Ancient Novels," *Arethusa* 27 (1994), 387–411 (here p. 402).

32. "Le choix de la prose," *Cahiers de recherches médiévales (XIIIe–XVe siècles)* 5 (1998), 7–13 (here p. 13).

33. Mikhail Bakhtin's descriptions of "prose-art" could easily include medieval prose—although, curiously, he does not mention it, instead casting bilingual poetry as

the precursor of the dialogic novel; see *The Dialogic Imagination: Four Essays*, ed. Michael Holquist, tr. Caryl Emerson and Michael Holquist (Austin: University of Texas Press, 1981), pp. 50–82, 276ff.

34. Through Tholomeus, Alexandrian histography becomes entangled with the Arthurian; see *Estoire del saint graal*, ed. Jean-Paul Ponceau (Paris: Champion, 1997), pp. 92–99.

35. "The Passing of Arthur in Malory, Spenser, and Shakespeare: The Avoidance of Closure," in *The Passing of Arthur: New Essays in Arthurian Tradition*, ed. Christopher Baswell and William Sharpe (New York: Garland, 1988), pp. 173–92 (here p. 174).

36. The open silence that closes the prose *Alexandre* is all the more striking when compared to the end of the verse narrative: "Ci fenissent li livre, des or mais est mesure . . . / Ci fenissent li ver, l'estoire plus ne dure" (*MFRA II*, p. 358, ll. 1690–98). Here, history can be measured and the *estoire* has a finite life.

37. Indeed, Gosman's conclusion that the prose *Alexandre* demonstrates that armies are lost without leaders and that royalty needs the support of nobles to succeed ("Le *Roman*," pp. 333, 337–38) could sustain arguments for either royalist or aristocratic interests.

38. I am grateful to Rebecca Biron for inspiring discussions about possession, and to Maytee Valenzuela for expert research assistance (supported by a General Research Grant from the University of Miami).

10

Alexander and Caesar in the *Faits des Romains*

Catherine Croizy-Naquet

With the *Faits des Romains*, a compilation from the beginning of the thirteenth century, the history of Rome makes a remarkable entry onto the horizon of French historiography. For the first time, Rome is at the center of a historical narrative, and this enterprise is all the more original because the author argues for the existence of a significant juncture in Roman history: the decisive transition from the Republic to the Empire.[1] In his prologue he had indicated that he would relate the lives of the twelve Caesars, but, for reasons unknown, he recounts only that of Julius Caesar, from birth to death. This focus on a founding period of Roman history does not rule out links to other segments of human history. Indeed, in the *Histoire ancienne* this technique, new to the vernacular, turns that work into a universal history: salvation history blends with Trojan and Greek legends, then with the history of Alexander and of Rome, so that for the Middle Ages legend is thrust irreversibly into a historical continuum.[2] It is thus scarcely surprising that its successor, the *Faits des Romains*, links the matter of Ancient Rome with the Trojan legend and the story of Alexander, by means of succinct references, allusions or comparisons, thus locating it within a more general context. This technique does not betoken a failure to adhere to the initial intention to compile ancient Latin sources on Roman subjects, for the writer in fact translates four works whose authors are named at the beginning of certain manuscripts: Suetonius's *Life of Caesar*, the *Conspiracy of Catiline* of Sallust, Caesar's commentaries on his campaigns in Gaul, and Lucan's *Pharsalia*. Onto these official sources, however, he grafts countless secondary sources, including those from the luxuriant matter of Greco-Trojan antiquity, including, implicitly or explicitly, the constant presence of Alexander the Great in the life of the Roman leader.[3]

The choice of Alexander is perfectly logical in a text that depicts Caesar's extraordinary rise, through conquest, to the summit of power. It is especially apt because Caesar himself was a fervent admirer of the Macedonian leader, according to the remarks of Alexandre de Paris in his *Roman d'Alexandre*:

"Enprés sa mort le dist Cesaires Jul̈iens/ Que ce fu tous li mieudres des princes terr̈iens"[4] (After Alexander's death, Julius Caesar affirmed that he was the greatest of the world's princes). In the *Faits des Romains*, the nature and sources of the references to Alexander allow us to elaborate a particular image of that mythic figure that derives its significance from the comparison established with that of Caesar. The references reflect the work of the compiler and the measures he took to ensure a proper "montage" of the Roman leader's portrait. Although the compiler follows tradition and closely adheres to the content of his sources, he redesigns the contours of two exemplary figures and offers in embryo a definition of the historical personage.

Apparent though it may be, the presence of the Macedonian hero is modest throughout the work. Through allusions or digressions, the compiler casts Alexander, at the outset of the story, as the perfect conqueror, the ideal of precocious physical and intellectual traits. This aspect partakes of the traditional representation of the character and stems from its principal source, Suetonius, for the account of Caesar's *questure* and his campaign in southern Spain.[5] It acquires prominence in Caesar's lament before the statue of Alexander. True to his source, the compiler nonetheless adds a special nuance to Caesar's speech: "Ha! Fist il a soi më̈smes, con sui mauves, qui n'ai anquore rien fet dont ge doie lox avoir! et cil dont ge voi ci l'ymage ot conquis pres que tot le monde quant il fu de mon aage" (p. 15, ll. 25–26; p. 16, ll. 1–2: Ah, he said to himself, how mediocre am I, who have yet to do anything worthy of praise, while he, whose image I see here before me, had conquered nearly the entire world when he was my age). He emphasizes the vivid impression Alexander makes on Caesar and ensures the Roman hero's awareness of a resemblance that will subsequently become apparent between two careers and two destinies, while making Alexander Caesar's acknowledged model. The devotional context of the temple of Hercules and the accompanying ritual surrounds the mythic figure of Alexander with an aura of sanctity and legitimizes Caesar's decision to emulate him: "Lors li crut ses hardemenz, et se pensa que il emprendroit greignors choses que il n'avoit fet ançois et voudroit monter en greignor pris" (p. 16, ll. 2–4: Then his courage swelled, and he thought that he would undertake greater things than he had thus far and would earn greater renown). This transposition into chivalric terms is merely a way of rendering Caesar's engagement more operative, while also defining the textual modalities the compiler intends to adopt in order to recount the Roman hero's conquests.[6] Evoked before Caesar embarks on his conquest of power, the figure of Alexander determines a strategy for reading and programs the work that will ensue, which the prologue has identified as a story of the *gestes as Romains*. This extensive comparison offers a way of perceiving the Roman leader; while authorizing him to make a name for himself in history, it also places him in the wake of prestigious conquerors who preceded him.

The parallel between the two leaders is rounded out by the account of Caesar's dream: "La nuit devant, li fu vis en dormant que il gisoit charnelment o sa mere. De ce fu il mout confus" (p. 16, ll. 5–6: The night before, he dreamed that he knew his mother carnally, and this he found very disturbing). In contrast with Suetonius (VII), the writer associates this dream with the lament in which Caesar envisages himself as a new Alexander, thus indirectly recalling the latter's own dream.[7] Though they differ in content, the two dreams lend themselves to the same interpretation: they foretell the conquest and domination of the world. In the *Faits des Romains*, the seers' response is unambiguous: "Ce que tu avoies ta mere souz toi senefie que tu avras toute terre en ta subjection et seras sire deu monde" (p. 16, ll. 9–10: That you had your mother beneath you signifies that you will have the whole earth under your dominion and will be lord of the world). This seems to be a direct echo of the predictions that Alexander's dream elicits, in the version by Alexander of Paris: "Que ce ert Alixandres qui tout le monde chaele,/ Tot avra desous lui, com faus la torterele" (Br. I, vv. 238–39: Alexander will rule the world, hold it beneath him, as the falcon holds the turtledove). This parallel shows how the compiler reworks the figure of Alexander introduced and modeled into the vernacular by Albéric, and how he puts it into perspective so as to establish a spiritual kinship between the two heroes.[8]

From Suetonius and the ancient and medieval traditions, the historian thus appropriates the conventional image of Alexander, quintessentially one of warlike power and glory. The statue depicting him, which a rapt Caesar contemplates admiringly, reduces him to a uniform and monolithic image. The compiler, however, injects an important corrective, in a digression which, inserted into the heart of the text, interrupts the character's idealization. While Pompey is marshaling the forces of the Orient against Caesar, the author relates the story of how Alexander's lieutenants, Mistones and Aristes, travel to the Terrestial Paradise, from the mere mention of Gion, *un des .IIII. fluns de Paradis* (one of the four rivers of Paradise).[9] The story is undoubtedly inspired by the *Iter ad Paradisum*, from the first half of the twelfth century. The editors also mention the influence of verse segments found in a certain number of manuscripts, including the *Prise de Defur* and the *Voyage d'Alexandre au Paradis terrestre*.[10] The dates are a problem, however, as the latter are dated 1260 and 1270 respectively, according to Gosman, whereas the *Faits des Romains* was most likely written in 1213 (*Légende*, p. 33). It is not impossible that the compiler knew intermediate versions, were there any, though nothing indicates what they would have been. In spite of the identical comprehensive format, the compilation presents major contrasts, in both context and detail, with the Latin and French texts.[11] In the *Faits des Romains*, Alexander's lieutenants undertake the voyage, and not Alexander himself along with his five hundred companions, as in the *Iter*, nor Alexander with his mariners and twenty knights—

two of them (Eumenides and Ptolemy) identified—as in the *Voyage*. As in the *Iter*, the author evokes the gift of a stone representing a human eye and endowed with marvelous qualities, whereas in the *Voyage* the gift is an apple. Finally, in the *Faits des Romains*, it is Aristotle, not the elderly Jew of the *Iter* nor the inhabitant of Paradise and then Aristotle as in the *Voyage*, who derives a meaning from this stone.

The compiler proposes two essential orientations in his version of the episode. In contrast with the other texts, he refrains from moralizing about greed, which is not suprising in a work that demonstrates a constant effort to restore spatio-temporal alterity and to seek objectivity.[12] On the other hand—and paradoxically, however, in view of the overall tone of the story—he Christianizes the episode. The guardian of Paradise alludes to Christ: "uns autres qui n'a point de pareill. Alissandres est ainz nez de lui, et neporquant il fu ançois que Alixandres" (p. 399, ll. 1–2: another who has no peer. Alexander was born before He was, and yet He lived before Alexander). The guardian reveals the nature of the Terrestrial Paradise and its tree of immortality, then evokes the admission of the patriarch Enoch and the prophet Elijah to Paradise and announces their departure to do battle with the Antichrist at the end of the world (p. 399, ll. 6–9). This Christianization, which to say the least is unexpected in a text that elsewhere refuses to espouse Christian values, is explicable in terms of the intellectual status accorded to the Bible.[13] The *Seinte Escriture* embodies a means of envisaging universal order; it is the scientific standard of reference from which all human events and behavior derive meaning, whereas its purely spiritual import normally remains obscure. Christianization provides a rational explanation of Alexander's failure, attributable to his status as pagan deprived of the light of Revelation, rather than to his status as pagan guilty of greed and excess. The radical breach between Alexander and Christianity and the impossibility of closing it are magnified in the biases of rewriting. Thus, not Alexander but his lieutenants set out for Terrestrial Paradise, while from the outset our hero denies himself the conquest of the knowledge he lacks and access to Christian truths. Nor does he derive any benefit from the insight of his envoys, whose knowledge about eschatology and metaphysics, however fragmentary and hazy, is never conveyed to him: his men merely give him the stone and describe its virtues (p. 399, ll. 29–30). The lesson dispensed by the stone is in any case merely evidential: it recalls the opposition between life and death and, derived from it, that between fame and oblivion. It offers Alexander no unutterable secret, no higher virtue to augment his power. Disappointing in that it is merely a reminder of common knowledge accessible to all, it is, in the faultless trajectory of the hero, a symbol of his limitations and the token of a futile quest and an illusory glory. Following Aristotle's interpretation, the hero prefers to reject the stone: "et quide l'en que ele rala la dont estoit venue" (p. 401, ll. 9–13: And it is thought that it returned whence it came). While lending the Macedonian the image of a pagan refusing humility, this gesture signals the impossibility of attaining divine Truth, which forever eludes him, just as it indicates his refusal to accept his human limitations or to allow for them in his actions. Without tarnisihing the representation of Alexander, even though it discloses his weaknesses, this digression in the heart of the text has the value of an *exemplum*. Thus redefined, it becomes a measure of the hero's failure. Above all, it allows us to identify, through Alexander, his Roman *alter ego* who, as a pagan driven by the same desires, is called upon to confront the same obstacles in his career as conqueror. The lesson valid for Alexander in fact also concerns, in specular fashion, Caesar and is justified, in a text focused on Roman history, only by the implicit comparison of the two heroes. The affinities that link them will be underlined in the *Voeux du Paon*, whose author places among the Nine Worthies, along with Hector in the series of pagans, Alexander and Caesar, according to chronological order and ties of heredity and/or spiritual filiation.[14]

Beginning with the opening lament, everything serves to place the two heroes on an equal footing; to make the Roman a double of the Macedonian in terms of exemplarity, so that the life of Caesar can be reflected and read in that of Alexander. There are remarkable similarities between their respective premonitory dreams that foretell their destinies and locate them within the sphere of the elect. In both cases, birth and death are marked by violence and accompanied by extraordinary signs;[15] in both, existence unfolds along a path of conquest leading to possession of the world and of glory. Like Alexander, Caesar is depicted as the model of a conqueror, while the parallel between the two heroes is emblematized by the attribute *par excellence* of the warrior, a horse. Although the author retains from Suetonius (LXI) the detail of feet resembling those of a man, with hooves split into five fingers, he looks to Bucephalus for the animal's extraordinary character, repeating a fundamental trait that is also a sign of election and the proclamation or promise of an exceptional destiny: like Alexander, Caesar alone is able to mount the horse, a feat that designates him as the future *sire dou monde*.[16]

The first virtue that unites the two heroes in the lineage of seasoned conquerors is their prowess, set forth in their behavior and their speech. Alexander's prowess, already extolled in the fragment by Albéric, is nuanced in various ways. Alexandre de Paris depicts it in the tradition of the *chansons de geste*, which helps turn Alexander into a paragon of chivalry. The hero is depicted in a variety of combats, skirmishes and duels, where he displays the audacity, temerity, and bravery that strike fear into his enemies and awaken the admiration of his friends and allies. His exceptional prowess is emphasized in the laments declaimed over his mortal remains. Thus Aristé, one of the twelve peers, observes: "Que de toutes proëces estiés la fontaine,/ Sor trestoutes estoit la vostre soveraine" (Br. IV, vv. 1242–43: that you were the wellspring of all prowess; among all others yours was supreme). The hero's portrait is condi-tioned by this major virtue in the world of epic and romance and is structured by the warlike values associated with it. Alexander's prowess finds its counter-part in his spiritual successor, Caesar. The numerous combats and battles, on land and at sea, bring the hero into the foreground, revealing his consummate mastery of the art of warfare and his propensity to thrust himself, body and soul, into every sort of confrontation. In this historical account, the prowess of the Roman leader and that of his adversaries is usually depicted according to conventions of epic and romance. Although the compiler is concerned with offering the most faithful image possible of the Roman past, he transposes the *res militaris* into medieval chivalry, while sometimes combining Roman and/ or Gaulish battle techniques, culled from his sources, with medieval methods.[17] Amidst his men, Caesar distinguishes himself through his prowess, while the text as a whole features a subtle and varied assortment of traits typical of Alexander's prowess as well: endurance, perseverance, physical force, a drive to fight and to exact submission.

An individual matter, prowess is uniquely consubstantial with the exer-cise of the power that determines its objectives. As exemplary models of prowess, the two leaders are in fact model governors as well, since the mastery of power entails the establishment of some form of government. Both are clever strategists and managers of men, who blend charismatic authority and uncompromising standards, tempered by good will toward their men. This attitude is defined by Nicolas's messenger with reference to Alexander: "A ciaus qui sont o lui est frans et de bon aire,/ Et vers ses enemis est fel et de put aire" (Br. I, vv. 625–26: With his allies he is loyal and kind; toward his enemies he is cruel and malevolent). Caesar's attitude is apparent throughout the text from his actions, and is synthesized in the final portrait, borrowed from Suetonius (*Faits*, pp. 724–25 [13]). Such qualities are subsumed under the rubric of dispenser of justice. Both know how to grant rewards and punish evil. In many anecdotes Alexander is a teacher of lessons, as he punishes the ruthless murderers of Darius or congratulates his good and loyal servants by giving gifts. In the *Faits des Romains*, the compiler recasts the profile of the dispenser of justice in terms of magnanimity by developing notations in Suetonius.[18] Above all, what associates the two characters and identifies them as leaders and conquerors is the quality of largesse, indissociably linked with Alexander, who is its living embodiment.[19] Throughout his life, the Macedonian king generously lavishes his possessions; he distributes the wealth of his parents; repossesses the holdings of usurers and restores them to their original owners; and gives away the spoils of his victories to youths and soldiers. His treatment of Porus, the most selfish of kings, best illustrates his conception and practice of largesse as a source of power and sovereignty (p. 435, vv. 2213–16). As a dynamic of conquest and a fundamental political principle, largesse determines both the image of a king who depends on his men and that of knights who are bound to their monarch. The establishment of a relation of interdepen-dence obscures the depiction of an authoritarian leader, in contrast to a Darius whose lack of exchange with his entourage is one cause of his failure (Br. III, l. 11). Frequently reflected upon in the *Faits des Romains*, largesse is similarly conceived as a key factor in the accession to power. Like Alexander, Caesar lavishes his possessions and the spoils of his conquests in order to forge and strengthen the solid entourage and the large circle of devoted warriors that he had lacked (p. 45, ll. 6–7). The Macedonian, and following him the Roman, elaborate an art of sovereignty based on conquest defined in terms of material growth and exchanges.

Such sovereignty would nonetheless remain incomplete and unsatisfactory without the addition of the quest for knowledge. Indissociable from the acquisition of power, it is an essential dimension of the personality of both heroes. In the twelfth century, the clerics at the court of Henry II Plantagenet included Alexander and Caesar in the list of educated monarchs.[20] Alexander in fact received training in all realms of knowledge from his prestigious master Aristotle. The content of his instruction varies according to versions. In Alexandre de Paris it is above all moral, based on learning sacred tongues, rhetoric and law, and on the acquisition of everything that contributes to his formation as an ideal cleric (Br. I, l. 15). Through his prowess and knowledge, Alexander embodies the union of chivalry and *clergie*, a medieval ideal whose fortunes are well-known. The latter favors and exalts chivalry: culture confers the superior wisdom necessary for the enlightened exercise of power. Inversely, prowess stems from an abiding desire for more knowledge. Chivalry and *clergie* are caught up in a circular relationship, while Alexander's actions also manifest his remarkable intelligence, poise, vivacity, as well as his ability to manipulate language and signs.[21] In this sense, Caesar is another Alexander. Although his wisdom is not of the same nature, it is nonetheless as diversified, as we see in the enumeration of his capabilities in the final portrait. He possesses the art of rhetoric and eloquence, revealing himself to be a talented, seasoned orator who is praised by Cicero. His intellectual precocity is remarkable, and he is the author of numerous works (*Faits*, pp. 723–24 [11]–[12]). The compiler sums up the way in which he wishes to lead his life: "Tot son tens voloit gaster ou en chevalerie ou en clergie, sanz les hores de boivre et de mengier et de solacier od dames" (p. 724, ll. 23–26: He wanted to lavish all of his time on chivalry or learning, not on idle hours of drinking and eating and womanizing). For both heroes, knowledge is a major, vital necessity. Will Caesar not go so far as to say that he prefers the possession of knowledge to that of power? As for the order of Alexander's conquests, does it not reflect a hierarchy of interests?

The two rulers show a perfect convergence of characteristics.[22] A comparative reading of the two destinies, based on Alexander's lament, would produce two portraits as mirror images of one another, at the heart of which lies a complex ideal of power. The similar itineraries, mind-sets and objectives that relate the heroes undoubtedly stem from a common character trait: pride and the greed it engenders, through a desire for total conquest. Alexander's extreme pride, which is noted in the earliest literary manifestations, is identical to the principal character trait of Caesar, especially in the portrait that closes the text (*Faits*, pp. 735–37). Pride is a source of strength, ascendancy, and success, in that it marshals all of the other qualities, but is also a source of weakness, loss, and failure through excess, whether it be Alexander's desire to rival the gods or Caesar's interpretation and manipulation of divine omens in his own interest, as in the famous episode in which he crosses the Rubicon.[23]

Pride as both strength and weakness explains, in the mode of government established, the flaws of a political ideal determined *a priori*. Alexander and Caesar share a nearly similar concept of exclusive authority, as we see in the relations they establish with their men. Their largesse is thus subject to profound fluctuations, because it is propelled only by greed. In Alexandre de Paris, rather than being the instrument of political conduct recommended by Aristotle (Br. I, vv. 680–81), it is a mode of being and of perceiving oneself as king, not in order to generate a series of exchanges within a circularity that, without neutralizing differences of rank, raises the royal figure to the status of *primus inter pares*, but in order to exalt and to isolate him in his sovereignty. Caesar's practice of largesse is much more ostensibly subversive and cynical. He gives freely to everyone, without discriminating between nobles and non-nobles. Traditionally a royal and aristocratic virtue reserved for the chivalric elite, largesse is here degraded and contributes, according to Gabrielle Spiegel, to a uniformly negative portrait of Caesar, one with which the compiler would have intended to denounce the inferior ruler, in this instance Philip Augustus, who is referred to in the text and who would be Caesar's double.[24] Such a parallel can doubtless be made between the two men in power and is prompted by the choice of the decisive point at which the passage from the Republic to dictatorship and the Empire begins; the author could be using Caesar to denounce royal absolutism and the marginalization of Northern French aristocracy. Nevertheless, this work is not a political pamphlet, and though it has a contestatory political dimension to it, it can be characterized overall as a search for a new objectivity with regard to earlier texts, one that attests to a concern with Roman alterity and reveals a new way of conceiving of history and of producing it.[25] This does not rule out an apparent critique of Caesar, whose utilization of largesse is perceived as nefarious and reprehensible, as well as dangerous to established order of any sort. Here the Roman differs from the Macedonian, who gives only to knights. Unlike Caesar, Alexander shuns dubious associates, a principle that joins largesse, as the other leitmotif in the text. And yet he strays but once from that principle and thus dies, poisoned by a serf (Br. IV, *laisse* 8 ff.).

Largesse—arising from greed and, whether deliberately or out of a momentary weakness, from reliance on a dubious entourage—is a major flaw in both rulers and reflects an authoritarian, if not a tyrannical, notion of power. In the context of an apology for a knight-king and cleric, Alexandre de Paris's romance conveys, through its silences, lacunae, and contradictions, an ambiguous image of the hero as a monarch absolute on account of his immoderation.[26] Despite the presence of the twelve peers, Alexander makes his decisions alone, rarely soliciting the counsel of his men and scarcely respecting it. Once he is even violent, with Perdicas, for recommending that the conquests cease (Br. II, *laisse* 124, vv. 2655–56). He appears as sovereign judge in the trial of Dares's murderers and imposes his will upon his peers (Br. III, *laisse* 15). A few discreet criticisms do in fact emanate from within his entourage with regard to his temerity, thirst for conquest, and insatiable pride.[27] All of this shows that self-centeredness spawns absolute authority with no other finality than satisfaction of a desire for omnipotence. Caesar's authoritarianism is of a similar nature: he confuses his own interests with those of Rome and strives to acquire personal power and glory. These are the reproaches addressed to him by Cato and Pompey, his arch rivals who serve Rome rather than have Rome serve their personal triumphs. Once he has reached the summit of power, Caesar introduces a dictatorship, the consummate form of absolutism; he makes the laws, mobilizes the armies, creates the games and amusements, and redefines space by erecting monuments designed to perennialize his glory. In sum, he models Rome in the image of his own desires and prestige: "Apres disoit [Cesar] que l'en devoit de totes besoignes prendre conseill a lui, et tenir por loi quamque il disoit" (p. 735, ll. 6–8: Then he specified that he be consulted concerning all initiatives, and that his word be law).

The limits revealed by the exercise of power are equally apparent in the realm of knowledge, which is the object of an incessant, always unfulfilled quest. For Alexander, the oriental venture—a disappointing experience if ever there was one—takes shape both as an impossible conquest of alien space and as a forbidden quest for immortality and divine secrets.[28] The voyage to the Terrestrial Paradise as depicted in the *Faits des Romains* gives some sense of this. While, with Achoreus, broadening the scope of his knowlege, Caesar, like Alexander before him, is unable to penetrate the secrets of the Nile: "Li soverains rois Alissandres envoia parmi le Nile . . . por trover le chief dou flum. Mes ce fu neenz . . . (p. 631, ll. 31–33; p. 632, ll. 19–20: The sovereign king Alexander sent a party up the Nile . . . in search of the river's source, but in vain). Then the compiler again compares the two heroes so as better to emhasize the utter powerlessness of leaders bent on rivaling the gods.

By incorporating the myth of Alexander as a substratum, the text offers a nuanced view of the Roman leader, whose portrait acquires unprecedented depth and is haloed in the aura of conquering hero. Alexander is both a foil for Casesar and the latter's preferred role model. When Caesar visits the ruins of Troy other heroes are cited, including Hector and Achilles, but their profiles solely as warlords, with no inclination to explore knowledge, do not make them "complete" models and sustain only partial, purely conventional comparison.[29] In this perspective, the parallel between Alexander and Caesar, in essence legitimate, creates a kind of continuity and initiates an affiliation that will continue with the historico-political figures of Louis XIV and Napoleon. Caesar's wish to become a new Alexander, however, cannot conceal the contrasts between them. By bringing in Alexander, the compiler, amidst an apparent convergence of traits, renders Caesar all the more unique in terms of his manner of governance. That the Macedonian hero is presented ambiguously, at times mistreated and reviled over time, scarcely tarnishes his luster; he passes brilliantly into posterity and remains the emblematic mythic figure of the conqueror. Caesar on the other hand escapes any categorisation whatsoever, as we see in the *Faits des Romains*.

For Alexander, conquering the world means founding cities—in this case, the twelve Alexandrias. Alexandre de Paris scarcely dwells on this essential characteristic; during the Oriental campaign the Macedonian founds not a single one, although this partakes of a desire to avoid enclosure within the confines of a city, precisely when it is a matter of extending the world's frontiers ever outward and enlarging the scope of knowledge. The hero nonetheless remains a natural "creator," founder of cities in which the values of civilization take shape. In this respect, Caesar is an "anti-Alexander": he conquers the world, from Gaul to the Near East, without it ever being a matter of founding cities. Above all, he wants to conquer Rome, a city already founded, inscribed into the course of history, and with a tradition that he wishes to appropriate and redefine. He is a pragmatic hero who tailors his ambitions to what already exists, to the point of altering its foundations and its values. The object and modalities of conquest thus contrast the two heroes, as well as their natures. These divergences emerge in characteristic fashion in the way the Orient is perceived.

For Alexander the Orient is suffused with marvels whose unheard-of profusion of treasures inspires both admiration and dreams, yet whose horrible monsters and extremely severe climate also cause repulsion and nightmares. The Orient is also a place of initiation where the hero discovers the paths of his destiny yet also the degree of his finitude, in adventures that are new with regard to the tradition of oriental discovery.[30] There is also a new awareness of alterity, in the perception of a vast and unknown world and of time governed by other laws, including that of chance. The Oriental expedition is thus an innovation in every respect, elaborated within an uncharted "before" and "beyond" and commensurate with the zeal of a hero who strives to surpass earthly limitations and break free of the yoke of his human condition. Alexander's itinerary is simultaneously horizontal, to the extent that he spans the entire world, and vertical, in that he strives to rise above the earth (Br. III, v. 4967) or to plunge into its depths (Br. IV, v. 4987). Both horizontal and vertical conqueror, the hero is obsessed with a desire to transcend his human nature, which prompts his ceaseless, unbridled wandering in quest of immortality. Yet even though he constantly pushes the limits of the forbidden and encounters failure in disappointment and finally in death, he succeeds in living out to its fullest extent a complete initiatory itinerary and the confrontation with a form of the sacred.

In comparison with Alexander, Caesar is a more down-to-earth hero. His conquest lies on a horizon of expectations which is known, or at least "realistic" and plausible. In the *Faits des Romains* the Orient is no realm of extraordinary marvels. It is a domain of luxury and every sort of possession, as we see in the description of Ptolemy's palace, in spite of its somewhat medieval, occidental quality.[31] It is also a locus of debauchery: through its furnishings, this palace lends itself to indolence and lust. It is also a place of horror, where one encounters terrifying serpents and must endure a very harsh climate. As a fascinating realm that inspires both admiration and disgust, the Orient is "read" and apprehended as part of an assimilable alterity, in comparison with the known and mastered space of reference, the medieval West. And without being expelled from the text, the marvelous remains describable and assimilable. Just as Caesar's Orient, a "historical" Orient, differs from Alexander's, so do the nature of his conquests take another direction. His itinerary leads to no disclosure of his destiny or the manner of his death, but is rather a stage on his march toward empowerment and the acquisition of knowledge. The decisive fact of his inability to penetrate the secret of the Nile's source confirms the fundamental alienation from the sacred and the impossibility of attaining any sort of transcendence. Moreover, his search for knowledge seems to stem only from his quest for pleasure, the same pleasure he finds in satisfying his desire for power or his sexual appetite. In sum, Caesar emerges as an earthly hero, immersed in his reality as a "historical" figure and reduced to his human condition, even though he is among the elect and undoubtedly superior.

The differences between Alexander and Caesar materialize in the representations to which they lend themselves. Alexander's status is always at issue: is he an epic or a romance hero? When the narrative works through an individual adventure or the hero fights for an idea he has of himself, he never struggles alone for a superior cause, and the texts variously set forth a collective ideal of imperial conquest, in the name of communal interests. With Caesar, the compiler engages a profound modification of the conquering hero figure. A leader guided by a religion that governs his pride and his desires, he struggles exclusively for himself alone, Rome being but the source that slakes his thirst for power. The ambiguity conveyed by this frenzied individualism is heightened by the emphasis on his lust and his ceaseless quest for pleasure. In the Egyptian episode where he meets Cleopatra, he is swept away by the appeal of sensual and sexual delights; in the final portrait, his bisexuality is described at length according to Suetonius, the remarkable innovation being that no unfavorable judgment or definitive condemnation is leveled against him. In contrast, perhaps on account of his ambiguous sexuality, Alexander's love relationships are usually veiled in cautious silence, with the notable exceptions in Alexandre de Paris's romance of the courtly episode of the Amazons and, to a lesser degree, of Alexander and Queen Candace. Both a mythic and an epico-romanesque figure, Alexander is the model for a Caesar who wishes to be caught up in the momentum of his illustrious predecessor and follow in his footsteps.[32] In the *Faits des Romains*, however, Caesar lacks the mythic aura surrounding Alexander. He is a complex, problematic character tormented by the intrinsic imperfection of his human nature. The compiler, availing himself of the devices of narrative in order to render the conduct of a major actor in Roman history more suggestive, casts him as a hero of romance, yet he remains an essentially historical personage, certainly exceptional yet also human. Whereas Alexander, problematic though he may be, travels in a different dimension of the imaginary, escaping confinement in a historical continuum.[33]

It is tempting to turn the Caesar of the *Faits des Romains* into a new Alexander. As a kind of preamble, the Roman leader's lament before the statue of his illustrious model effectively inaugurates a parallel reading of the two destinies whose similarities are constantly in evidence, thus prompting discovery of a previously marginal hero in vernacular literature. This notwithstanding, Caesar is no Alexander, but a historical figure portrayed in terms of his individualism and ambiguities, his single-minded search for pleasure, which power and knowledge no less than lust can procure. He stands apart from the stylized image the compiler reserves for the Macedonian, who serves as the standard for measuring the Roman's "heroic" quality. Working on a key period in Roman history, the compiler thus does not overlook the mythico-legendary dimension in order to create an image of Caesar that goes well beyond text and context. Juxtaposition of the two heroes provides a means of inscribing the Roman leader into the lineage of worthies, of whom Alexander is the most brilliant representative. The comparison also enables the compiler to integrate, in a decisive way, the personage of Caesar into history, making him into the perfect incarnation of an ambivalent man in whose exemplary strength, marked by an indomitable fragility, we discover the quintessence of the human condition.

Notes

1. *Li fet des Romains, compilé ensemble de Saluste et de Suetoine et de Lucan, texte du XIIIe siècle*, ed. Louis-Ferdinand Flutre and Karl Sneyders de Vogel, 2 vols. (Paris: Droz; Groningen: Wolters, 1938; Geneva: Slatkine Reprints, 1977); here abbr. *Faits*.

2. Cf. Emmanuèle Baumgartner, "Romans antiques, histoires anciennes et transmission du savoir aux XIIe et XIIIe siècles," in *Mediaeval Antiquity* (Leuven: Leuven University Press, 1995), pp. 219–35.

3. Cf. Flutre, *Les Manuscrits des "Faits des Romains"* (Paris: Hachette, 1932), pp. 1–2.

4. *MFRA II*, Br. I, vv. 203–4.

5. Suetonius, *Vies des douze César*, ed. and trans. H. Alloud (Paris: Les Belles Lettres, 1967), I, 1.

6. On anachronism in the *Faits*, see Catherine Croizy-Naquet, *Ecrire l'histoire romaine au début du XIIIe siècle: "l'Histoire ancienne jusqu'à César," les "Faits des Romains"* (Paris: Champion, 1999), pp. 154–87.

7. The dream about the serpent that emerges from a broken egg, thrice circles the bed, then goes back in; see *RA*, Br. I, *laisse* 9.

8. Cf. Emmanuèle Baumgartner, "La Fortuna di Alessandro nei testi francesi medievali del secolo XII e l'esotismo nel *Roman d'Alexandre*," in *Le Roman d'Alexandre: Riproduzione del ms. Venezia, Biblioteca Museo Correr 1493*, ed. Roberto Benedetti (Udine: Roberto Vattori, 1998), pp. 11–28.

9. *Faits*, pp. 397–99. On the misidentification of Gion as the Ganges instead of the Nile, see vol. 2, p. 162.

10. *Faits*, vol. 2, p. 162. See the edition of the *Iter Alexandri Magni ad Paradisum* in *Prise*, pp. XLI–XLVII. For comparison of the two texts, see Martin Gosman, "*Le Roman d'Alexandre*: les interpolations du XIIIe siècle," in *Le Roman antique au Moyen Age*, ed. Danielle Buschinger (Göppingen: Kümmerle, 1992), pp. 61–72; and Gaullier-Bougassas, *Frontières*, pp. 478–84.

11. Cf. the analysis by Flutre, p. 20.

12. See Croizy-Naquet, *Ecrire l'histoire romaine*, pp. 125–54.

13. Ibid., pp. 102–24.

14. Jacques de Longuyon, *Les Voeux du Paon*, ed. R. L. Graeme Ritchie, in *The Buik of Alexander*, by J. Barbour, vols. 2, 3, and 4 (Edinburgh and London: The Scottish Text Society, 1921–1929).

15. See in particular *MFRA II*, Br. I, vv. 22–29; Br. IV, l. 23–32; *Faits*, p. 8, ll. 1–2; pp. 738–40.

16. *Faits*, pp. 489–90 [19]; p. 726 [17]; cf. vol. 2, pp. 181; 218. AdeP, Br. I, ll. 18–22.

17. On this complicated practice, see Croizy-Naquet, *Ecrire l'histoire romaine*, pp. 218–64.

18. See AdeP, Br. I, ll. 13–17; *Faits*, pp. 728–32.

19. On Alexander's largesse, see Gaullier-Bougassas, *Frontières*, pp. 324–30; on Caesar's, see Croizy-Naquet, *Ecrire l'histoire romaine*, pp. 218–64.

20. On the model of the literate knight-prince, see in particular Reto R. Bezzola, *Les Origines et la formation de la littérature courtoise en Occident (500–1200)*, 3 vols. (Paris: Champion, 1944–1963), vol. 2, pp. 326–66; 517–37.

21. On the way in which he reinterprets the gifts from Darius, see Croizy-Naquet, "Darius ou l'image du potentat perse dans le roman d'Alexandre de Paris," in *Alexandre*, pp. 161–72.

22. The brief portrait that closes the text of Alexandre de Paris could apply to Caesar as well: see *MFRA II*, Br. IV, vv. 1669–72.

23. Cf. Gaullier-Bougassas, *Frontières*, pp. 493–50. For the crossing of the Rubicon, see the *Faits des Romains*, pp. 347–50.

24. On Caesar's largesse, see *Faits*, pp. 340–41 [7]–[9]; see also Gabrielle Spiegel, *Romancing the Past: The Rise of Vernacular Prose Historiography in Thirteenth-Century France* (Berkeley and Los Angeles: University of California Press, 1993), pp. 99–213.

25. See Croizy-Naquet, *Ecrire l'histoire romaine*, pp. 125–87.

26. The author formulates no direct criticisms of the hero, yet the latter's amibvalence is constantly manifested in an atypical agenda based on strictly personal use of royal prerogatives in service to absolute power.

27. Cf. Br. I, *laisse* 112; Br. II, *laisse* 82; Br. III, *laisse* 60.

28. Cf. Gaullier-Bougassas, *Frontières*, pp. 423–519.

29. *Faits*, Caesar's pilgrimage to Troy, pp. 614–15.

30. See also Emmanuèle Baumgartner, "L'Orient d'Alexandre," *Bien dire et bien aprandre* (*Le Roman d'Alexandre*) 6 (1988), 7–15.

31. See Croizy-Naquet, "Un exemple de l'imaginaire oriental dans les *Faits des Romains*," *Pris-Ma*, 13 (1997), 157–67.

32. See also François Suard, "Alexandre est-il un personnage de roman?," *Bien dire et bien aprandre* (*Autour du Roman d'Alexandre*), 7 (1989), 77–87; and Gaullier-Bougassas, *Frontières*, pp. 343–520.

33. In spite of the efforts of the author of the *Histoire ancienne* who, by juxtaposing the different segments of human history, effectively neutralizes the presentation of the heroes, who are stylized and reduced to a few characteristics borrowed from ancient traditions.

11

Alexander the Great as the Icon of Perfection in the Epigones of the *Roman d'Alexandre* (1250–1450): The *Utilitas* of the Ideal Prince

Martin Gosman

According to legend, Alexander was very much aware that his conquests were to change the course of history. For this reason he ordered his historiographers to draw up an account of his exceptional deeds. We know that accounts were made by Callisthenes, the official historiographer, as well as by Aristobulus, Cleitarchus, and Ptolemy. Unfortunately their texts are lost, but some indications of their points of view can be detected in the works of Plutarch, Quintus Curtius, and many others. In them, however, the evaluation of Alexander's exploits varies enormously: some praise him, while others see his enterprise as a manifestation of sheer *hybris*. Whatever the nature of their judgments, it is evident that all give a tropological interpretation of the conqueror's adventures. His deeds have also been interpreted in a soteriological way; in the Book of *Daniel*, written in the second century before Christ, his empire is considered the third *regnum* in the history of mankind. There is even a strictly historical perception: the Book of *Maccabees*, which seems to have been begun c. 100 B.C., considers the Macedonian adventure as the beginning of the history of the Seleucids.[1]

Legend, however, has been quick to take possession of history's legacy. Most important here is Quintus Curtius's *History of Alexander* (first century A.D.), in which the author admits to having introduced facts which he himself considers unbelievable.[2] This creative attitude was adopted by later writers of romance and pseudohistorians who occupied themselves with the life and deeds of the famous conqueror. The presence of the Macedonian army in what was considered the *oikoumènè* provided the necessary authoritative framework—enriched through information about the strange people and the marvelous flora and fauna believed to be characteristic of the unknown parts of Asia—for which they found the details in the works of Pliny the Elder, Solinus, Isidorus, and many others. The last stage in the transformation process is the admiration for the successful ruler himself, for his extraordinary capacities as a general and a ruler. This last aspect is vital to medieval Alexander literature, since it turns his adventure into an example typologically exploitable by propagandists in the service of medieval rulers.

Of course, the Macedonian is not the only hero with whom medieval rulers like to be compared. There are also Caesar, Hannibal, Charlemagne, and many others. The problem, however, was that the real nature of the models was not known, since the past with all its heroes is but a psychological and even theological construct that can do without any empirically verifiable points of reference. Until the fifteenth century, history seems to be a collection of moral precepts which, in one way or another, always evoke a lost perfection.[3] Small wonder that classical moralism, as expressed by clichés such as *historia magistra vitae* or *aurea aetas,* is easily combined with Christian soteriological notions as evoked by the well-known *laudatio temporis acti* and *degradatio temporum* clichés. Not only does this explain why the excellence manifested by an individual hero in a specific context is considered to be the result of a divine intention; it also justifies a typological approach to historical facts. Analogy seems to be the key: Charlemagne is depicted as an *alter David* and as an *alter Christus* and Henry II Plantagenet is presented as *Alexander occidentalis.* Typology can also be of concern to collectivities: the illustrious Trojans are cast as the ancestors of the Romans and also of the French, the English, and the Germans. There is no end to all this: in the sixteenth century, Etruscan civilization becomes a model as well as a political excuse for both Florentine independence and Medicean rule,[4] while sixteenth-century French propaganda recognizes the political possibilities of ancient Gaul's legendary heroism. It is clear that the past, having a "wax nose" (Alain of Lille), can serve any situation and any purpose.[5]

An analysis of the way medieval French Alexander texts adapt the legacy of the Latin writers reveals that the *narratio* itself is never changed. Taking into account that any reshuffling of facts necessitates an adequate knowledge of the contexts evoked in the sources exploited, this is only logical. Since medieval authors do not know what Alexander's society was like, they totally ignore its sociopolitical and military characteristics; even the exact localization of Macedonia seems to have generated difficulties. This, however, in no way bothers the authors who are supposed to produce a functional—that is to say, a sociologically "readable"—text.[6] Their product has to guarantee three important things: a recognizable polysystem (hence the importance of anachronisms); a perfect ruler whose conduct can be imitated; and presentation of a sociopolitical behavior capable of generating the required successes. In our case the first element is Alexander's Macedonia, the second concerns the hero himself. The third, however, cannot but insist on the harmonious relationship between the ruler and the ruled.

The last element is the most important of the three, since medieval rulers are only interested in approaches that might help them to strengthen their *potestas* and impose their *auctoritas* over others.[7] Within this context facts are not really important, since everyone knows that Alexander's deeds—like the successes of other historical heroes—cannot be repeated, and everyone is much aware that the third *regnum* is no more. Even the fourth, embodied by the Roman Empire, has become part of history's legacy, and has been integrated into the Christian *oikoumènè*. Thus the poet has to take over from the historian. Medieval rulers (and, of course, the people in their service) are interested only in obtaining a good answer to the question of why Alexander had been so successful in liberating (and channelling) the energy by means of which he realized a sociopolitical consensus of which medieval princes could only dream. For the latter, the Macedonian was a model ruler whose status benefited from God's consent, whose authority was uncontested, and whose political and military projects were wholeheartedly supported by his people— a ruler whose successes were due to the fact that his men not only recognized his extraordinary qualities but manifested an unquestioning obedience. It is hardly surprising that the propagandists in the service of medieval rulers saw him as the *rex utilis* par excellence, as a type to be imitated.[8]

It is worth noting that most medieval adaptations of the life of the Macedonian are euphoric, since negative examples are inimitable.[9] The basis of his success seems to have been an uncontested authority in an adequately structured sociopolitical system—precisely what all the texts suggest. The problem, however, is that the descriptions of how that perfect system presumably allowed him to enforce both his *potestas* and *auctoritas* are essentially ambivalent. Sometimes portrayed as a ruler who seems to stand at the top of a vertically organised power structure demanding strict obedience from all subjects (here Roman legal traditions seem to exercise their influence), at other times he is seen as ruling a society with "feudal" traits, and is but the *primus inter pares* who cannot impose anything at all. However, since Alexander's political and military expediency is all that counts, the ambivalence seems unimportant, and indeed explains the legend's ontological adaptability to a great many different contexts: medieval society, feeding on the power of connotation, can live with incomplete descriptions, with "icons."

The Vulgate *Roman d'Alexandre* of Alexandre de Paris generated a whole series of interpolations in alexandrine verse written, *grosso modo*, between 1250 and 1350; in the fifteenth century, two prose compilations combine material taken from it with elements drawn from most of the interpolations. While the epigones tend to respect both the framework and the themes offered by the Vulgate version, they introduce changes in the relationship between the Macedonian and his men. Whether these are deliberate or not seems unimportant; what counts is the fact that they echo the changes in the factual relationship between the kings of France and their subjects. Of course, the echoes are vague—after all, we are dealing with literary texts—but their presence and functionality are undeniable. Their differences in perception are sometimes striking, but their evolution is slow and hesitant, and neither rectilinear nor systematic. In fact the changes only manifest themselves on the micro-level: a typical word or a curious formula may reflect either the growing impact of Roman legal theory or the factual reshuffling of the cards in the political arena in which the text is generated. The most significant changes, however, can be detected in the way the epigones describe (better: evoke) life at court, where the noble warrior is disciplined[10] and transformed into a noble courtier—a process that in some ways anticipates the basic philosophy of Baldassare Castiglione's 1528 *Cortegiano*.

This evolution is evident in the correspondences between sociopolitical reality on the one hand and, on the other hand, the "descriptions" of Macedonian society in the epigonal texts: the anonymous *Prise de Defur* of the second half of the thirteenth century; the *Voeux du Paon* written in 1313–14 at the request of Thibaud, bishop of Liège, by Jacques de Longuyon; the *Restor du Paon* finished before 1338 by a certain Jean Le Court dit Brisebarre who seems to have lived in Douai; the *Parfait du Paon* made, before 1348, by Jean de Le Mote for the goldsmith Simon of Lille; and in prose the *Histoire du bon roy Alexandre*, written at the behest of Jean de Bourgogne before 1448 by Jean Wauquelin (= *Histoire*), and *Les Fais et Concquestes du Noble roy Alexandre* (= *Fais*) produced by an anonymous compiler between 1450 and 1470.[11] Analysis of these correspondences not only illuminates the traditional permeability of literary texts, but also reveals transformations in the relationship between the ruler and his companions. Depicted in the earlier texts as a classical *dux* with the characteristics of a Germanic "Heerführer," Alexander is slowly transformed into a *persona* who represents an *institutio* in which medieval feudal traditions definitively yield to Roman legal principles.[12] The differences noted also indicate the nobles' loss of autonomy. All these adaptations of the Macedonian's *vita* are narrative illustrations of the same syllogism. Its major premise claims that the historical Alexander was able to play his historical role because he benefited both from God's consent and from the unconditional loyalty of his subjects.[13] The minor states that the literary Macedonian's *modus operandi* is in perfect accord with the traditions of the past as well as with the political conceptions of medieval French society. The conclusion imposes itself: the successful way in which Alexander exercises his *auctoritas* is the best way to implement the God-given royal *potestas* in medieval—that is to say French— society.[14]

It goes without saying that any consideration of whether the epigonic texts echo the evolution of their sociopolitical context has to take into account that literary texts cannot but produce yet another interpretation of "historical reality." This is particularly true in medieval literature, which tends to ignore the necessity of empirical verification. It must also allow for another fact: the epigones, who pretend to fill the narrative gaps of their source text, have to respect the basic perceptions and conditions of that text. Alexander has to remain the model hero whose deeds generate typological possibilities; if ever his companions come to the fore, their activities can be interpreted only as the consequence of some temporary delegation of power. In other words, nothing happens without the master's consent. It is hardly surprising that all the texts insist on the alleged political stability and social harmony in Macedonia's (noble and military) society. Even if the "icon" Alexander is transformed from a traditional "Germanic" army chief into what might be interpreted as a "Roman" ruler, the change will never be complete. The Macedonian actor (in the Greimassian sense) is either a feudal prince with "monarchical" characteristics, or a monarchical ruler with "feudal" traits. Whatever the option chosen by the authors of the epigonic texts, their Macedonian nobles adhere to the precepts of the medieval literary canon: they are unconditionally loyal to each other as well as to their master; they ignore fear, reject discourteous behavior, and consider a lavish lifestyle to be a sign of true chivalric nobility.

Even if the literary product depends on the magic of the (supposedly) correct formula, Alexander's personal qualities are never really described, since any specification of the typologically perfect is essentially limited. Standard qualifications, however, stimulate connotations. The Macedonian is handsome, strong, capable, trusted and loved by his soldiers, etc. This, of course, is hardly surprising. Much more important is the bond between the hero and his noble companions, because it explains the focus, by both Alexandre de Paris and the authors of the epigonic texts, on the narratively less important details which readers/listeners will recognize and accept as being identical with their own sociopolitical and emotional standards. This is the integration mechanism well-known in propaganda: after having identified in the message those elements with which they are familiar, or of which they dream, people tend to accept the remainder of the information provided.[15]

There is, however, a serious psychological problem. Even if some specific formulas can be explained by the fact that in the period in question the political cards are being reshuffled, the changes are never complete. There are two reasons for this: 1) history is, as Braudel has noted, a process of which the ad-hoc event is only a constituent part, and 2) although propagandists are aware of this fact, they never try to describe the situation or the process with which they are supposed to deal, but prefer the creative possibilities of the suggestive formula. Here too, connotation is preferred. It is, however, also a fact that, even if major changes occur, propaganda will try to conceal them. Rulers in the Middle Ages and the Renaissance, while most keen on strengthening their position, always refuse to acknowledge openly that the familiar context no longer exists. Thus monarchical society maintains the traditional feudal ritualism as long as possible, since it needs the support of key societal figures who, traditionally conservative, cling to old values. The psychology of politics demands that age-old ritualism mask society's new dynamism.[16] This explains, for example, the conservative *modus scribendi* of medieval and Renaissance

authors whose audiences (nobles and/or bourgeois) dislike "nouvelletés" (nov-
elties) in sociopolitical reality.[17] But changes do occur, and they are nowhere
more manifest than in the way the nobles have to behave at court.

This is already noticeable in the Vulgate, where Alexander's appeal to the
juvenes to avenge the insults to Macedonia's honor by Darius III of Persia not
only generates a remarkable enthusiasm but also establishes Alexander's authority
as leader, as a *dux*. Moreover, his personal desire to punish the Persian's arrogance is immediately perceived as a duty that the (noble) collectivity has to
assume. It is, of course, possible to detect traces of the anthropomorphic
conception of society: the head decides, the body follows; sociopolitical harmony seems to be the key. There is, however, a snag: although the young
nobles accept the consequences of their personal relationship with their liege
lord, their enthusiasm is motivated primarily by the possible material security
which, one day, will reward their unconditional support of the latter's cause.
The episode of the *Val Périlleux*, where the Macedonians fear for their master's
life after he decides to sacrifice himself in order to save his men, is a perfect
illustration of the catastrophic consequences to be anticipated from a disappearance of the king, for with him they would also lose their economic
security. This particular fact must have been understood in medieval society
where political or administrative continuity was only a haphazard phenomenon. Apart from the activities in the first part of the text, where the gathering
of the *juvenes* and Alexander's knighting can only refer to the existence of a
court, and the events at Babylon, where the hero organises a typical
"*Festkrönung*,"[18] the Vulgate ignores the court as the symbol of royal *auctoritas*.
Of course, one has to admit that an attempt to conquer the *oikoumènè* can
hardly be considered an invitation to a sedentary life. Taking into account the
modus vivendi at Arthur's court as evoked, for instance, in the romances of
Chrétien de Troyes, the absence in the Vulgate of a stable power structure is
somewhat surprising. The same may be said of the rather technical presentation
of chivalry: the Amazon episode in Alexandre de Paris is the only one that reveals
what might be interpreted as courtly behaviour (*Légende*, pp. 243–65).

A rather significant element suggests that things are changing. When
the compiler refers to Alexander's wish to be crowned at Babylon, he does
not specify the status of the crown the conqueror is to wear. Is it a *corona
regis* or a *corona regni*? Answering this question is difficult, since the whole
episode is connotated by the tradition of the four *regna* as evoked by the
prophet Daniel. Given the fact that the crown is definitely linked to Alexander's
status as *dominus mundi*, the second option (*corona regni*) might be favored. But
again, the modern interpreter has to be careful: there is no sign of a coherent
and stable sedentary power structure in the Macedonian empire. There is
something that might be considered to be a court, but there seems to be no
identification between the ceremonial court and some recognizable architectural structure.

At first glance the *Prise* does not introduce any significant variations, any clear signs of a different perception of the relationship between the king and his men. Alexander is presented as the "seignor des seignours et des vassaus la flour" (king of kings and the most illustrious knight, l. 27). The formula is rather ambivalent, since it is not clear whether it refers to an authentic desire for total sovereignty ("seignor des seignours") or to a hyperbolic perfection ("des vassaus la flour"); but whatever the author intended, it combines *auctoritas* and *militia* and thus confirms the traditional solidarity between the crown and the nobility.[19] The scene in which the king, whose heroic deeds are watched by his men, flings his lance into the door of Defur's main gate is a real piece of bravado (the hero proves that he is really the "flour") and it announces the theatrical side of chivalry, which will be so important in the texts belonging to the *Paon* cycle. The highly ritualized performance announces the dramatized emulation which, in the centuries that follow, will characterize the life of the nobleman.

Other scenes in the *Prise* reveal changes in royal behavior: Alexander no longer participates in all combats, but prefers to play chess in his tent and let his men do the fighting. To Floridas, a young noble captured by the Macedonians, Alexander admits that he owes his victories to his loyal vassals: "Batailles ai jou faites, et Dieu en doi loër, / Et mes bons compaignons servir et merchïer, / Qui m'ont fait par lor armes seignor du mont clamer" (ll. 466–68: I have fought [many] battles, for which I have to thank God as well as my loyal companions, who with their arms have made me the lord of the whole world). Together with the formula "seignor des seignors," the passage reflects the basic ambivalence already noted: Alexander is both a traditional liege lord who is accustomed to fight his battles together with his vassals, and a ruler who lets the latter take care of his interests. The very fact that he separates himself from his men, who are supposed to prevail, announces the slow but undeniable change in the position of medieval kings.[20] His behavior shows monarchical traits.

The theatrical side of noble life, as embodied in the *Prise* by Alexander's heroic act, becomes even more manifest in the texts centered around the peacock vows: the *Voeux*, the *Restor* and the *Parfait*. Whether they are in the palace of Ephezon or on the battlefield before that town, the nobles do their utmost to perform their role as perfectly as possible. In the *Chambre de Vénus*, a reserved space where the elite of chivalry engage in courtly conversation with noble ladies or play typical society games, *amor* inspires *militia*. On the battlefield, however, things are the other way round: there, the second element of the binomial provokes the first or finds its inspiration in it. The whole siege as described by Jacques de Longuyon is a hyperbole of coded *aemulatio*. The real master of the scene is Alexander who, from a promontory on the other side of the river, oversees the combats before the city. The nobles engaged in the fighting know that the king is observing everything, and that he judges his men's deeds as well as those of the noble knights of Ephezon. Moreover, since real nobility ignores "international" barriers, the king appreciates the deeds of the noble (and worthy) enemies. All noble actors (here in the theatrical sense of the word) try to please the royal spectator. The horizontal as well as vertical distance between the latter and the former suggests changes in sociopolitical structure: the nobles can no longer function without the king's approval.[21] The gallant discussions and the games in the *Chambre de Vénus*, moreover, are not innocent at all, since the acting talents of the noble lords and ladies now determine their position. Self-discipline and emotional control are the key factors in the noblemen's lives.[22] If they want to distinguish themselves from the crowd and please their lord, their performances have to reach the standards set by their society's code, which, in actual fact, is the prince's.

It is striking that the courtly lifestyle evoked in the *Chambre de Vénus* announces the simulated and coded correctness that Baldassare Castiglione will evoke in his *Cortegiano*. Since the military side of noble life has no need of motivation—tradition is the best guarantee the nobleman can offer—the verbal jousts in the *hortus conclusus* of the Ephezon court reveal themselves as one of the many obligatory occupations of the leisured class. In the centuries that follow, the verbal and emotional sophistication displayed in these discussions will be a perfect substitute for the nobleman's sociopolitical ambitions. This, of course, is the behavior that princes will stimulate as much as possible. It is clear that Jacques de Longuyon's interpolation enthusiastically trumpets the new ritualistic order of what one day will be the prince's monarchical absolutist *auctoritas*. The latter's court will be a stage where the noble actors have to play the role the prince is prepared to assign them.

This tendency is even more evident in the *Restor* and the *Parfait*, where noble emulation centers around the "restoration" of the peacock which, after having generated the well-known vows, was eaten. Since the noble damsel Edéa, who had sworn to restore the bird, had not been able to keep her word (the bird had to be eaten first), the author of the *Restor* makes Ephezon's goldsmiths produce a peacock of gold and precious stones. This generates considerable excitement: the noble lords and ladies try to outbid each other by offering gold and precious stones for the fabrication of the masterpiece ordered by Edéa. Even Alexander participates in the game. Moreover, the nobles pay for the right to enter the forge where the goldsmiths create the peacock; they seem to do this voluntarily, but in reality they cannot refuse the "entrance fee." Once the peacock is "restored," the circle is closed: everybody has done what he or she had promised to do.

The circularity that dominates the texts of the peacock cycle is symbolic of the situation at the prince's court. The whole ceremony, which practically resembles a religious service, is centripetal, since there is no external referentiality (ll. 158–99; 1309–1405). This becomes even more manifest in the discussion immediately following, where the different vows as well as the ways in which they have been implemented are judged in order to award a prize to the best contender. This, of course, is a rather sensitive matter, since the nobleman's touchiness—a sign of both his pretensions and his social and economic vulnerability—is proverbial. Taking into account the basic euphoria of the peacock texts, however, the dream is not to be shattered: *mirabile dictu*, the prize is awarded to Cassamus, Ephezon's *éminence grise* who had died in front of the city which he was defending against the intruder Clarus (ll. 2436 ff).

The whole episode confronts us with a different Alexander, since it is he who, in order to avoid any reproach of partiality, performs the ceremony and draws the lot that designates Cassamus as winner of the contest. The king is also the person before whom the nobles kneel when they want to address him (l. 971). It is he who organizes the marriages and orders the organization of court festivities, including a ball at which the conqueror himself begins the dance: ". . . quant vint au karoler / Li fors rois Alixandres por sa gent rescrïer / Commencha voiant tous, premerains a fester" (ll. 1101–3: . . . when the dancing started, the mighty king Alexander, who wanted to please his noble company, was the first who, in front of everybody, opened the ball). It goes without saying that the splendor of the ceremonial activities does not deceive anyone: the king's *auctoritas* is of a strictly political nature, and Alexander's every wish is the nobles' command. The example of line 2455, "Car par vos [= Alexandre] est li drois approuvés et descris" (Because it is by you that the law is approved and promulgated), is highly significant, since it evokes the Roman perception of the ruler as *fons legis* (see Pennington, pp. 119–64; 203–37).

The code the nobleman has to respect at his master's court is very much accentuated in the *Parfait*. Here the enemy Mélidus, whose men have captured three of Alexander's peers, informs the latter that even if someone bears a grudge against another person (noble, of course), he will never show this in court, since the master's residence is only a place for ". . . esbatemens, deduis, solaz et jus / Car qui est avec dame coiement a repus; / . . . doit parler d'amours . . ." (ll. 324–26: . . . entertainment, amusement, recreation and games / Because he who finds himself in the peaceful company of a lady . . . can only speak of love). This is "Affektkontrol" at its best.

The perspective introduced by Jacques de Longuyon into his *Voeux* has become the essence of the canon: the nobleman is now an actor who plays his master's game and who never forgets that the latter always observes him. The circularity of court(ly) life is emphasized further by two other elements. First is the *chambre amoureuse* in Mélidus's palace, dominated by his four daughters who pull all the strings. It is a perfect counterpart of Ephezon's *Chambre de Vénus* and this architectural imitation underlines, once again, the inescapable circularity of the nobleman's life in which changes ("nouvelletés") are to be avoided. There is even more: like the palace in the *Voyage de Charlemagne à Jérusalem et à Constantinople*, the room rotates on its axis. In the epic text Charlemagne and his men were unpleasantly surprised, but in the *Parfait* the rotation causes great merriment (ll. 1498–514). The second fact also confirms the basic circularity of life at court: the walls of the *chambre amoureuse* are covered with iconographical representations of Alexander's deeds. There is his descent to the bottom of the sea as well as his celestial journey (ll. 404–11). There is also—and the paint is still fresh ("Encore y rot on fet, pas .xv. jors n'avoit," l. 420: They had made the paintings not even two weeks before)— a picture of the peacock ceremony in the palace of Ephezon as described by Jacques de Longuyon. The court is a place where people remember, discuss, and judge excellent performances. The past motivates the present. Small wonder that the courtiers—and the qualification finally seems appropriate—also compose poems. Even Alexander, whom we have already seen dancing in the *Restor*, composes a ballad that he himself sings. Again, prizes are awarded: the first is given to one of Mélidus's daughters, and the second, a "vert chapel" (laurel wreath), to the Macedonian himself (ll. 983–1369).

Circularity, however, is a narrative's greatest enemy and it is precisely for this reason that the euphoria manifested in the different *chambres* is rapidly destroyed. The enemies who, after their defeat by the combined armies of Ephezon and Macedonia, had initially recognized Alexander as their liege lord, now rebel against his authority. The ferocious battle that follows is another sign that things are changing. In the *Voeux* it was not really the result that counted, but only the quality of the nobleman's performance; the elegant skill with which the knight unhorsed the adversary inspired love in the ladies who were watching the activities from Ephezon's walls, *militia* generating *amor*. Now the enemies betray Alexander, and they have to be punished. When the fighting is over, everybody has to mourn the death of a loved one. Reality dominates the scene, since the prince cannot tolerate any contestation whatsoever of his *auctoritas*.

The two fifteenth-century prose compilations, by Jean Wauquelin and an anonymous compiler, contain interesting indications of both the evolution in political theory and the changes in contemporary reality. Given the fact that these texts are even more voluminous than the interpolations mentioned above, I shall limit myself to a few examples. Both authors respect the macro-structure of the Macedonian adventure, but the changes they introduce (*nolens volens?*) into their compilations provide useful information about the way fifteenth-century authors perceived (or had to evoke) the relationship between the ruler and the ruled. Wauquelin wrote his *Histoire* in a Burgundian context.[23] As far as the anonymous *Fais* is concerned, it is impossible to determine the context in which it was produced, since the first leaves and the last ones of the manuscript are lost.[24] Remarkable, however, is the way in which both compilations reduce both the number and the size of the traditional battle scenes and favor description of court activities. The anonymous compiler of the *Fais* is more active here than Wauquelin, whose reworking is definitely less consequential.[25] Another significant contrast can be detected in the vocabulary of the two compilers; even if not consistent and certainly not systematic, it echoes the changes in the way fifteenth-century authors were putting contemporary ideas into words. Here again the compiler of the *Fais* has made a significantly greater effort than Jean Wauquelin.

Two examples will illustrate this. The first, taken from Wauquelin's *Histoire*, echoes day-to-day reality. In the reworking of the *Fuerre de Gadres* episode, which is the main body of the second *Branche* of Alexandre de Paris, Corneüs, the nephew of Alexander's lieutenant Emenidus, wants to meet his uncle. Wauquelin notes that Emenidus is "haultement recommandé en la court du roy Alixandre" (fol. 32v: highly recommended in king Alexander's court). Since the Vulgate ignored the existence of a court, the remark is interesting. The second example stems from the *Fais*. Jacques de Longuyon had introduced court life into the Alexander tradition, and since life at court can only be euphoric, sadness was qualified as the courtier's greatest enemy (see *supra*). The anonymous compiler of the *Fais* retains the descriptions of court life but adapts the passage in question by noting that court festivities are meant "pour joye commenchier et dechassier merancolie" (p. 174: to favor merriment and dispel melancholy). Textually the change is of minor importance, but it makes explicit that the court is a *hortus conclusus* to which only the nobles have access, and the court is a place where any manifestation of social or emotional noncon-formity is refused.[26] This, of course, is a perfect example of the emotional control mentioned earlier. These apparently minor alterations in fact reveal a new perception of life at court, where the nobles have to deal either with the physical presence of the ruler or with the latter's *auctoritas* as signified in a strictly hierarchical codification.

The same can be noted of the vocabulary used by the two compilers. It is indeed remarkable to find feudal terminology replaced by qualifications that derive their essence from a Roman legalistic perception of political struc-tures. While recounting the well-known conflict between Philip of Macedon and King Nicolas—the first in which Alexander is able to show his qualities as a military leader—Wauquelin qualifies Philip as a *"subget"* who has to pay a tribute to Nicolas's *"noble majesté"* (fol. 13v).[27] In the Vulgate Philip was only the latter's vassal. In the passage describing his marriage to Roxane, Alexander's dignity is marked as *"magesté imperiale"* (fol. 121v). Elsewhere, his robe is "d'un fin pourpre comme a son estat roial appartenoit" (fol. 87v: made of purple of the highest quality befitting his royal status). While addressing the "bourgeois" of Babylon, Alexander says that if these *"citoijens"* reveal themselves as his good *"subgiés"* he will be their *"bon seigneur"* (fol. 200v). In the same fragment Wauquelin refers to traditional feudal elements like the *"hommaige"* Sanson pays to his *"souverain seigneur* Alexander" (fol. 15v). While Wauquelin's terminology is somewhat inconsistent, that in the *Fais* is more coherent, and even more "Roman." A qualification like *"princes"* (pp. 133–34, 159, 166) replaces *"compaignon"* and *"seigneur"* (*Voeux*, ll. 327, 490). The court has become a *"court de prince"* (p. 136); a traditional formula like *"mauvaistié de baron"* (*Voeux*, l. 1204) becomes *"tyrannie de prince"* (p. 160), and *"malvais marchis"* is now *"parvers tyrant"* (p. 187). Alexander's "homes" are his *"subgetz,"* etc. Even if terms like *"tyrant"* and *"subgetz"*—and I limit myself to these examples—were already used in twelfth-century texts, the frequency with which they occur in the *Fais* can only signify that the perception of sociopolitical reality has changed.

Since literary and historiographical texts offer only virtual parallels with real society, it is impossible to draw any pertinent conclusion about the way contemporary medieval society was perceived by the elite who, in one way or another, was confronted with texts like those here discussed. However, if such texts were to be understood and accepted by their intended audience, there had to be a plausible relationship between the details of the *integumentum* (Alexander's adventure which is part of the past) and the context ("France" between, *grosso modo,* 1250 and 1450) which generated and consumed the products of the interpolators and compilers of the Alexander texts. And, in fact, there are significant details suggestive of a correspondence between the epigonic texts on the one hand, and their possible context on the other. The epigones definitely relegate the divine to the background and focus on the technical and legal aspects of the relationship between the ruler and his men. This movement can be explained by the evolution in the contemporary political arena, where the interest of medieval rulers in Roman legal constructions accounts for the transfer from a God-given *status aparte*, which can do without explanation, to a legal excellence (here in the etymological sense of the word) as embodied by, among others, the *legibus solutus* principle. In the course of time, human society is no longer perceived as the result of a divine decision, but as the consequence of an analytical reasoning largely indebted to recently (re)discovered Aristotelian thought and to the return of Roman law.

One way or another, the epigones respect the "historical" and legendary framework of the Macedonian adventure. The texts of the peacock cycle, however, are the result of a very creative invention process. Their interpolation into the Vulgate gives them an undeniable authenticity that—and this is vital— does not exclude the introduction of "nouvelletés." As noted, changes can only manifest themselves on the micro-level. The examples produced have shown that the military aspects of the Macedonian expedition are perceived differently by the authors of the epigonic texts. Alexandre de Paris, the compiler of the Vulgate, did not ignore the possibilities offered by the *amor et militia* topos, but he preferred the second element of the binomial; the hero's brief encounter with Candace and the charming episode in which two of his peers fall in love with Amazons are exceptions. The most significant absence in the Vulgate, however, is the court which, after all, is the *sedia regis/regni*. The epigones, on the contrary, emphasize the description of life at court; the changes they introduce not only concern the growing impact of *amor*, but also highlight the refinement of court ceremonial. The nobleman's prestige no longer depends exclusively on his performance on the battlefield, but also, and probably even more, on his correct behavior at court. Since the court is the *sedia regis*, the "Affektkontrol" as manifested by the noble knights and ladies is the consequence of the growing authority of medieval rulers who want to exercise a *potestas publica rotunda et plena* (Krynen, pp. 79, 87).

The intellectuals in the king's service understand this very well. Even if their own sociopolitical reality is far from euphoric, the legists as well as the authors of literary and historiographical documents exploit as much as possible the rediscovered principles of Roman law and present them as keys to stability, even to happiness. It goes without saying that both the frequency and the precision with which they do so depends on the political power of the rulers they serve. Well-known theorists like Jean de Paris, Pierre Dubois, and Marsilius of Padua boldly claim vertical and authoritarian power for their master, Philip the Fair. Their approach is rather direct. Charles V, however, prefers the indirect way: in 1376 he orders Evrard de Trémaugon to reformulate royal rights. The result is the *Somnium Viridarii*, which is translated very rapidly into the vernacular. In all legal texts the well-known statement "Quod principi placuit, legis habet vigorem" (*Digest*) is considered the very basis of royal authority.

Political success, however, can only be the result of sociopolitical consensus, since in this period royal power is certainly not strong enough to impose itself. The *utilitas regis* of which Alexander is supposed to have been the living incarnation is still part of the dream. It is for this reason that the principle "Quod omnes tangit ab omnibus tractari et approbari debet" remains so important in literary and historiographical texts and even in the ceremonial of royal entries, where the theoretical aspects of society's structure seem to retreat into the background. Moreover, the psychological effectiveness of this type of cultural product is based on the assumption that the "system" these products are supposed to evoke is beyond all theorizing: it is simply there. This explains why the implications of the "Quod principi placuit" principle are presented as taken for granted by the authors as well as by their audience. The "authoritative" formula is accepted because its essence is hidden by the suggestion of total sociopolitical harmony, which refers to an agreement between the ruler and the nobles.

Whatever the situation of the nobles, the ruler never leaves them without an occupation. The maxim "cessante causa, cessat effectus," which in so-called feudal society led to an effective reduction of royal *auctoritas*, seems to have been endowed with a new interpretation. Once the traditional *consilium et auxilium* had been provided, the vassals could leave their (liege) lord's dwellings and return to their fiefs, since there was no longer a *causa* necessitating their presence at the ruler's court or in his army. In the course of time, however, things changed: the rulers tried to exercise full control over their noble vassals and preferred not to leave them without a *causa*. The latter had to serve at court (even if only for a short period), where the ruler's presence seemed to take the sting out of traditional noble jealousy and transform life into some innocent courtly *aemulatio* that could only reach its fulfillment in restricted areas like the *Chambre de Vénus* or the *Chambre amoureuse*. The changes detected in the epigonic Alexander texts—and the same can be said of other literary texts of the period—concern only minor and suggestive details, since direct statements in a politically sensitive environment are always counterproductive.

I have pointed out that the courtly behavior of Jacques de Longuyon's heroes prefigures that of Baldassare Castiglione's nobles. It is evident that the noble protagonists in the *Voeux* lack the *sprezzatura* that in Castiglione's text characterizes the discussions and the behavior of the nobles during the Urbino soirées, but the heroes in the *Voeux* know how to play their role. Like his predecessor, the author of the *Cortegiano* describes what seems to be a voluntary participation of the nobles in court life, but neither the games in the Alexander epigonic texts nor the essentially open-ended "Ciceronian" dialogues in Castiglione's famous conduct-book should be considered as descriptions of a voluntary presence. On the contrary, as part of an imposed ceremonial, they imply submission and obedience. The courtiers can talk about their master's *potestas* and *auctoritas*, but they cannot discuss it.[28] The monarchical society of early modern Europe will show that the nobles have become courtiers, and that the games they are allowed to play are not only at their master's pleasure; they also symbolize his perfect *utilitas*.

Notes

1. *Daniel* 8, 3–21; *Maccabees* I, 1, 1–8. Cf. André-Marie Girard, *Dictionnaire de la Bible* (Paris: Robert Laffont, 1989), pp. 822–26; and Cary, *Parfait,* pp. 108, 289.

2. See John Yardley, trans., and Waldemar Heckel, intro. and notes, *Quintus Curtius Rufus. The History of Alexander* (Harmondsworth: Penguin Books, 1984), ch. IX, 1, 34.

3. Janet Coleman, "The Science of Politics and Late Medieval Academic Debate," in *Criticism and Dissent in the Middle Ages*, ed. Rita Copeland (Cambridge: Cambridge University Press, 1996), pp. 181–214.

4. See my "La 'reconstruction' du passé et la construction du pouvoir: le cas des Médicis," in *Ensi firent li ancessor. Mélanges de philologie médiévale offerts à Marc-René Jung,* ed. Luciano Rossi et al.(Milan: Edizioni dell'Orso, 1996), II, pp. 831–44.

5. For the "wax nose" see Jacques Le Goff, *La civilisation de l'Occident médiéval* (Paris: Flammarion, 1982), p. 299. The role of Gaul in sixteenth-century propaganda is discussed in Colette Beaune's *Naissance de la nation France* (Paris: Gallimard, 1985).

6. Cf. Paul Zumthor, *Essai de Poétique médiévale* (Paris: Seuil, 1972), pp. 31–36.

7. The problem is age-old: the great Augustus saw himself only as *princeps civium,* a status which gave a real *auctoritas*. However, he had no more *potestas* than the average

magistrate. See Theodor Eschenburg, *Uber Autorität* (Frankfurt am Main: Suhrkamp, 1976), p. 27; Kenneth Pennington, *The Prince and the Law, 1200–1600. Sovereignty and Rights in the Western Legal Tradition* (Berkeley: University of California Press, 1993), pp. 9, 32–33, 202–37.

8. For the *utilitas*, see Edward Peters, *The Shadow King. Rex Inutilis in Medieval Law and Literature* (New Haven: Yale University Press, 1970).

9. The tradition as embodied by Orosius and his epigones interprets the deeds of the Macedonian as manifestations of sheer hubris.

10. See Werner Paravicini, "The Court of the Dukes of Burgundy. A Model for Europe," in Ronald G. Asch and Adolf M. Birke, eds., *Princes, Patronage and the Nobility* (Oxford: Oxford University Press, 1991), 69–102; Jacques Krynen, *L'Empire du roi. Idées et croyances politiques en France, XIIIe–XVe siècles* (Paris: NRF/Gallimard, 1993), pp. 319–28; Norbert Elias, *Uber den Prozess der Zivilisation. Soziogenetische und psychogenetische Untersuchungen* (Bern/Munich: A. Francke, 1956), chapter III. In the period discussed, the term "court" seems to refer to a clear-cut concept everyone is assumed to know. In reality, however, it refers to an ad-hoc structure. See J. Hirschbiegel, "Der Hof als soziales System," *Mitteilungen der Residenzkommission der Akadamie der Wissenschaften zu Göttingen* 3 (1993), 11–25.

11. I do not consider the *Vengement Alixandre* by Gui de Cambrai or the *Venjance Alixandre* ascribed to Jean le Nevelon, since these texts composed towards the end of the twelfth century do not concern, at least not directly, Alexander himself. Nor will the *Voyage au Paradis terrestre* (second half of the thirteenth century) be discussed, since in the adventure described the hero suffers some kind of defeat. Wauquelin's *Histoire* has not yet been edited; I have consulted the version in Paris, Bibliothèque Nationale fonds français 1419, which differs little from that in Petit Palais, MS 456, Collection Dutuit. For the *Fais* see Renée Nicolet Liscinsky, ed., *Les Fais et Conquestes du Noble Roy Alexandre. Edition du manuscrit 836 de la Bibliothèque Municipale de Besançon* (Ann Arbor: University Microfilms, 1980). For an overall discussion of the twelfth-century texts see my *Légende*.

12. See Ernst H. Kantorowicz, *The King's Two Bodies. Studies in Medieval Political Thought* (Princeton: Princeton University Press, 1957), pp. 44–45.

13. In the period discussed (c. 1250–1450) the term "subject" < *subjectus* is not to be interpreted in a strictly etymological sense. That will only be the case in sixteenth-century treatises, e. g., *Les six Livres de la République* by Jean Bodin.

14. See Paul, *Romans* 13, 1: "Omnis anima potestatibus sublimioribus subdita est: non est enim potestas nisi a Deo."

15. See A. P. Foulkes, *Literature and Propaganda* (London: Methuen, 1983); Garth S. Jowett and Victoria O'Donnell, *Propaganda and Persuasion* (Newbury Park: Sage Publications, 1986).

16. New laws are always presented as "corrections" or "improvements." See Fritz Kern, *Recht und Verfassung im Mittelalter* (Darmstadt: Wissenschaftliche Buchgesellschaft, 1992), pp. 38–42.

17. The antagonism provoked by Louis XI's "monarchical" policy illustrates this very well. The *modus operandi* of the Valois was considered as different, as "new." The nobility and the clergy, as well as the important representatives of the *Tiers Etat*, did not like the king's centralism at all. See Paul Murray Kendall, *Louis XI "L'universelle araigne,"* trans. Eric Diaton (Paris: Marabout, 1974), pp. 404–37.

18. Percy Ernst Schramm, *Herrschaftszeichen und Staatssymbolik: Beiträge zu ihrer Geschichte vom dritten bis zum sechzehnten Jahrhundert*, 3 vols. (Stuttgart: Hierseman, 1954–1978), III, pp. 916–19, 963.

19. The formula "seignor des seignours" has Christological connotations (e.g., *Apostles* 19, 16: "Rex regum et Dominus dominantium"), but the setting of the *PD* does not allow for any soteriological interpretation.

20. The expedition into the region of Gadres to search for provisions in Alexander's absence is understandable, but elsewhere, distance between him and his men generates emotions. In the *Val Périlleux* as well as in his descent to the bottm of the sea or his aerial flight, his men fear for their material safety (AdeP III, 2471–895; 389–541; 4949–5078). Emenidus, Alexander's lieutenant, in the *Voyage au Paradis terrestre* advises his master not to expose himself to dangerous situations: "Pau fait rois a prisier qui s'ocist par outrage" (A king who kills himself because of foolish behavior will not be thought of very highly, l. 87).

21. See my "L'exploitation de la 'reflexion' dans les *Voeux du Paon*. Une technique expositionnelle," *Bien dire et bien aprandre* 5 (1987), 73–88.

22. For the game "Le roi qui ne ment" (the king who does not lie) and other leisure activities at court, see Jean-Michel Mehl, *Les jeux au royaume de France du XIIIe au XVIe siècle* (Paris: Fayard, 1990), pp. 109–10, 195–209.

23. See Paris, Bibliothèque Nationale fonds français 1419, fol. 17r, where Wauquelin notes that he has made the text "a la requeste et principallement au commandement de treshault, noble et puissant seigneur monseigneur Jehan de Bourgoigne" (at the request and especially by order of the very high, noble and powerful lord John of Burgundy). See also MS 9342, vol. 127v where our compiler refers to "Philip par la grace de Dieu duc de Bourgogne, de Brabant et conte de Flandres, et duquel pays de Picardie je sui natif" (Philip by the grace of God duke of Burgundy and Brabant and count of Flanders, in whose country Picardy I was born).

24. For Wauquelin see Ross, p. 17, as well as my "Les Fais et Concquestes du noble roy Alexandre: dérimage ou remaniement?" in *Actes du IVe Colloque du Moyen Français*, ed. Antonij Dees (Amsterdam: Rodopi, 1985), pp. 315–26.

25. The importance of the reshaping process is marked by the space allotted to the rewriting of Jacques de Longuyon's *Voeux* in the *Fais*: the nucleus of the *paon* cycle occupies over fifty percent of the text. Since there is as yet no edition of Wauquelin's text, I can supply no verifiable information about the *Histoire* in order to make a reliable comparison.

26. ". . . merancolie n'y pouoit avoir quelque lieu ou sejour, car a ce estoit elle anchiennement ordonnee" (p. 246: melancholy was not allowed in those places, because

so it had been decreed in ancient times): a pseudo *auctoritas* is introduced as the guarantor of tradition.

27. The ms. is Paris, BNF, fr. 9342.

28. We see this when the ill Guidobaldo da Montefeltro retires early; those remaining are free to discuss the type of *potestas* and *auctoritas* he represents. See Baldassare Castiglione, *Il Libro del Cortegiano*, ed. G. Carnazzi, intro. S.Battaglia (Milan: Biblioteca Universale Rizzoli, 1987), pp. 57–58.

12

Ekphrasis and Memory in the Fourteenth-Century *Parfait du Paon*

Renate Blumenfeld-Kosinski

Dedicated to the memory of Alfred Foulet, 1900–1987

Jean de le Mote's *Parfait du Paon* of 1340 in many ways represents the endpoint of a tradition. The *Parfait*, which is inserted into the *Prise de Defur* and thus fits chronologically between the end of Branch III and the beginning of Branch IV of the Vulgate *Roman d'Alexandre*, is skillfully woven into a whole network of references to previous Alexander texts. As the last text of what one could call the Paon Cycle it features the same cast of characters as the *Voeux du Paon* by Jacques de Longuyon (ca. 1312), minus Cassamus and Clar[v]us who in the *Voeux* died and were buried. I have shown elsewhere how this late Alexander cycle exemplifies an extremely sophisticated aesthetics of continuation and cycle formation.[1] Here I shall focus on the notion of memory as it is embodied in various artifacts—particularly through ekphrasis—expressing a kind of nostalgia, a feeling that Martin Gosman has seen in the *Voeux du Paon* as linked to "les exigences d'une société où la noblesse perd du terrain" and where we witness "la fin du noble héros épique."[2] What we see in the *Parfait*, I would argue, is not so much the end of our noble epic hero as a transformation (or at least a temporary transformation): at a crucial point in the *Parfait* Alexander is called upon—for a brief span of time—to become a poet.

This pivotal moment occurs in the *chambre amoureuse*, a room with elaborate wall paintings, described in a lengthy ekphrasis. While in the earlier *Restor du Paon* the poet Jean le Court (or Brisebarre) had introduced a gold peacock, an artifact that recalled in an emblematic manner the earlier *Voeux du Paon* and an unfulfilled vow, the *chambre amoureuse*'s paintings provide through ekphrasis a history of reading both the *Alexander* and *Paon* cycles. The *chambre*'s images establish a generic framework by showing scenes from the *romans antiques*, and also bring to life Alexander's own past by depicting his submarine and aerial adventures. The *chambre* represents an emblem of literate society, and, in the midst of the horrible bloodshed that pervades the *Parfait*, a kind of last stand of civilized mores. Ekphrasis represents a pause in the narrative, which calls upon readers to engage in interpretation, and here the *chambre* invites readers to reflect on notions of memory and literary traditions.[3] In addition it generates new texts, since the *Parfait*'s characters, including Alexander, enter into a poetic contest. By turning Alexander into the figure of a writer at the very place and moment of the commemoration of his own literary tradition, Jean de le Mote underlines the generative function of ekphrasis. The textual memory is activated in the service of continuing literary creation.

Ekphrasis as a rhetorical device questions and reevaluates the power of language. Essentially it questions, as Murray Krieger puts it, "the capacity of language to do the work of the visual sign" and, further, whether language can or should do this work; generally, ekphrasis is a "verbal replacement for a visual image"; it expresses the "desire to have the world captured in the word."[4] In ancient literature writers were aware of its generative force. The Byzantine writer Nikolaos Mesarites, for example, stated in his *Ekphrasis of the Church of the Holy Apostles*: "Unless the Lord builds for me through you [meaning the Apostles] this building which I have undertaken to construct with the material of words and the skill of my intellect, so that I and all the lovers of the Apostles may be able to gaze upon the beauty of your house more acutely and purely, my human thoughts and words have labored in vain."[5] The kind of "word painting" we find in ekphrasis, then, has the potential to make a work of art or a building present in a purer and livelier form than the gaze upon the actual object could afford. It is the writer who recreates and revitalizes a visual experience. In the Byzantine tradition of which I just quoted an example, ekphrasis often masquerades as a kind of objective description found in guidebooks of churches and other buildings. But, as Ruth Webb has recently shown, these ekphrases appeal to the imagination in a different way. The trajectory the viewer takes in, say, a church, may be arranged by theological principles—that is, the ekphrastic writer already interprets—and thus surpasses ordinary time and perceptions.[6] The reader becomes a viewer for whom the spatial fixity of a building dissolves into "the freedom of the temporal flow" afforded by language.[7]

In medieval literature ekphrases most often depict elaborate art objects, such as tombs, cups, or saddles. Most often these ekphrases provide some thematic commentary or highlight the literary concerns of a given text.[8] In Chrétien de Troyes's *Erec et Enide*, for example, the depiction of the story of Aeneas and Dido on Enide's saddle allows for an intrusion of the potentially destructive aspects of passionate love into the initially festive atmosphere of the couple's courtship.[9] For medieval culture, Aeneas's contemplation of his own story on Juno's temple in Carthage in *Aeneid* 1 was the *locus classicus* of ekphrasis. Here the ekphrastic moment signals a profound tension, as Stephen G. Nichols has demonstrated: a tension between past and future, between history and desire.[10] The images of the Trojan war, by their very presence in a work of art, already represent an interpretation of the events. But this "re-enactment of the past," as Lee Patterson calls it, also points to the future, since Carthage foreshadows Rome. Aeneas's story as told in the ekphrasis is incomplete and exhorts him to further deeds.[11] His bygone deeds become static at the very moment the ekphrastic description ends; his future must necessarily detach itself from this stasis. A moment of commemoration thus generates a renewed—and newly energized—plot.

Ekphrasis can also function as "compensatory mimesis," as Michel Zink argues, for Lancelot's frescoes in the *Livre de Lancelot del Lac*.[12] Signaling a moment of contemplation, the static fresco can do no more here than make a painful past present. Dante has perhaps found the best term for ekphrasis when he calls it, in *Purgatorio* X, *visibile parlare*—"visible speech," which represents, in Kevin Brownlee's words, "a miraculous fusion of visual image and verbal expression."[13] The "entranced gaze upon a significant image" thus stops the narrative flow, fuses past and present, and signals, finally, a different type of understanding, even a "nostalgic evasion of understanding" (Patterson, n. 11, p. 458). Thus in Gautier de Châtillon's *Alexandreis* the tomb ekphrases point to Alexander's lack of understanding, as Maura Lafferty has shown.[14] Alexander does not have the necessary knowledge of key Jewish and biblical texts in order to understand that his ambition to transcend human boundaries—the very boundaries defined in the tomb ekphrases—will lead to his death.

Yet, at the same time, we saw that ekphrases (such as the one in *Aeneid* 1) can create a new understanding of the past—arranged and *already* interpreted—that can reenergize and reorient the narrative. Ekphrastic moments can, through their momentarily apparent stasis, become important turning points in any narrative since they both represent and activate memory. This memory is frequently that of another text. In *Erec et Enide*, as we saw, the *Aeneid* resurfaces; this epic's themes and central problematics must now be confronted with the developments in Chrétien's romance. In Jean le Court's *Restor du Paon* the central function of the gold peacock, fashioned on Edea's orders, is "metre les hardis en memoration" (commemorate the brave).[15] The gold peacock thus brings back and continues, in an emblematic manner, the previous text, the *Voeux du Paon*. Painting plays an even more complex role in relation to memory. Richart de Fournival's famous *dictum* on *painture* and *parole* (in his mid-thirteenth-century *Li Bestiaires d' Amours*) as equally important roads of access to the "house of memory" must of course be considered here.[16] For Richart the two cannot be separated: "Car quant on voit painte une estoire, ou de Troies ou d'autre, on voit les fais des preudommes ki cha en ariere furent, aussi com s'il fussent present. Et tout ensi est il de parole. Car quant on ot .i. romans lire, on entent les aventures, aussi com on les *veïst* en present"[17] (When one sees painted a story, whether of Troy or something else, one sees the deeds of noble men who lived in the past just as though they were still present. And it is the same thing with hearing [a text], for when one hears a story read aloud, one hears the events just as if one *saw* them in the present). It is the writer who wants to be present by these two means: "Car je vous envoie en cest escrit et painture et parole, pour che ke, quant je ne serais presens, ke cis escris par sa painture et par sa parole me rende a vostre memoire comme present" (I am sending you in this text both painting and writing, so that, when I am not present, this text may make me present to your memory through both painting and writing, pp. 6–7). The writer thus wants to make himself present by the two *chemins* of the eye and the ear. But Richart in some way privileges the visual, for we saw in the earlier quote that the reading aloud of a story is supposed to make past events *visually* present. The shape of the letters (part of *painture*) creates sounds that are retranslated into the visual, as it were. Ekphrasis appears to skip the auditory part as well as the retranslation and makes past events directly visually present.

This more contemplative mode of consumption creates moments of stasis that are more conducive to interpretation. The rhetorical function of the trope *enargeia,* or set-piece description, is to bring "a scene before our eyes" (Fowler, n. 8, 26), and it does so in a more totalizing fashion than a linear narrative. Medieval images often work out the so-called "linearization problem,"[18] confronting any speaker by depicting a series of actions simultaneously in one image. A good example has been highlighted by Mary Carruthers in her *Book of Memory* (p. 228 and fig. 13). In the intial D of Psalm 52 ("Dixit insipiens in corde suo non est deus"—incidentally the iconographic commonplace for the depiction of madness in the Middle Ages) one can read counterclockwise the contents of this Psalm (Revised Standard Version). The images of God in the upper center looking down upon two praying men on the right, two men lying nestled spoon-like at the bottom, and a man holding a club and biting into a piece of round bread on the left correspond to the verses: 1) "The fool says in his heart, 'There is no God.' They are corrupt doing abominable iniquity; there is none that does good." 2) "God looks down from heaven upon the sons of men to see if there are any that are wise, that seek after God." 3) "They have all fallen away; they are all alike depraved; there is none that does good, not one." 4) "Have those who work evil no understanding, who eat up my people as they eat bread, and do not call upon God?" Although this is not an example of ekphrasis, it shows clearly the difference in visual versus aural consumption: that is, the circumvention of the constraints of linearity.

Let us now take a closer look at the *chambre amoureuse* itself. Recalling in its elaborate construction the *Chambre de beautés* of the *Roman de Troie* and various tombs of the *Roman d'Enéas*, the *chambre* sits on a pillar without any particular fastening. On an ivory altar two trumpeters, automatons like the sculpted young women in *Troie*, produce the most harmonious music, night and day. The *chambre* turns three times every hour. Jean de le Mote stresses several times the ingeniousness of the construction of this artifact: "Moult fu

faite d'ouvrier de scïence engingneuse" (l. 397, it was made by a most ingenious craftsman) who had a "teste soustilleuse" (l. 398, subtle brain) and knew
how to construct an "euvre scïenteuse" (l. 402, ingenious work of art). In
addition to countless ingenious aspects of its construction, the *chambre* boasts
a series of paintings on walls of alabaster with ebony carving: "Toute y estoit
pourtraite la matere crueuse" (l. 403, the entire curious subject matter was
portrayed there). With the typical formula introducing many a medieval ekphrasis
(or a résumé of a story, for that matter) the poet tells that here we can see how
Alexander went underwater in a glass barrel and how the griffins took him
away high into the heavens.[19] Underneath we can see further images that go
around the room in bands, perhaps like the series of paintings Christine de
Pizan contemplates in the *salle du château de Fortune*.[20]

The images clearly link the *Parfait* to the *matière antique*, focusing on love
and death: "La roÿne Dydo en figure y estoit / Et Eneas aussi, mais Dydo la
monstroit / L'example en quel maniere pour li tuee estoit" (ll. 415–17, There
was a figure of queen Dido and also of Aeneas, but it was Dido who showed
there as an example how she was killed for him). Dido thus serves as an
exemplar of a woman who died for the sake of a man. This scene is shown
in one of the six miniatures of the *Parfait* in BNF fr. 12565 (fol. 286v), the only
complete manuscript of the *Parfait* (the one in Douce 165 is incomplete). That
is, this manuscript illustration reproduces part of the ekphrastic description
within the text rather than a part of the plot. For the story of Troy we see only
Paris and Helen, exchanging amorous glances, without any mention of the
Trojan war—death and destruction are still in the future. After these links to
the *romans antiques* we are led into the very recent past, to events that occurred
not even two weeks ago. The paintings show how Alexander besieged Phezon;
how Porus killed the peacock; how everyone sat around the table and made
his or her vow; how Gadifer gave out the prize and Aristes cut up the peacock;
how Lyoine accomplished his feat and then one by one how each person who
made a vow fulfills it completely, "de chief en chief" (l. 430). This summary
statement refers us to the *Voeux du Paon*, for without knowledge of that text
we could not fill in the gaps left by this description in the *Parfait*.

The poet insists on the uncanny mimetic power of these images when
he stresses that we are tempted to greet the people around the table "au voir,"
in truth (l. 435)—as if they were real. In a lively imagined scene Jean suggests
that the viewer might say: "Taisiez vous, cilz sires parler doit" (l. 438, be quiet,
it is this gentleman's turn to speak). These paintings, then, are like a book come
to life. Going back to Richart de Fournival, we can say that the viewer's or
reader's memory is activated here. The book "speaks." As Carruthers points out
for the translation of the *Ad Herennium* by Bono Giamboni: "[he] adds to the
Latin original the rule that memory images should not be 'mute,' 'silent.' They
must speak" (*Book of Memory*, p. 229). The figures in the *chambre*'s paintings,
then, are the memory of a previous textual tradition seemingly come to life.

Finally, our poet provides a mythological framework: in the four corners of the room we see Venus and Mars, Cupid and Diana, Jupiter and Saturn, and the "gods of nature" who hold up the entire firmament, including earth, heaven, air, water, and all the created people.

As far as the images from the *Roman d'Alexandre* and *Paon* cycle are concerned, we see that they represent the most popular manuscript illuminations, such as the submarine and the "griffin plane." In the many manuscripts of the *Voeux* and the *Restor* that I have examined and that have illustrations, there are always the scenes of Porus shooting the peacock, of the banquet and the vows, and of the gold peacock on a pedestal. We can thus see the walls in the *chambre* as some kind of gigantic manuscript pages whose images as a key to memory recapitulate prominent episodes of the Alexander cycle; they "speak" to us of past greatness and of past texts.

This *merveille* is not only a static description depicting a room in a castle. It has a particular *"destinee"* (purpose) and that is that anyone who enters there has to *"parler"* et *"argüer"* (l. 978, speak and debate), or at the very least compose a ballad. Writing poetry is thus a response to the artistic stimuli provided by the *chambre*. Alexander admits right away that he has no talent for this kind of work: "Elas, dist Alixandres, j'ai a non Fol y bee" (l. 981, Alas, says Alexander, I can be called a stupid fool). But the young women of the castle will not accept this statement of poetic impotence: "Sire, font les pucelles, ce ne puet remanoir. / Il vous convient par force a canter esmouvoir" (ll. 984–84, My lord, the young women say, we cannot leave it at this. You have to get on with singing something). Alexander finally relents, but will need some time: "Dames, fait Alixandres, ci faut grant estudie; / Je n'ai pas ma matere si tost appareillie" (ll. 1018–19, Ladies, says Alexander, this needs some effort. I do not have a ready-made subject matter). Alexander "pense et melancholie" (l. 1021, thinks and becomes melancholy) and eventually begins to write while everybody is watching him. To add to the intensity of the moment, the participants now lock the *chambre amoureuse* and decorate it with even more art work, "d'ymages entailliez d'or fin et de pierrie" (l. 1034, with images engraved into pure gold and precious stones). Now Alexander has to present his ballad and let it be judged in the competition.[21] But first he has to swear that this ballad is original and has never been recited or heard before. He does so and begins his recitation of a ballad focused on the "plaisir" (pleasure) he gets from his "douce dame" (sweet lady).

This rather standard ballad underlines Alexander's identity as a lover and a writer, an identity absent in the images painted on the walls of the *chambre amoureuse*. As we saw, the paintings show the same subjects as the most popular manuscript illuminations, evoking Alexander as adventurer and warrior. But he succeeds in his new guise of poet and is awarded the "couronne verte" (the green [laurel] crown) which is here the second prize, while Clarete receives the "couronne d'or" (the gold crown), or first prize (stanza 50). This celebration of poetic creativity gives rise to an emotional outburst on the part of the

author of the *Parfait* itself: Jean de le Mote exclaims that the princes here do
not resemble those who do not appreciate a poet's (i.e., his) efforts and "qui
se vont des faiseurs par le païs moquant / Et si appellent 'rusez' leur ouvrage
poissant" (ll. 144–45, who go around the country mocking the poets and
calling their powerful works tricks). Only Simon de Lille, his patron, sufficiently
appreciates Jean's work, his "soutil oevre" (l. 1450, subtle work)—a term recalling the *chambre amoureuse*.[22] He loves subtle writings, as is evidenced by his
supplying to Jean "vivre, chambre et clerc escrisant / Pour faire li biax dis" (ll.
1456–57, livelihood, a room, and a scribe so that he can compose beautiful
poems). Jean's insistence on his own artistry—and the reward due to him—
at the end of the poetic competition positions him in the lineage of the noble
participants and demonstrates the coherence of the poetic production that
begins with Alexander and the other contestants. Further, since Jean himself
incorporates characters and continues events of the previous *Paon* texts, as do
some of the wall paintings in the *chambre*, we can read this artifact as a *mise
en abyme* of a poetics of continuation in pictorial terms. The implied painter
of these scenes created a visual complement to what Jean is doing in this final
installment of the *Paon* cycle.

The poetic competition is followed by a scene, familiar from the *Voeux*
and from the *Restor du Paon*, of the taking of vows on a peacock, here the gold
peacock that had been constructed in the *Restor*. As John L. Grigsby observed,
already in the *Voeux du Paon* "hostility jars the polite vowing session."[23] The
vows, in fact, center on the continued war between the different factions and
on future bloodshed. Marcien, for example, vows that he will twist the neck
of anyone who comes to Alexander's aid during a surreptitious attack he is
planning (stanza 70); Melidus vows to vanquish Alexander, and although
Alexander praises Melidus's heroic spirit (stanza 63), it is clear that new hos-
tilities will erupt and wipe out most of the heroes who have just participated
in the ballad contest. And indeed, the next fifty stanzas or so (of a total of 127)
are devoted to descriptions of horrendous battles which claim, one after the
other, most of the protagonists, including Porus (stanza 121) who in the *Voeux*
had shot the peacock and thus set in motion the striking—and influential—
ceremony of the vows.[24]

In an epic context, death provides the ultimate closure, while a romance
often culminates in a marriage. In the *Parfait* we have both: most of the heroes
die, and the few who are left are married off by Alexander to the remaining
daughters of Melidus, brother of Clarus and uncle of Porus. As I observed
elsewhere, except for Alexander the only "survivors of the *Parfait* are characters
who only appear in this . . . text" ("Poetics of Continuation," p. 446), while the
complex cast of characters created in the *Voeux* and the *Restor* vanishes.

The two types of ending incarnate the deep conflict between different
value systems in the *Parfait du Paon*. Grigsby pointed out for the *Voeux* that
they "reflect an ancient warrior tradition at a crossroads." The vows, "an

expression of hostility," are juxtaposed to an "almost unbelievable courtesy"; this contrast is "built on the base of a real historical phenomenon: the four-teenth-century sacrifice of military effectiveness to courtesy" (p. 575). In the *Parfait* we have the additional dimension of an artistic tour de force: the ekphrasis of the *chambre amoureuse* as the locus of memory. The *chambre* comes to represent a kind of last stand of civilized society in the face of renewed carnage. Its paintings emphasize love and adventure, the (still) civilized scene of the vows and the mythological (learned) framework of these adventures. The *chambre* thus elides the more bloody aspects of the warrior life that come to the fore later in the text and pit civilization—celebrated in the form of artistic excellence—against death and destruction.

The function of ekphrasis as an acme of artistic achievement—a perfect blending of the visual and verbal arts—is of course not unique to the *Parfait du Paon*. I have shown recently with regard to the paintings on the temple in the *Roman de Thèbes* that an ekphrastic moment like this can celebrate a culture's past while at the same time calling attention to the dangers this culture faces,[25] and I would argue that the *Parfait's chambre amoureuse* functions in a similar way. Its vivid evocation of a literary past, the activation of a cultural memory, reconfigures Alexander as a writer at a crucial juncture in the text. But it is a role he cannot sustain: before long he again turns into the well-known conqueror and killer of men. The possibility that a world of literature and art could be safeguarded is there, but it remains fixed on the walls of the *chambre amoureuse*, and as the characters finally turn their backs on this *locus amoenus*, the audience as well has to close the door on this last, best hope for a life of peace, love, and poetry.

Notes

1. See my "The Poetics of Continuation in the Old French *Paon* Cycle," *Romance Philology* 39 (1986), 437–47; for the text see *Parfait*. On the production of one manu-script and the connection to the patron, the goldsmith Simon de Lille, and his possible manufacture of a real gold peacock see Mary A. Rouse and Richard Rouse, "The Goldsmith and the Peacock: Jean de le Mote in the Household of Simon de Lille, 1340," *Viator* 28 (1997), 281–303.

2. Martin Gosman, "Au carrefour des traditions scriptuaires: Les *Voeux du Paon* et l'apport des écritures épique et romanesque," in *Au carrefour des routes d'Europe*, *Senefiance* 20, 2 vols. (Aix-en-Provence: CUERMA, 1987), vol. 1, pp. 551–65 (here pp. 561–62).

3. On images as "conduit for memory" (with a focus on the *Chambre de beautés* in the *Roman de Troie* and the *salle aux images* in the Prose *Lancelot*), see Paul Rockwell, "Remembering *Troie*: the Implications of *Ymages* in the *Roman de Troie* and the Prose *Lancelot*," *Arthuriana* 7 (1997), 20–35.

4. Murray Krieger, *Ekphrasis: The Illusion of the Natural Sign* (Baltimore and London: Johns Hopkins University Press, 1992), pp. 4, 11.

5. Nikolaos Mesarites, *Description of the Church of the Holy Apostles at Constantinople*, ed. Glanville Downey in *Transactions of the American Philosophical Society* n.s. 47 (1957), 855–924; Greek citation in 12.4., p. 900. I use the translation provided by Ruth Webb on a handout (see next note).

6. Ruth Webb, "Byzantine Ekphrases of Church Buildings." Lecture, Princeton University, April 15, 1998.

7. See Krieger, *Ekphrasis*, pp. 10–11.

8. See Linda Clemente, *Literary objets d'art: Ekphrasis in Medieval French Romance, 1150–1210* (New York: Peter Lang, 1992), p. 92. On the narratological implications of ekphrasis see D.P. Fowler, "Narrate and Describe: The Problem of Ekphrasis," *Journal of Roman Studies* 81 (1991), 25–35. Note 1 provides an extensive bibliography of recent work on ekphrasis (mostly for classical literature).

9. See Joseph S. Wittig, "The Aeneas-Dido Allusion in Chrétien's *Erec et Enide*," *Comparative Literature* 22 (1970), 237–53 and Clemente, *Ekphrasis*, pp. 68–73.

10. Stephen G. Nichols, "Ekphrasis, Iconoclasm, and Desire," in *Rethinking the Romance of the Rose*, ed. Kevin Brownlee and Sylvia Huot (Philadelphia: University of Pennsylvania Press, 1992), pp. 133–66.

11. See Lee Patterson, " 'Rapt with Pleasaunce': Vision and Narration in the Epic," *English Literary History* 48 (1981), 455–75 (here p. 456).

12. Michel Zink, "Les toiles d'Agamanor et les fresques de Lancelot," *Littérature* 38 (1980), 43–61 (here pp. 54–55).

13. Kevin Brownlee, "The Image of History in Christine de Pizan's *Livre de la Mutacion de Fortune*," in *Contexts: Style and Value in Medieval Art and Literature, Yale French Studies*, Special Edition, 1991, ed. Daniel Poirion and Nancy Freeman Regalado, pp. 44–56 (here p. 52).

14. Maura K. Lafferty, "Mapping Human Limitations: The Tomb Ekphrases in Walter of Châtillon's *Alexandreis*," *Journal of Medieval Latin* 4 (1994), 64–81.

15. *Restor*, l. 284.

16. On this topic see Mary Carruthers, *The Book of Memory: A Study of Memory in Medieval Culture* (Cambridge: Cambridge University Press, 1990), pp. 223–24.

17. Richart de Fournival, *Li Bestiaires d'Amours*, ed. Cesare Segre (Milan: Riccardi, 1957), p. 5 (my emphasis).

18. Term used by W.J.M. Levelt and quoted by Fowler, "Narrate and Describe," p. 29.

19. On illustrated Alexander manuscripts see Ross, pp. 14–17 for the *Paon* cycle.

20. See for example BNF fr. 603, fol. 127v. There Christine looks at bands of paintings showing battle scenes. They are divided by narrower white bands featuring captions.

21. Generally on this competition see Friedrich Gennrich, "Der Gesangswettstreit im *Parfait du Paon,*" *Romanische Forschungen* 58–59 (1947), 208–32.

22. On Simon, see Rouse and Rouse 1997.

23. See John L. Grigsby, "Courtesy in the Voeux du Paon," *Neuphilologische Mitteilungen* 86 (1985), 566–75 (here p. 575).

24. In particular, the *Voeux de l'Epervier* and the *Voeux du Héron.* On the former see my "Historiography and *matière antique*: The Emperor Henry VII as a New Alexander in the Fourteenth-Century *Voeux de l'Epervier,*" *Medievalia et Humanistica* n.s. 14 (1986), 17–35; on the latter text see B. J. Whiting, "The Vows of the Heron," *Speculum* 20 (1945), 261–78.

25. See my *Reading Myth: Classical Mythology and Its Interpretations in Medieval French Literature* (Stanford: Stanford University Press, 1997), pp. 27–30.

13

Conquering Alexander:
Perceforest and the Alexandrian Tradition

Michelle Szkilnik

Twelfth- and thirteenth-century writers of Arthurian romances showed little interest in Alexander. The emperor appears as Philip of Flanders's distorted figure in the *Conte du Graal*; in *Erec et Enide*, he is only a reference by which to measure Arthur's superior generosity. Indeed, early on, Alexander and the corpus of texts dedicated to him remain foreign to Arthurian romance. To Chrétien and his epigones, they must have looked like exotic "others" who did not rightly belong to romance. Thus François Suard and Catherine Gaullier-Bougassas have legitimately raised the question of Alexander's identity as a romance hero in the twelth and thirteenth centuries.[1] Yet in the fourteenth century, with the *Roman de Perceforest*,[2] Alexander has undoubtedly become a romance character. This *entrée en roman*—his entry into the Arthurian romance at least—takes three forms: first, the hero founds an illustrious lineage; second, he establishes a brilliant civilization; third, he initiates the practice of recording important events, those that constitute the material of romance. Alexander can be proud of his new conquest: Arthurian romance itself. But who has conquered whom? Is it not Alexander who, upon landing in Great Britain, has changed completely?

Perceforest integrates Alexander into the Arthurian tradition in a way that might seem abrupt but is actually skillful. At first, the romance recounts the history of Great Britain, following more or less faithfully Geoffrey of Monmouth's *Historia Regum Britanniae*. It stops suddenly at King Pir's death to explain, in an impressive prolepsis of several centuries, how the manuscript containing the "Chroniques de Grande-Bretagne" has miraculously reappeared in the fourteenth century. Immediately after this deferred prologue Alexander enters the romance. The time warp imposed obscures the subsequent drastic change of place: returning to the time of King Pir, the author whizzes us from England to Macedonia to tell us first about Philip's coming to power, and then, twenty-six years later, about Alexander's. This new chapter opens with a date, "four hundred years after the foundation of the noble city of Rome," followed by a second, "four hundred and twenty-six years after the foundation of the aforementioned city" (*Perceforest* I, pp. 124–25). These dates echo others that the romance has evoked earlier: that of Helen's abduction (I, p. 63), of the sack of Rome (I, p. 109), of Edward III's wedding (I, p. 120). The solemnity with which all these events are inscribed in time gives them special significance. The Trojan war, the sack of Rome, Edward's wedding, Alexander's accession to the Macedonian throne, all are essential landmarks for the reader of *Perceforest*. And to consolidate his historical frame, the author borrows a short summary of Alexander's career from Orosius, a historian he used earlier to describe Great Britain and to recount the sack of Rome.

Protected by Orosius's authority, by the seriousness of the "anciennes hystoires" (the ancient histories), the writer can then turn to fictional works to give flesh and blood to his character. Two episodes from the *Roman d'Alexandre* provide the necessary details: *Fuerre de Gadres*, which recounts how one of Alexander's lieutenants, Euménide (Permenio according to *Perceforest*), kills Gadiffer, father of the future kings of England and Scotland, during a raid near the city of Gadres; and the *Voeux du Paon*, written by Jacques de Longuyon before 1312. *Perceforest* summarizes *Fuerre de Gadres* very quickly, though faithfully. The way it transforms the *Voeux du Paon*, however, reveals a bias that Jeanne Lods has clearly identified:[3] whereas in Jacques de Longuyon's work Alexander stays in the background and remains more or less a spectator, in *Perceforest* he is brought into the foreground. First, in three pages that correspond roughly to two hundred and fifty lines, the author stages a confrontation between Alexander and his proud enemy Cassamus. Like the Cassamus of the *Voeux du Paon*, the old man in *Perceforest* wears Chaldean dress, carries a walking stick and is on his way to Mars's temple where he will pray for strengh to avenge his brother Gadiffer. Although the dialogue is somewhat different from that in the *Voeux*, its gist and even some specific arguments are retained: Alexander calls on his mother to witness his good faith; he reminds Cassamus that the laws of war sometimes allow good knights to perish; finally he offers his help to the old man. In both works, Cassamus is full of hate and arrogance when he first recognizes the emperor, but is then touched by Alexander's peaceful entreaties and generosity.

Having rewritten in detail this opening scene from the *Voeux*, the author summarizes in one and a half pages the ensuing nine thousand lines of that work, giving only the result of the battles that constitute a major part of it: Alexander's resounding victory (although he does mention that Cassamus kills the Indian king Clarvus). More surprisingly, he passes over all the courtly scenes that take place in the city of Ephezon, omitting even the one that gave the work its title: the peacock ritual. Alexander, having installed his camp on the outskirts of the city and merely sent emissaries to its people, does not attend the ceremony in the earlier text, and indeed he is not a main character in the *Voeux*: from his lofty position, he appears godlike, contemplating the action rather than taking part in it.[4] Only at the beginning, when he meets Cassamus, and at the end, when he marries the heroes of the romance, does he occupy a prominent position. These are the episodes that *Perceforest*'s author emphasizes. As he had rewritten Alexander's conversation with Cassamus, he inserts the speech Alexander pronounces when he gives each knight his beloved. Yet the weddings are not described: "Aultre est qui bien le sçara mettre en escript, car trop est la matiere grande et longue que sur cestuy commencement je entend a traittier" (I, p. 131: Someone else will write that down, for large and long is the subject I have undertaken to treat on this beginning). Is this an allusion to Brisebarre, the author of the *Restor du Paon*, this "someone else" who indeed has taken the time to retell the weddings that Alexander organizes without being personally involved? Whatever the case, this biased rewriting of the *Voeux* prepares an exceptional position for Alexander in *Perceforest*.

Even though, following Orosius, *Perceforest* recalls that Alexander "fut envenimé dedans la cité de Babiloine" (I, p. 125: was poisoned in the city of Babylon), the romance designs a destiny for the emperor that is original and unique in the Alexander tradition, but less so in regard to the fate befalling other heroes such as those of the *romans antiques* or Brutus, the founder of Great Britain, as recounted by Geoffrey of Monmouth and Wace. *Perceforest* invites us, indeed compels us, to compare Alexander to Brutus, since the romance translates the *Historia Regum Britanniae* and recounts how Brutus and his troops first colonized England. At first sight, Brutus's destiny seems quite different from Alexander's. Cursed yet nonetheless guaranteed an illustrious future, expelled from Italy where he was the accidental cause of his parents' death, Brutus liberates Helenus's lineage reduced to bondage by the Greek king Pandrasius, and thus, by his prowess and his qualities as leader, wins himself a people. He needs only a land to settle: after many long and perilous adventures, he arrives in Great Britain where he founds a new Troy, *Troiam Novam*, a name later changed to Trinovatum according to Geoffrey and the *Perceforest*. Far from being in search of a land in which to settle his people, Alexander, when he enters the romance, is already the leader of a gigantic empire. Not a poor, powerless exile (like so many literary founders of new societies), he is at the apex of his power and his glory. Accompanied by his new allies and friends, he is on his way to the city of Glodofar where he will attend the coronation of Porrus, Clarvus's son. *Perceforest* will have to tear him away from the comfort of his victories in order to change his destiny and make him a new Brutus.

Both the Trojan and the Macedonian receive a sign from the gods that they have been chosen. After drifting at sea with his people, Brutus lands on a desert island where he discovers an ancient temple dedicated to the goddess Diana. He offers her a sacrifice and prays that she will reveal what country is reserved for him. He falls asleep before the altar and, in a dream, the goddess reveals that an island is awaiting him "dessoubz soleil couchant/ Oultre le royaume de Galle" (I, p. 77: towards the setting sun, beyond the kingdom of the Gauls). As for Alexander, when he has almost reached Glodofar he decides to make a pilgrimage to an island where people worship Venus. The romance does not bother to explain his whim, stating merely that the island was a very famous pilgrimage site. Is Alexander simply curious, or is his sudden "devotion" the work of the gods? In any case, he too, not having prayed for anything particular, is granted a vision. Asleep, like Brutus, in the temple, he dreams that having embarked on an amazingly large vessel he is caught in a terrible storm. A man dressed in black[5] reassures him, and soon he lands on a beautiful island. The inhabitants come to him and ask him to give them a king. He divides the island in two, and to each half assigns a king. His dream will come true in every detail, and the emperor can then fully measure how much Venus presides over his destiny. At the very place where he reaches the coast of Great Britain—for such is the beautiful island awaiting him—stands another sanctuary dedicated to Venus, in which have gathered all the island's major dignitaries in the hope that the goddess will show them the way after the death of their king Pir. Venus advises them to go to the shore, for there "ilz auroient fortune pour eulx qui les pourverroit de roy souffisant" (I, p. 135: Fortune would provide the king they needed). Thus does Alexander experience the discomfort and necessary wandering that open new horizons. The storm plays the same role as the exile imposed on Brutus: the hero, pushed away by the violence of the winds or of his fellow citizens, is condemned to roam the world before reaching his promised land.

Brutus implores Diana; Alexander is cherished by Venus. This substitution is not gratuitous. Diana, as Brutus states in his prayer, is the goddess of forests, hunters, wildlife—in other words, of a primitive world. Venus, goddess of love, represents the forces of civilization; it is thanks to her that courtly manners develop and chivalry shines.[6] By choosing Diana as his protector, Brutus immediately shows the limits of his colonizing achievement. The Trojan is indeed a good warrior, but the romance does not dwell on his qualities as a ruler of his land. After his death, the country is divided into three parts and at once threatened by neighboring peoples. *Perceforest*, still following the *Historia Regum Britanniae*, then retells a long history of wars, pillage, and fratricide that leads to the decadence of Great Britain by the time Alexander reaches it. Geoffrey's narrative thus provides a dark backdrop against which to view the Macedonian's magnificent civilizing enterprise. Book I still describes numerous battles, but they pit the forces of good against the forces of evil, the forces of civilization against the forces of anarchy. An episode at the beginning of Book II underlines the difference between Brutus's endeavor and that of Alexander and his companions. Gadiffer, the new king of Scotland, is exploring his country with his men when they are attacked by savages. Naked or clad in skins, hairy and shaggy, armed with sticks, eating raw meat because they have not discovered the use of fire, these wild men nonetheless speak some kind of corrupted Greek. Gadiffer discovers to his amazement that they are of Trojan descent (ms. Arsenal 3485 fol. 7–9). The text does not state whether they came with Brutus, but we may suppose that they did. The first Greeks in Great Britain have thus reverted to a pitiful state of nature. The second colonizing wave, led by Alexander, restores the light of civilization and their lost dignity to Priam's children: indeed among the wild men lives Priande, grand-daughter of King Laomedon, who will marry Estonné and give birth to Passelion.

By showing Alexander worshipping Venus, *Perceforest* suggests the power the goddess will exercise both in the romance as a whole and in Alexander's life in particular. Whereas Diana, after speaking to Brutus, recedes into the background, Venus is one of the most important pagan divinities venerated in the romance. Far from threatening the superiority of the *Dieu Souverain* (the supreme God, i.e., the foreshadowing of the Christian God), she appears as a beneficent power preparing the triumph of the true God of Love. In addition, she assures the hero's individual happiness, for in Great Britain Alexander will experience an exceptional love. In Geoffrey of Monmouth's work and in the Great Britain before Alexander, women are subjected to the male rules of abduction, exchange, and booty; Brutus lands in England with a wife who does not forget that she had been married for political reasons only, a token in the deal between her father and her husband. Alexander's arrival changes the relations between the sexes and establishes harmony and peace, introducing the religion of love that will flourish in the last book.

As Alexander succeeds where Brutus failed, *Perceforest* replaces Geoffrey of Monmouth's founding hero with its own. Alexander is triply a founder: of an illustrious lineage culminating in Arthur; of a splendid and harmonious civilization that unites courtesy and chivalry; and, last but not least, of the romance that celebrates the luster of this new age.

The genealogy that makes Alexander Arthur's ancestor is complicated. In the forest of Darnantes where he is looking for Perceforest, Alexander meets the enchantress Sebille with whom he falls in love, and shortly thereafter leaves her pregnant with a son. The romance then announces that "de ce lignaige yssy le roy Arthus" (I, p. 242: King Arthur descends from this lineage). The boy, born after his father's death, is called "Remanant de Joie," since he was his mother Sebille's last comfort. Secretly raised by the enchantress, he is dubbed by Perceforest in Book II and learns at this moment that his real name is Alexander, but not until Book IV, through a posthumous letter from the emperor, does the court learn of his noble origin. Perceforest then marries the young Alexander to his own daughter Bethoine (IV-1, pp. 50–55). Remanant de Joie is killed along with all the other good knights, during the battle of Franc-Palais, but not before he has fathered a daughter. Later lost, she is found again in Book VI where we learn her name: Alexandre-Fin de Liesse, since she

was her mother's last joy, as Remanant de Joie was Sebille's last comfort.[7] She
marries her cousin Gallafur, grandson of Gadiffer king of Scotland. Their children thus have Alexander's, Perceforest's, and Gadiffer's blood, and it is from this
prestigious lineage that Arthur is born. Although—because of the tradition inherited from the *Roman d'Alexandre*—it was impossible to imagine Alexander
ruling in person over Great Britain, and equally difficult to substitute his son for
Perceforest's son—for, as Perceforest states, "je n'en puis desheriter le droit hoir"
(IV-1, p. 54: I cannot disinherit the rightful heir of Great Britain)—, at least his
granddaughter, the third Alexander, will accede to the throne of that land.

Alexander is not simply Arthur's magnificent ancestor. He also lays the
foundations of a splendid civilization, noble, strong, concerned with justice and
truth, which survive all the catastrophes that follow. Moreover, he establishes
the important rites of Arthurian society. Recognizing that the English had
been invaded many times and enslaved by tyrannical leaders because they did
not know how to fight, he creates an athletic game inspired by what he had
seen under the sea: "il avoit veu une maniere de poissons que on appelloit
chevaliers de mer, qui ont les testes façonnees a maniere de heaulme et au
dessus tenant une espee par le pumel et par dessus le dos ung escu. La veyt
le gentil roy ces poissons tournoier et bataillier les ungs aux autres tant fort
que merveilles estoit a veoir" (I, p. 167: He had seen some sort of fish that were
called sea knights, whose heads were shaped like helmets; on top they hold a
sword and on their back a shield. There the noble king had seen these fish
tourney and fight each other so vigorously that it was a marvel to behold).
With this explanation of the origin of tournaments, *Perceforest* links a well-
known episode of the *Roman d'Alexandre* to one of the most common motifs
of Arthurian romance,[8] while also giving a moral meaning to this martial
game: the tournament "sera destournement de oyseuse, exaulcement de proesse,
nourrissement de hardiesse, exaulcement d'armes et d'amours" (I, p. 168: will
keep away idleness, boost prowess, nourish boldness, enhance arms and love).
Alexander thus institutes knighthood.

Remarkably, Alexander connects love and prowess from the very beginning; love is indeed the second field where he dictates new laws. Protected, as
we have seen, by Venus, the king embodies in Book I the model of the
fin'amant. Perceforest, Gadiffer, Porrus, and Cassiel, like Brutus before them,
landed in Great Britain with their wives. Alexander himself had presided over
their weddings (I, p. 130), and in the *Voeux du Paon* Porrus and Cassiel, for
example, had shown that they had the makings of *fins amants*. But *Perceforest*
does not include any of the courtly scenes from the *Voeux du Paon*. As for
Gadiffer, he is wed to Lidoire, Eumenide-Permenio's niece, and the romance
explains that this wedding is a way of making amends for the death of old
Gadiffer, killed by Eumenides in *Fuerre de Gadres*; the detail demonstrates the
same logic that had prevailed for Brutus's wedding. But in Great Britain this
logic no longer applies. First, all the marriages turn out to be happy ones, and

women, Lidoire in particular, play a prominent role that was formerly denied to them. Second, and most important, the mode of conquering ladies changes radically. Alexander sets a new example when falling in love with the enchantress Sebille. This love story holds no surprises for readers of Arthurian romances or *lais*. Its main episodes—the hero staying fifteen days with his lady while thinking that he has spent only one night in her castle; the engraving of his name on an oak to let Sebille know who he is without breaking his word; his second, longer and most pleasant stay with Sebille—seem to come straight from Marie de France's lais or an anonymous *lai* such as *Guingamor*. But it is Alexander who is the first hero of a love story in *Perceforest*, and his adventure provides a model for all its subsequent love stories, for example that of Marmona who casts a spell on Passelion (IV-2, p. 903).[9] *Perceforest* thus bestows on Alexander the title of first *fin'amant* in Arthurian romance.

There is a third connection between Alexander's destiny and that of the Arthurian romance: the emperor institutes the writing process. When in Book I, Sarra, a damsel of the forest Darnantes, regrets that all the feats of arms accomplished by Perceforest and his knights have not been recorded, Alexander supports her claim:

> "Certes, la demoiselle Sarra dist moult bien car de ma part je consens que tous les fais qui sont advenus puis que j'entray en Engleterre, a ceste fois soient mis en memoire pour ceulx qui sont vivans et pour tous aultres qui vendront aprez nous car ilz ne le pourroient sçavoir se l'en ne leur disoit ou s'ilz ne le trouvoient par escript. Et quant a ma part, j'en diray au vrai ce qui m'en est advenu combien que ce soit plus a mon blasme que a mon honneur car je y ay si petitement besongnié qu'il n'est ja nécessité d'en faire memoire. Mais je suis content que de mon costé je y aie ung petit de honte et ceulx qui y ont achevé les haultes emprises par prouesse en aient l'onneur. Si vous prometz, noble damoiselle, que sans en riens celer ne adjouster sinon le vray, je confesseray franchement tout ce qu'il m'en est advenu et je requier a tous les autres qu'ilz promettent d'en faire ainsi." (Ms. Arsenal 3484, fol. 403r°)

(The damsel Sarra speaks the truth. As for me, I accept that the memory of all that has happened since I came to England, be now saved for the living and for all those who will come after us; for they cannot know it unless they are told or they find it written down. And as for me, I will tell the truth about what befell me although it will be more shameful than glorious since I have accomplished so little that it is not worth remembering. But I am content that some shame be mine and that the ones who achieved high undertakings thanks to their prowess have the honor. I thus promise you, noble damsel, that without hiding or adding anything, but adhering to the truth, I will frankly confess everything that has happened to me and I ask all the others to promise to do the same") (translation mine).

Then king Perceforest calls his cleric Cresus and asks him to be ready to record Alexander's testimony:

> "Cressus, il fault que vous aiés parchemin et encre et quant Alexandre vous huchera vous soiés prest pour mestre par escript ce qu'il vous devisera et pareillement ferez aux autres noeuf et en general de toutes les adventures qui sont advenues en cestuy paÿs depuis que le noble empereur y est venus et nous aussi, et non point seulement ce qui est advenu jusques a present mais ce qui advendra d'ores en avant en Angleterre de jor en jor." En la maniere que le bon roy le commanda, Cressus le bon clerc s'i emploia et ce que nous en sçavons nous vient de lui. Car selon la relation des nobles barons, il mist par escript toutes leurs adventures, au mains celles qui estoient dignes de memoire. (Ms. Arsenal 3484, fol. 403r°)

> ("Cresus, you must have parchment and ink ready and when Alexander calls you, you must be prepared to write down what he will dictate and to do the same with the other nine [knights]; and in general you will write down all the adventures that have happened in this country since the noble emperor came here, not only what has happened until now but also what will happen from now on in England, day by day." Cresus, the good cleric, did as the king had ordered him, and whatever we know comes to us from him. For, following what the noble barons reported, he wrote down all their adventures, at least the ones worth remembering) (translation mine).

Thus it is Alexander who invents the means of saving the memory of all feats of arms, a means that Arthur's clerics will imitate several generations later.[10]

Three persons initiate the process of writing the chronicles of Great Britain: Sarra, Alexander, and finally Perceforest. Sarra suggests the idea, but does not have the authority to carry it out. Alexander's intervention is then essential, not only because his desire becomes an order for Perceforest but also because he sets an example for the other knights by being the first to tell his adventures and by emphasizing the truthfulness of his confession. Indeed, the prologues opening the next five books prove that Alexander plays a major role in the realization of the project, for at the beginning of each major section the narrator states that he is faithfully following Cresus the cleric and that the latter was merely complying with Alexander's order: "Cressus [. . .] estoit de l'ostel du tresexcellent prince Alexandre le Grant, lequel par bon advis lui bailla avecques plusieurs autres roys charge de ce (= compiler les chroniques) faire" (III-1, p. 1: Cresus belonged to the retinue of the excellent prince Alexander the Great, who, with other kings, had the good idea to make him chronicle the history of Great Britain). "Le saige et venerable clercq Cressus la compila (cette matière) par le commandement et ordonnance du tresexcellent empereur Alexandre le Concquerant" (IV-1, p. 1: The wise and venerable cleric Cresus compiled this material on the order of the excellent emperor Alexander the conqueror)[11]—a wording that sounds very much like that of Chrétien de Troyes at the end of his prologue to the *Conte du Graal*: "Crestïens qui entant et poine / Par lo *commandement* lo comte / A rimoier lo meillor conte . . ." (Chrétien aims and strives by command of the count to put into rhyme the greatest story . . .).[12] *Perceforest* humorously corrects Alexander's negative image in the prologue to the *Conte* by raising the Emperor to the status of Cresus's patron (the resemblance between the names Crestïen and Cresus might not be a coincidence), while the "real" patron is instead Perceforest, the king whom the cleric serves.

Alexander is also a patron in the second sense of the term: his qualities shape the narrative as those of Philip of Alsace shaped the *Conte*.[13] Philip's charity makes him a new model of *prodomie* to which all the other characters of the *Conte* must be compared. Likewise, in the *Perceforest*, Alexander is "le dieu de prouesse, de gentillesse, de largesse, d'onneur, de constance, le bieneuré, la fleur de chevalerie, de hardement et de grant emprise" (Ms. Arsenal 3485, fol. 54v°: the god of prowess, nobility, generosity, honor, constancy, the blessed and the flower of chivalry, of bravery and of great undertakings), as described by the messenger who announces his death to Perceforest's court. He is the model of the perfect knight, a better model than Perceforest, who sometimes abandons himself to despair for his kingdom's doom, better too than Gadiffer, the maimed king who, after his accident in Book II, will no longer be able to demonstrate his prowess.

True, a major obstacle stands between Alexander and perfection: his paganism. How can the Emperor be a perfect model if he never discovers the Sovereign God? Unlike Perceforest and Gadiffer, Alexander never renounces his pagan gods. Perhaps it was inconceivable, at the time *Perceforest* was composed, to make him convert. In any case, the tradition sees in Alexander the example of *hybris* rightly punished: his tragic death in Babylon is the proof that Fortune is indeed all powerful and does not spare the mighty. *Perceforest* links Alexander's paganism to his *hybris*, and condems both through the words of a servant attached to the hermit Dardanon. The hermit had prophesied that a Greek bird would cover the world with its wings just before being destroyed; the narrator indicates that the prophecy applies to Alexander, and the emperor himself guesses its meaning (I, pp. 252–57). This prediction of Alexander's fall curiously echoes Lancelot's vision in the *Queste del Saint Graal* in which he sees a king turning a young knight into a winged lion. The lion then takes flight "et devenoient ses eles si granz et si merveilleuses que toz li monz en estoit coverz" (his wings became so big and so marvelous that they covered the whole world).[14] The lion is Galaad, who is destined to a glorious future: "si s'en aloit contremont vers les nues; et maintenant se ovroit li ciex por lui recevoir" (He flew towards the clouds and immediately the sky opened to receive him). The contrast between the two destinies seems irredeemably to condemn Alexander.

Yet sometimes the romance forgets Alexander's paganism. Right after his landing in England, for example, he addresses his troops in these words: "Seigneurs, moult devons regracier le Dieu Souverain que de la grant tempeste ou nous avons esté nous a delivrez [. . .] Sy en regracie le Dieu Souverain et tous les autres dieux qui regnent par dessoubz luy" (I, p. 145: Lords, we must give many thanks to the Sovereign God who has saved us from the terrible storm we experienced (. . .) I thank the Sovereign God and all the other gods who reign under him). Perhaps this "Sovereign God" who rules over many other gods is not the "Only God" that Perceforest will worship later, but the phrase *Dieu Souverain* is usually reserved for the Christian God. Besides, in *Perceforest*, all kinds of evil spirits, like Zephir, end up favoring the coming of the new religion. Pagan gods, although evil, help the good knights and minister to the progress of the true religion. Thus it is not impossible that Alexander was granted some confused revelation about the new God; in any case the profound modifications of his character in this romance allow the reader to forget that the emperor, unlike Perceforest, was not touched by grace.

Connecting Alexander to Arthur not only enhances Arthur's prestige but also gives Alexander the status of a romance character. Alexander can be proud of his new conquest: the Arthurian romance itself. What type of romance emerges from this alliance between Alexander's tradition and Arthur's? How does it renew thirteenth-century prose romance? Can we not say that in a way Alexander benefits more than Arthur from the connection? Taken away from his oriental world and acclimated to the Darnantes Forest, Alexander enters a new literary genre; Arthur, even though he has acquired an illustrious ancestor, will remain the well-known hero and the embodiment of a type of romance named after him.

We have seen how little *Perceforest* used *Fuerre de Gadres* and the *Voeux du Paon* in Book I. The Alexander material, however, intrudes again in Book II, when bad news arrives from the East: Porrus and Cassiel, the sultan of Badres, have been killed by the traitor Antipater; then Perceforest's court learns that Alexander himself has been poisoned by Antipater and Juvenispater.[15] *Perceforest* then invents its own version of the *Venjance Alixandre*: Lyonnel du Glat, Gadiffer's future son-in-law and one of the most noble heroes of the second generation, engages in battle the enemies who have taken over Royalville, a harbor founded by Gadiffer. After his victory, he hears that the enemy leader whom he had killed in the midst of the battle is none other than Juvenispater, the murderer of Alexander, Porrus, and Cassiel.[16] Forced to accommodate the previous tradition especially as it deals with Alexander's death, *Perceforest* forges a strong link between the destinies of the oriental and the occidental heroes. Here, contrary to Jean le Nevelon's account or other reports of the *Venjance Alixandre*,[17] it is not Alexander's Eastern relatives or friends who avenge the Emperor, but the Britons: Lyonnel is the grandson of Gelinant du Glat, the enchanter Darnant's only rational brother.

Like the *Historia Regum Britanniae*, like the *romans antiques* and the *Estoire del Saint Graal*, *Perceforest* tells the story of a *translatio imperii*.[18] With the foundation of occidental kingdoms, the center of gravity of the Macedonian Empire has shifted. When Alexander realizes that his power is threatened in the East, he takes comfort in the thought that his Occidental Empire is flourishing under Perceforest's wise rule. In his posthumous letter addressed to the king of England, Alexander, who felt that his end was near, confided to his friend: "je laisse ma povre puissance et retourne a ceulx dont je vaulz de mieulx et par lesquelz j'avray pouoir tant qu'il leur plaira, en especial a vous, noble roy, qui estes l'une des coulompnes qui soustiennent mon honneur" (IV-1, p. 2: I relinquish my meager power and come back to those who increase my worth and through whom I will retain power as long as it pleases them, especially to you, noble king, who are one of the columns supporting my honor). In the East, Alexander's empire is doomed to collapse: although *Perceforest* gives few details, it appears that after Alexander's death, all he had accomplished in this part of the world was destroyed. Porrus's and Cassiel's widows, robbed of their kingdoms, are forced to take refuge in the West where they will remain for the rest of their lives.[19] The kingdom of India, deprived of its legitimate lord, endures difficult years as the Romans threaten to invade it. It will again find a legitimate king: Porrus's son, whom Indian messengers come to seek in the West. It is remarkable, however, that it is now Perceforest who officially invests the young prince with his inheritance, and thus plays the role of father and protector that Alexander had taken upon himself when Perceforest and Gadiffer were orphaned. Perceforest declares to the Indian knights: "Et au regard de Porrus mon nepveu je lui rens son roiaulme et l'en mes en posession et saisine" (Ms. Arsenal 3486, fol. 410v°: As for my nephew Porrus, I give him back his kingdom and put it in his hands and his power). In Great Britain, on the contrary, despite the numerous difficulties encountered by the two kings, their power increases, and through them Alexander's prestige still shines.

Why do the two parts of Alexander's empire, although founded at the same time, not prosper equally? Because, as it seems to me, in *Perceforest* Alexander is no longer the conqueror he was in the *Roman d'Alexandre*. Alexander did not conquer England by force, but won it thanks to his moral and humane qualities. When the English lords, confused and troubled after King Pir's death, meet him on the shore, he wisely and peacefully advises them to take as their kings Betis and Gadiffer, his friends and allies. Following the

Voeux du Paon, which had already altered Alexander's moral portrait, *Perceforest* turns the proud conqueror into a moderate, peace-loving, caring man; humble, he acknowledges the role played by Fortune in his remarkable rise. The long speech he addresses to the English lords is strikingly lucid: Alexander sees himself as a mere instrument in the hands of the gods. Responsible for chastising the proud and the traitors, he knows that the time is near when Fortune will cast him down from the pinnacle of his glory. All he wants now is to act "au vouloir des dieux qui ce luy remeriront en leur saint paradis" (I, p. 148: according to the gods' will who will reward him in their holy paradise). Alexander is not ashamed of confessing his submission to the gods because he has been touched by the humility of the Britons who, following Venus's advice, relied on his wise decisions. Thus Alexander redeems his earlier flawed preference for Asia over Europe, for which Gautier de Châtillon blamed him in his *Alexandreis*.[20] The unquenchable thirst for conquest that prompted him to annex the whole of Asia and brought about his downfall, according to Gautier, is balanced, or better, *atoned for* by the wisdom and the genuine generosity (akin to Philip of Alsace's charity) that he demonstrates in England. These qualities have saved his name, and his enterprise.

Alexander changed because he trod on English soil, because he entered Arthurian romance, spontaneously adopting its values. Of course the Emperor and *Perceforest* would like us to believe that the opposite happened, that a corrupt, decadent Great Britain is going to be regenerated by this infusion of oriental blood: "Sy dist [Alexandre] a soy mesmes que le bon sang en gentillesse et en prouesse estoit tout corrompu et aliené, et de necessité seroit qu'ilz eussent prince souverain estrange et de gentil sang qui les gentilz hommes du pays renouvellast en toute gentillesse par bons exemples et par chevaleureuse vie, car par nice seigneur et enfrun empire tout ung pays" (I, p. 144: Alexander said to himself that good blood, noble and full of prowess, had been corrupted and degenerated. It was necessary for them to have a foreign king of noble blood who would renew the nobility of the country by setting good examples and leading a chivalrous life, for a country deteriorates if its prince is stupid and stingy). But in the "literary reality," it is the *matière de Bretagne* that regenerates the Alexandrian tradition. Is it not Arthurian romance that has conquered Alexander?

Yet, why bother introducing Alexander into Arthurian romance if finally Alexander alone is changed? Can we not argue that this new conquest also increases the authority of Arthurian romance? After all, through Arthur's veins runs the blood of Sebille, the *Dame du Lac*, who lives in a castle surrounded by water and mist, and the blood of the Macedonian conqueror, from whom emanates an aura of Oriental prestige. The Arthurian world can proclaim that it descends from Aeneas, from Brutus and the Trojans that he brought with him, from Alexander and the Greeks, and from the Britons. In it, yesterday's enemies are reconciled, and all the qualities of all the prestigious ancestors combine harmoniously. Arthurian romance is the rich heir of many traditions (*matière de Rome, matière de Bretagne*, and Alexandrian romance). And Alexander brings one more gift to *Perceforest*. Although turned into a romance character, he still remains a historical figure, and to make him Arthur's ancestor supports the author's project: to chronicle the history of Great Britain. Alexander gives the romance a much-wanted ring of historical truthfulness. Paradoxically, Alexander becomes a romance character to guarantee the historicity of *Perceforest*.

A brave and courtly knight, a *fin'amant*, a wise and generous king, an honorable patron—Alexander embodies all the values of the Arthurian world before it even exists. His only flaw is his paganism, but it is difficult to blame his not embracing a religion that did not yet exist and toward which all his qualities would surely have driven him if the time had been propitious. The only shadow across this altogether laudatory portrait is the hero's obstinate determination to undertake the conquest of Babylon despite the many forebodings of his tragic fate. The conqueror seems to recover his former haughtiness when he declares to a weeping Sebille:

> "Je vous promets que dés mon enfance, j'ay desiré d'avoir en ma domination toute la terre autant qu'elle comprent et veu que maintenant j'en ay submis la plus part se je ne achevoie le demourant veu qu'il n'y a que Babilone, l'en me devroit bien tenir pour lasce et de peu de valeur et me oster ce que j'ay conquis jusques a maintenant." (Ms. Arsenal 3484, fol. 439v°)

> (I assure you that since childhood I have wished to dominate the entire earth and all it encompasses; and since I have now subjected most of it, if I did not achieve my undertaking since only Babylon remains, I should rightly be considered recreant and worthless and all that I have conquered so far should be taken away from me.)

Perceforest attempts to attenuate its hero's defect by presenting the conquest of Babylon as a point of honor. Yet the shadow remains. Torn between the Alexandrian tradition and its admiration for the Emperor, the romance, in its effort to maintain a balance, does not always avoid contradiction.

Notes

1. They conclude, however, that he was indeed a romance hero. See François Suard, "Alexandre est-il un personnage de roman?," *Bien dire et bien aprandre* 7 (1989), 77–87; Catherine Gaullier-Bougassas, *Frontières*.

2. I refer to the following editions: *Le Roman de Perceforest*, première partie, ed. Jane H. M. Taylor (Geneva: Droz, 1979); *Le Roman de Perceforest*, quatrième partie, ed. Gilles Roussineau, 2 vols. (Geneva: Droz, 1987); *Le Roman de Perceforest*, troisième partie,

ed. Gilles Roussineau, 3 vols. (Geneva: Droz, 1988–1994). The Roman numeral indicates the part, the Arabic numeral the volume. For the unedited parts of the romance, I use the twelve manuscripts from the Bibliothèque de l'Arsenal: Paris, Arsenal, fr 3483–94. Each of the six parts of the romance is contained in two manuscript volumes. Part I: mss. 3483 and 3484; Part II: mss. 3485 and 3486; Part V: mss. 3491 and 3492; Part VI: mss. 3493 and 3494.

3. Jeanne Lods, *Le Roman de Perceforest* (Geneva: Droz, 1951), p. 41.

4. On Alexander's role in the *Voeux du Paon*, see my "Courtoisie et violence dans le *Cycle du Paon*" in *Alexandre*, pp. 321–39.

5. The man "vestu d'une noire cape" (cloaked in a black cape) who intervenes in Alexander's dream is Zephir, a fallen angel who will reappear in Book II and play a very prominent role in the destiny of Great Britain. He will be the one who will prepare Arthur's coming. The fact that he first—if only briefly and in a dream—assists Alexander links Arthur to Alexander, from the very outset of the romance.

6. It is true that this image of Venus does not correspond to the one inherited from the thirteenth-century *Roman de la rose* by Jean de Meun, where, as is well-known, Venus represents carnal desire and not especially refined *mores*. It might be one of the originalities of *Perceforest* to transform a somewhat ambiguous Venus into a symbol of courtly love and, moreover, a helper of the Christan God.

7. See L. F. Flutre, "Etudes sur le Roman de *Perceforêt*," *Romania* 91 (1970), pp. 204–5.

8. Alexander's undersea expedition inspires another episode of the *Perceforest*. The Blanc Chevalier, son of Perceforest, is carried to a strange island where he has to fight the famous sea knights (III-2, pp. 273–85). He attends a tournament between the fish, and thus witnesses the very game that Alexander copied. At the end of the fourteenth century another prose romance, the *Chevalier au Papegau*, also uses the motif of the sea knight: Arthur fights a terrible sea knight who regularly ravages the lands of a fairy. See F. Heuckenkamp's edition (Halle: Niemeyer, 1897), pp. 14–18.

9. One can hardly say, of course, that Passelion embodies the model of the *fin amant*! Nonetheless, the use of magic powers by women in love, so common in *lais*, is also a feature of the love stories in *Perceforest*.

10. See my "Le Clerc et le ménestrel: prose historique et discours versifié dans le *Perceforest*," *Cahiers de Recherches Médiévales* 5: "Ecrire en prose (XIIIe–XVe siècles): histoire et fiction" (1998).

11. The prologue of Book V uses almost the same wording: "Cresus le sage clerc et venerable poete la compilla et ordonna par le commandement et ordonnance du tresexcellent empereur Alexandre le conquerant" (Ms. Arsenal 3491, fol. 7rº: Cresus the wise cleric and venerable poet compiled it and organized it following the order of the very excellent Emperor Alexander the conqueror).

12. *Le Conte du Graal*, ed. Charles Méla (Paris: Librairie Générale Française, 1990), vv. 60–62; ed. W. Roach (Geneva: Droz, 1959), vv. 64–65. English translation by William Kibler in *Arthurian Romances* (London: Penguin Books, 1991), p. 382.

13. On the role of patrons, see Douglas Kelly, "Le Patron et l'auteur dans l'invention romanesque," in *Théories et Pratiques de l'écriture au Moyen Age*, ed. E. Baumgartner et C. Marchello-Nizia (*Littérales* 4: Paris X- Nanterre, 1988), pp. 25–39.

14. *La Queste del Saint Graal*, ed. A. Pauphilet (Paris: Champion, 1978), p. 131. The explanation for the vision is given on p. 137.

15. We hear the news twice: first from the queen of India, Fezonas, sister of Perceforest and Gadiffer, and her friend Edea of Gadres; then from the sailors who brought Juvenispater's troops to Royalville (ms. Arsenal 3485, fol. 69r° and v°). On the borrowings from the *Roman d'Alexandre* in this part of *Perceforest*, see Flûtre, "Etudes sur le *Roman de Perceforêt*," pp. 482–84.

16. The captain of the sailors tells Alexander that Antipater has remained on the island of Venus where he had committed his crimes.

17. We know seven versions of Alexander's death: Jehan le Nevelon, *La Venjance Alixandre* (c. 1180), ed. Edward Billings Ham, Elliott Monographs 34 (Princeton: Princeton University Press, 1931); Gui de Cambrai, *Le Vengement Alixandre*, ed. Bateman Edwards, Elliott Monographs 23 (Princeton: Princeton University Press, 1928); and five later accounts: in a manuscript in Venice, in a manuscript in Parma, in the adaptation offered by Jean Wauquelin (fifteenth century), in a passage of *Renart le Contrefait* (1328–1342), and in the version in the manuscript of Besançon (fifteenth century). See Edward Billings Ham, ed., *Five Versions of the Venjance Alixandre*, Elliott Monographs 34 (Princeton: Princeton University Press, 1935).

18. Up to modern times, since Perceforest's crown passes down to King Edward of England. See Sylvia Huot, "Chronicle, Lai and Romance: Orality and Writing in the *Roman de Perceforest*," in *Vox Intexta: Orality and Textuality in the Middle Ages*, ed. A. Nick Doane and Carol Braun Pasternak (Madison: University of Wisconsin Press, 1991), pp. 203–23, esp. pp. 220–21.

19. At the beginning of Book IV, for instance, they attend the solemnities organized by Perceforest in honor of the Sovereign God (IV-1, p. 3).

20. On this point see Douglas Kelly, *The Art of Medieval French Romance* (Madison: University of Wisconsin Press, 1992), pp. 45–47.

14

Alexander Amoroso: Rethinking Alexander in the *Roman de Perceforest*

Jane H. M. Taylor

> No interpretation can be effectively disqualified on its own terms
> by a simple enumeration of inaccuracies or omissions, or by a list
> of unanswered questions.[1]

Like all those ingenious late-medieval writers who perform contortionist
feats to make a space in the Arthurian canon for new Arthurian adventures—
the continuators, the interpolators, the constructors of cycle-codices—the writer
of the *Roman de Perceforest* is an encyclopedic reader for whom the repertoire of
his predecessors is a mine of theme and motif. To say this unqualified, however,
is to play into the hands of those who would see the *Perceforest*, or Froissart's
Meliador, or *Ysaïe le Triste*, as drearily unoriginal and shamelessly opportunistic, no
more—the medieval equivalent, as it were, of *Nightmare on Elm Street* numbers
9, and 10, and 11. I have argued repeatedly that this is to misunderstand late-
medieval intertextuality in general, and the narrative projects of these writers in
particular; late-medieval narrative art consists not in "originality" as we understand it, but rather in harnessing the potential of sources, eliciting, and in the
strictly etymological sense *explicating*, what is latent in them.[2] We should see these
late-medieval *romanciers*, then, as mature and expert readers who use their inter-
pretative and exegetical skills to map out and engage with the work of their
predecessors, redeploying the constituent elements of the latter at the service of
new coherences. This essay is intended as another building block in the construction of that argument: another plea for a better understanding of these still-
neglected and maligned edifices. I shall suggest that just as the writer of the
Perceforest, expertly decoding his sources, capitalizes on the meaning-potential of
the Vulgate Arthurian romances, so he "maps" Alexander the Great, isolating what
serves his purpose in the latter's distinctive characteristics and adapting it, expertly,
to the genealogical and teleological narrative that he wants to construct. More

particularly, I shall suggest that his characteristically dexterous, adaptive reading of the Alexander corpus feeds on and feeds into an Alexander of a particular sort, one who serves, ideally, his textual—and even metatextual—strategies.

But let me start, simply, with Alexander the Great in the *Roman de Perceforest*. As Michelle Szkilnik shows in this volume, his role is political and, more important, genealogical. Fresh from his conquest of Gadres and Fezon, Alexander is brought to the English coast by a providential storm, just in time to nominate kings of England and Scotland to take the place of the weak and incompetent King Pir, lately deceased. The new king of England, Betis de Fezon, later known as *Perceforest*, disappears into the great forests of the country to impose his good government on the brutal and dissident *lignage de Darnant*; Alexander and some of his court follow, swearing never to spend more than one night anywhere until they have found him. Alexander is badly wounded in combat with some of Darnant's clan; he is succored by a certain Sebille, with whom he enjoys a secret and idyllic love affair: the result is a child, known as Remanant de Joie, who is, distantly, the ancestor of King Arthur.[3]

Now, of course, several elements here must surprise the informed reader: that Alexander should be directed, however providentially, to England; that his visit should remain so resolutely secret; finally, and the point in which I am primarily interested here, that he should indulge in what I called an "idyllic love affair." Nothing, after all, in the Vulgate *Alexandre* would seem to offer the remotest precedent. True, there are women—there are even hints of love affairs—in Alexander's legendary *vita*, but they remain resolutely marginal, oddly unsatisfactory,[4] to the extent that to make them a topic at all is to decenter the romances in which they appear so fleetingly. Consider, for instance, Alexander's curiously unsubstantial queen, Roxane.[5] Most readers, it is probably safe to say, are astonished to discover, at Alexander's coronation and in the maelstrom of grief at his death, a grieving *roïne*[6] of whose existence they had been previously unaware.[7] Her name is *Rosenés*, and the Latin histories, which are by contrast perfectly clear (Gosman, *Légende*, p. 256), have explained that *Roxane* is the daughter of the Emperor Darius, and that Alexander had married her after the defeat of her father. Darius's daughter, it turns out, we have met before in the Vulgate *Alexandre*—but anonymously, and in ways that are studiously obfuscating. After her father's defeat, she is attached to Alexander's travelling court, but with an odd phrase (What else was he *supposed* to do with her?), which cannot but sound rather offhand and perfunctory: "Mais sa [Darius's] fille estoit bele et ot cler le viaire, / Sa colour samble rose et soleil qui esclaire; / Aveuc soi l'en mena, *q'en deüst il el faire?*" (*MFRA II*, Br. II, vv. 3069–71: But his [Darius's] daughter was beautiful and fair of face, her coloring rose-pink and bright as the sun; he took her with him: what else was he to do?).

No suggestion here of a marriage, still less of love—even the faintly courtly description seems no more than conventional, and although the possibility of marriage with Alexander is raised, it is in passing, as if the poet were quite uncommitted to the prospect; marriage to Alexander is just one of the ways in which a magnanimous conqueror might dispose of a beautiful and politically valuable captive.[8]

Alternatively, consider the case of *la reine Candace* (Gosman, *Légende*, pp. 253–56, and "L'élément féminin"). True, she is more developed as a personality and figures more substantially in the *Roman d'Alexandre*, but she is paradoxically marked by ambivalences of the same order as those that make Roxane so insubstantial. Alexandre de Paris is firm: Alexander spends no more than half a day with her, and what is at issue is less love than sexuality: "Grant joie font ensemble par bien et par amor,/ Desus un lit paré *se jurent demi jor*" (*MRFA II*, Br. III, vv. 4842–43 emphasis mine: They were very happy together, from joy and love; they spent half a day lying on a fine, well-decked bed). But how meaningful, then, is that phrase *par amor*? How seriously ought we to take Alexander's messages to her when he thanks her for her opulent gifts: "Li message revienent, la novele ont contee / Que *li rois Alixandres l'a tant fort aamee / Plus que nisune feme qui de mere soit nee.*" (vv. 4449–51, The messengers return bearing the news that King Alexander loves her more than any other mortal woman). Is Candace right to be, as she is made to say, *boneürée* (v. 4452)? Has she not *mis*read a politeness formula? This is, surely, no more than a *repos du guerrier*, not to be treated as more than an interlude: Alexander having left immediately for his next conquest, we hear no more of any attachment to the lovesick queen.

That said, I am of course simplifying; there is more to Alexander's women than mere irrelevance, and the bland version of Alexander's Vulgate love affairs that I have just given is, to a degree, incomplete. To be precise: I have adopted Alexandre de Paris's relatively innocuous account—and while Alexandre makes Roxane and Candace marginal, some of his avatars, more seriously, make them threatening. There are, for instance, those ominous images that, Ross says, must have encapsulated oral traditions in the north of France and which seem to have attributed attempted murder of Alexander to Roxane: in a series of northern French manuscripts, an illuminator has shown her—or at least a queen—armed with a knife, about to cut the chains that attach Alexander's submarine to a boat on the surface.[9] There is also the odd and unsettling story of the portrait that so angers Alexander (*MFRA II*, Br. III, vv. 4770–82), and the way in which the Candace episode veers so decisively, in the English tradition for instance, toward Candace as a scheming woman who entraps Alexander and preens herself on the cunning with which, like Delilah gulling Samson or Eve Adam, she has drawn Alexander into her net.[10] Candace and Roxane, in other words, become not merely marginal but puzzling and problematical:[11] dangerous distractions to male autonomy and a warrior career.

I labor these points because my bland summary of Alexander's idyll with Sebille in the *Roman de Perceforest* was just as misleadingly brief and incomplete: Sebille too is problematic, and in ways, however vestigial, which seem to suggest very similar pressures in operation.[12] Take, for instance, the loaded terms in which she makes her first appearance in the romance. Like so many of the *demoiselles de la forest*, she is adept, it seems, in magical illusions: not only is her castle made secure from marauding members of the *lignage Darnant* by *espés air*[13] but, much more seriously, she is able to divert Alexander, with cheerful lack of scruple, from his proper, chivalric path by circumventing the solemn and binding oath that he and all his followers have sworn: when he tells her, as he must, that he has promised not to spend more than one night in any particular place until he and Floridas, his companion, have found Betis, she—and the choice of the verb is surely significant—"pensa qu'elle en *joueroit* autrement et aussy fist elle, car le roy et Floridas y demourerent *quinze jours* sy n'y cuidoient avoir demouré que une nuyt" (*Perceforest* I/i, p. 242, ll. 6334–7: She thought that she would play a different game, and so she did, for the king and Floridas spent fifteen days in her company while convinced that they had been there only one night). Any well-informed reader of the Vulgate version of the Arthurian romances will, of course, recognize all sorts of intertextual resonances—starting with Sebille's name (or names, since she is also known as the *Dame du Lac*). It is, after all, a certain *Sibylle l'enchanteresse* who conspires with Morgue la Fée and the *reine de Sorestan* to kidnap Lancelot— they are, says the writer of the Prose *Lancelot*, "les .III. fames ou monde qui plus savoient d'anchantement et de charaies sanz *la Dame del Lac*"[14] (the three women who, in the whole world, and apart from the Lady of the Lake, knew most of spells and enchantments)—and merely to link her, via this means, with Morgue is to tap into a complex of narrative motifs, largely associated with the latter,[15] whereby mortal heroes are seduced into an erotic otherworld where time passes unnoticed. We might perhaps also draw analogies between Alexander's involuntary paternity on the one hand, and on the other hand the sort of subterfuges to which Merlin resorts to engineer the birth of Arthur himself—or indeed, those that allow Lancelot to engender Galaad, and Bors Helain le Blanc.[16] But even allowing for intertextualities, Sebille's unscrupulous female artifice strikes a discordant note that it is wrong to set aside: the author of the *Perceforest* is rarely random or unthinking in his borrowings, and if the idyll with Sebille starts off in circumstances so particular, it is wiser for our analysis to take account of it.

To attempt to do so, of course, is to return to the texts comprising the Vulgate *Alexandre*, and to wonder why it is that the roles women play in them are so very ambivalent—why it is that women are so carefully occluded in the masculine, military, empire-conquering society that romances devoted to Alexander project, why it is that, so consistently, Alexander has to be enchanted or hoodwinked or diverted into an attachment. And I should like to propose, in response, a hypothesis: that what the Alexander romances and their avatars explore and crystallize is the conflict—which the writers themselves, no doubt, would have been unable to articulate conceptually[17]—between the public persona and the private self of the charismatic leader. I use the word "charismatic" here in the sense in which Max Weber coined (or more precisely popularised) it—prefacing what I have to say by pointing out that what Weber himself says remains rather rudimentary and inexplicit.[18] Charisma, for Weber, is a very particular type of authority that can exist only *in community*, because it implies a symbiosis between a particular leader and his adoring followers, and only *in contradistinction to normal political processes*, because it emerges from circumstances or emergencies that transcend the everyday. Charismatic authority attaches to a person who, because he appears to possess superhuman, or at least unaccustomed, powers, is seen as providential or exemplary;[19] it generates a passionate, and unqualified, personal devotion that has no ground in logic or rationality, and whose prime characteristic is self-sacrifice, gladly assumed, in the service of the cause that the leader embodies, endorsed by what appear to be authenticating manifestations. Authority and devotion of this sort can exist in all sorts of different spheres, but Weber makes most of what he calls "the *brotherliness* [Brüderlichkeit] of war, and of death in war,"[20] and this underscores something that is particularly valuable for my purposes here: the fact that his universe is fundamentally binary. What he calls *brotherliness* stands on the one hand, self-abnegating, inclusive, heroic, and on the other stands erotic love, subjective, irrational, unenduring, exclusive, individual. Weber—and I quote Roslyn Bologh's aptly named book *Love or Greatness*[21]—tends to pit "action and success in the world against love and withdrawal from the world": the conflicting claims of love and conquest, lineage and empire-building, are irreconcilable.

What I am suggesting is that Alexander is configured in all the Alexander romances as just such a charismatic authority. His mission of conquest is, of course, divinely inspired (Gosman, *Légende*, pp. 200–3): was he even, as Plutarch had suggested, of divine birth—the son of Apollo? or of Zeus? His very birth, says Pseudo-Callisthenes,[22] avidly followed by Alexandre de Paris, is marked by premonitory signs and marvels:

> A l'eure que li enfes dut de sa mere issir
> Demostra *Dieus* par signes qu'il se feroit cremir,
> Car l'air estut müer, le firmament croissir (. . .)
> Ce fu senefiance que *Dieus* fist esclarcir
> Por mostrer de l'enfant q'en devoit avenir
> Et com grant segnorie il avroit a baillir. (*MFRA II*, Br. I, vv. 22–24,
> 27–29)

(At the very hour when the child was to issue from his mother's womb, God showed by signs that he would make himself feared, for the very air shook, the firmament was torn apart (. . .) All these were God's signs, to show what destiny awaited the child, and how great was the empire he was to rule).

It is not—maintain the histories and romances—that his conquests are self-interested: on the contrary, he is concerned only by "proëce, segnorie et barnage" (*MFRA II*, Br. III, v. 2230: prowess, lordship and honor), and gives away castles, cities, whole countries, to his followers as soon as he has acquired them. This remarkable and disinterested generosity creates, of course, the other dimension of charismatic leadership as Weber conceives it: an unqualified mutual devotion that unites Alexander and his men, a symbiosis against which nothing can prevail—one in which Martin Gosman, significantly, sees analogies with the Germanic *Blutbrüderschaft* (*Légende*, pp. 220–42). Our cynical twentieth-century imaginations may impute more self-seeking motives to Alexander's barons—*juvenes* in pursuit of nice little fiefs? (*Légende*, pp. 239–41)—but overtly at least, and as Alexandre de Paris and his colleagues paint them, they are a very model of generous selflessness, chivalric discipleship.

But that symbiotic closeness creates a binary world—one analogous to that of Max Weber's charismatic leader, in which "women, love, mysticism fall on one side, men, action, and accomplishment on the other," and in which erotic love is at a polar opposite from "brotherliness" (Bologh, p. 165). The ideal social order of the Alexander romances (something like what Karl Uitti calls an "ideal *communitas*"[23]) is based on a masculine chivalric identity which is, necessarily, threatened by the incursion of the female: at the very least, that a woman might divert the political ambitions of the charismatic warrior leader; at the worst, that her intervention might change, irrevocably, the idyllic warrior bonding between him and his men. Is it, then, altogether surprising that Alexander's women are configured as adventitious desiring *subjects* who manipulate him, and not as the *objects* of his unprompted, unmanipulated desire? That Alexandre de Paris directly prefaces Candace's intrusion into his romance with yet another firm reminder of Alexander's manifest and ineluctable *destinee?*

> Par trestout Oriant est la novele alee
> Que li rois Alixandres a si fort *destinee*
> Que sous ciel n'a cité de si haut mur fondee
> Qu'a lui puisse durer nisune matinee;
> Il est teus de son cors, c'est verités provee,
> C'un chevalier armé trenche tout a s'espee. (*MFRA II*, Br. III, vv.
>   4429–34, my emphasis)

> (Throughout the East the news went that King Alexander's destiny was so exalted that no city, however great its walls, could resist him for as much as a morning; he is so physically powerful, and this is proven, that he can cut an armed warrior in two with his sword).

Or is it surprising that Candace is, as we have seen, so persistently associated with the dispiritingly ubiquitous catalogue of scheming women? That there is that nagging little tradition of the knife-wielding Roxane? Women become, to borrow a phrase from Dorothy Dinnerstein,[24] the "carnal scapegoats" who, if indulged, would threaten Alexander's "clean, world-conquering humanity," in Alexander romances that negotiate (I use the distinction that Sarah Kay makes in her recent, excellent book on the *chanson de geste*[25]) the difficult boundaries between epic—collective experience, and romance—individual achievement:[26] the masculine brotherhood firmly understood within charismatic leadership must remain inviolate.

This may seem to have taken me dismayingly far from the *Roman de Perceforest*, but what I want to suggest is that the latter makes manifest just these issues of eros as against empire building, private as against public; it addresses them *explicitly*, and weaves them into a satisfyingly rational hermeneutic configuration. Its author takes as a springboard the tradition of the Vulgate that Alexander's mission is god-given: "je ne suis pas a moy, ains suys sergent des dieux ne je ne puis fors par eulx" (I/i, ll. 2782–83: I am not my own man, but rather the servant of the gods, and I can do nothing without them) and that his followers are, in a sense, selflessly his disciples: "[J]e de moy pou vaulx se *les dieux* n'estoient et *la bonne chevalerie qui par la bonté qui en eulx est me servent*, et qui par leur proesse et leur chevalerie acquierent les terres et les fiefz dont je suys souverain" (I.i, ll. 2955–59: For I am worth little in my own right, were it not for the gods and the fine knights who of their worthiness serve me, and who by their prowess and their chivalry acquire the lands and the fiefs of which I am lord). Rather than leaving the gods' purpose unmotivated and mysterious, however, in a typical adaptive manoeuvre, he lends the king an ethical role that explains and justifies the gods' endorsement of what could look like mere self-aggrandisement, and creates a new role for the emperor whereby he is deputed by the gods to be the scourge of the proud and the godless: "ja soie je si grant (. . .) c'est par la bonté des dieux qui font de moy leur sergent et leur verge pour chastier les felons princes et eslevés qui ne recongnoissent ne dieu ne homme par leur grant orgueil" (I/i, ll. 2951–55: If I have reached such heights (. . .) it is by the goodness of the gods who make me their servant and the rod with which they punish the wicked and arrogant princes who, of their overweening pride, recognize the authority of neither god nor man). The romance thus becomes a *political* fiction[27] that deflects Alexander toward a motivated purposefulness that he did not possess in, say, the *Roman d'Alexandre*: the signs and portents that continue to pursue him, the ardor of his followers, are rationally explained, rather than a mythical given.

It is with that political reorientation of Alexander's mission in mind that we should approach his affair with Sebille. There is no doubt in the author's mind but that this is a genuine love. "Force d'amours," Alexander writes to her, "m'amaine a ce que je suy et voeuil estre le sien tresloial amy et chevalier" (I/i, ll. 7260–61: The force of my love draws me most willingly to be her very loyal friend and knight). And it is, says the *romancier*, revealingly, the most painful emotional experience of Alexander's career: "Quant il deut partir du pays (. . .) il n'avoit oncques esté a sy grant peine pour chose qui luy avenist"[28] (When he was obliged to leave the country, he had never been so unhappy for anything else that had happened to him). But it is precisely for that reason that the dialectic of public and private becomes particularly acute—and this author, unlike the authors of the earlier Alexander romances, makes that dilemma explicit.

Take, for instance, their crucial leavetaking in the latter part of Book I. Sebille has flown to the help of Alexander, seriously wounded once again—but this time quite aware of Sebille's dangerously spell-binding proclivities.[29] Sebille's skill cures him, in all joy, of his wounds, and they are walking one day in the garden when Alexander notices that she is weeping in anticipation of his leaving. Alexander confects a *demande d'amour*:[30] if she were able to exercise so powerful an influence that he would abandon his god-given, empire-building mission and remain with her, would she choose to ask him to do so? Like all the best heroines, Sebille, of course, subordinates any private needs or desires that she may feel to the public Alexander: "Sire," dist Sybille, "je vous jure par le dieu qui fait mieulx a aourer, que ja par moy denree de honneur ne perderez. Car certainement vous ameroie mieulx arriere de moy conquerant honneur que prez de moy deffaillant a proesse. . . . " ("Sire," said Sebille, "I swear by the god who most deserves praise that never by my fault shall you lose a scrap of honor. For naturally, I would love you better far from me and conquering honor, than close to me and abandoning prowess"), and Alexander is captivated precisely by this display of selflessness: "Je vous ay en convenant que sy tost que je auray achevee l'emprinse que j'ay encommencee, que je vous reviendray veoir comme vostre amy se les dieux me sauvent la vie" (BNF fr. 345, f. 184v.: "I promise you that, as soon as I have achieved the enterprise on which I have embarked, and assuming I am alive, I shall come back to you as your lover"). Their discussion, however, has reflected and articulated a masculine anxiety about the security of man's control over women's sexuality, about the irreconcilable disparity between man's political power and his emotional vulnerability. Sebille is made to accept a role that will, in the context of Alexander's conquering career, remain marginal: she will be visited in secrecy and only, as it were, when Alexander can spare the time from his career of conquest; she will bear his child, but without his presence or his acknowledgement; she will never impinge on the homosocial[31] bond that unites him with the paladins, whose unquestioning loyalty is the *sine qua non* of his success.

In conclusion, I should like to speculate by briefly exploring the possibility that the Alexander romances, including the *Perceforest*, are a reflection of a wider anxiety manifest in other legend clusters of the Middle Ages: the anxieties of an epic, essentially warrior society as it sees its values subverted by the pressures that we know as "romance," anxieties about the ways in which collective identities based on charismatic leadership are threatened by the advent of a queen or a consort.[32] Take, for instance, the case of Charlemagne. Sarah Kay has warned us (*Chansons de geste*, pp. 25–30), of course, not to take the *Chanson de Roland* as a benchmark, but it does, surely, epitomize that idealized, even ecstatic collective experience, masculine experience, of which the *chanson de geste* is a record: the twelve peers, the Christian army, united in the unconditional service of an emperor marked out by God to be the vehicle of His triumph over evil. And what happens when Charlemagne in other poems, usually unwisely, allows himself to be diverted by a woman shows how far women are—to return to the description I used earlier—"carnal scapegoats."[33] Charlemagne's fictional queens are shadowy, and consistently problematic.[34] Take *his* Sebille, for instance—is the ubiquity of the name a sign in itself?—who survives only incompletely, in a French fragment or two and in the fourteenth-century Franco-Italian *Macario*.[35] She herself is innocent enough, of course—but disruptive, provoking disharmony, via the traitor Macaire, in the Emperor's household. Or the Duchess of Burgundy in *Girart de Vienne*, whom Charlemagne is unwise enough to marry in spite of having promised her to Girart, who is the instrument of the latter's humiliation, and who provokes a seven-year war of secession between the Emperor and Girart.[36] Take—finally and it may be incongruously—the legend of the *péché de Charlemagne*:[37] not articulated with absolute clarity before the fourteenth century, with *Tristan de Nanteuil*,[38] but a permanent lurking threat to the integrity and authority of the charismatic, unquestioned leader whom the Emperor otherwise is. To quote Sarah Kay again, in the world of the *chanson de geste* "the desire of/for women introduces an excess which cannot be accommodated" (p. 137): a charismatic king who withdraws from public life to indulge private desire represents a danger to the social and political fabric, and the ideal kingdom can only be one in which, the objects of such desire having been studiously erased, the homosocial bond between warrior leader and warrior band is inviolate.

But the Charlemagne epics and the Alexander "romances"[39] do share an epic agenda; romance, it might be thought, will be more accommodating. However, to quote Simon Gaunt, in romance too "sexuality (. . .) has the potential to destroy social cohesion" and "[t]he hero of romance is a divided self, split between an impulse towards social integration and a counter-impulse towards socially alienating, but privately fulfilling desires."[40] Take—of course— Guenevere, ultimately the agent of the fall of Arthur's kingdom and the destruction of that pattern book of masculine collective identity, the Round Table.[41] But what interests me is less this eschatological role, significant though it is, than the ill-focused unease that she generates, at intervals, precisely within that tight-knit masculine circle.[42] Take, in that connection, the cloud that hangs over Guenevere's identity, after the odd, discomfiting episode of the False Guenevere;[43] here even we are left uneasy, especially given the startling alacrity with which Arthur himself and much of his Round Table repudiate what we

assume to be the real Guenevere (*La Fausse Guenièvre*, pp. 236–38): might we
not see this, as Sarah Kay sees this and other doubles, as figuring "une opposition évidente entre une féminité désirée par le héros, et une autre qu'il
redoute"?[44] And what about the very similar eagerness with which the entire
Round Table—including those like Bors or Yvain or Gauvain, whom one
might expect to be allies—unquestioningly assumes Guenevere's guilt in the
episode of the poisoned apple in *La Mort le roi Artu*? Of course, there *are*
reasons for this: notably and legally, the question of ocular evidence and of laws
pertaining to responsibility.[45] But it is difficult for us not to sympathize with
Lancelot's incredulous dismay: if so many of the Round Table were present, did
none of them leap to the Queen's defense and endorse her innocence? "Et
comment fu ce donc, fet Lancelos, qu'il soufrirent que madame la reïne ot
honte devant eus, qu'il n'i ot qui l'en deffendist?"[46] ("And how could it have
happened," said Lancelot, "that they suffered that my lady the queen be shamed
before them, and that not one of them defended her?"). But his interlocutor's
self-satisfied conviction of Guenevere's guilt ("il n'i ot qui i feïst si grant force;
si *orent droit* . . ." (Not one of them was prepared for the challenge; and they
were right, *La Mort*, p. 75) is a telling image of a male court closing ranks
against an outsider whom they have long distrusted: Is it significant that when
her innocence is established and guilt is therefore presumably imputed where
it belongs, to Arvarlen who had intended the poisoned apple for Gauvain (*La
Mort*, p. 61), we hear nothing of his punishment, indeed nothing more of his
fate? It is as if the Round Table's idealization of itself, finally, was less a matter
of the erotic ethos to which it pays lip service, than of preserving the male,
homosocial ethos that minor matters like attempted poisoning must not be
allowed to disturb.

   I even wonder whether that imperative is not echoed in the writers'
satisfaction, in those snide little pseudo-fabliaux the *Lai du cor* and the *Conte
du mantel*, when Guenevere so signally fails a chastity test.[47] The Queen is
marginalized, socially and politically,[48] in ways which surely betray a resentment of her very being:[49] a resentment which is, I think, a political one, and
unites her with the Sebilles and Roxanes and Candaces of the Charlemagne
and Alexander groups. It is true, of course, that we are no longer accustomed
to thinking of Arthur as a "leader": in the romances in which his court is the
ideological and narrative center, he himself has largely become a figurehead,
almost a cipher.[50] But it is after all as a charismatic leader, of a devotedly loyal
warband, that Geoffrey and Wace initially construct him,[51] and traces of the
collective bond between leader and Round Table remain, surely, in some of the
earlier romances devoted to him, in Beroul's *Tristan*, for instance, with its all-
encompassing Round Table "qui tornoie conme le monde,"[52] or in the vision
to which Perceval subscribes, until he finds Arthur full of gloom, of Arthur's
court as *par excellence* the shining, idyllic, center where knights are made.[53] And
may it perhaps be significant that those nagging images of an Arthur declining

to lead are so often focused on Guenevere—like the moment where, at the beginning of *Yvain*, Arthur has retired to bed with his Queen and, to the outrage of the remainder of the Round Table, cannot be awakened to direct the activities of the court?[54]

These are very large questions, and I cannot begin to explore them fully here. My point, however, remains: that Sebille, like Candace, like Roxane, like all the women who intrude, briefly, into the emotional and personal ambits of the charismatic heroes of medieval epic and romance, is in essence and potentially a challenge to the ideological foundations of empire. She is given—like them—no fixed or authoritative position from which to speak; she is—like them—systematically excluded from the public arena. The author of the *Roman de Perceforest*, like the Alexander-writers who precede him, has imagined a binary, dichotomous universe, a universe in which erotic love is found to be incompatible with "brotherliness." What Max Weber calls then "the extraordinary quality of brotherliness of war, and of death in war" which is "shared with sacred charisma and the experience of the communion with God" (*From Max Weber*, p. 336) is—must be—exclusive of women: in a society that values just such charismatic relationships, and which sets at its fictional centers charismatic leaders like Alexander, the queen—the woman—must at best be hurriedly—and gratefully—set aside, eliminated from discourse,[55] and at worst, discredited.

Notes

1. Fredric Jameson, *The Political Unconscious: Narrative as a Socially Symbolic Act* (Ithaca, NY: Cornell University Press, 1982), p. 13.

2. Starting with "The Fourteenth Century: Context, Text, Intertext," in *The Legacy of Chrétien de Troyes*, ed. Norris Lacy, Keith Busby, and Douglas Kelly (Amsterdam: Rodopi, 1987), 267–332, and most recently in the first chapter of my *The Poetry of François Villon: Text and Context* (Cambridge: Cambridge University Press, 2001).

3. On the genealogical implications of this, see my "Arthurian Cyclicity: the Construction of History in the Late French Romances," *The Arthurian Yearbook* 2 (1992), 209–23; "Order from Accident: Cyclic Consciousness at the End of the Middle Ages," in Bart Besamusca et al., eds, *Cyclification: The Development of Narrative Cycles in the Chansons de Geste and the Arthurian Romances* (Amsterdam: North-Holland Publishing Company, 1994), 59–73; "The Sense of a Beginning: Genealogy and Plenitude in Late Medieval Narrative Cycles," in *Transtextualities: Of Cycles and Cyclicity in Medieval French Literature*, ed. Donald Maddox and Sara Sturm-Maddox (Binghamton, NY: Medieval and Renaissance Texts and Studies, 1995), 93–123.

4. See Gosman, *Légende*, ch. xi, pp. 243–65.

5. See Martin Gosman, "L'élément féminin dans le 'Roman d'Alexandre': Olympias et Candace," in *Court and Poet. Selected Proceedings of the International Courtly Literature Society, Liverpool, 1980*, ed. Glyn S. Burgess (Liverpool: Francis Cairns, 1980),

167–76, and cf. also Gerrit H. V. Bunt, "A Wife There Was for Alexander the Great," in *"A Wyf Ther Was": Essays in Honour of Paule Mertens-Fonck*, ed. Juliette Dor (Liège: Département d'Anglais, 1992), 41–48.

6. She appears briefly, ravishingly dressed (*MFRA II*, Br. IV, v. 68) at Alexander's coronation, and then distraught with grief, at the very end of Alexander's life: "Qui lors veïst sovent la roïne pasmer/ Et ses chavaus desrompre et ses dras descirer . . ." (*MFRA II*, Br. IV, vv. 610–11); their text is also used in the excellent bilingual edition by Laurence Harf-Lancner (*RA*).

7. Other than in one, idiosyncratic, manuscript, ms. L (BNF, fr. 789); see Alfred Foulet's note in *MFRA I*, p. 390, and E. C. Armstrong's remarks in *Mélanges de linguistique et de littérature offerts à M. Alfred Jeanroy par ses élèves et ses amis* (Paris: Droz, 1928), 131–40.

8. See the reassuring words with which an escaped prisoner reports to her anxious father Darius: "vostre fille est bele si a molt cler le vis; / S'il veut, si la prendra au los de ses amis, / Et s'il ne la veut prendre, ja n'en fera pis: / Donra li a segnor duc ou conte ou marchis" (*MFRA II*, Br. II, vv. 3026–29).

9. D.J.A. Ross, "Alexander and the Faithless Lady: A Submarine Adventure," in *Studies*, pp. 382–403.

10. See *King Alisaunder*, ed. G. V. Smithers, 2 vols. (London: Oxford University Press, 1952–57), ll. 7703–10. Thomas of Kent likewise prefaces the Candace episode with a misogynist diatribe (*RTC* ll. 7631–40); see Gosman, *Légende*, pp. 311–12.

11. The same could be said of any of the women of the Alexander legend: Alexander's mother Olympias, of course (on whom see Gosman, *Légende*, pp. 246–53), but also such incidental females as the *filles-fleurs* and the *filles de l'eau* (on whom see Philippe Ménard, "Femmes séduisantes et femmes malfaisantes: les filles-fleurs de la forêt et les créatures des eaux dans le *Roman d'Alexandre*," *Bien dire et bien aprandre* 7 [1989], 5–17), and even the Amazons (see Aimé Petit, "Le traitement courtois du thème des Amazones d'après trois romans antiques: *Enéas, Troie et Alexandre*," *Le Moyen Age* 89 [1983], 63–84).

12. On Sebille see Anne Berthelot, "La Dame du Lac, Sebile l'enchanteresse, la dame d'Avalon . . . et quelques autres," in *Europäische Literaturen im Mittelalters: Mélanges en l'honneur de Wolfgang Spiewok à l'occasion de son 65ème anniversaire*, ed. Danielle Buschinger (Greifswald: Reineke-Verlag, 1994), 9–17.

13. See *Le Roman de Perceforest: première partie*, ed. Jane H. M. Taylor (Geneva: Droz, 1979), pp. 236–37 (references: *Perceforest* I/i, with page or line numbers as appropriate).

14. See *Lancelot*, iv, ed. Alexandre Micha (Paris and Geneva: Droz, 1979), pp. 173–76 (where she is called *Sedile*); cf. *Les Prophécies de Merlin*, ed. L. A. Paton (New York: D. C. Heath/ London: Oxford University Press, 1926), i, pp. 388–89.

15. See especially Laurence Harf-Lancner, *Les Fées au moyen âge: Morgane et Mélusine: La naissance des fées* (Geneva: Slatkine, 1984), pp. 263–88.

16. See Howard Bloch, *Etymologies and Genealogies: A Literary Anthropology of the Middle Ages* (Chicago: University of Chicago Press, 1983), p. 210, on the odd way in which "within the Grail corpus bastardy is an even more pressing concern than incest."

17. I am therefore following Fredric Jameson in contending that "the production of aesthetic or narrative form is to be seen as an ideological act in its own right, with the function of inventing imaginary or formal 'solutions' to unresolvable social contradictions (. . .) resolutions of issues that [peoples] are unable to articulate conceptually" (*The Political Unconscious*, p. 79).

18. The concept—the term itself was borrowed, in fact, from Rudolf Sohm—is most fully dealt with in two chapters from larger enterprises: "Die charismatische Herrschaft und ihre Umbildung," in *Wirtschaft und Gesellschaft: Grundriss der verstehenden Soziologie*, ed. J. Winckelmann (Tübingen: J. C. B. Mohr, 1956), part III, ch. 9, and "Die Wirtschaftsethik der Weltreligionen," in *Gesammelte Aufsätze zur Religionssoziologie* (Tübingen: J. C. B. Mohr, 1922), i, 237–75; translations are in *From Max Weber: Essays in Sociology*, trans. and ed. H. H. Gerth and C. Wright Mills (New York: Oxford University Press, 1946). I should acknowledge debts to the following: Julien Freund, *The Sociology of Max Weber*, trans. Mary Ilford (New York: Pantheon Books, 1968); Reinhard Bendix, *Max Weber: An Intellectual Portrait* (New York: Anchor Books, 1962), and particularly Charles Lindholm, *Charisma* (Oxford: Blackwell, 1990).

19. "Es soll bei den nachfolgenden Erörterungen unter dem Ausdruck: 'Charisma' eine (ganz einerlei: ob wirkliche Qualität eines Menschen verstanden weden. Unter 'charismatischer Autorität' also eine (sei es mehr äusserliche oder mehr innerliche) Herrschaft über Menschen, welcher sich die Beherrschten des Glaubens an diese Qualität dieser bestimmten Person fügen" ("Wirtschaftsethik der Weltreligionen," p. 269: "Charisma" shall be understood to refer to an *extraordinary* quality of a person, regardless of whether this quality is actual, alleged, or presumed. "Charismatic authority," hence, shall refer to a rule over men, whether predominantly external or predominantly internal, to which the governed submit because of their belief in the extraordinary quality of the specific *person*": *From Max Weber*, p. 295).

20. See Weber's essay "Zwischenbetrachtung," in *Gesammelte Aufsätze*, i, pp. 536–73 (p. 551).

21. Roslyn Wallach Bologh, *Love or Greatness: Max Weber and Masculine Thinking—A Feminist Inquiry* (London: Unwin Hyman, 1990), p. 165.

22. See Jacques Lacarrière with Christiane Raynaud, *Le Conquérant de l'absolu: Alexandre le Grand: La vie légendaire, traduite du grec* (Paris: Editions du Félin, 1993), pp. 41–43, on "L'homme-dieu."

23. Karl Uitti, *Story, Myth and Celebration in Old French Narrative Poetry 1050–1200* (Princeton, NJ: Princeton University Press, 1973), p. 79.

24. Dorothy Dinnerstein, *The Mermaid and the Minotaur: Sexual Arrangements and Human Malaise* (New York: Harper Colophon, 1977), p. 133.

25. Sarah Kay, *The "Chansons de geste" in the Age of Romance: Political Fictions* (Oxford: Clarendon Press, 1995), p. 3.

26. On these taxonomic complexities, see the useful summary in Harf-Lancner, *RA*, pp. 27–43.

27. I borrow the term from Kay, *"Chansons de geste."*

28. I quote from my own transcription of the latter part of Book I (from BNF fr. 345, f. 183v).

29. He accepts her ministrations, but only after she has promised that, this time, she will not delude him in any way (I/i, ll. 8109–18).

30. See, most notably, Margaret Felberg-Levitt, *Demandes d'amour* (Montréal: CERES, 1995). It is intriguing that in Thomas de Saluce's *Le Chevalier errant*, Alexander himself figures, incongruously, alongside Venus, as one of the "judges" for a *demande*; see the unpublished critical edition by M. J. Ward (Ph.D, University of North Carolina at Chapel Hill, 1984), pp. 605–11. I am grateful to Dr. Nadia Margolis for allowing me to look at her copy of the dissertation.

31. I borrow the term from Eve Kosofsky Sedgwick, *Between Men: English Literature and Male Homosocial Desire* (New York: Columbia University Press, 1985). Sedgwick, however, explicitly declines to discuss the sort of bonds that I am talking about here— the "crucially important male homosocial bonds that are less glamorous to talk about— such as the institutional, bureaucratic, and military," because she finds "feminist theoretical paradigms" more pertinent in writing about "eros and sex" (p. 19).

32. Here I follow the example of Peggy McCracken's recent, excellent, *The Romance of Adultery: Queenship and Sexual Transgression in Old French Literature* (Philadelphia: University of Pennsylvania Press, 1998), esp. chs. 3 and 4. I am particularly impressed by the way in which she relates the sort of pressures I am talking about here to the broader political debates and anxieties about twelfth- and thirteenth-century queenship; such readings could be made also of the texts with which I am concerned here.

33. Thus I do not quite agree with Dominique Boutet, who sees Charlemagne himself as largely responsible for his own political problems; in my view, the fact that the "trigger" is a woman is significant. See his "L'origine des conflits," in *Charlemagne et Arthur, ou le roi imaginaire* (Paris: Champion/Geneva: Droz, 1992), 368.

34. See Kay, *"Chansons de geste,"* chapters 4 and 7, and her article "Kings, Vassals and Queens: Problems of Hierarchy in the Old French *Chansons de geste," Journal of the Institute of Romance Studies* 1 (1992), 27–47.

35. See the editions by F. Guessard (Paris: Franck, 1866) and Adolfo Mussafia, *Altfranzösische Gedichte. 1. La prise de Pampelune. 2. Macaire* (Vienna: C. Gerold's sohn, 1864).

36. *Girart de Vienne*, ed. Wolfgang van Emden (Paris: Firmin Didot, 1977), on which see notably Kay, *"Chansons de geste,"* pp. 132–37.

37. See most recently Rita Lejeune, "Le péché de Charlemagne et la *Chanson de Roland,"* in *Studia Philologica. Homenaje ofrecido a Dámaso Alonso* (Madrid: Gredos, 1961), II, pp. 339–70. For a review of the scholarship on the subject, see Aurelio Roncaglia, "Roland e il peccato di Carlomagno," in *Symposium in onorem prof. M. de Riquer* (Barcelona: Universidad-Quaderns Crema, 1986), pp. 315–47.

38. *Tristan de Nanteuil*, ed. K.V. Sinclair (Assen: Van Gorcum, 1971), *laisse* CDLIV.

39. I put "romances" in inverted commas because they are, of course, composed in the assonanced *laisses* that are the marker of the *chanson de geste*—but it is nevertheless traditional to call them "romances."

40. Simon Gaunt, *Gender and Genre in Medieval French Literature* (Cambridge: Cambridge University Press, 1995), p. 109.

41. See Roberta L. Krueger, *Women Readers and the Ideology of Gender in Old French Verse Romances* (Cambridge: Cambridge University Press, 1993), and McCracken, *The Romance of Adultery*, esp. chs. 3 and 4. Is Guenevere even Arthur's only queen? See Maurice Delbouille, "Guenièvre fut-elle la seule épouse du roi Arthur?" *Travaux de linguistique et de littérature* 6 (1966), 123–34.

42. The episode is already adumbrated in Geoffrey of Monmouth and Wace, with her hinted complicity in Mordred's betrayal: see Peter Korrel, *An Arthurian Triangle: A Study of the Origin, Development and Characterization of Arthur, Guinevere and Modred [sic]* (Leiden: Brill, 1984), p. 102; cf. Fiona T. Neuendorf, "Negotiating Feminist and Historicist Concerns: Guenevere in Geoffrey of Monmouth's *Historia Regum Britanniae*," *Quondam et Futurus* 3/2 (1993), 26–44. On the rapidity with which surface virtue is revealed to be delusive, see Maureen Fries, "Female Heroes, Heroines, and Counter-Heroes: Images of Women in Arthurian Tradition," repr. in *Arthurian Women: A Casebook*, ed. Thelma S. Fenster (New York: Garland, 1996), pp. 59–73.

43. See François Mosès, ed., *La Fausse Guenièvre: Lancelot du Lac* (Paris: Librairie Générale Française, 1998), and also *Lancelot do Lac: The Non-Cyclic Old French Prose Romance*, ed. Elspeth Kennedy (Oxford: Clarendon Press, 1980), p. 584. See Alexandre Micha, "Etudes sur le *Lancelot en prose*, I: Les épisodes du Voyage en Sorelois et de la Fausse Guenièvre," *Romania* 76 (1955), 334–41, and the response by Elspeth Kennedy, "The Two Versions of the False Guinevere Episode in the Old French Prose *Lancelot*," *Romania* 77 (1956), 94–104; Laurence Harf-Lancner, "Les deux Guenièvre dans le *Lancelot* en prose," in *Lancelot: Actes du colloque des 14 et 15 janvier 1984*, ed. Danielle Buschinger (Göppingen: Kümmerle Verlag, 1984), pp. 63–73; Paul Rockwell, "The Falsification of Resemblance: Reading the False Guinevere," *The Arthurian Yearbook* 1 (1991), 27–42 and his *Rewriting Resemblance in Medieval French Romance: "Ceci n'est pas un graal"* (New York: Garland, 1995), pp. 43–60; E. Jane Burns, "Which Queen? Guinevere's Transvestism in the French Prose *Lancelot*," in *Lancelot and Guinevere: A Casebook*, ed. Lori J. Walters (New York: Garland, 1996), pp. 247–65.

44. Sarah Kay, "La représentation de la féminité dans les chansons de geste," in *Charlemagne in the North: Proceedings of the Twelfth International Conference of the Société Rencesvals*, ed. Philip E. Bennett et al. (Edinburgh: Société Rencesvals British Branch, 1993), pp. 223–40 (here p. 224).

45. See Yolande de Pontfarcy, "Source et structure de l'épisode de l'empoisonnement dans *La Mort Artu*," *Romania* 99 (1978), 246–55, and especially Howard Bloch, *Medieval French Literature and Law* (Berkeley: University of California Press, 1977), ch. 1.

46. *La Mort le roi Artu*, ed. Jean Frappier (Paris: Droz, 1936), p. 75.

47. *Mantel et cor: deux lais du XIIe siècle,* ed. Philip Bennett (Exeter: University of Exeter Press, 1975).

48. I am thus inclined to agree with Jean-Charles Payen's argument that in Guenevere survive traces of the enchantress who manipulates Arthur—and Lancelot; see his "Plaidoyer pour Guenièvre: la culpabilité de Guenièvre dans le *Lancelot-Graal,*" *Les Lettres romanes* 20 (1966), 103–14, and "La *Charrette* avant la charrette: Guenièvre et le roman d'*Erec,*" in *Mélanges de langue et de littérature du Moyen Age et de la Renaissance offerts à Jean Frappier* (Geneva: Droz, 1970), I, pp. 419–32. Might one add the way in which the question of her maternity is also left problematic? See Keith Busby, "The Enigma of Loholt," in *An Arthurian Tapestry: Essays in Memory of Lewis Thorpe,* ed. K. Varty (Glasgow: French Department of the University of Glasgow, 1981), pp. 28–36.

49. Of course, it could be argued that by the time of the poisoned-apple episode, the court and the Round Table are painfully aware of her adultery, and that the court's eagerness simply represents its moral outrage—but that seems not to be the case with the False Guenevere episode.

50. To track this evolution, see for instance Rosemary Morris, *The Character of King Arthur in Medieval Literature* (Woodbridge, Suffolk: Boydell and Brewer, 1982), and Barbara N. Sargent-Baur, "*Dux bellorum / rex militum / roi fainéant,*" *Le Moyen Age* 90 (1984), 357–73.

51. See, for instance, Geoffrey's eulogy: "Arthur then began to increase his personal entourage by inviting very distinguished men from distant kingdoms to join it. In this way he developed such a code of courtliness in his household that he inspired peoples living far away to imitate him. The result was that even the man of noblest birth, once he was roused to rivalry, thought nothing of himself unless he wore his arms and dressed in the same way as Arthur's knights." *History of the Kings of Britain,* trans. Lewis Thorpe (Harmondsworth: Penguin Books, 1996), p. 222.

52. *Le Roman de Tristan,* ed. Alfred Ewert (Oxford: Blackwell, 1939), line 3380.

53. Chrétien de Troyes, *Le Roman de Perceval ou le Conte du Graal,* ed. Keith Busby (Tübingen: Max Niemeyer, 1993).

54. See Chrétien de Troyes, *Yvain: Le Chevalier au Lion,* ed. T. B. W. Reid (Manchester: Manchester University Press, 1967), vv. 42–52.

55. This is what I meant by saying, in the opening of this essay, that the author of the *Perceforest* had configured an Alexander for his metatextual purposes: after all, he has to find some convincing, if not rational, reason why no one has heard that Arthur is descended from Alexander.

15

From Alexander to Marco Polo, from Text to Image: The Marvels of India

Laurence Harf-Lancner

Alexander the Great and Marco Polo are two discoverers who pushed the exploration of the mysteries of the Orient to the farthest limits of the known world. The texts that recount their travels, however, often sacrifice historical truth to exotic revery. Alexander's expedition concluded in 326 B.C. on the banks of the Hyphase, a sub-tributary of the Indus: confronted with the refusal of his army to proceed farther, the Macedonian descends the Indus and returns to Babylonia, following the shore of the Persian Gulf. But a text whose earliest version, now lost, was presumably written in Greek shortly after Alexander's death and translated into Latin before the seventh century, the *Letter of Alexander of Macedonia to his Teacher Aristotle on his Expedition and the Description of India*, evokes at length the hero's discovery of the marvels of India.[1] This is one of the sources of the French Alexander romances in the twelfth century; under its influence, Alexander's itinerary, from one text to the next—from the first version of the *Letter to Aristotle* to the medieval French romances—is reduced in its Persian segment to the advantage of the Indian segment, a mythic space in which the hero did not set foot.[2]

As for Marco Polo, reservations have long been expressed about the authenticity of his tribulations in China, in Indochina, and in India. There is no agreement about the route followed by the two Polo brothers on their first voyage (1252–69), about that of the two brothers accompanied by their son and nephew Marco on their second voyage (1271–95), nor on the comings and goings of Marco during his stay at the court of the Great Khan. The very authenticity of Marco Polo's voyages has recently been again called into question, casting him as an armchair explorer, a precursor of Jean de Mandeville.[3] Did Marco really make all the voyages he is assumed to have dictated to Rustician of Pisa in his Genoese prison in 1298? It matters little, for the interest of the book lies elsewhere, in the evocation of a new type of *merveilleux*. India, for the occupants of the medieval Occident as for the Greeks before them, is the eastern extremity of the earth. It covers a great part of Asia: "Greater India, which includes the largest part of our India, is framed by an India Minor that stretches from the north of the Coromandel coast and encloses the peninsulae of southeast Asia, and a Southern India that includes Ethiopia and the coastal regions of southwest Asia."[4] Since antiquity, descriptions of India have been inseparable from the evocation of marvels—*mirabilia*—those phenomena that defy the usual course of nature and inspire the amazement of the Western world. Marco Polo's *Devisement du monde* transfers the interest from India, a land of marvels "endowed with the prestige associated with antiquity, authority and writing," toward China, land of unrecorded and unheard-of marvels.[5]

The figure of Alexander haunts travelers' accounts, that of Marco Polo in particular.[6] But we must not forget the fundamental differences that separate the texts. The principal French Alexander romances span the years from 1180 (the Vulgate of Alexandre de Paris, the *Roman de toute chevalerie* of Thomas of Kent) to 1448 (*Histoire du bon roi Alexandre* by Jean Wauquelin), through the prose *Roman d'Alexandre* of the thirteenth century, without counting multiple interpolations and continuations. Marco Polo probably dictated his account in 1298. From the twelfth to the fifteenth centuries, relations between East and West are in continual flux, from the great fear that prevails until the middle of the thirteenth century to the ambassadorial missions of the period from 1250 to 1368, the year in which the Chinese Empire closes itself off from the West with the ascension to power of the Ming dynasty.[7] In addition, although the boundary between various literary forms is fluid in the Middle Ages, the Alexander romances, which oscillate between *chanson de geste* and romance, emphasize the supernatural in their evocation of the marvels of the East. The prodigious things reported by the voyagers, on the other hand, are recorded as so many fantasies of nature, deriving from the encyclopedic tradition of marvels as defined by Gervaise of Tilbury at the beginning of the thirteenth century: "By marvels, we understand that which, although natural, escapes our understanding; what makes it a marvel is our inability to account for the cause of the phenomenon."[8]

Comparison of the texts allows us to discern two approaches to the marvels of India and to cast light on the originality of Marco Polo and his tendency to demystify the Oriental *merveilleux*. It also reveals, in certain manuscripts, distortions between text and image. Alexander and Marco Polo, moreover, are found together in two collections devoted to the evocation of the Orient: the manuscript Oxford, Bodley 264, which brings together the *Roman d'Alexandre* by Alexandre de Paris and the *Devisement du monde*, and the manuscript London, B.L. Royal 19 D1, which juxtaposes the prose *Roman d'Alexandre* and Marco Polo's text.[9] The confrontation of text and illustration reveals divergent interpretations by the illustrators in their creation of images of the marvels of India. Whereas the illuminators of the Alexander romances faithfully illustrate a text that, adhering to the literary tradition of *mirabilia*, allows them to connect with the same tradition on the level of iconography, so does Marco Polo's originality trouble the illustrators, who do not hesitate to contradict the text in favor of the iconographic tradition of *mirabilia*.

★ ★ ★

Alexander and the Literary and Iconographic Tradition of the Marvels of India: Overinterpretation of the Text by the Image

The clerics who, from the twelfth century, "mettent en roman" the legendary biography of Alexander deriving from the Latin versions of the Pseudo-Callisthenes inherit, with regard to the hero's discovery of India, a rich ancient tradition, represented in particular by the *Natural History* of Pliny the Elder (first century A.D.) and the *Collectanea rerum mirabilium* of Solinus (third century), whose chapters on Asia feed the medieval encyclopedias, prominent among them the *Etymologiae* of Isidore of Seville.[10] They also exploit more fantastical writings, such as the *Letter to the Emperor Hadrian on the Marvels of India*[11] and especially the *Letter from Alexander to Aristotle*. In the latter, Alexander recounts to his teacher his exploration of the farthest regions of India and his confrontation with natural or supernatural forces: struggle against the elements; droughts or floods; blizzards and firestorms. But the marvels arise often in the form of monsters: monstrous animals (hippopotami, serpents of the most diverse and frightening forms, or the mysterious odontotyrannus, bigger than an elephant, with a horse's head armed with three horns), but also monstrous peoples, at the border of the animal and human kingdoms (the Ichthyophages, the Cynocephales, the fearsome water sprites who smother men in their embrace and lead them to the watery depths). All of these adventures reappear, with considerable amplification, in the French romances.[12] In that of Alexandre de Paris, interlaced with other episodes, they become so many signs of excess on the part of the hero, who seeks to extend his empire "from the Occident to the Orient" (according to the *Letter to Aristotle*) and whose quest is destined to fail.[13] In the thirteenth century the prose *Roman d'Alexandre*, following its Latin source the *Historia de Preliis*, integrates the evocation of the same prodigious occurrences, as does, in the fifteenth century, the *Histoire du bon roi Alexandre* written by Jean Wauquelin for Philippe le Bon, Duke of Burgundy.[14] The romance that makes the most of the marvels of the East, however, is the *Roman de toute chevalerie* (=*RTC*) of Thomas of Kent (c. 1180), which differs from the other Alexander romances in its didactic project and encyclopedic nature. Here the description of *mirabilia* is considerably developed. Thomas, like the other Alexander authors, utilizes the Latin adaptation of the Pseudo-Callisthenes by Julius Valerius and its *Epitomè*, the *Letter to Aristotle*, but also other authorities whose names he regularly cites, such as Solinus and Aethicus Ister, the pseudo-author of a *Cosmography* composed around the eighth century.[15]

The introduction of the descriptions of India gives rise in Thomas to a change in writing:[16] here *laisses* of several verses offer the reader a list of curiosities, among which the monsters, as in the ancient tradition, have pride of place. The term *"mostre, mustre, monstre*," moreover, is used several times by Thomas in its modern sense and applied indifferently to animals and to peoples, linked to epithets that connote fright.[17] The fabulous bestiary (unicorns, dragons, griffins) keeps company with various fantastic human races. The typology of these monsters permits an assessment of the different forms of alterity.[18] The difference is first of all morphological: in this case monstrosity arises from excess or from lack (cyclops of Maritimos endowed with four eyes, sciapodes with a single foot used as an umbrella, and Arcabatistes with four feet, giants and dwarfs, Blemmyes with no heads but with eyes and a mouth on their chests: vv. 4716, 6725, 4717, 6736, 4636, 6079, 4749) or from a mixture of the animal and the human (cynocephales, sirens, centaurs: vv. 4711, 4638, 4637, 5690). But it may equally be attached to behavior: alimentation, habitat, religion, or relation to time, to sexuality, and to death. Thus the Ichthyophages or Faunos eat raw fish, another people eat garbage, others are cannibals; another, on the other hand, lives on the odor of an apple (vv. 5758, 6021, 5990, 4720). Yet others inhabit water or the forest, knowing no civilized habitat; adore the star Saturn; live a hundred years or eight years; share women; hide themselves to die (vv. 6842, 6742, 6035, 4635, 4736, 6708, 4709). One people combines in itself alone all the traits of savagery: that of Gog and Magog, who lives in caves, feeds on human flesh, and dreams of invading the universe in order to destroy all civilization, until Alexander isolates it from the rest of the world (vv. 5966–67, 6344–51). The image of the Orient, in the *Roman de toute chevalerie* as elsewhere in medieval literature, is thoroughly ambivalent, juxtaposing the most extreme idealization and the most frightening spectacle. But all ambivalence is proscribed in the illustration, which overinterprets the text to reinforce the terrifying vision of the Orient.

From ancient times, a pictorial tradition of monsters develops in parallel with the literary tradition.[19] We find it in the Middle Ages in maps and *mappemondes*, in the illustrated manuscripts of the Alexander romances and in accounts of voyages. The illustration of the *Roman de toute chevalerie* is particularly representative. Two manuscripts offer the same magnificent iconographic cycle: BNF fr. 24364 (the only one containing the whole cycle) and Cambridge, Trinity College, O.9.34 (1446).[20] BNF fr. 24364 is a London manuscript of ca. 1308–1312, containing 311 small miniatures placed below the columns of text, in the text itself or in the vertical margins; first painted, the images were colored in wash-painting beginning with folio 48, then executed in grisaille beginning with folio 68. This manuscript reproduces the text, rubrics and illustration of the Cambridge manuscript (mid-thirteenth century). It seems to have been commissioned by Jean d'Engaigne, whose shield is reproduced ten times, and all of the coats of arms identified belong to English knights living at the beginning of the fourteenth century. Two artists collaborated in the illustration: the style of the first is close to that of the first Master of the Psalter of Robert of Lisle, that of the second evokes an artist who participated in a collection of scientific works associated with a bestiary, which explains the encyclopedic aspect of certain folios.[21] In fact, of the 87 leaves many are illustrated recto and verso,[22] and in those dedicated to the description of the peoples of the Orient the text is really sacrificed to the image which takes over the space of the page, with a miniature for each *laisse* of a few verses: we find as many as eight miniatures per page.

The first impression is that of scrupulous fidelity to the text. Thus most of the elements of *laisse* 244 find their place in the images (folio 50, figure 1):

> Mult i ad riches isles e plusors rois mananz,
> Monstres e centaures e dragons e geanz,
> Sireines qe deceivent les homes par lur chanz.
> Indus i est un fluvies e Ganges le coranz;
> De trois cenz pez de long i ad pessons noanz.
> En cel fluvie ad un isle e pople combatanz.
> Si li rois vet en ost qui les est guianz,
> Cinquante quatre mile avera des combatanz,
> Cinquante mil a pié od gavelos trenchanz,
> Tuyt devers orient ou le regne est finanz.

> (There are many rich isles and several reigning kings, monsters and centaurs and dragons and giants, sirens that seduce men by their song. Indus is a river and the swift Ganges; fish three hundred feet long swim in it. In that river there is an island with a belligerent people. If the king leads out his forces, there will be fifty-four thousand combatants, fifty thousand on foot with sharp javelins, all toward the East where the realm ends.)

At the bottom of folio 50, a colored design sketch includes a giant armed with an ax who invades the margin and the text, two sirens and an enormous fish in the waters of a river, and, on an island, the warrior people mentioned in the text, and some monstrous animals. The meticulous artist does not stop with illustrating the rubric. Folio 51 (figure 2) regroups eight *laisses* (249–56), each preceded by a rubric and by an image colored in wash-painting that scrupulously illustrates the text:

—"Of Cauden, where only women reign" (the rubric figures on the preceding folio): a gigantic queen dominates a group of women who kneel before her;
—"Of the people who live on venison and on fish": the image, like the text,

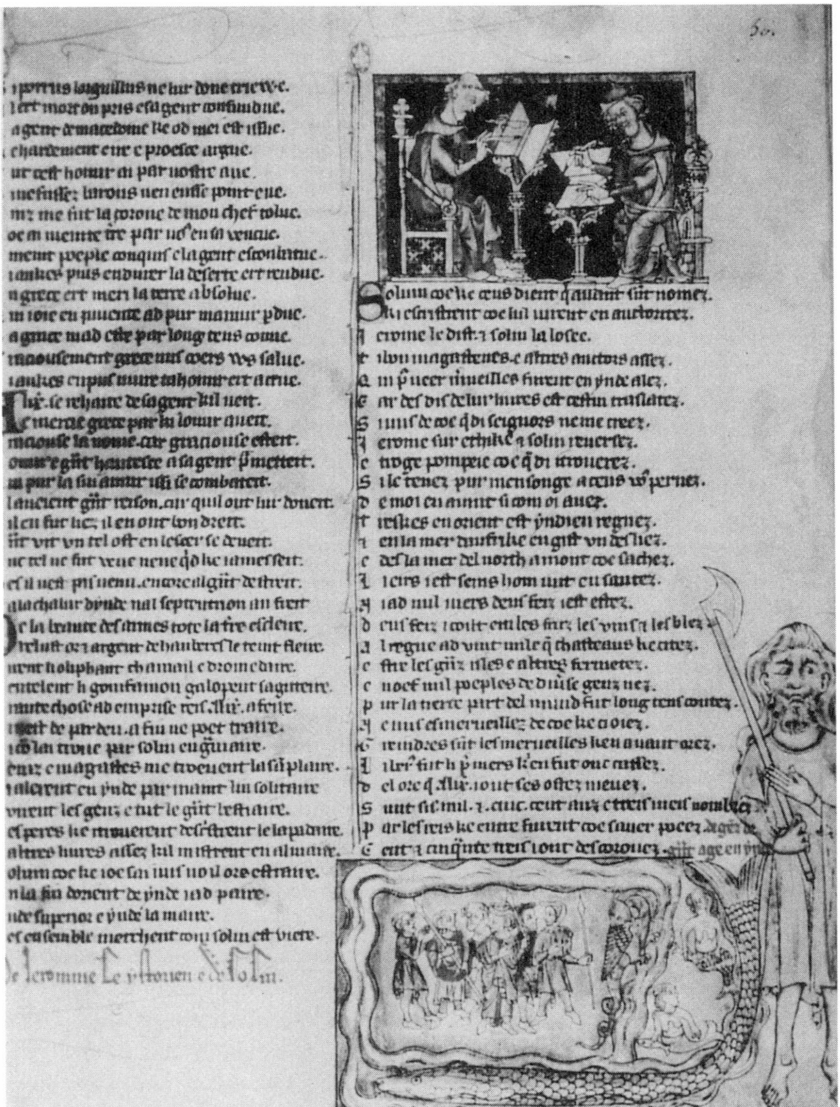

Figure 1
Paris, BNF Fr. 24364
Folio 50

underscores the savagery of these two peoples who eat raw flesh: a naked man devours a deer's leg; another holds in his hand a fish he has just caught in the water.

—"Of the porcine people who live on acorns": this people, "who seem porcine," is figured in the form of monsters with heads and bodies of boars and the arms and legs of men, gathering acorns.

—"Of those who kill their aged fathers": two naked young men kill their equally naked parents by cutting off their heads with a sword and piercing their sides with a lance.

—"Of those who die in the wilderness": a naked man lies dead on his back in a forest.

—"Of people half dog and half man": a cynocephalus devours a goat, in accord with the indication in the text ("and they eat goat flesh").

—"Of the people with a single foot that protects them from everything": a sciapode shelters himself from the sun with his foot.

—"Of the people who live on the odor of an apple": a man dressed in an animal skin gathers apples, which he collects in a basket; he brings one of them to his nostrils.

The illustrator seeks to render the details of the text faithfully in the language of the image, relying on the pictorial tradition of the monsters of the Orient, for the cynocephale and sciapode of folio 51 and the Blemmye (headless man) of folio 51v.[23] He also underlines the elements of the text that associate the image of the Oriental with that of savage man, such as hairiness.[24] The iconographic representation of cannibalism reinforces the effect of horror created by the text (vv. 5967, 5990, folios 60v, 61). Folio 61 (figure 3) thus presents successively a gigantic, hideous man devouring a corpse in the water (*laisse* 372), and eaters of repugnant animals: three wild men, one of whom kills a mouse with a spade while the other two eat mice and moles (*laisse* 373), and a monstrous man devouring the remains of a dog (*laisse* 375). In addition, the illustrator does not hesitate to abandon the text to reinforce the element of savagery and bestiality in the representation of the Orient. In four of the illustrations of folio 51 (figure 2), monstrous peoples are depicted naked: the eaters of raw flesh, the parricides, the men who isolate themselves to die, and the sciapodes. This trait, however, is not mentioned in the text: Thomas of Kent only rarely evokes the nudity of the Oriental peoples (vv. 4733, 6842).[25] The illustrator adds this trait on his own initiative, and furthermore often endows these personages with an enormous sex organ to suggest an unbridled sexuality.[26] The contorted bodies, off balance, reinforce the pejorative connotation. The grimacing faces, with enormous mouths opening over huge teeth, relate these monsters to demons and reinforce the obsession with devouring, omnipresent in Thomas of Kent's text. Another discrepancy between image and text allows the evocation of incest: the representation of the Mastiens "who knew

Figure 2
Paris, BNF Fr. 24364
Folio 51

Figure 3
Paris, BNF Fr. 24364
Folio 61

their mothers." The illustrator represents this lustful people where "tuit sunt commun entr'els cum bestes in pasture" (all commingle with each other like livestock in pasture) under the form of two cynocephales: a mother and her infant, their legs interlaced. Thomas of Kent's text does not evoke cynocephales, but the illustrator seeks to make explicit the bestiality of the Mastiens (*laisse* 417, BNF 24364, f. 66v).

Thus the *Roman de toute chevalerie*, like all the Alexander romances, gives its readers a traditional vision of the Orient and its monsters; the originality of Thomas of Kent lies in the amplification of this description. The illustrators rely on the pictorial tradition of the monsters of India to support the encyclopedic vein of the text.

Marco Polo: The Distortion of Text and Image

After a prologue of eighteen chapters that constitutes the only travel account properly so-called and the only narrative part of the text, the *Devisement du monde* offers three substantial descriptions which, in the French redaction, each open with an introductory rubric:

—"Ore, puis que je vous ay conté tout le fait du prologue ainsi comme vous avez oy, si commenderai le livre du devisement des diversitez que messire Marc Pol trouva et son oncle ou païs et ou chemin" (XIX, p. 74: Now that I have told you the contents of the prologue as you have heard, I shall begin the book giving account of the diverse things that Marco Polo and his uncle found in the land or on the journey). There follows the description of the lands that extend from the Black Sea to the Persian Gulf, then from the Persian Gulf to China.

—"Cy devise des granz faiz du Grant Kaan qui orendroit regne, qui Cublay Kaan est appellez et deviserons de touz les grans faiz de sa court et comment il maintient ses gens" (LXXV, p. 188: Here I set forth the great deeds of the Great Khan now reigning, who is called Kublai Khan, and we shall note all the great deeds of his court and how he governs his people). There follows a description of the Mongol Empire and of the wise administration of the Great Khan.

—"Cy commence le livre d'Ynde et devisera toutes les merveilles qui y sont et les manieres des gens aussi" (CLVII, p. 374: Here begins the book of India, and it will describe all the marvels found there and the customs of the people as well).

Thus we would find opposed a "civilized" China and a "marvelous" India, but this opposition we owe to the rubricators or the *maîtres d'oeuvre* responsible for the composition of the manuscripts, for whom India is synonymous with *merveille*.

The text that immediately follows the second rubric cited in fact announces the "great marvels of the Great Khan," which are identified for Marco Polo with the "new things" he wants to reveal to his readers (LXXV, p. 188 and CV, p. 256). P.-Y. Badel has highlighted this: "It is the choice between the well-known and the new that aligns on the one side Isidore, Rabanus and Honorius, and on the other Giraud (de Barri), Gervaise (de Tilbury) and Marco Polo . . . Marco is on the side of the unknown, of the not-yet-heard-of."[27] It is in effect Giraud de Barri who, in 1188, set in opposition in his *Topographia Hibernica* the *nova* and the *nota*. The marvels presented by Marco Polo in the book of India in fact involve the strange more than the supernatural.

The evocation of new marvels passes first through the negation and rationalization of the ancient ones. Accounts of voyages contributed to a reexamination of the traditional belief in the existence of Oriental monsters.[28] In this Marco Polo's critical judgment echoes that of other voyagers. Thus the salamander is for Alexandre de Paris, in conformity with the bestiary tradition, an animal that "always lies in fire, it has no other dwelling"; thus its pelt adorns Alexander's tent to extinguish any eventual fire.[29] For Marco Polo, the salamander is not an animal that lives in fire but a "vein of earth," a mineral that is pounded to extract a thread of which cloth is made, i.e., asbestos (LIX, p. 148). The unicorn is almost the size of an elephant and has a thick black horn in the middle of its forehead: it is a very ugly beast "quite the opposite" of its portrayal in the West (CLV, p. 396). As for the griffin, "they say that it has different manners than we attribute to it, and those who have been there recounted to Marco Polo that [these beasts] are also like eagles, but extraordinarily large, for the wingspan is a good thirty feet and the feathers of those wings are twelve feet long" (CLXXXV, p. 452). Here Marco Polo does not substitute a real referent for a fabulous one (as in the case of the salamander or the unicorn) but another fantastic referent, the Oriental tradition of the Roc bird, that had been "told him."[30] As Jean-Claude Faucon points out, Marco "divests the fabulous animal of its *merveilleux* and seeks to demythify it (unicorn, salamander, griffin)," and "clothes in the colors of the marvelous the animal which, if not familiar, is at least real and well known to Europeans": sheep and dogs as big as donkeys, elephants coupling in the human manner, livestock fed on fish.[31] The monstrous peoples of India are reduced to the men of the Isle of Angamanan, who "have heads and teeth and mouths like dogs, for their faces all seem like those of large mastiffs" (CLVII, p. 404): we find again the cynocephales.

The marvels of the *Devisement du monde* concern less nature than culture. In China, a "great marvel" is the Tartar's custom of killing the servants of the dead Khan so that they may continue their service in the Otherworld (LXVII, p. 162). As for the book of India, its first chapter opens on a first "marvellous thing": the merchant boats that circulate among the islands, prodigious in their size and their solidity; the second describes the "great marvel" of the palace of the lord of Sypangu (Japan), all covered in fine gold (CLVII, p. 374; CLVIII, p. 378). With regard to the "little isle of Java" (Sumatra), the "great marvel" lies not in the presence of men with long tails but in the existence of "trees that produce flour that is very good to eat" or in the provisions of pearls and precious stones of the king of Malabar (CLXV, p. 402; CLXIX, p. 416). Two traits deriving from the "savage" vision of the Orient, however, are common to the *Roman de toute chevalerie* and the *Devisement du monde*: nudity and cannibalism. Marco Polo mentions the nudity of the peoples of the isles of Gavenispola, Necoran (Weh and Nibobar) and of Ceylon, and the cannibalism practiced in the realm of Fuguy (Fuzhou), the China Sea islands and Sumatra (CLXVI, p. 404; CLXVIII, p. 406; CLIV, p. 366; CLX, p. 386; CLXV, pp. 396, 401). The contrast is thus great between the ancient marvels of the *Roman d'Alexandre* and the "new things" reported by Marco Polo. It is greater still between the text of the *Devisement du monde* and the illustration of certain manuscripts, which deliberately refuse to transcribe Marco Polo's *noveletés* in iconographic language in order to remain faithful to the pictorial tradition of the marvels of the Orient.

In a study devoted to the relations between text and image in a number of manuscript accounts of Asia, Christine Bousquet points out a double disparity:

—between the writing of the text (end of the thirteenth century for Marco Polo) and the composition of the manuscripts (end of the fourteenth, beginning of the fifteenth century);
—between the text written by a traveler and the illustration due to an illustrator who does not know the Orient.[32]

Four illustrated manuscripts of Marco Polo compel attention for the richness of their iconographic program. The most famous is BNF fr. 2810, *Le Livre des merveilles*, created for the Duke of Burgundy in 1407 and offered by him to Jean de Berry in 1415.[33] Marco Polo's account opens the collection, followed by the books of Oderic de Pordenone, of Guillaume de Boldensele, and of John de Mandeville, Hayton's *Fleur des histoires d'Orient* and Ricold de Monte Croce's *Livre de la pérégrination*. Of the 265 large miniatures, by the hand or the workshop of the Flemish painter Jacques Coene (the Boucicaut Master), eighty-four illustrate the *Devisement du monde*. The manuscript British Library Royal 19 D1 (second half of the fourteenth century) contains the *Roman d'Alexandre* in prose followed by the *Vengeance Alexandre* of Jean Le Nevelais, *Le Devisement du monde*, *Les Merveilles de la terre d'outremer* (a translation by Jean de Vignay of a part of the *Speculum historiale* of Vincent de Beauvais that takes up again the *Voyage* of Jean de Plan Carpin), Jean de Vignay's translation of the *Passage* by Burchard du Mont Sion and his translation of a part of Primat's *Chronique de France*, and finally extracts from the *Bible historiale*: battles of the kings of Israel against the Philistines and the Assyrians. We see that the common theme of all these texts is the Orient, whether the biblical Orient or the Far East. Marco Polo's book (the *Livre du Grant Caan*) immediately follows the *Roman d'Alexandre* in prose and the *Vengeance d'Alexandre* of Jean le Nevelais.[34] Of the 164 illustrations, thirty-eight are devoted to Marco Polo's account. Manuscript Bodley 264 presents, after the *Roman d'Alexandre* of Alexandre de Paris and some interpolations, the *Livre du Grand Can*. *Le Roman d'Alexandre* (110 illustrations) was illustrated in Flanders by Jehan de Grise between 1339 and 1344, *Le devisement du monde* around 1400 in England by a certain Johannes (thirty-seven illustrations) and bound with *Alexandre* at the beginning of the fifteenth century.[35] MS Arsenal 5169 was copied by Robert Frescher at the end of the fifteenth or the beginning of the sixteenth century, perhaps for Louise de Savoie, and adorned with 197 miniatures that are characterized, unlike those of MS 2810, by their remarkable fidelity to the text.[36]

Bousquet underlines the contrast, in the iconographic programs of these four manuscripts, between BNF 2810, which emphasizes marvels and monsters, and the three manuscripts Royal 19 D1, Bodley 264, and Arsenal 5169, which reduce the attention to marvels (no representation at all in the Royal MS, very little in the other two) in favor of the political and everyday Orient. On the other hand, as Wittkower has noted, the paintings of MS 2810 "obviously deviate from the text they are supposed to illustrate. They seek to interpret it, even to correct it, so as to make it conform to current conceptions and representations."[37] Thus the unicorn that Marco Polo depicts with the features of an ungraceful rhinoceros reassumes, for the illuminator of MS 2810, the model of the Western pictorial tradition, as does the griffin, with its lion's body, wings, and eagle's head (MS 2810, f. 85, 59v, 88). The image is thus in flagrant contradiction with the text. The giant serpents of the region of Caraian (Yunnan) strongly resemble crocodiles in Marco Polo's description; in the illustration they become winged dragons (MS 2810, f. 55v). As for the salamander, the enigmatic image of folio 24, showing an old man on a pyre spared by the flames, seems to tend in the same direction. For Wittkower, "one can imagine that the man is protected from burns by a shirt of salamander skin," but an allegorical interpretation is equally possible: "in the Christian allegories, the salamander represents the virtuous man who does not allow himself to be consumed by the fire of cupidity and lust."[38] For Bousquet, it is "a salamander of human appearance attached to a pole and plunged into flames intended to cleanse it" (p. 313). It is further possible that the illustrator recalled the funeral pyres evoked two chapters earlier and illustrated on the preceding folio (Marco Polo LVII, p. 144; BNF 2801, f. 23).

The same lack of accord between text and image characterizes the vision of the oriental peoples. Of the monstrous peoples of ancient tradition, Marco Polo mentions only the men with dogs' heads, the cynocephales, which are indeed found in the illustration (f. 76v). But even in the absence of all description of savage peoples, the painter represents different monstrous races that have no reference in the text but rather reproduce the monsters of Thomas of Kent: a wild man covered with hair (f. 15v); a Blemmye, a sciapode and a cyclops (f. 29v). In the two paintings devoted to the monsters of India, the painter of the Bodley manuscript adopts the same procedure: the book of India, where Marco Polo begins by marveling at the merchant boats, opens in this manuscript with an image that attempts the synthesis of the marvels of India (folio 260, figure 4). On three islands are pictured monstrous creatures: a Blemmye accompanied by a dragon on the first; then a cyclops covered with hair and an erect sciapode, he too covered with hair and armed with a mace, in the tradition of the wild man; and finally a cynocephale armed with a lance and an anthropomorphic shield. A bit farther, the inhabitants of Cochinchina, idolaters according to the text, who pay a tribute to the Great Khan and offer all their wives to their king, become wild men on an island (folio 264, figure 5): one treats himself to a human hand and foot; another, with hooves and a horn on his forehead, tears off the foot of a living stag; the third, gigantic, armed with a spear and an anthropomorphic shield and endowed with two horns on each side of his face, stands before the closed gate of a citadel, observed from the ramparts by a group of armed soldiers: this is the very image of a barbaric Orient seen from afar, with fright, by the Western world (Marco Polo, pp. 374, 390; Bodley 260, f. 264, 262). Bousquet has moreover made clear the desire in all the manuscripts to "moralize the text by means of the image," to give a pejorative vision of the Orient through the use of colors (yellow, green, brown), the deformation of faces, the presence of spots and stripes, the dark skin of the men, the scanty dress of the women, and, curiously, "very prominent latrines" on the city remparts (p. 377).

The comparison of the texts and their iconographic programs thus allows us to discern a double opposition:

—between a traditional vision of the Orient in the Alexander romances, on both the literary and iconographic planes, and a new vision in the account of Marco Polo;

—between this original vision of Marco Polo and the conventional vision reproduced by the illuminators of the manuscripts of the *Devisement du monde*. But this opposition must be nuanced. The illuminators of Marco Polo do seek on occasion to capture the exoticism of the text, and one could not, as would be tempting when confronted with the monsters in the manuscripts of the *Devisement du monde*, reduce the relation between text and image to an oppositional one for the iconographic programs as a whole. The painters of all the manuscripts are most often very faithful to Marco Polo's text and, like him, privilege the representation of the daily life of the peoples of the Orient. They also seek on occasion to translate into the language of iconography marvels of another type that run through the *Devisement du monde*. Among these new marvels we find first of all the city, in conformity

Figure 4
Oxford, Bodley 264
Folio 260r

Figure 5
Oxford Bodley 264
Folio 262r

with a tradition that goes back to the Western discovery of Constantinople. The space of Asia is an urbanized space, and the cities, symbols of political power but also of wealth and refinement, are the object of innumerable descriptions and innumerable illustrations.[39] The Orient is rich: both text and image dwell at length on gold and silver, silk, pearls, precious stones, and spices. And the Mongol Empire in particular offers a model of society that impressed the voyager but also the painters, who translate in the image the omnipresence of the Khan and the sophistication of the socioeconomic organization: the mail system, the exchange of gold and silver for paper money (BNF 2810, f. 46v, 45; Bodley 264, f. 242v). The sexual tolerance attributed to the Orient, moreover, is evidently the object of a fantasy in the Western world. Already the illustrators of Thomas of Kent's romance lent their wild men an unbridled sexuality. Marco Polo evokes polygamy (which he identifies with lust), but also sexual freedom (LVIII, p. 146; LXI, p. 150; LXVIII, p. 164; XCV, p. 238; CXV, p. 274; CXVI, p. 280; CXXVI, p. 308; CLXXIV, p. 436), and here the painters willingly follow his lead. The Great Khan is represented with all his wives and children; the young women of Tibet do not find a husband until they have slept with the greatest possible number of foreigners (BNF 2810, f. 36, 39, 52v; Bodley 264, f. 239). The illuminators reinforce the exoticism of the first scene in showing, depending on the case, three or four crowned queens, entirely westernized, seated side by side; in the second, they represent the negotiation between fathers, who push their daughters forward to offer them to voyagers, and the latter, who hold out a jewel in exchange.

We even find in MS BNF 2810 two really fantastic tableaux: the cynocephales of the Isle of Andaman and the ichthyophagous sheep. Marco Polo makes the men of Andaman into true "savage beasts":

> "Et si vous dy que tous les hommes de ceste isle de Angamanam ont chief comme de chiens et dens et yeulx aussi, car il semblent des visages tous comme grans chiens mastins. Il ont espiceries assez et sont moult crueulx gens, car il menguent tous ceulz que il puent prendre, mais que il ne soient de leurs gens. Ils vivent de ris et de char et de lait et si ont fruis assez devisez aux nostres" (CLXVII, p. 404; BNF 2810, f. 76v).

(Thus I tell you that all the men of this island of Andaman have heads and teeth and eyes like dogs, for their faces resemble those of large mastiffs. They have spice markets and are very cruel people, for they eat all those they can catch, who are not of their own people. They live on rice and flesh and milk, and have fruits quite like ours.)

These dog-headed wild men practice cannibalism, but otherwise their alimentation is entirely civilized. The painter plays on the juxtaposition of these
elements: his cynocephales are peacefully occupied in their rustic decor, some
transacting business, others discussing around two sacks of spices (one of which
contains pepper). But "the great find of the miniaturist . . . was to clothe these
beings, then to give them the head of a wolf-dog and especially a leaden
color."[40] From this coexistence of the monstrous and the banal is born the
fantastic character of the image. In the same way, the inhabitants of the city
of Estier (Shihr) have curious livestock:

> "toutes leurs bestes, si sont roncins, bués, chameus, touz menguent
> petiz poissons et ne vivent d'autre chose, car ce est toute leur viande.
> Et ce est pour ce que en tout ce païs n'a herbe ne viande, ains est
> le plus sec lieu du monde. Les poissons que les bestes menjuent sont
> moult petiz, et les prent l'en de mars et d'avril et de may, et en
> prennent tant que c'est merveilles, et puis les sechent, et metent en
> mesons et les donnent a mengier a leurs bestes tout l'an. Et encores
> les menguent les bestes aux poissoniers touz vis si comme il issent de
> l'yaue" (CLXXXIX, p. 464; BNF 2810, f. 91).

> (all their animals, whether they be horses, oxen, or camels, all eat small
> fish and live on nothing else, for that is their only food. And this is
> because in the whole country there is neither grass nor food: rather
> it is the most arid place in the world. The fish that the animals eat
> are very small, and are caught in March, April and May; they catch
> a marvelous quantity and then dry them, and store them in buildings
> and feed them to their animals all year round. And they even give the
> animals live fish to eat just as they come from the water.)

There again the painter plays upon the juxtaposition of the strange and the
everyday (figure 6). In a city that has no Oriental touches, located on the bank
of a river with boats loaded with cargo, we see, at the water's edge, a peasant
woman pouring out a basketful of fish to three sheep, who devour them
eagerly. In the interior, a man repeats the same gesture for three horses, who
equally appreciate this curious repast. The iconographic fantastic can thus arise
from the desire of painters to transcribe the novelty of Marco Polo's text into
the language of the image.

★   ★   ★

The tableaux of the Orient, in the text as in the illustration of the
Alexander romances, are in the direct line of the mythic India of tradition. But
if Alexander resurfaces in many accounts of voyages, it is because he is for the
Middle Ages the emblematic figure of the discoverer thirsty for knowledge—

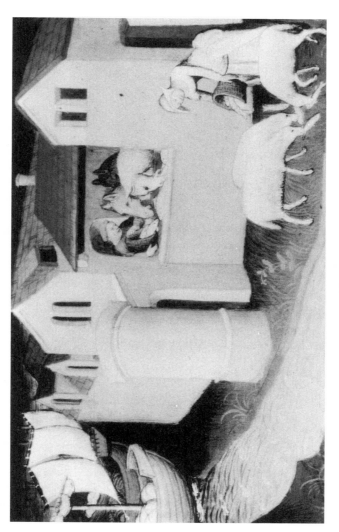

Figure 6
Paris, BNF Fr. 2810
Folio 91

because the Alexander romances offer the first manifestations, in French literature, of a scientific *merveilleux* linked to the need to know. As for Marco Polo, he "freed the marvels of India from the mythic connotations of the *Roman d'Alexandre*; he reduced the mythic to the exotic by making it the space for a description that calls for other attempts at more complete description."[41] His illustrators were not able to break free of the pictorial tradition of the monsters of the Orient. But in the iconographic programs devoted to the *Devisement du monde*, the monsters occupy a reduced space; the image, like the text, gives the victory to exoticism.

Notes

1. *Epistola Alexandri ad Aristotelem*, ed. W. W. Boer, *Beiträge zur klassischen Philologie* 50 (1973); *Alexander's Letter to Aristotle*, study and trans. L. L. Gunderson, *Beiträge zur klassischen Philologie* 110 (1980), French trans. in Pseudo-Callisthène, *Le Roman d'Alexandre*, trans. G. Bounouré and B. Serret (Paris: Les Belles Lettres, 1992) and trans. A. Tallet-Bonvalot (Paris: GF–Flammarion, 1994).

2. Gioia Zaganelli, "Alessandro Magno in India: storia di un'epistola e di un'immagine del mondo," in *Medioevo Romanzo e Orientale: oralità, scrittura, modelli narrativi*, ed. A. Pioletti and F. Rizzo Nervo (Catanzaro: Soveria Mannelli, 1995), pp. 139–53.

3. Frances Wood, *Did Marco Polo go to China?* (London: Secker & Warburg, 1996), concludes that only the first voyage of the Polo brothers seems likely to have occurred.

4. Jacques Le Goff, "L'Occident médiéval et l'Orient indien: un horizon onirique," in his *Pour un autre Moyen Age* (Paris: Gallimard, 1977), pp. 280–98 (here p. 291).

5. Marco Polo, *La Description du monde*, ed. and trans. Pierre-Yves Badel (Paris: Librairie Générale Française, 1998), Introduction, p. 12, and P.-Y. Badel, "Lire la merveille selon Marco Polo," *Revue des Sciences Humaines* 183 (1981/3), 1–16.

6. Michèle Guéret-Laferté, *Sur les routes de l'empire mongol* (Paris: Champion, 1994), pp. 342–51.

7. Jacques Heers, *Marco Polo* (Paris: Fayard, 1983).

8. Gervais de Tilbury, *Otia Imperialia*, ed. G. W. Leibniz, *Scriptores rerum Brunsvicensium*, I, and *Emendationes et supplementa*, II (Hanover, 1707 and 1709), complete edition; ed. F. Liebrecht (Hanover: Carl Rümpler, 1856), partial edition, preface to the third part: "Mirabilia vero dicimus quae nostrae cognitioni non subiacent, etiam cum sint naturalia, sed et mirabilia constituit ignorantia reddendae rationis, quare sic sit"; trans. A. Duchesne, *Le Livre des merveilles* (Paris: Les Belles Lettres, 1992), p. 20. Cf. Jacques Le Goff, "Le merveilleux dans l'Occident médiéval," in his *L'imaginaire médiéval* (Paris: Gallimard, 1985), 17–39 and idem, "Le merveilleux scientifique au Moyen Age," in J. B. Berger, ed., *Zwischen Wahn, Glaube und Wissenschaft* (Zurich: Verlag der Fachvereine, 1988), 87–113.

9. On the manuscripts see *infra*, notes 35 and 36.

10. Pliny the Elder, *Histoire naturelle*, ed. and trans. J. André and J. Filliozat (Paris: Les Belles Lettres, 1980); Solinus, *Collectanea rerum memorabilium*, ed. T. Mommsen (Berlin: Nicolai, 1864, reed. 1895), trans. M. A. Agnant (Paris, 1847). See Jacques Le Goff, "L'Occident médiéval et l'Orient Indien," pp. 285–89; Gioia Zaganelli, *L'Oriente incognito medievale* (Soveria Mannelli-Catanzaro: Rubbettino, 1997). This Latin tradition itself of course goes back to a Greek tradition represented in particular by the *Indica* of Ctésias (fourth century B.C.).

11. " Lettre à Adrien sur les merveilles de l'Inde," ed. E. Faral, *Romania* 43 (1914), 199–215, 353–70, and *De rebus in oriente mirabilibus*, ed. Claude Lecouteux (Meisenheim am Glan: Anton Hain, 1979).

12. Alexander Cizek, "Ungeheuer und magische Lebewesen in der *Epistola Alexandri ad magistratum suum Aristotelem de situ Indiae*," in *Third International Beast Epic, Fable and Fabliau Colloquium*, ed. J. Goossens, *Niederdeutsche Studien* 30 (1981), 78–94; Emmanuèle Baumgartner, "L'Orient d'Alexandre," *Bien dire et bien aprandre* 6 (1988), 7–15; Philippe Ménard, "Femmes séduisantes et femmes malfaisantes: les filles-fleurs de la fôret et les créatures des eaux dans le *Roman d'Alexandre*," *Bien dire et bien aprandre* 7 (1989), 5–17; Francis Dubost, *Aspects fantastiques de la littérature narrative médiévale* (Paris: Champion, 1991), Ch 11; Catherine Gaullier-Bougassas, *Frontières*, 239–75; Laurence Harf-Lancner, "La quête de l'immortalité: les fontaines merveilleuses du *Roman d'Alexandre*," in *Sources et fontaines du Moyen Age à l'âge baroque* (Paris: Champion, 1998), pp. 31–45.

13. See *Lettre à Aristote*, trans. G. Bounouré, p. 138; *MFRA II*; *RA*.

14. *Prosa*, pp. 160ff; Jean Wauquelin, *Histoire du bon roi Alexandre*, ed. Sandrine Hériché (Geneva: Droz, forthcoming). I thank Sandrine Hériché for making her text available to me before publication.

15. Aethicus Ister, *Cosmographia*, ed. O. Prinz, Munich: *Monumenta Germaniae Historica* 14, 1993. See J. Weynand, *Der Roman de toute chevalerie des Thomas von Kent in seinem Verhältnis zu seinem Quellen* (Bonn, thesis, 1911). Thomas multiplies the references to his sources: see vv. 4594, 4606, 4611, 6657 (Solinus); 4611, 6622, 6659 (Aethicus Ister); P 42 and P 46 (*Letter to Aristotle*).

16. Catherine Gaullier-Bougassas, "La description du monde dans le *Roman de toute chevalerie* de Thomas de Kent," *Bien dire et bien aprandre* 11 (1993), 191–205.

17. V. 4637, "Monstres e centaures e dragons e geanz"; 4921, "un monstres greignur qe olifant" (the hippopotamus); "un mustre orgoillus" (the odontotyrannus); 6069 (the messenger with one eye and one foot); 6353, "ces enfernals mostres" (Gog and Magog); 6752, "mostres contrefez e mult orrible gent" (men without noses); 6804 (Sephus); 6820 (monoceros); 6924, "Ne remaint a veer nule merveille seue,/ De mostre ne d'engin ne de beste mue." The term is found also in several rubrics: CLIII, CLXXXVII, CLXXXVIII, CLXXXIX, CCXXXIII.

18. Gaullier-Bougassas, *Frontières*, pp. 254–60. Cf. Claude Kappler, *Monstres, démons et merveilles à la fin du Moyen Age* (Paris: Payot, 1980); Claude Lecouteux, *Les Monstres dans la littérature allemande du Moyen Age* (Göppingen: Kummerle, 1982).

19. R. Wittkower, "Monstres et merveilles de l'Orient," in *L'Orient fabuleux* (Paris: Thames and Hudson, 1991), pp. 23–100; reprint of "Marvels of the East," *Journal of the Warburg and Courtauld Institute* 5 (1942), 159–97.

20. *RTC*, pp. 6–12; M. R. J. James, *The Western Manuscripts in the Library of Trinity College* (Cambridge, 1902), Vol. III, notice 1446, pp. 482–91; David J. A. Ross, "A Thirteenth Century Anglo-Norman Workshop Illustrating Secular Literary Manuscripts," in *Mélanges Rita Lejeune* (Gembloux: Duculot, 1969), pp. 689–94; François Avril and Patricia Stirnemann, *Manuscrits enluminés d'origine insulaire VIIe–XXe siècles* (Paris, Bibliothèque Nationale Française, 1987), n. 171, pp. 126–38.

21. See Avril and Stirnemann.

22. The non-illustrated folios are grouped at the beginning and at the end of the romance; those corresponding to the discovery of the Orient are the most heavily illustrated.

23. Wittkower, "Monstres et merveilles," figures 10, 11, 12, 13, 14, 23, 24, 25, 26, 27, 28, 44, 45, 16, 22, 30, 36.

24. *RTC*, vv. 5756, 5953, 5996, 6026, 6740, 6755; cf. folios 59, 60v, 61, 67.

25. Only the nudity of the Seres suggests, in the image as in the text, another vision of the Orient, that of the time of origins and of pre-lapsarian innocence: v. C 140 and f. 73.

26. BNF fr. 24364, folios 50v (the men of Mont Maleus), 50 (the eaters of raw flesh, the parricides), 51v (the Blemmye and the one-legged man), 60v, 61, 66v, 67.

27. Badel, p. 13. See also Gioia Zaganelli, "Viaggiatori europei in Asia nel Medioevo. Note sulla retorica del mirabile," in *Lo Straniero*, ed. M. Domenichelli and P. Fasano (Bologna: Bulsoni, 1997), pp. 389–99.

28. M. Guéret-Laferté, *Sur les routes de l'empire mongol*, pp. 257–82: "La rationalisation du merveilleux."

29. Alexandre de Paris, v. 1973; Pliny, *Histoire naturelle* X, LXVII, pp. 188–89: "Sicut salamandrae, animal lacertae figura, stellatum, numquam nisi magnis imbribus proveniens et serenitate desinens. Huic tantus rigor ut ignem tactu restinguat non alio modo quam glacies" (Such is the salamander, an animal that has the form of a lizard with a star-studded body; it appears only in times of great rains and disappears in fair weather; it is so cold that contact with it extinguishes fire, just as ice would do). See Gabriel Bianciotto, trans., *Bestiaires du Moyen Âge* (Paris: Stock, 1980), p. 55 (Pierre de Beauvais) and p. 111 (Guillaume le Clerc), and M. F. Dupuis and S. Louis, trans., *Le Bestiaire* (Paris: Ph. Lebaud, 1988), p. 153 (Ashmolean Bestiary).

30. R. Wittkower, "Le roc: un prodige de l'Orient dans une gravure hollandaise," *L'Orient fabuleux*, pp. 131–39.

31. Jean-Claude Faucon, "La représentation de l'animal par Marco Polo," *Médiévales* 32 (1997), 97–117 (here p. 103). Cf. Brian Levy, "Un bestiaire oriental: le monde animal

dans le *Devisement du monde*," in *Les animaux dans la littérature*, ed. H. Matsubara et al. (Tokyo: Keio University Press, 1997).

32. Christine Bousquet, *Les Voyageurs et l'Orient. Etude des rapports entre les textes et les images dans quelques récits manuscrits sur l'Asie aux XIVe and XVe siècles*, thesis, Tours, Université François Rabelais, 1994. See also Philippe Ménard, "L'illustration du *Devisement du monde* de Marco Polo. Etude d'iconographie comparée," in *Métamorphoses du récit de voyage* (Paris: Champion, 1988), pp. 17–31.

33. Marco Polo, *Le Livre des merveilles, le manuscrit Français 2810 de la Bibliothèque Nationale de France* (Lucerne: Ed. Facsimile, 1996), 2 vols.; Bousquet, pp. 48–54.

34. On Royal 19 D1 see G. F. Warner and J. P. Gilson, *British Museum, Catalogue of the Western Manuscripts in the Old Royal and King's Collections* (London, 1921), II, p. 341, and D. J. A. Ross, "Methods of Book Production in a XIVth Century French Miscellany," *Scriptorium* 6 (1952), 63–75; C. Bousquet, pp. 55–59.

35. On Bodley 264 see O. Pächt and J. J. Alexander, *Illuminated Manuscripts in the Bodleian Library* (Oxford: Clarendon, 1973), Vol. 3, British School, p. 70, n. 792; R. Marks and N. Morgan, *The Golden Age of English Manuscript Painting (1200–1500)* (New York: G. Braziller, 1981), p. 27; on the *Alexandre* portion, M. R. James, *The Romance of Alexander* (Oxford: Milford, 1993, facsimile); Bousquet, pp. 60–66.

36. See Bousquet, pp. 66–77.

37. Wittkower, "Marco Polo et la tradition picturale," pp. 101–30.

38. Wittkower, "Monstres et merveilles de l'Orient," p. 57.

39. See Bousquet, pp. 289–302.

40. See Ménard, p. 29.

41. Friedrich Wolfzettel, *Le discours du voyageur* (Paris: PUF, 1996), p. 31.

16

"Codices manuscriptos nudos tenemus": Alexander and the New Codicology*

Keith Busby

The textual history of *Le Roman d'Alexandre* is, frankly, a mess. For despite an apparent sense of order generated by the series published under the general title of *The Medieval French "Roman d'Alexandre,"* anything other than a cursory examination reveals that the contents of the manuscripts vary enormously with respect to which "branches" are actually included, as well as interpolations, omissions, the order of *laisses*, *remaniements*, and so on. Moreover, some manuscripts are illustrated while others are not; while most contain only the *Roman d'Alexandre* or its individual sections, a few also contain apparently unrelated texts. Something similar is true, of course, for many, if not most, medieval texts, and anyone looking at the manuscript corpus of the *chanson de geste* or *Le Roman de Renart*, to cite just two examples, will come to similar conclusions.

For this kind of codicological transmission, any form of modern edition is by definition an anachronism, and bound to be a failure if its aim is to present the modern reader with a faithful image of the medieval text. However, if *The Medieval French "Roman d'Alexandre"* is a failure, it is a magnificent one, like William Roach's Continuations of the *Perceval*, Emanuel Mickel's Old French Crusade Cycle, or the Dutch *Nouveau Recueil Complet des Fabliaux*. Nor would anyone who edited Chrétien's last romance ever admit that he wasted nine years of his life doing so, for the critical edition will remain for most scholars the basic means of access to the medieval text, which reveals some of its aspects more clearly away from the "clutter" of the manuscript page. And nothing teaches us about medieval textuality better than the letter-for-letter, word-for-word, line-for-line examination of a text in multiple manuscripts, in other words, the kind of work that has to be carried out in the preparation of an edition. In this sense, the process is as important to the editor as the end result might be to scholars for whom an edition is intended. Only by such

---

*I treat the manuscripts of *Le roman d'Alexandre* more extensively in Chapter 4 of my *Codex and Context: Reading Old French Verse Narrative in Manuscript* (Amsterdam: Rodopi, 2002).

work can one come to grips with the monster *variance*.[1] Cerquiglini's monster, however, was only a textual one, and one that in any case has been largely misunderstood, I believe. My own *Ungeheuer* has many more heads and is altogether more unruly.

Unruliness is one of the prime characteristics of the manuscript transmission of medieval French literature, and one with which it is extremely difficult to come to terms. In addition to the textual and codicological features mentioned above, manuscripts are often acephalous, or defective at the end or somewhere in the middle, sometimes all three; even when complete, some seem to be factitious or otherwise composite. The modern edition disguises this unruliness in the form of a modern book, and divorces the text from the variety of its contexts, usually ignoring illustration and rubric, furnishing no information on *mise en page* or *mise en texte*. The critical edition is a reductionist product that renders the medieval text unidimensional and anodyne, colorless and odorless. If the purely textual transmission can be satisfactorily articulated by the presentation in parallel of transcriptions of all manuscripts (and even this is practical only in the case of relatively brief texts), nothing short of holistic reproduction can approach the reality of the medieval manuscript which is, after all, our only point of contact with the object of our study.

In his basic article on *Le Roman d'Alexandre*,[2] Paul Meyer listed twenty-eight complete manuscripts or fragments; if one adds fragments discovered since 1882, as well as manuscripts of the *Paon*-poems and *Le Roman de Toute Chevalerie*, the number rises to somewhere near sixty. Clearly, I cannot examine all of them here, but I would like to offer a brief typology of the *Alexandre* manuscripts and comment selectively on some features that may cast light on the reception of the texts. And it is important to note that we are dealing here with secondary reception at the time of the production of the manuscripts rather than reception by primary audiences.

Scholars of *Le Roman d'Alexandre* habitually refer to "the Arsenal-Venice version" as a means of indicating a particular state of the text. While this grouping is textually indisputable, it conceals a serious contrast in the material transmission of Paris, Arsenal 3472 and Venice, Museo Civico VI, 665 (B. 5. 8.). The former, from the mid-thirteenth century, is the kind of unillustrated small-format manuscript (13 cm × 8.5 cm, 1 × 27) that used to be called a "manuscrit de jongleur," although its quality of execution is generally better than the usual run of such manuscripts. I have no intention of reopening the debate about the validity of this classification, but it is worth pointing out that such modest manuscripts, usually decorated only with red capitals at the beginning of the *laisses* and made from quite poor-quality materials, were produced from the late-twelfth through the fourteenth centuries and are clearly not all early in date. BN fr. 15094 and 15095 (both mid-thirteenth century) belong to this category (19.6 cm × 12.2 cm, 1 × 28; 17.5 cm × 11.5 cm, 1 × 36); the Oxford fragment (Bodleian, Hatton 67; 19 cm × 13 cm, 1 ×

20), attributed by Meyer to the same textual constellation, is even later (from the latter part of the fourteenth century). There is quite a large group of some thirty such manuscripts containing *chansons de geste*, but very few of romance texts (Tours, BM 942 of Chrétien's *Cligés* would seem to be an exception). If these are not "manuscrits de jongleur," they at least prove that customers got what they paid for when commissioning manuscripts, in this case, plain and unadorned texts. While monastic and ad hoc copies cannot be ruled out, certain features, such as the marginal decorations of Arsenal 3472 and the right justification of the text block in fr. 15095, do suggest routine professional production. They also locate *Le Roman d'Alexandre* codicologically in close proximity to the epic, confirming evidence of a more properly textual nature.

The presence in the same textual group as fr. 15094 and 15095 of the larger format fr. 787 (latter third of the thirteenth century; 28.2 cm × 21.7 cm, 2 × 36), a manuscript that conforms more strictly to the dominant model of verse codices of the period, argues for a less evolutionary view of manuscript production in the period preceding the fifteenth century. In other words, although the range of formats and degrees of decoration no doubt increased with time, some may have purposely been produced to suggest a deliberate measure of archaism. Manufacture, in the thirteenth and fourteenth centuries, of copies in the "manuscrit de jongleur" format would underline the relationship of *Le Roman d'Alexandre* to the epic, originally transmitted in modest monastic productions. The larger, two-column format is essentially that of verse romance, and its use for *Le Roman d'Alexandre* and the *chanson de geste* goes part of the way to disguising the individualistic nature of the texts in question, grounding them fully in the larger intertext of Old French literature, at a time when generic parameters are becoming indistinct textually. Thus, the very format chosen by a patron or a planner for a manuscript can be crucial to the meaning generated by the text it preserves. Illustrated and rubricated manuscripts take this development even further, although the progression is again not a purely chronological one. The choice of scenes for illustration and the precise wording of rubrics create an even greater potential for the generation of meaning. These modest manuscripts may be seen as proudly proclaiming the respectability of the Alexander legend as an epic *matière*, while those in the larger format, sometimes illustrated, could assert its modernity and suitability as the stuff of romance.

The fourth manuscript Meyer relates textually to fr. 15094, 15095, and 787 is Parma, BN 1206. Like the Venice manuscript, Parma 1206 is an Italian product of the fourteenth century, and is further testimony to the importance of French literature in Italy at the time. In point of fact, even Arsenal 3472, not generally regarded as Italian, shows clear signs not only of having been in Italy in the fourteenth century (the rewritten ff. 9 and 16), but of actually having been copied there in the first instance. Some attention has been paid to manuscripts of prose romances, particularly the prose *Tristan*, copied in Italy, but relatively little to the copying of verse texts. I believe that a thorough investigation of what might be termed "the geography of the codex" would have a good deal to tell us about the reception of French literature at the courts of Italy in the thirteenth and fourteenth centuries. While it is true that prose romance and epic seem to have been the genres most favored by medieval Italian audiences, the *romans d'antiquité* were also copied (the best-known manuscript being Milan, Ambrosiana D. 44 of *Le Roman de Troie*). There is here an interesting triangular relationship to be explored between continental France, Italy, and the Norman-Angevin domains, the last of which often provided exemplars for texts copied in Italy. It was doubtless the consciousness of Italy as the repository and guardian of classical antiquity, to become so much more pronounced in the second half of the fourteenth century, that was largely responsible for the interest shown there in *Le Roman d'Alexandre*. The *translatio studii et imperii* topos, which has been shown to be central to so much of Old French literature and its own subjectivity, has almost retraced its steps here: if learning and chivalry moved from Greece through Rome to France and Norman England, it is now back in Italy largely thanks to political and military influences from the other side of the Alps and of the English Channel.

BN fr. 786 has been attributed to Tournai in the second half of the thirteenth century. It contains *Le Roman d'Alexandre* followed by the first Crusade cycle, although the original intended order seems to have been the reverse. A number of factors would seem to authorize the conjuncture of these two texts in a manuscript from the northeast of France. First of all, the majority of Crusade-cycle manuscripts seem to have been written at this time in this region, some for members of the Boulonnais aristocracy, probably because of the local dynastic associations with Godefroi de Bouillon, the Chevalier au Cygne. *Le Roman d'Alexandre* complements the Crusade epics not only because of a basic generic similarity (epics with romance/mythological elements) but also because of the associations with the Orient and primarily, I would have thought, because Alexander, like Godefroi, was one of the Nine Worthies. It is therefore no coincidence that the closing *laisse* of *Le Roman d'Alexandre* on f. 91rb of fr. 786 mentions another worthy, this one from a trio not represented by Alexander (antiquity) or Godefroi (contemporary):

> Et puis que li baron vinrent en lor resnés
> Ne fu li uns de l'autre ne cieris ne amés,
>Ançois se gueroierent par lor grans poestés
> Tres c'al jour kes ocist tous Judas Macabés
> Et conquist lor roiaumes, çou dist l'autorités.

(And after the peers returned to their realms, no love was lost between them, but rather they made war on one another with their great might until the day Judas Maccabeus killed them all and conquered their kingdoms, so says the authority.)

A similar motivation doubtless lies behind the inclusion in BN, fr. 789 (dated 1280 on f. 218rb) of *La Chevalerie Judas Machabé* (ff. 105r–218r) with *Le Roman d'Alexandre* (ff. 1r–103r). Although J. R. Smeets argues that the two texts were bound together by Bourdelot at the beginning of the seventeenth century,[3] there is enough codicological evidence, despite the separate fascicles, to confirm that the manuscript was planned essentially as it appears today. The association of Alexander with two of the other eight Worthies in manuscripts before the end of the thirteenth century is particularly significant, as it is generally agreed that the topos does not become established as such before the celebrated passage in *Les Voeux du Paon* (before 1312). While we do not have the complete list of Nine Worthies here, it is clearly visible *in statu nascendi*. This is therefore an example, minor as it may be, of how manuscript study might contribute to the revision of literary history.

This raises the general question of context as a generator of meaning in those manuscripts where *Le Roman d'Alexandre* is accompanied by other texts (for the time being, I will consider the *Paon*-poems as part of *Le Roman d'Alexandre*). BN fr. 368 (second half of the fourteenth century) is a much larger format manuscript than most (40 cm × 30.75 cm, 3 × 50), containing *Partonopeu de Blois* (ff. 1r–40v), *Le Roman d'Alexandre*, *Les Voeux du Paon*, and *La Mort Alixandre* (ff. 41r–88v, 89r–119r, 119r–120v), *La Chanson des Saisnes* (ff. 121r–139v), *Simon de Pouille* (ff. 140r–160v), and *chansons de geste* from the Guillaume cycle (ff. 161r–280r).[4] Scholars have pointed out that although this manuscript is complete, many of the texts it contains are truncated. In the light of what Delbouille, McMillan, and Tyssens pointed out some years ago in the great debate on the manuscripts of the Guillaume cycle, I would suggest that what we have here is a manuscript complete but for the transitional passages between texts, where adjustments are made and links forged, and awaiting the continuation of its final fragment, *Anseïs de Cartage* (f. 280r). This is a manuscript that would probably repay closer textual and codicological analysis than I have been able to afford it here. The context is primarily epic, with the position of *Partonopeu* at the head of the manuscript anchoring the whole collection in the tradition of *translatio studii et imperii*, Partonopeu being the favourite nephew of Clovis, whose genealogy is traced back to Priam of Troy. *Le Roman d'Alexandre* explores another aspect of the Greek legacy through Aristotle's tutoring of Alexander and the latter's military career. With *La Chanson des Saisnes*, we return to the legacy of Priam through the connection of the Carolingian dynasty to the descendants of Clovis (Pepin helped put Childeric III on the throne before deposing him and acceding in 751). As an ancestor of Guillaume (Garin de Monglane's great grandson), Simon de Pouille is also a Carolingian, and the epic that bears his name also relates to *Le Roman d'Alexandre* in that much of its action takes place in the Orient. The connection of Apulia with the Normans in general and with the family of Tancrède de Hauteville in particular may point in the direction of an early owner or even patron. Such dynastic and territorial concerns form the *conjointure* for a good number of romance and epic collections from this time. Although the movement is not always strictly chronological and unidirectional, it tends to legitimize claims, both notional and real, of the French monarchy to most of the known world, from the Near East and the Holy Land to France, Norman Britain, and even Ireland.

On BN fr. 375 I shall be brief, as this manuscript is relatively well-known.[5] *Le Roman d'Alexandre* is to be found in the second part of this huge Artesian collection, the part dated 1288 by the signature of Jehan Madot, nephew of Adam de la Halle, on f. 119v. It contains part of the rhymed table of contents by Perrot de Neele (ff. 34r–35r), *Le Roman de Thèbes* (ff. 36r–67v), *Le Roman de Troie* (ff. 68r–119va), *Athis et Prophilias* (ff. 119vb–162r), Jean Bodel's *Congés* (ff. 162r–163r), *Le Roman d'Alexandre* (ff. 164r–216r), and a genealogy of the Counts of Boulogne (ff. 216r–216vb). This manuscript is particularly significant for a number of reasons, not the least of which is its clearly northeastern character and probable patronage in the house of Boulogne (it also includes some distinctly northeastern texts such as Jean Bodel's *Congés*, *Ille et Galeron* by Gautier d'Arras, and *Le Vengement Alixandre* by Gui de Cambrai). The context of *Le Roman d'Alexandre* here is clearly that of the *roman antique* rather than that of the *chanson de geste*. The *Congés* and the genealogy may seem out of place, but their presence is due to purely practical considerations. Manuscript planners had a *horror vacui*, and as *Athis et Prophilias* and *Le Roman d'Alexandre* ended before the end of a gathering, as so often, "fillers" were added to take up the space. If we discount the first thirty-three folios as certainly extraneous, there is a clear movement visible between the part of the manuscript containing the classical matter and the next, which starts with Wace's *Rou* and consists mainly of romances (including some by Chrétien) before closing with a number of religious texts. In this context, *Le Roman d'Alexandre* is the bridge between the ancient and the medieval worlds in both the chronological and literary senses.

One of the basic structural principles of the Old French epic, and of secular story telling generally, is a genealogical one according to which the popularity of heroes was exploited by the addition to the core narrative of tales relating to the hero's childhood, the deeds of his offspring, or his ancestors. Examples of this are legion, and it is clearly visible not only as a compositional principle, but also as one that determined the manufacture and ordering of cyclical manuscripts. It is clearly responsible for the content of BN, fr. 792 (last quarter of the thirteenth century; 34.5 cm × 23 cm, 3 × 48), where *Le Roman d'Alexandre* is preceded by Aimon de Varennes's *Florimont*. Composed in 1188, *Florimont* was enormously popular, judging by the number of surviving manuscripts. Like many romances of the period, it is dynastic, and relates the found-ing of Phillipopolis by Florimont, great grandfather of Alexander. Its place in a manuscript of *Le Roman d'Alexandre* is thus secure. BN fr. 792 thus provides a context both for *Florimont* as the foundation romance of Alexander's dynasty and for *Le Roman d'Alexandre* as a continuation of Florimont's line. The *explicit* to *Florimont* is clear: "Explicit l'istoire de Florimont pere de Philippe de Macedoine pere du grant Alixandre" (f. 50v). As such, this kind of linkage effectively precludes narrative or codicological closure of any kind, providing both author and manuscript planner with a wealth of creative opportunity.

If a number of manuscripts of *Le Roman d'Alexandre* belong to the modest, small-format type I have discussed above, by far the majority belong to the routined, professional production that began to flourish in the second half of the thirteenth century. The provenance of these manuscripts covers a wide geographical area: for example, Tournai (BN fr. 786), Arras (BN fr. 375), Paris (BN fr. 1590), Burgundy-Lorraine (BN fr. 1635), and Italy (Venice and Parma). Curiously, perhaps, no surviving copy of *Le Roman d'Alexandre* seems to have been produced *outre-Manche*, but the range does extend to England if one includes Thomas of Kent's *Le Roman de Toute Chevalerie*. The three primary manuscripts of this text are illustrative of a number of issues relating to manu-script production in the thirteenth and fourteenth centuries. While insular production can be no surprise in a text of insular origin, the existence of the continental BN fr. 24364 alongside Durham, Cathedral Library C.IV.27 B, and Cambridge, Trinity College O. 9. 34 serves as a reminder of the French linguistic community on both sides of the Channel as late as the early-fourteenth century.[6] The Durham manuscript, the only unillustrated one of the three, has a whole gathering at the beginning devoted to "chapeteres" that are in fact transcriptions of rubrics corresponding to those that accompany the illustra-tions in the Cambridge and Paris copies. The collection (and often duplica-tion) of rubrics/*tituli* into tables of contents is quite common, although far from universal, starting in the thirteenth century, and is an important step in the evolution of the book. It also has implications for the user in that it suggests the possibility of individual rather than public reading, through a perceived necessity to organize and offer the opportunity to read in relatively short installments and to find one's place again.

The Durham manuscript, in fact, has a good deal more to tell us about the way it was read in the middle of the fourteenth century, its period of production. The "chapeteres" are carefully numbered from .i. ("le prolong") to .cclxxxxvij. in both the table and the text itself, and the use of blue capitals in the table indicates that the "chapetere" in question is one that relates a battle; Alexander's battles, of course, are one of the basic structuring elements of the text, where they are further noted as "1 bellum," "2 bellum," etc. This kind of methodical *mise en livre* is found elsewhere, mainly in manuscripts of chronicles, and in collections of short narratives, such as *La Vie des Pères*,

Gautier de Coinci's *Miracles Nostre Dame,* or the *Ovide moralisé,* all works that have learned origins. Although *Le Roman de Toute Chevalerie* owes much to the continental *Roman d'Alexandre,* its organization in the Durham manuscript underlines its ties with the classical tradition of Alexander rather than its status as a vernacular romance. This is further illustrated by the frequent occurrence of near-contemporary Latin glosses that are essentially references to Orosius and Josephus pertaining to the battles, many of which add details not present in the French text. This procedure, so typical of a learned, clerical environment, argues strongly in favor of ownership in a clerical establishment of some kind where a reader had access to copies of the Latin histories. In other locations, the word "No^a" (Nota) occurs in the margin beside a proverbial expression, a particularly important speech or other passage deemed to be especially significant (for example, the eagle dropping the egg into Philip's lap [f. 12v], a reference to the black arts [f. 92r], and antifeminist outbursts [ff. 22v, 184r]).

Cambridge, Trinity College O. 9. 34 was dated 1250 by M. R. James and attributed on palæographical and art-historical grounds to St. Alban's Abbey.[7] Its 152 pen-wash drawings are certainly in a characteristic English style of the time, related to the work of Matthew Paris, and found in a number of vernacular codices, such as the fragments of the Becket life (J. P. Getty, on permanent loan to the British Library), the manuscript of Matthew's lives of St. Alban and St. Amphibalus (Dublin, Trinity College, E. i. 40), and particularly closely to London, BL, Lansdowne 782 of *La Chanson d'Aspremont.*[8] Later developments of this style are found in epic manuscripts such as London, BL, Egerton 3028 and Hannover, Niedersächsiche Landesbibl. IV 578 (*Fierabras* and *La Destruction de Rome*),[9] and in parts of the Paris manuscript of *Le Roman de Toute Chevalerie.* Ross argued that these epic manuscripts must have been made in a secular workshop since the subject matter of some of the miniatures would scarcely have met the approval of a monastic establishment (p. 694), although there is a long-standing and persistent connection of epic poetry and religious institutions, with respect to both ownership and production. Certainly, some of the illustrations in the Cambridge manuscript are strictly speaking *risqué,* but it may be dangerous to impose modern sensibilities here, particularly in the light of the kind of obscenities often found in the margins of medieval religious art. Nevertheless, the relationship between text, image, and rubric is particularly complex in Trinity College O. 9. 34, and provides a salutory example of the importance of considering the manuscript in all its aspects and their interrelations (as a *Gesamtkunstwerk*) rather than its text alone. Since there are 152 illustrations in this manuscript, I obviously cannot look at them all in detail here, but will simply indicate by a few examples exactly how they complement and manipulate the text.[10]

Many of the illustrations, particularly those in the first part of the text, relate to the battles, and show jousts, combats, sieges, messengers, councils of war, and so on. Later sections represent the marvels of the Orient, Alexander's exploration of the universe, his relationship with Candace, the struggle against Porus, his death, and the dispersal of his lands to the twelve peers. By and large, this gives a fair representation of the narrative and its concerns, particularly as the illustrations are so frequent, averaging more than three per folio, but it is through their detail that they are significant. For example, the final illustration on f. 22rb of the section of the text attributed in the manuscript to "Eustace de Kent" is of a tonsured monk seated at a writing desk, wielding a quill and a knife with which he holds down the unruly parchment. The rubric reads: "La conclusion del livere Alisandre / De maistre Eustace ki translata cest livere" (The conclusion of the book of Alexander by master Eustace who translated this book), referring to the text on f. 22va ("Ki mon nun demande, Eustace ai non de Kent": If anyone asks my name, I am called Eustace of Kent). This clearly marks a major articulation of the text, and is likewise marked by illustration or *titulus* in the Paris and Durham manuscripts. The net effect of this illustration is to underline and consolidate the creative act as one which includes the intellectual-verbal process of translation from Latin into the vernacular and the physical endeavor of putting quill to parchment to produce the exemplar from which the codex is finally made. It also inscribes the text as a product of a monastic and learned environment, anticipating the Latin glossing present in the Durham manuscript.

This form of "subjectivité littéraire" is apparent elsewhere in the illustrations to Trinity O. 9. 34, as for example on f. 9ra, where a messenger from Alexander holds before Darius a letter inscribed as in the text (l. 1496) "Sachez ke jeo governer dei tote ta grant honur" (Know that I shall govern all your great domains). And on f. 30va, a messenger from Candace hands Alexander a letter inscribed with two lines as found in the text itself (ll. 6960-61): "Nule ren coveit tant en mun desirer / Come vus prendre a seinur et vus mai a muiller" (I desire nothing so much as to take you for my lord and for you to take me as your wife). The illustrator clearly has a penchant for this kind of ekphrastic *mise en abime*, although it is not limited to representation of the verbal. On f. 36vb, Candace takes Alexander by the hand and shows him a statue of a king holding a scepter, with the rubric: "Coment Candace mostra a Alisandre sa ymage" (How Candace showed Alexander his own image). D. J. A. Ross, who thought that the illustration on f. 37ra of Alexandre and Candace together in bed was one of those that made it unlikely that O. 9. 34 was a monastic production, might have pointed to that on f. 36va, accompanied by the rubric "Coment Candace mostra a Alisandre ses tresors" (How Candace showed Alexander her treasure). Heaps of crowns and brooches on the right represent the treasure, to which Candace, in the center, points; Alexandre, however, points to Candace's knee, as if to say: "No. This is the kind of treasure I want." Both figures are seated with their knees apart in a suggestive posture. Such immodesty is not present in the text and indeed would be inappropriate given its more or less serious nature, but it can be expressed through the accompanying visual medium. It is also practically impossible to convey in a critical edition, short of the reproduction or extensive description of all illustrations.

I reserve for elsewhere a fuller study of the relationship between word and image in the manuscripts of *Le Roman d'Alexandre*; here I would simply like to provide a cursory examination, concentrating more on their general physical appearance than on interpretive detail. Few of the illuminated manuscripts are particularly luxurious, and most can be grouped with other codices of other works in both general appearance and specific provenance. I have already mentioned that BN fr. 786 was probably made in Tournai in the second half of the thirteenth century and that it is related to other manuscripts of the Crusade Cycle. Although it is of fairly large dimensions (23 cm × 34 cm, 2 × 60 lines) and contains more than twenty miniatures and historiated capitals, its general aspect is quite modest; its rubrics are of the "Si dist si con . . ."-type. BN fr. 789 (1280) can be grouped with fr. 786 because of its dimensions (22 cm × 32.75 cm, 2 × 51 lines), style of miniatures, and because it also links Alexander with another of the Nine Worthies. BN fr. 790 and fr. 1590 have both been attributed by Alison Stones to the workshop of Thomas de Maubeuge, thus locating their provenance as Paris, first third of the fourteenth century.[11] The two manuscripts are of identical format and dimensions (22.8 cm x 30.8 cm [21.2 cm × 29.8 cm], writing block 18 cm × 24 cm, 2 × 40 lines), and the miniatures are of about the same frequency, although fr. 790 has rubrics while fr. 1590 does not.

The importance of this identification is multiple. Thomas de Maubeuge was a *libraire* first sworn to the University of Paris in 1316, and is known to have supplied vernacular manuscripts to such aristocratic and royal patrons as Mahaut d'Artois, the Count of Hainaut, Charles IV, and the Duke of Normandy (the future Jean le Bon).[12] In addition to indicating the type of patron for whom these manuscripts may have been intended, the grouping of manuscripts proposed by Stones argues forcefully in favor of an inclusive rather than an exclusive view of the corpus of vernacular literature at the time. The manuscripts on which the Maubeuge artist is thought to have worked include copies of the *Grandes Chroniques de France*, *Le Roman de la Rose*, lives of saints, *Le Roman de Renart*, the Arthurian Vulgate Cycle, and the prose *Tristan*. He also seems to have collaborated with the so-called "sub-*Fauvel* painter" and an artist associated with the workshop of Richard and Jeanne de Montbaston. Stones, following François Avril, has also attributed BN, fr. 24365 to the *Fauvel* master and the sub-*Fauvel* master, locating it once more to Paris in the early-fourteenth century. Expanding the orbit of *Le Roman de Fauvel* only slightly, there emerges an extraordinary picture of vernacular manuscript production dependent on the patronage of royalty and the court circle, the provincial nobility, and other relatively wealthy individuals such as lawyers.

Probably the best known of the illustrated manuscripts of *Le Roman d'Alexandre* is Oxford, Bodleian, Bodley 264, published in facsimile by M. R. James.[13] Apart from the richness of its decoration (large multicompartment miniatures, detailed marginalia) and the detailed formulation of its rubrics, this manuscript is particularly interesting for what it reveals about its own manufacture. The main text was completed on December 18, 1338, as per the colophon on f. 209r:

> Chi define li romans du boin roi Alixandre et les veus du pavon, les acomplissemens, le restor du pavon et le pris, qui fu parescrit le .xviij^e. jor de decembre l'an .m. ccc. xxxviij.
>
> Explicit iste liber. Scriptor sit crimine liber.
> Christus scriptorem custodiat ac det honorem.

(Here ends the romance of good King Alexander and the vows of the peacock, the fulfillings, the restoration and prize of the peacock, the copying of which was finished on December 18, 1338.

> Here ends this book. May the scribe be free from reproach.
> May Christ protect the scribe and give him honor.)

On the same folio, another, incomplete, colophon reads:

> Laus tibi sit, Christe, quoniam liber explicit iste.
> Nomen scriptoris est Thomas plenus amoris.[14]
> Qui ultra querit

(Praise be to Thee, o Christ, for this book ends here. The scribe's name is Thomas full of love. If anyone seeks more . . .)

This is the most elaborate of all the Alexandre manuscripts in most respects, textually as well as artistically, and seems to have been produced in three stages, possibly in as many locations. Another inscription on the same folio, in gold letters, reads: "Che livre fu perfais de le enluminure au xviij^e jour d'avryl per Jehan de Grise, l'an de grace .m. ccc. xliiij" (The illumination of this book was completed by Jehan de Grise on April 18, the year of grace 1344). It is not immediately clear whether or not the decoration took six years to complete or whether there was a hiatus after the writing of the main text before Jehan de Grise and collaborators started work. To complicate matters further, the language of the rubrics reveals Anglo-Norman features, while that of the text is Franco-Picard. While it is not impossible that an English rubricator (Thomas Pleindamour?) worked in northeastern France, or that northeastern artists and scribes worked in England, it is more likely, I would have thought, that the rubrics were added in England sometime shortly after 1344. Bodley 264 was certainly in England in 1466 when it became the property of Richard de Widville, Lord Rivers.

This is one of the very earliest copies of *Le Restor du Paon*, for which the scribal colophon provides the *terminus ad quem*, and the manuscript in general is the ultimate Alexander romance, a kind of verbal and visual *summa Alexandriana*, for it contains, in addition to *Le Roman d'Alexandre*, lavishly illustrated texts of *La Prise de Defur*, the first two of the three peacock poems, the *Voyage*, and the *Vengeance*; only *Le Parfait du Paon* is not included.

Like so many medieval works, *Le Roman d'Alexandre* is preserved only in manuscripts produced many decades after its composition. If we can posit a certain popularity at the end of the twelfth and beginning of the thirteenth centuries, the manuscript evidence points, roughly speaking, to two more waves of dissemination, namely the last quarter of the thirteenth century, and the third and fourth decades of the fourteenth. One might attribute the first of these in part to the conditions of commercial book production in the northeast and the second to a renewed interest in the older material spurred on by the writing of the *Paon* sequence. *Les Voeux du Paon* is in fact the most lavishly illustrated of the *Alexandre* texts, although only eight of its more than thirty extant copies have more than a handful of miniatures. The nineteen miniatures in Vatican City, BAV, vat. lat. 3209 and the twenty in Liverpool, Public Library 9. 841. i are relatively modest, while the twenty-two miniatures in New York, Pierpont Morgan Library, Glazier 24 are of much higher quality and accompanied by detailed and lively marginalia. In Paris, BN fr. 12565, where the *Voeux* is presented as the continuation of *La Prise de Defur* and followed by the other two peacock poems, it is accompanied by eighty miniatures; the ex-Sabin manuscript now in the New York Public Library, Spencer 9, contains eighty-one miniatures, and Amsterdam, Rijksmuseum 3042, eighty-seven.[15] Apart from Bodley 264, another Oxford manuscript, Douce 308, is the most frequently illustrated, with 145 for the *Voeux* alone.

Glazier 24 has been attributed to Tournai (mid-thirteenth century) by François Avril,[16] while at least two of the others, Douce 308 and Rijksmuseum 3042, have close ties with Lorraine.[17] While it is clear that the geography of the codex reveals that many manuscripts were produced and owned in regions that feature in the texts (for example, Lorraine manuscripts of the Lorraine cycle of *chansons de geste*) or the homelands of their heroes (northeastern manuscripts of the Crusade cycle; a southern manuscript of *Joufroi de Poitiers* in Copenhagen, KB, Gl. kgl. saml. 3555, 8°), thereby catering to a need to express pride in the accomplishments of local heroes or their lineage, others seem to proclaim the achievements of local authors. Numerous Artesian or Parisian anthology manuscripts illustrate the point, and it is surely no coincidence that many of the manuscripts of Girart d'Amiens or Adenet le Roi are of northeastern provenance. Both literary activity itself and manuscript production are intimately bound up with the state of the aristocracy and the urban classes in the various regions of France, and although the northeast and Paris are the clearest indications of how the codicological map needs to be drawn, other areas, such as the Lyonnais-Burgundy and Lorraine, would need to be included. The correlation between literature and the manuscripts in which it was transmitted changes quite radically in the late-thirteenth and early-fourteenth centuries, as the notion of authorial identity evolves and authors take a more active role in the supervision of the books in which their works are preserved. Poets such as Machaut and Froissart are the most obvious and best documented examples of this development, but it is doubtless true of Girart, Adenet, and others. Consequently, the interval between dates of composition and production of the earliest extant manuscripts is reduced and in many cases eliminated altogether. Something similar may be the case with Jacques de Longuyon and *Les Voeux du Paon* and is almost certainly so for Jehan de le Mote and *Le Parfait du Paon*, as Mary and Richard Rouse have recently argued.[18]

The lavishness of the illustrated *Voeux du Paon* manuscripts can be at least partly explained by its nature as a poem commissioned from Jacques de Longuyon by Thibaud de Bar, Bishop of Liège, and even if we cannot identify the presentation copy, it is likely that it would have been a luxurious item and would have provided an illustrated model for later copies. Oxford, Bodleian, Douce 308 is an anthology of works associated with Lorraine and Lorraine authors, and the presence of *Les Voeux du Paon* (Longuyon, Meurthe-et-Moselle) needs no further justification; Rijksmuseum 3042 is clearly written in the dialect of Lorraine. As for *Le Parfait du Paon*, it was written by Jehan de le Mote for Simon de Lille, the king's goldsmith, to accompany (if the Rouses' speculations are correct) the presentation of an elaborate gold peacock, as described in the text of *Le Restor du Paon*, made by Simon to Philippe de Valois in 1340. The illustrations in Oxford, Bodleian, Douce 165 are by Jeanne de Montbaston, wife of the *libraire* Richard de Montbaston, who are both known to have worked for the royal court in this very period, and the Rouses argue that this is indeed the copy presented along with the peacock to Philippe. This is an interesting case of life imitating literature and realizing that imitation in an *objet d'art* accompanied by a codex containing the text which verbally describes the same *objet d'art*; the presence of a miniature depicting the golden peacock in most of the illustrated manuscripts of the *Restor* adds further depth to the ekphrastic perspective. Whether the Rouses' speculation is correct or not, the example of the interaction between artistic and literary forms in the fourth decade of the fourteenth century is instructive, as is that of a poet protected by someone not a member of the aristocracy, but who by all accounts behaved and lived like one.

I do not suggest we all burn our Lettres Gothiques in a postmodern *auto da fé*, but that we try to enrich our understanding of the reception of medieval literature, in this case *Le Roman d'Alexandre*, by returning to the manuscripts in a more positive, perhaps even positivistic, act of faith. After all, *codices manuscriptos nudos tenemus.*

Notes

1. See Bernard Cerquiglini, *Eloge de la variante* (Paris: Seuil, 1989).

2. Paul Meyer, "Etude sur les manuscrits du *Roman d'Alexandre*," *Romania* 11 (1882), 213–330.

3. J. R. Smeets, ed., *La chevalerie de Judas Macchabee de Gautier de Belleperche (et de Pieros du Riés)*, 2 vols. (Assen: Van Gorcum, 1991), I, p. 11.

4. For a good recent description of fr. 368, see Annette Brasseur, "Les manuscrits de *La chanson des Saisnes*," *Olifant* 19: 1–2 (Fall 1994–Winter 1995), 57–99, esp. pp. 73–81.

5. See especially Charles François, "Perrot de Neele, Jehan Madot et le ms. B.N. fr. 375," *Revue Belge de Philologie et d'Histoire* 41 (1963), 761–79, and Sylvia Huot, *From Song to Book: The Poetics of Writing in Old French Lyric and Lyrical Narrative Poetry* (Ithaca: Cornell University Press, 1987), pp. 21–27.

6. The manuscripts have been described by Brian Foster (with the assistance of Ian Short) in *RTC*, II, pp. 3–14.

7. M. R. James, *Western Manuscripts in the Library of Trinity College, Cambridge: A Descriptive Catalogue*, 4 vols. (Cambridge: Cambridge University Press, 1900–1904), III, p. 482.

8. See D. J. A. Ross, "A Thirteenth-Century Anglo-Norman Workshop Illustrating Secular Literary Manuscripts?" in *Mélanges Rita Lejeune*, 2 vols. (Gembloux: Duculot, 1969), I, pp. 689–94.

9. On these manuscripts, see Louis Brandin, "La *Destruction de Rome* et *Fierabras*: ms. Egerton 3028 du Musée Britannique à Londres," *Romania* 64 (1938), 18–100, and "Le manuscrit de Hanovre de la *Destruction de Rome* et de *Fierabras*," *Romania* 28 (1899), 489–507; Ida Wirtz, *Studien zur Handschrift IV. 578 der Provinzialbibliothek zu Hannover, der chanson de geste "Fierabras d'Alixandre"* (Diss. Göttingen, 1935); Helmar Härtel, *Handschriften der Niedersächsischen Landesbibliothek Hannover*, II, Beschreibungen (Wiesbaden: Harrassowitz, 1982).

10. The rubrics have been transcribed by James (loc. cit.), who also gives brief descriptions of the illustrations.

11. Alison Stones, "The Stylistic Context of the *Roman de Fauvel* with a note on the *Fauvain*," in *Fauvel Studies: Allegory, Chronicle, Music, and Image in Paris, Bibliothèque Nationale de France, MS francais 146*, ed. Margaret Bent and Andrew Wathey (Oxford: Clarendon Press, 1998), pp. 529–67, 558–59.

12. Stones, pp. 542–43 and the literature cited there.

13. *The Romance of Alexander. A Collotype Facsimile of ms. Bodley 264* (Oxford: Clarendon Press, 1933).

14. Cf. the "Hamonicus plenus amoris" who signed BN fr. 542 (f. 339v) and Vatican City, BAV, vat. lat. 986 (f. 137v).

15. On Rijksmuseum 3042, see J. J. Salverda de Grave, "Un manuscrit inconnu des *Voeux du Paon*," *Studi Medievali* 1 (1928), 422–37.

16. "Un chef d'oeuvre de l'enluminure sous le règne de Jean le Bon: la *Bible moralisée* (le ms. fr. 167 de la Bibliothèque nationale)," *Monuments et mémoires publiés par l'Académie des Inscriptions et Belles-Lettres* 58 (1973), 91–125.

17. See *Écriture et enluminure en Lorraine au Moyen Âge (Catalogue de l'exposition "La plume et le parchemin," Nancy, 29 mai–29 juillet 1984)* (Nancy: Société Thierry Alix, 1984), pp. 186–88.

18. Mary A. Rouse and Richard H. Rouse, "The Goldsmith and the Peacocks: Jean de le Mote in the Household of Simon de Lille, 1340," *Viator* 28 (1997), 283–303.

Contributors

Emmanuèle Baumgartner is professeur de Littérature française du Moyen Age at the Université de Paris III—Sorbonne Nouvelle. She is particularly interested in twelfth- and thirteenth-century narrative in verse and prose and has published numerous books, including studies on Villon's works, the Tristan romances, Chrétien de Troyes, Arthurian prose romance, especially the *Quête du saint Graal* and the Prose *Tristan,* as well as several literary-historical syntheses, including *Le Récit médiéval (XIIe–XIIIe siècles)* (Hachette, 1995).

Renate Blumenfeld-Kosinski is professor of French and Director of the Medieval and Renaissance Studies Program at the University of Pittsburgh. She is the author of *Not of Woman Born: Representations of Caesarean Birth in Medieval and Renaissance Culture* (Cornell, 1990), *The Writings of Margaret of Oingt* (Focus Press, 1991), and *Reading Myth: Classical Mythology and its Intepretations in Medieval French Literature* (Stanford, 1997).

Keith Busby is professor of French at the University of Wisconsin, Madison. He is the author of *Gauvain in Old French Literature* (Rodopi, 1980). He has edited Raoul de Houdenc's *Le Roman des eles* and the anonymous *Ordene de chevalerie* (Benjamins, 1983) and Chrétien de Troyes's *Le Conte del graal* (Niemeyer, 1993); he coedited *Les Manuscrits de Chrétien de Troyes* (Rodopi, 1993).

Catherine Croizy-Naquet is professeur de Littérature française at the Université de Lille III. Her publications on medieval French literature include *Thèbes, Troie et Carthage: Poétique de la ville dans les romans antiques* (Champion, 1994) and *Ecrire l'histoire romaine au début du XIIIe siècle: 'L'Histoire ancienne jusqu'à César,' les 'Faits des Romains'* (Champion, 1999).

Catherine Gaullier-Bougassas is Maître de Conférences en littérature médiévale at the Université de Paris III—Sorbonne Nouvelle. She has published many studies on the medieval French Alexander tradition, including a major synthesis, *Les Romans d'Alexandre: Aux frontières de l'épique et du romanesque* (Champion, 1998), which deals extensively with the versions by Alexandre de Paris and Thomas de Kent.

275

Martin Gosman, Univeristy of Groningen, has authored some two dozen articles on Alexander the Great in medieval literature, as well as a major synthesis on the earliest French texts in the tradition: *La Légende d'Alexandre le Grand dans la littérature française du 12e siècle* (Rodopi, 1997).

Laurence Harf-Lancner is professeur de Littérature française du Moyen Age at the Université de Paris III—Sorbonne Nouvelle. Author of *Les Fées au Moyen Age: Morgane et Mélusine* (Champion, 1984), she has also published an edition and translation into modern French of the *Roman d'Alexandre* of Alexandre de Paris, and of the *Lais* of Marie de France, as well as numerous collective volumes. She is coeditor of *Alexandre le Grand dans les littératures occidentales et proche-orientales* (Nanterre, 1999).

Douglas Kelly is Professor Emeritus of French and Medieval Studies at the University of Wisconsin, Madison. He has published extensively on medieval literature and medieval poetics. Among his recent books are *The Art of Medieval French Romance* (Wisconsin, 1992); *Medieval French Romance* (Twayne, 1993); *Internal Difference and Meanings in the 'Roman de la rose'* (Wisconsin, 1995); and *The Conspiracy of Allusion: Description, Rewriting, and Authorship from Macrobius to Medieval Romance* (Brill, 1999).

William W. Kibler is Superior Oil—Linward Shivers Centennial Professor of Medieval Studies and Professor of French at the University of Texas at Austin. He has written extensively on medieval literature and is the author of *An Introduction to Old French* (MLA, 1984). He coedited *Lion de Bourges* and *Medieval France: An Encyclopedia* (Garland, 1995) and edited collective volumes on Eleanor of Aquitaine and on the Prose *Lancelot*.

Donald Maddox is professor of French and Italian Studies at the University of Massachusetts, Amherst. Among his books are *Semiotics of Deceit: The Pathelin Era* (Bucknell, 1984); *The Arthurian Romances of Chrétien de Troyes* (Cambridge, 1991) and *Fictions of Identity in Medieval France* (Cambridge, 2000). With Sara Sturm-Maddox he has coedited numerous collective volumes, including *Literary Aspects of Courtly Culture* (Cambridge: D. S. Brewer, 1994); *Transtextualities: Of Cycles and Cyclicity in Medieval French Literature* (Medieval and Renaissance Texts & Studies, 1996); *Melusine of Lusignan: Founding Fiction in Late Medieval France* (Georgia, 1996); and *Froissart Across the Genres* (Florida, 1998).

Rupert T. Pickens is professor of French at the University of Kentucky. His books include a study of Chrétien de Troyes's *Conte del graal,* critical editions of the *Conte del graal* and of Jaufré Rudel's songs, and a translation of the Lancelot-Grail *Merlin*. He has edited three volumes of scholarly essays and published articles on a wide range of medieval and critical topics. He is currently at work on a comparative study of Marie de France's *Lais* and *Fables* and a scholarly translation of texts from the William of Orange Cycle.

Sara Sturm-Maddox, professor of French and Italian Studies at the University of Massachusetts, Amherst, writes on the medieval and Renaissance literature of both France and Italy. Among her books are *Petrarch's Laurels* (University of Missouri Press, 1985); *Petrarch's Metamorphoses* (Pennsylvania State University Press, 1992); and *Ronsard, Petrarch, and the 'Amours'* (University Press of Florida, 2000). Among the collective volumes she has coedited with Donald Maddox are *Literary Aspects of Courtly Culture* (Cambridge: D. S. Brewer, 1994); *Transtextualities: Of Cycle and Cyclicity in Medieval French Literature* (Medieval and Renaissance Texts & Studies, 1996); *Melusine of Lusignan: Founding Fiction in Late Medieval France* (Georgia, 1996); and *Froissant Across the Genres* (Florida, 1998).

François Suard, Emeritus Professor de littérature française at the Université Paris X—Nanterre, is coeditor of *Alexandre le Grand dans les littératures occidentales et proche-orientales* (Nanterre, 1999). He has published widely on medieval French literature, with many contributions on the epic, including *Guillaume d'Orange: Etude du roman en prose* (Champion, 1979); *Les Chansons de geste* (Presses Universitaires de France, 1993); and an edition-translation of *La Chanson de Guillaume* (Bordas, 1991).

Michelle Szkilnik is professeur de Littérature médiévale at the Université de Nantes and has authored *L'Archipel du Graal: Etude de 'l'Estoire del Saint Graal'* (Droz, 1991); *L'Histoire des moines d'Egypte de Wauchier de Denain* (Droz, 1993); and *Lecture du Conte du Graal* (Gallimard, 1998), as well as many articles on medieval French literature. With Emmanuèle Baumgartner, she coedited volume 6 of the *Roman de Tristan en Prose* (Droz, 1993).

Jane H. M. Taylor, Principal of Collingwood College at the University of Durham, has published extensively on the literature of the later Middle Ages: romances (the *Roman de Perceforest* and *Le Petit Jean de Saintré*), historians (Froissart and Joinville), and lyric poets (Charles d'Orléans, Machaut, and François Villon). Her most recent book is *The Poetry of François Villon: Text and Context* (Cambridge, 2001).

Michelle R. Warren is associate professor of French at the University of Miami. Her recent book, *History on the Edge: Excalibur and the Borders of Britain, 1100–1300* (Minnesota, 2000), examines the Arthurian tradition and medieval history through the lens of postcolonial theory. Among her current research projects is a major study of the nineteenth-century reception of medieval works and traditions.

Stephen D. White is Asa G. Candler Professor of Medieval History at Emory University. He has published *Sir Edward Coke and 'The Grievances of the Commonwealth,' 1621–1628* (University of North Carolina Press and University Press of Manchester, 1979); *Custom, Kinship and Gifts to Saints: The Laudatio Parentum in Western France, 1050–1150* (University of North Carolina Press, 1988), and *Feuding and Peacemaking in Early Medieval France* (University of North Carolina Press, forthcoming).

Michel Zink, of the Académie des Inscriptions et Belles-Lettres, holds the chair in medieval French studies at the Collège de France and has published many studies on medieval literature, including several literary histories, and books on the *pastourelle*; the *chansons de toile*; *Guillaume de Dole* of Jean Renart; the medieval sermon, and literary subjectivity in the age of Louis IX. Among his recent titles are *Froissart et le temps* (Presses Universitaires de France, 1998) and a novel based on the troubadours, *Le Tiers d'Amour* (Editions de Fallois, 1998).

Index